Robert Wilkinson

The law of prisons in England and Wales

Robert Wilkinson

The law of prisons in England and Wales

ISBN/EAN: 9783337113360

Printed in Europe, USA, Canada, Australia, Japan

Cover: Foto ©Suzi / pixelio.de

More available books at **www.hansebooks.com**

THE
LAW OF PRISONS
IN
ENGLAND AND WALES,

BEING

THE PRISON ACT, 1865 (28 & 29 VICT. C. 126),

AND

THE PRISON ACT, 1877 (40 & 41 VICT. C. 21),

WITH AN ANALYSIS OF THE ACTS;
NOTES;
A SELECTION OF OTHER ACTS, AND PORTIONS OF ACTS STILL IN
FORCE RELATING TO PRISONS;
AND A FULL INDEX.

BY

ROBERT WILKINSON, ESQ., M.A.,
Of Jesus College, Cambridge; and of Lincoln's Inn, Barrister-at-Law.

EDITOR OF THE "REFORMATORY AND THE INDUSTRIAL SCHOOLS ACTS, 1866;"
"THE REPRESENTATION OF THE PEOPLE ACT, 1867," ETC.

London:
KNIGHT & CO., 90 FLEET STREET.
1878.

TO THE

RIGHT HONOURABLE RICHARD ASSHETON CROSS, M.P.,

HER MAJESTY'S

PRINCIPAL SECRETARY OF STATE FOR THE HOME DEPARTMENT,

BY WHOM THE BILL

WHICH NOW FORMS THE PRISON ACT, 1877,

WAS INTRODUCED INTO PARLIAMENT,

AND TO WHOSE EXERTIONS THE EXISTENCE OF THAT ACT

IS MAINLY TO BE ATTRIBUTED,

THIS WORK IS (BY HIS PERMISSION) RESPECTFULLY DEDICATED.

PREFACE.

The Bill which formed the foundation of The Prison Act, 1877, was first introduced into the House of Commons in the month of June, 1876; but, although it became the subject of several long and able debates, and passed a second reading by the large majority of 199 votes, its withdrawal was subsequently rendered necessary by the pressure of other business, and by the lateness of the period at which the Session of Parliament had then arrived.

At the commencement of the Session of 1877, the Bill was again introduced, and after being subjected to an amount of criticism and discussion, both in and out of the Legislature, such as few measures have of late years encountered, it ultimately passed through both Houses of Parliament, and received the Royal assent on the 12th of July in that year.

The object of the Act, as indicated in Her Majesty's speech, and as afterwards explained by Mr. Secretary Cross on introducing the Bill, is twofold—viz., to promote economy and efficiency in the management of prisons, and to effect a relief of local burdens.

The Prison Act, 1865, although it wrought a considerable improvement not only in the discipline, but also in the entire general management of our prisons, and although it was found in many respects to work very well, failed to secure that uniformity of discipline and management which is essential to the efficiency of a system of prison administration. By making provision for such a construction of prisons as would accomplish the effectual separation of prisoners; by better and more clearly defining hard labour, and laying down rules for its enforcement; and by establishing a comprehensive code of regulations relating to the details of prison management generally, the Act effected a great and an important step in advance of the state of things previously existing. It introduced, in fact, a system where no system had existed before. But the Act, at the same time, created a number of separate local jurisdictions, and entrusted the immediate supervision of the management of the prisons in them to distinct and independent bodies, under the title of "Visiting Justices," who were directly responsible, not to one central authority, but to a number of dispersed authorities, in the form of the "Justices in Sessions assembled" in their respective prison jurisdictions.

Between the bodies thus existing in the various jurisdictions there was, generally speaking, no bond of union; and the magistrates acting in one locality had usually no means of knowing what was being done by the magistrates acting in another. It is hardly surprising, therefore, that it should have been found impossible for the different bodies to arrive at the adoption of any uniform mode of carrying out the various details of the system which the Act of 1865 inaugurated, or that, in the attempt to work out that system, differences should have arisen of such a nature as entirely to defeat the attainment of the uniformity which the Act was intended to establish. Thus there were great differences with regard to hard labour, both as to the daily number of hours of employment, and as to the character of the work the prisoners were required to perform. The term "hard labour" meant, consequently, very different things in different places. There were also great differences as to diet, discipline, instruction, supervision, and other matters. Sentences, therefore, nominally alike, involved in reality different punishments; although it could not be doubted that the punishment of offences ought not, as well in the interests of justice as in other respects, to be dependent upon or to vary with the opinions or the theories entertained by particular persons or prevailing in particular localities, but that it should be the same and be administered with equality and certainty in every part of the country.

A want of uniformity and certainty, and consequently of efficiency, were not, however, the only objections to which the state of things existing under the Act of 1865 was open.

The number of prisons had become excessive, and their distribution was unequal and inconvenient, whilst the cost of maintaining them was not only very heavy, but also, to a large extent, unnecessary. With all these matters, and with others of a like kind, The Prison Act, 1877, is intended to afford the means of effectually dealing, in order to accomplish both a saving of expense and an increase of efficiency.

The two principal features of the Act are, the transfer of the entire management of the prisons from the various local jurisdictions to the State, and the removal of the cost incidental to their maintenance from the local rates to the Imperial Exchequer.

The Government, instead of supplementing the local rates by a grant from the Treasury, for the purposes of prisons, will in future take the whole expense of the prisons upon itself, and hold in its own hands their entire control. Power will thus be given to redistribute the prisons; to provide for their existing or being built only where they are needed, and for their being adapted to the requirements of the populations in which they may respectively be situated; as well as to provide for numerous other details, so as to secure a system of discipline and management being practically and equally carried out in all the prisons in the country.

The Act will further afford the means of closing unnecessary prisons, and consequently of effecting, in that respect alone, a considerable saving of expense. It will, moreover, give power for more satisfactorily dealing with the important question of prison labour, by enabling the labour of prisoners to be more usefully and profitably employed than hitherto,—the Act of 1865 having been defective in giving far too great a prominence to penal as opposed to industrial labour.

Not a little fear was at one time entertained that the new Act would to a large extent, if not wholly, supersede the authority of the magistrates in relation to prisons. A glance at the provisions of the Act itself, and at the Rules which have been framed under it by the Secretary of State—as well those relating to certain classes of prisoners, and to the general government of prisons, as those specially relating to the duties of Visiting Committees—will, however, suffice to show that the authority referred to is very far from having been taken away. The Rules, moreover, made under The Prison Act, 1865, will also, except in some few instances in which new Rules have taken their place, remain in force. The old title of "Visiting Justices" will, it is true, disappear, but under the new title of the "Visiting Committee of Prisons" the magistrates will still have a great deal of important work to do. Their duties, if not identical with those which they heretofore discharged (and discharged, it should be observed, in a manner such as to confer benefit on others and to reflect credit on themselves, for they were in no way responsible for the inherent defects of the Act of 1865), will not differ very widely from them, whilst they will certainly be neither lighter nor less dignified.

In all matters of urgent necessity, or requiring to be done by authorities on the spot, the magistrates, under the title of the "Visiting Committee," will still, as heretofore, have to act. They will also, as heretofore, have to see that all the Rules laid down by the Secretary of State are duly carried out by the officers. They will likewise have, from time to time, to make reports, and upon them the Secretary of State must still depend, in no slight degree, for the proper working of the system of prison administration throughout the country. The principal difference in their position may, indeed, be said to consist in the fact that they will in future possess the supervision of the prisons under the Secretary of State, instead of being subject to the authority of the "Justices in Sessions assembled."

I have endeavoured, in the preparation of the work, to render it practically useful, both to members of the legal profession, and to those persons who may be either employed in, or in any way connected with, the management of prisons.

In the analysis of the two principal Acts, the order of arrangement of the Acts themselves has not been adhered to. But, with the object of rendering the state of the law as clear as possible at one view, their various provisions have been brought together under separate heads, so as to be read as one Act.

The Prison Acts, 1865 and 1877, will not, however, be the only Acts still in force relating to prisons.

In order, therefore, to make the work as complete as the nature of its subject and the want which it is designed to meet seemed alike to require, a selection of such other Acts, and portions of other Acts, as appeared to possess the greatest practical utility, has been included in an Appendix. The Rules made under The Prevention of Crimes Act, 1871, and The Prevention of Crimes Amendment Act, 1876, with respect to the registration and photographing of Habitual Criminals, as well as the Rules settled and approved by the Secretary of State under The Prison Act, 1877, and which relate to the appointment and duties of Visiting Committees; to prisoners awaiting trial; to misdemeanants of the first division; to debtors; to the general government of prisons; and to other matters, have also been included.

A copious Index to the entire work, which will, it is hoped, be found to render the requisite assistance to all who may consult its pages, has likewise been added.

ROBERT WILKINSON.

18th *March*, 1878.

TABLE OF CONTENTS.

                                                                  PAGE

AN ANALYSIS OF THE PRISON ACTS, 1865, 1877   . 1

THE PRISON ACT, 1865 (28 & 29 VICT. C. 126)   . . . 60
(*An Act to Consolidate and Amend the Laws relating to Prisons.*)

THE PRISON ACT, 1877. (40 & 41 VICT. C. 41)   . . . 149
(*An Act to Amend the Law relating to Prisons in England.*)

THE 5 GEO. IV. C. 12   199
(*An Act to facilitate, in those Counties which are divided into Ridings or Divisions, the Execution of an Act of the last Session of Parliament, for Consolidating and Amending the Laws relating to the Building, Repairing, and Regulating of certain Gaols and Houses of Correction in England and Wales.*)

THE 5 & 6 WILL. IV. C. 38 204
(*An Act for effecting greater Uniformity of Practice in the Government of the several Prisons in England and Wales; and for appointing Inspectors of Prisons in Great Britain.*)

THE 5 & 6 WILL. IV. C. 76 206
(*An Act to provide for the Regulation of Municipal Corporations in England and Wales.*)

xiv   TABLE OF CONTENTS.

                                                                               PAGE

THE 7 WILL. IV. & 1 VICT. C. 78.   208
    (*An Act to Amend an Act for the Regulation of Municipal Corporations in England and Wales.*)

THE 5 & 6 VICT. C. 98.   210
    (*An Act to Amend the Laws concerning Prisons.*)

THE 17 & 18 VICT. C. 115.   216
    (*An Act to Amend the Law relative to the Removal of Prisoners in Custody.*)

THE 21 & 22 VICT. C. 92.   218
    (*An Act to provide for the Conveyance of County Property to the Clerk of the Peace of the County.*)

THE 25 & 26 VICT. C. 44.   220
    (*An Act to Amend the Law relating to the giving of Aid to Discharged Prisoners.*)

THE 26 & 27 VICT. C. 79.   222
    (*An Act for the Amendment of the Law relating to the Religious Instruction of Prisoners in County and Borough Prisons in England and Scotland.*)

THE 29 & 30 VICT. C. 100.   223
    (*An Act for the Amendment of the Laws relating to Prisons.*)

THE 31 VICT. C. 21.   225
    (*An Act to provide Compensation to Officers of certain discontinued Prisons.*)

THE 31 VICT. C. 24.   226
    (*An Act to provide for carrying out of Capital Punishment within Prisons.*)

THE 32 & 33 VICT. C. 71.   230
    (*An Act to Consolidate and Amend the Law of Bankruptcy.*)

THE 34 & 35 VICT. C. 112.   230
    (*An Act for the more effectual Prevention of Crime.*)

TABLE OF CONTENTS.

THE 39 & 40 VICT. C. 23. 233
(*An Act to Amend the Prevention of Crimes Act,* 1871.)

THE 40 VICT. C. 7. 236
(*An Act for punishing Mutiny and Desertion, and for the better payment of the Army and their quarters.*)

THE 40 VICT. C. 8. 242
(*An Act for the Regulation of Her Majesty's Royal Marine Forces while on shore.*)

THE PRISON RULES, 1878 250

INDEX 294

ARRANGEMENT OF THE ANALYSIS.

	PAGE
Preliminary Sections	1
Definition of Terms	2
Maintenance of Prisons	7
Contracts and Debts of Prison Authorities	11
Administration of Prisons	14
Visiting Justices, Visiting Committee of Justices, and Visits to Prisons by any Justice	20
Appointment, Status, etc., of Prison Officers	23
Jurisdiction over Prisons, and Commitment and Classification of Prisoners	29
Custody of Prisoners	31
Discipline of Prisoners	34
Offences in relation to Prisons	40
Removal of Prisoners from one Prison or place of Confinement to another	42
Discharge of Prisoners	43
Death of Prisoners in Prison	44
Regulations and Rules as to Government of Prisons	45
Actions, Arbitration, and Arrangement	46
Discontinuance of certain Prisons	48
Repeal of Statutes and parts of Statutes	52

AN ANALYSIS

OF

THE PRISON ACT, 1865,

Entitled "An Act to consolidate and amend the Law relating to Prisons" (28 & 29 Vict. c. 126).

[6th of July, 1865.]

AND OF

THE PRISON ACT, 1877,

Entitled "An Act to amend the Law relating to Prisons in England" (40 & 41 Vict. c. 21.)

[12th of July, 1877.]

PRELIMINARY SECTIONS.

Short Title of the Acts.—The Acts may respectively be cited for all purposes as "The Prison Act, 1865," and "The Prison Act, 1877" (P. A., 1865, s. 1, and P. A., 1877, s. 1).

Commencement of the Acts.—The Prison Act, 1865, came into operation on the 1st of February, 1866; and The Prison Act, 1877, is, except in certain cases provided for by the Act, and except as to the making of rules by the Secretary of State, which rules may be made at any time after the passing of the Act, to come into operation on the 1st of April, 1878 (P. A., 1865, s. 2, and P. A., 1877, s. 2).

Application of the Acts.—The Acts are not to extend to Scotland or Ireland, nor are they to apply to the

1

prisons for convicts under the superintendence of the Directors of Convict Prisons, or to any military or naval prison, but they are to apply to all prisons belonging to any prison authority as defined by The Prison Act, 1865 (P. A., 1865, s. 3, and P. A., 1877, s. 3).

Definition of Terms.

The following expressions are to have the meanings hereinafter attached to them, unless there is something in the tenor of the Acts inconsistent with such meanings.

Municipal Borough and Borough.—" Municipal borough " is to mean any place for the time being subject to the Municipal Corporation Act, 5 & 6 W. IV. c. 76, and any Acts amending the same, and " borough " is to include a municipal borough; and in The Prison Act, 1877, the term " borough " is also to mean any place which is for the time being subject to The Municipal Corporation Act, and to be inclusive of any county of a city or county of a town (P. A., 1865, s. 4, and P. A., 1877, s. 59).

Prison.—"Prison" is to mean a gaol, house of correction, bridewell, or penitentiary; and is also to include the airing grounds or other grounds or buildings occupied by prison officers for the use of the prison, and contiguous thereto (P. A., 1865, s. 4); and in The Prison Act, 1877, the term, in addition to the meaning thus attached to it by The Prison Act, 1865, is to include any land or building bought or contracted to be bought before the commencement of the Act (1st of April, 1878) by a prison authority, for the purpose of enlarging or altering any prison, or adding to the appurtenances of any prison; subject to a proviso with regard to the manner in which the Secretary of State is to deal with any portion of the lands so bought or contracted to be bought, which was not, in his opinion, at the time of the passing of the Act (12th of July, 1877), necessary for the then subsisting purposes of the prison (P. A., 1877, s. 60).

Gaoler.—"Gaoler" is to mean the governor, keeper, or other chief officer of a prison (P. A., 1865, s. 4).

Clerk of the Peace.—"Clerk of the Peace" is to include any officer performing similar duties to those of a clerk of the peace (P. A., 1865, s. 4).

Treasurer.—"Treasurer" is to include any officer performing duties similar to those of treasurer (P. A., 1865, s. 4).

Quarter Sessions.—"Quarter Sessions" are to include "general sessions" (P. A., 1865, s. 4).

Criminal Prisoner and Prisoner.—"Criminal Prisoner" is to mean any person charged with or convicted of a crime (P. A., 1865, s. 4); and the term "Prisoner" is, for the purposes of The Prison Act, 1877, to mean any person committed to prison on remand or for trial, safe custody, punishment, or otherwise (P. A., 1877, s. 57).

Prison Authorities.—The Prison Act, 1865, declares that the following persons shall be "Prison Authorities;" that is to say,

(1) As respects any prison belonging to any county, except as below mentioned, or to any riding, division, hundred, or liberty of a county, having a separate court of quarter sessions, the justices in quarter sessions assembled:

(2) As respects any prison belonging to a county divided into ridings or divisions, and maintained at the common expense of such ridings or divisions, the justices of the county assembled at a court of gaol sessions held in the manner provided by the Act 5 Geo. IV. c. 12:

(3) As respects any prison belonging to the city of London, or the liberties thereof, the court of the Lord Mayor and Aldermen:

(4) As respects any prison belonging to a municipal borough, the council of the borough :
(5) As respects any prison belonging to any district, liberty, borough, or town, having a separate prison jurisdiction, and not before mentioned, the justices, council, or other persons having power at law to build, enlarge, or repair such prison, assembled at any gaol sessions or other formal meeting of their body (P. A., 1865, s. 5).
And The Prison Act, 1877, declares that the term shall have the same meaning also in that Act (P. A., 1877, s. 61).

Justices in Sessions assembled.—The expression "Justices in Sessions assembled" is to mean, with reference to the prisons respectively mentioned in the five classes of prison authorities enumerated in the preceding definition :
(1) The justices in quarter sessions assembled;
(2) The justices of the county assembled at gaol sessions;
(3) The court of the Lord Mayor and Aldermen;
(4) The justices of the borough assembled at sessions, to be held by them at the usual time of holding quarterly sessions of the peace, or at such other time as they may appoint;
(5) The justices or other persons having power at law to make rules for the government of such prison (P. A., 1865, s. 6, and P. A., 1877, s. 61).

Separate Prison Jurisdiction. — Every county, riding, division, hundred, liberty, franchise, borough, town, or other place, is to be deemed to have a separate prison jurisdiction which maintains a separate prison, or which would be liable to maintain a separate prison if accommodation were not provided for its prisoners in the prison of some other jurisdiction. And where a county is divided into ridings or divisions, and a prison is maintained at the common expense of such ridings or divisions, the county is, in relation to such prison, and for the purposes thereof, to be deemed to have a separate prison jurisdiction, notwithstanding a separate county rate is not levied in the county at large (P. A., 1865, s. 9).

Visiting Justices.—The Prison Act, 1877, enacts that the term "Visiting Justices" shall have the same meaning in that Act as it has in The Prison Act, 1865. The last-mentioned Act does not contain any distinct definition of the term; but provision is made by it for the appointment of certain justices of the peace as "Visiting Justices" (P. A., 1877, s. 61, and P. A., 1865, s. 53). The provision referred to is, however, repealed (P. A., 1877, s. 13) from the commencement of The Prison Act, 1877.

Meaning of the term "Gaol Act."—In the construction of the 25 & 26 Vict. c. 44 (*An Act to amend the Law relating to the giving of Aid to Discharged Prisoners*) the expression "Gaol Act" is to mean "The Prison Act," 1865, instead of the Act therein referred to (P. A., 1865, s. 77).

Furniture and Effects belonging to a Prison.—The expression "Furniture and effects belonging to a prison" is to include all furniture, beds, bedding, clothes, linen, implements, machinery, and stores, except goods manufactured for sale, and materials in store for the purposes of such manufacture; also all books, papers, registers, and documents whatsoever relating to such prison or to the prisoners therein; also all articles whatsoever, whether or not of the same kind as those previously described, belonging at the commencement of The Prison Act, 1877, (1st of April, 1878,) to the prison authority of any prison for the purposes of the prison (P. A., 1877, s. 56).

Maintenance of a Prisoner.—"Maintenance of a prisoner" is to include all such necessary expenses incurred in respect of a prisoner for food, clothing, custody, safe conduct, and removal from one place of confinement to another, or otherwise, from the period of his committal to prison until his death or discharge from prison, as would, if The Prison Act, 1877, had not been passed, have been payable by a prison authority; with this proviso, that nothing in that Act is to exempt a prisoner from payment of any costs or expenses in respect of his conveyance to prison or otherwise, which he would have been liable to pay before the passing of the Act (P. A., 1877, s. 57).

Sufficient Accommodation for Prisoners.—" Sufficient accommodation " for the prisoners belonging to a prison authority is, for the purposes of The Prison Act, 1877, as nearly as can be ascertained, to be deemed to be the average daily number of prisoners maintained at the expense of such authority, whether in its own prison or in a prison belonging to some other prison authority, during the five years immediately preceding the 1st of January, 1877 (P. A., 1877, s. 57).

Cell Accommodation for a Prisoner.—" Cell accommodation for a prisoner" is to mean a cell for the separate confinement of a prisoner certified in pursuance of The Prison Act, 1865 (P. A., 1877, s. 57).

County.—" County" is to mean, in The Prison Act, 1877, unless there is something inconsistent in the context, a county at large, inclusive of a riding, division, or parts of a county having a separate court of quarter sessions (P. A., 1877, s. 58).

Riding.—" Riding" is similarly to mean any riding, division, or parts of a county having a separate court of quarter sessions (P. A., 1877, s. 58).

The City of London is to be deemed to be a county, and any prison belonging to the City is to be deemed to be situate within the limits of the City (P. A., 1877, s. 58).

Except as thus provided, all counties of cities, counties

of towns, liberties and franchises of counties, are to be
considered as forming part of the county by which
they are surrounded, or, if surrounded by two or more
counties, then as forming part of that county with
which they have the longest common boundary (P. A.,
1877, s. 58).

Expressions defined in The Prison Act, 1865.—In
addition to the special provision made, as already
noticed, by The Prison Act, 1877, with regard to the
meaning of the expressions "Prison Authorities,"
"Justices in Sessions assembled," and "Visiting Justices," the Act declares that all expressions defined
in The Prison Act, 1865, shall have the same meaning
also in that Act (P. A., 1877, s. 61).

MAINTENANCE OF PRISONS.

Maintenance of Prisons by Separate Prison Jurisdiction.—By The Prison Act, 1865, it was required
that there should be provided, at the expense of
every county, riding, division, hundred, liberty, franchise, borough, town, or other place, having a separate
prison jurisdiction, adequate accommodation for its
prisoners in a prison or prisons constructed and regulated in such manner as to comply with the requisitions of that Act in respect of prisons; and that all
expenses incurred by a prison authority in carrying
into effect the provisions of that Act should be
defrayed out of the county rate, or rate in the nature
of a county rate, borough rate, or other rate leviable
in the county, riding, division, hundred, liberty, franchise, borough, town, or other place, having a separate
prison jurisdiction, and applicable to the maintenance
of a prison, or out of any property applicable to that
purpose (P. A., 1865, s. 8). Ample provision was also
made by the Act for empowering prison authorities to
build new prisons or to alter, enlarge, or rebuild existing prisons, and for enabling them to obtain the money

requisite for any such purpose (P. A., 1865, ss. 23-30, and ss. 44, 45). A penalty was likewise imposed by the Act for the existence of inadequate prisons, and power was given, in very stringent terms, to the Secretary of State to close such prisons (P. A., 1865, ss. 35, 36).

Provision was moreover made for enabling one prison authority to contract with any other prison authority, having a prison in conformity with the requisitions of the Act, that the latter authority should receive into and maintain in its prison, or in one of its prisons, all prisoners maintainable at the expense of the former authority, or any particular class or classes of such prisoners (P. A., 1865, ss. 31, 32).

Maintenance of Prisons, &c., out of Public Funds, and Termination of Local Obligation to Maintain Prisons, &c.—But The Prison Act, 1877, enacts that on and after its commencement (1st of April, 1878) all expenses incurred in respect of the maintenance of prisons to which the Act applies, and of the prisoners therein, shall be defrayed out of moneys provided by Parliament; and that the obligation of any county, riding, division, hundred, liberty, franchise, borough, town, or other place, having a separate prison jurisdiction, to maintain a prison, or to provide prison accommodation for its prisoners, shall cease (P. A., 1877, ss. 4, 16). As the several provisions of The Prison Act, 1865, just referred to, will consequently become superseded on the commencement of The Prison Act, 1877, it is unnecessary to mention them further in this analysis.

Compensation to be made in the Place of Prison Accommodation.—Where at the time of the passing (12th of July, 1877) of The Prison Act, 1877, any prison authority had not a prison of its own, or had not a prison or prisons of its own, adequate to the accommodation of its prisoners, the authority is to pay (P. A., 1877, s. 17) into the Exchequer one hundred and twenty pounds, in respect of each prisoner belonging to it for whom cell accommodation (which expression means—P. A., 1877, s. 57—a cell for the separate confinement of such prisoner certified in pursuance of The Prison Act, 1865) had not, at the time named, been provided by the authority in a prison of its own. Any sum of money so payable by a prison authority is to be deemed to be a debt due from the authority to the Crown, and is to be recoverable accordingly. Where one prison authority has contributed a sum of money towards the construction by some other prison authority of cell accommodation for the use of the prisoners of the contributing authority, and such cell accommodation has been constructed accordingly, the contribution so made is to be taken into consideration in assessing the sum payable into the Exchequer by the contributing authority, and a proportionate deduction is to be made from that sum for it. For the purpose of paying any such contribution, a prison authority is empowered to borrow, and the Public Works Loan Commissioners are empowered to lend, any sum of money that may be required (P. A., 1877, ss. 17, 46, 47).

Compensation to be made to Prison Authority in respect of Accommodation provided for Prisoners of some other Authority.—Where before the 1st of January, 1877, any prison authority (and any public department of State which has made contracts with respect to prisoners, is, for this purpose, to be included under that term), having more than sufficient cell accommodation for the number of its own prisoners, which authority is termed the receiving authority, has contracted with another prison authority, termed the sending authority, that the receiving authority is to receive into its prisons any prisoners belonging to the sending authority, and the receiving authority has, in performance of the contract, provided cell accommodation for the prisoners of the sending authority, the amount of any loss which the receiving authority may have sustained in relation to such contract by reason of the passing of The Prison Act, 1877, is to be paid to that authority out of moneys provided by Parliament, but so that the expense of providing cell accommodation for any one prisoner shall not in any case be held to have exceeded the sum of one hundred and twenty pounds. If it appears, however, that any such contract is intended to be renewed at the expiration of its subsisting term, the intention of renewal is also to be taken into consideration in estimating the loss sustained by the receiving authority. Where a prison authority has provided a prison or prisons of its own more than adequate for the accommodation of its prisoners, it is to be entitled to receive, out of moneys to be provided by Parliament, compensation to the extent of one hundred and twenty pounds in respect of each cell provided in such prison or prisons over and above the number of cells required for the average maximum number of prisoners maintained at the expense of the authority in its own prison or prisons during the five years immediately preceding the 1st of January, 1877. But, in case the Prison Commissioners shall report to the Secretary of State that the prison accommodation is in excess of the probable requirements (a term which means the probable future requirements of a prison authority calculated as from the passing of the Act) of such prison authority for its own prisoners, or that the buildings are dilapidated or unsuitable, the Secretary of State is empowered to decline to recommend to the Treasury to make such compensation, either in the whole or in part, as the circumstances of the case may demand. No compensation is, however, to be payable under the provision last mentioned, in respect of any prison discontinued within two years after the commencement of The Prison Act, 1877 (1st of April,

1878); and a prison authority is not to be entitled to receive, under either of the foregoing provisions, more than one hundred and twenty pounds in the whole in respect of the same cell. The average maximum number of prisoners of a prison authority maintained in any prison in the period of five years, is to be calculated by finding the greatest number of such prisoners confined therein on the day on which the prison contained most of such prisoners in each of the said five years, and dividing the aggregate so found by five, excluding fractions (P. A., 1877, s. 18).

Allowance to be made to Prison Authority in respect of Uncompleted Prison.—Where at the time of the passing of The Prison Act, 1877 (12th of July, 1877) a prison authority has contracted to construct a building to be used as a prison, but such building shall not at the commencement of the Act (1st of April, 1878) have been completed or become a prison within the meaning of the Act, the Secretary of State may, if he thinks fit to do so, allow the prison authority time to complete the building as a prison, and when so completed it is to pass over to and vest in the Secretary of State as a prison completed at the commencement of the Act; but, if the Secretary of State should not think fit so to allow time, he is, nevertheless, in assessing the amount of compensation payable in respect of cell accommodation, to make, with the consent of the Treasury, such deduction from the compensation, as, having regard to all the circumstances of the case, may be agreed upon, or as may, in the event of disagreement between him and the prison authority, be determined by arbitration (P. A., 1877, s. 19).

CONTRACTS AND DEBTS OF PRISON AUTHORITIES.

How Contracts, &c., by Prison Authorities are to be made.—The provisions of the Act 21 & 22

Vict. c. 92 (*An Act to provide for the Conveyance of County Property to the Clerk of the Peace of the County*) are to apply to all contracts, mortgages, or conveyances entered into or executed by or on behalf of or with the justices of any county, riding, division, hundred, or liberty of a county in general or quarter sessions assembled, in pursuance of The Prison Act, 1865; and, in construing the Act first mentioned, the expression "Justices in Quarter Sessions assembled" is to include the justices of the county in gaol sessions assembled in pursuance of the Act 5 Geo. IV. c. 12, and the bailiff and justices of the liberty of Romney Marsh assembled at any sessions or meeting; and all contracts, etc., entered into or executed in pursuance of The Prison Act, 1865, by or on behalf of or with any other prison authority, are to be entered into and executed in the manner in which such instruments or deeds are usually entered into by the authority (P. A., 1865, s. 7).

General Saving of Rights of Creditors.—Any right or claim of any creditor of a prison authority under any contract legally made or in respect of any dealing legally had before the commencement of The Prison Act, 1877, is not to be affected by any of the provisions of that Act (except contracts and obligations between prison authorities themselves), but between any creditor and the prison authority of which he is a creditor any such contract may be enforced in the same manner in all respects as if that Act had not passed (P. A., 1877, s. 20).

Determination of Contracts between Prison Authorities.—But any contract made or obligation undertaken by any prison authority with any other prison authority for or in relation to the maintenance of any prison or prisoners, or any matter relating to such maintenance, is to be deemed to be determined on and after the commencement of The Prison Act, 1877, without prejudice nevertheless to any moneys which may have accrued due under or in respect of the contract or obligation at or before that time (P. A., 1877, s. 21).

Existing Debts to be defrayed by Prison Authorities.—A prison authority is, however, to defray in the same manner as if The Prison Act, 1877, had not passed:

(1) All debts due and sums of money payable in respect of contracts performed, dealings completed, or any matter or thing done before the commencement of the Act; and

(2) All mortgage debts (together with interest from time to time accruing thereon) contracted in respect of any prison.

A mortgage debt in the foregoing provision is to include any moneys which at the commencement of The Prison Act, 1877, have been borrowed or contracted to be borrowed by a prison authority on the security of any prison, or on the security of any rate applicable to the payment of the expenses of a prison, and also any debt or liability contracted before the period just mentioned, for the payment of which debt or liability money is authorised to be borrowed in pursuance of the 23rd section of The Prison Act, 1865 (P. A., 1877, s. 22).

Provision as to continuing Contracts.—Where any contract or dealing, in which a prison authority is concerned, is a continuous contract or dealing, to be performed partly before and partly after the commencement of The Prison Act, 1877, and is neither a contract nor dealing which is declared by that Act to have determined, nor a mortgage debt, as already defined, such contract or debt is to be deemed to be divisible, and as to so much of it as is performable before the commencement of the Act, it is to create a debt or obligation to be discharged or performed by the prison authority concerned in it, and as to so much of it as is performable after the commencement of the Act, it is to create a debt or obligation to be discharged or performed out of moneys provided by Parliament (P. A., 1877, s. 23).

ADMINISTRATION OF PRISONS.

Hitherto the numerous duties connected with the provision, maintenance, and administration of prisons in counties, boroughs, and other places, have devolved upon the different prison authorities, the justices in sessions assembled, and the visiting justices, subject to the exercise, for their guidance and control, of various powers on the part of the Secretary of State, and to the inspection of the prisons by Inspectors appointed by him.

Prisons to Vest in Secretary of State.—The Prison Act, 1877, enacts, however, that subject as therein mentioned, the prisons to which the Act applies, and the furniture and effects belonging to them; and the appointment of all officers, and the control and safe custody of the prisoners in those prisons; and also all powers and jurisdictions at common law, or by Act of Parliament, or by charter vested in or exerciseable by prison authorities, or the justices in sessions assembled, in relation to prisons or prisoners within their jurisdiction, shall, on and after the commencement of that Act (1st of April, 1878), be transferred to, vested in, and exercised by the Secretary of State (P. A., 1877, s. 5).

Saving as to Reformatory and Industrial Schools. —But nothing contained in the Act is to affect the powers or jurisdiction of a prison authority in relation to any reformatory school or to any industrial school under The Reformatory Schools Acts, 1866, and The Industrial Schools Act, 1866, or either of those Acts, or any Act amending them, or either of them (P. A., 1877, s. 52).

Appropriation of Court Houses situate within the Precincts of a Prison.—Town-halls, court-houses, or other rooms situate within the curtilage of a prison, or forming part of a prison, as defined by The Prison Act, 1877, and which are used for holding assizes or petty sessions, or for purposes other than those connected with the management of a prison, are not to be transferred to or vested in the Secretary of State under the Act, but the Secretary of State is empowered, if he thinks it desirable, and with the consent of the Treasury, to purchase them from the local authority to whom they belong, and provision is made as to the manner in which the purchase is to be effected (P. A., 1877, s. 49).

Legal Estate in Prison.—And the Act further declares that the legal estate in every prison to which it applies, and in the site and land and the furniture and effects belonging to any such prison, shall, on and after its commencement, be deemed to be vested in the Prison Commissioners, and not in the Secretary of State, but that the disposal of the same by the Commissioners shall be made in such mode as the Secretary of State, with the consent of the Treasury, may direct (P. A., 1877, s. 48).

Protection of Prisons in the Nature of National Monuments.—Any buildings which being in the nature of national monuments may, as to certain portions of them, be used as prisons, are, as to the portions so used and during the time they are used by the Secretary of State, to be maintained in such a manner as to prevent their being defaced or injured in their character of national monuments (P. A., 1877, s. 50).

Appointment of Prison Commissioners.—For the purpose of aiding the Secretary of State in carrying out the provisions of The Prison Act, 1877, Her Majesty is empowered to appoint, on the recommendation of the Secretary of State, at any time after the passing of the Act, by warrant under her sign manual, any number of persons to be commissioners during

Her Majesty's pleasure, so that the whole number of Commissioners appointed do not at any one time exceed five, and on any vacancy arising in the office of any Commissioner by death, resignation, or otherwise, in like manner to appoint some other fit person to fill the vacancy. The Commissioners are to be a body corporate, having a common seal; are to have power to hold land without licence in mortmain, so far as may be necessary for the purposes of the Act; and are to be styled " The Prison Commissioners." The Secretary of State may from time to time appoint one of the Commissioners to be chairman; and any act required or authorised to be done by the Prison Commissioners may be done by any one or more of them, as the Secretary of State may by general or special rule direct (P. A., 1877, s. 6).

Appointment of Inspectors, Officers, and Servants.—The Prison Commissioners are to be assisted in the performance of their duties by such number of inspectors, store-keepers, accountants, and other officers and servants as may, with the sanction of the Treasury as to number, be determined by the Secretary of State. The Inspectors are to be appointed by the Secretary of State, the other officers and servants of the Prison Commissioners by the Commissioners themselves, subject to the approval of the Secretary of State (P. A., 1877, s. 7).

Transfer of Duties of existing Inspectors of Prisons.—On and after the commencement of The Prison Act, 1877, however, any duties required by Act of Parliament or otherwise to be performed by an Inspector of Prisons appointed under the Act 5 & 6 W. IV. c. 38, may, subject to any directions to be given by the Secretary of State, be performed by any Prison Commissioner or Inspector appointed under that Act. And the Inspectors of Prisons holding office at that period, under the Act 5 & 6 W. IV. c. 38, are to become

Inspectors under The Prison Act, 1877, in the same manner, and liable to the performance of the same duties, as if they had been appointed under it; but subject to the following qualifications:
(1) That every such Inspector is to hold his office by the same tenure, and upon like terms and conditions, as if The Prison Act, 1877, had not passed, and is to receive a salary of not less amount than that which he has hitherto received; and
(2) That any duties such Inspector may be required to perform under The Prison Act, 1877, shall be the same as or analogous to the duties which he performed previously (P. A., 1877, s. 45).

Inspector of Prisons to Report by Letter to Visiting Justices.—The Prison Act, 1865, required the Inspector, upon visiting or inspecting a prison under that Act, to call the attention of the visiting justices, by letter addressed to them, to any irregularity he may have observed therein, or any complaint he may have to make against the buildings, the officers, or the discipline of the prison; and the visiting justices were required to enter a copy of the letter in their minute book (P. A., 1865, s. 22). Under The Prison Act, 1877, the Prison Commissioners will, it would seem, as regards this report of the Inspector, take the place of the visiting justices (P. A., 1877, s. 9).

Salaries of Commissioners, Inspectors, and other Officers.—Such salary may be paid, out of moneys provided by Parliament, to all or any one or more of the Prison Commissioners as the Secretary of State may, with the consent of the Treasury, determine; and it is further directed that there shall be paid to the Inspectors and other officers and servants of the Prison Commissioners, such salaries as the Secretary of State may, in like manner, determine (P. A., 1877, s. 8).

Duties of Prison Commissioners.—The general

superintendence of prisons under The Prison Act, 1877, is, subject to the control of the Secretary of State, to be vested in the Prison Commissioners. The Commissioners are, subject to the approval of the Secretary of State, to appoint all such officers of a prison as are by The Prison Act, 1865, declared to be subordinate officers of a prison, such appointments to be for the general prison service. The Commissioners are also to make contracts, and to do all other acts necessary for the maintenance of the prisons and prisoners within their jurisdiction. They are also, either themselves or by their officers, to visit and inspect the prisons within their jurisdiction, to examine into the state of the buildings, so as to form a judgment as to the repairs, additions, or alterations which may appear necessary, regard being had to the requisitions of The Prison Act, 1865, as amended by The Prison Act, 1877, with respect to the separation of prisoners and enforcement of hard labour; and they are further to examine into the conduct of the respective officers and the treatment and conduct of the prisoners, the means of setting them to work, the amount of their earnings, and the expenses attending the prison; and to inquire into all abuses within the prison, and to regulate all matters required to be regulated by them. The Commissioners, or any one or more of them, may, in addition to any powers otherwise conferred on them by The Prison Act, 1877, exercise in relation to any prison under the Act, and the prisoners therein, all powers and jurisdiction by any Act of Parliament or at common law, or by charter, exerciseable by visiting justices, or a visiting justice, of a prison.. And any reports, acts, or things required to be made or done to or by or in relation to the visiting justices, or a visiting justice of a prison, at common law, or by any Act of Parliament or by charter, are, except in so far as The Prison Act, 1877, otherwise provides, to be made or done to or by or in relation to the Prison Commissioners, or any one or more of them, or to or by or in relation to such persons or person as the Secretary of State may from time to time appoint. With reference to all these matters the Prison Commissioners are to be subject to the control of the Secretary of State, and they are required, in the exercise of their powers and jurisdiction under The Prison Act, 1877, to conform to any directions, which may from time to time be given to them by the Secretary of State (P. A., 1877, s. 9).

Reports by Prison Commissioners.—The Prison Commissioners are, at such time or times as the Secretary of State may direct, to make a report or reports to him of the condition of the prisons and prisoners within their jurisdiction, and an annual report to be made by them with respect to every prison within their jurisdiction is to be laid before both Houses of Parliament (P. A., 1877, s. 10).

Report to contain Information as to Manufacturing Processes in Prison.—The Prison Act, 1877, after reciting that it is expedient that the expense of maintaining in prison prisoners who have been convicted of crime should in part be defrayed by their labour during the period of their imprisonment, and that, with a view to defraying such expenses, and also of teaching prisoners modes of gaining honest livelihoods, means should be taken in promoting in prison the exercise of and instruction in useful trades and manufactures, so far as may be consistent with a due regard on the one hand to the maintenance of the penal character of prison discipline, and on the other to the avoidance of undue pressure on or competition with any particular trade or industry, enacts that the annual Report of the Prison Commissioners shall state the various manufacturing processes carried on in each of the prisons within the jurisdiction of the Commissioners, and that such statement shall contain such particulars as to the kind and quantities of, and as to the commercial value of the labour on the manufactures, as to the number of prisoners employed, and otherwise, as may, in the opinion of the Secretary of State, be best calculated to afford information to Parliament (P. A., 1877, s. 11).

Return of Punishments and Offences of Prisoners to be made Yearly.—The Prison Commissioners are also to make a yearly return to Parliament of all punishments of any kind whatsoever which may have been inflicted within each prison, and of the offences for which such punishments were inflicted (P. A., 1877, s. 12).

VISITING JUSTICES, VISITING COMMITTEE OF JUSTICES, AND VISITS TO PRISONS BY ANY JUSTICE.

Appointment of Visiting Justices.—By The Prison Act, 1865, the justices within every prison jurisdiction, in sessions assembled, were required to nominate two or more justices, with their consent, to be visitors of each prison within their jurisdiction; and one or more of the justices so appointed was required from time to time to visit and inspect each prison, and to perform certain other duties in connexion with the prisons, and also to make a report, once, at least, in each quarter of a year, to the justices in sessions assembled (P. A., 1865, s. 53).

Power to make Rules as to Visiting Justices.—The justices in sessions assembled were likewise empowered to make rules with respect to the duties of the visiting justices, and from time to time to repeal or alter any rules so made (P. A., 1865, s. 54). The Prison Act, 1877, however, enacts that on and after its commencement (1st of April, 1878) the sections of The Prison Act, 1865, relating to the appointment and duties of visiting justices, shall be repealed (P. A., 1877, s. 13).

Appointment of Visiting Committee of Prisons.—
Instead of the visiting justices, a visiting committee
is to be annually appointed for every prison under
the Act, consisting of such number of persons, being
justices of the peace, to be appointed at such time and
by such court of quarter sessions or such bench or
benches of magistrates as the Secretary of State, having
regard to the locality of the prison, to the justices heretofore having jurisdiction over the prison, and to the
class of prisoners to be confined in the prison, may
from time to time by any general or special rule
prescribe. The appointment of the visiting committee is to be made in the following manner, that is
to say, the justices of any county, riding, or liberty
of a county having a separate court of quarter sessions
are to appoint members of a visiting committee when
assembled at such general or quarter sessions as may
be prescribed by the Secretary of State; and the
justices of a borough are to hold special sessions, at
such time as may be prescribed by the Secretary of
State, for the purpose of appointing any members of
a visiting committee they may be required to appoint.
It is, however, provided, with regard to the Worcester
Prison, as constituted by The Worcester Prison Act,
1867, that, so long as that prison is continued as a prison
for the purposes of The Prison Act, 1877, the appointment of such number of justices of the city of Worcester
as the Secretary of State may in pursuance of the
provision already noticed prescribe to be appointed to
serve on the visiting committee of that prison shall
be vested in the corporation, acting by the council of
the city. Nothing in The Prison Act, 1877, or in any
rules to be made under that Act, is to restrict any
member of the visiting committee for any prison from
visiting the prison at any time, and any such member
is at all times to have free access to every part of the
prison and to every prisoner therein (P. A., 1877, s. 13).

Duties of Visiting Committee.—The Secretary of State is, on or before the commencement of The Prison Act, 1877, to make and publish rules with respect to the duties of a visiting committee, and is empowered hereafter to repeal, alter, or add to such rules. The visiting committee are required to conform to any rules so made and for the time being in force, but, subject as before mentioned, the members of such a committee are from time to time and at frequent intervals to visit the prison for which they are appointed, and hear any complaints which may be made to them by the prisoners, and, if asked, they are to hear such complaints privately. They are also to report on any abuses within the prison, and on any repairs which may be urgently required in the prison, and they are further to take cognizance of any matters of pressing necessity and within the powers of their commission as justices, and to do such acts and perform such duties in relation to a prison as they may be required to do or perform by the Secretary of State (P. A., 1877, s. 14).

Punishment of Prisoners (P. A., 1865, Regs. 58, 59).—For all the purposes of the 58th and 59th regulations, contained in the first schedule of The Prison Act, 1865, relating to the punishment of prisoners, or either of such regulations, the visiting committee are to be deemed to be the visiting justices, and any member of a visiting committee may exercise any power, or do any act, or receive any report which any one justice may exercise, do, or receive, under those regulations or either of them. But an offender is not to be punished under the regulations in question, or either of them, by personal correction, except in pursuance of the order of two justices of the peace, after such inquiry upon oath and determination concerning the matter reported to them as is mentioned in the 58th regulation. The visiting committee are also to report to the Secretary of State any matters with respect to which they may consider it expedient to report, and are to report to him, as soon as may be, and in such manner as he may direct, any matter respecting which they may be required by him to report (P. A., 1877, s. 14).

Visits to Prison by any Justice.—The 55th section of The Prison Act, 1865, empowered any justice of the peace having jurisdiction in the place to which a prison belonged, to visit the prison for the purpose of examining the condition of the prison or of the prisoners in it, and made various provisions with regard to the power thus conferred. That section is, however, repealed by The Prison Act, 1877, which provides instead, that any justice of the peace, having jurisdiction either in the place in which a prison is situate, or in the place where the offence in respect of which any prisoner may be confined in prison was committed, may, when he thinks fit, enter into and examine the condition of the prison and of the prisoners therein, and may enter any observations he may think fit to make in reference to the condition of the prison, or abuses therein, in the visitors' book to be kept by the gaoler; and it is to be the duty of the gaoler to draw the attention of the visiting committee, at their next visit to the prison, to any entries made in that book; but the justice of the peace is not to be entitled, in pursuance of the provision in question, to visit any prisoner under sentence of death, or to communicate with any prisoner, except with reference to the treatment in prison of the prisoner, or to some complaint that the prisoner may make as to such treatment (P. A., 1877, s. 15).

APPOINTMENT, STATUS, ETC., OF PRISON OFFICERS.

Appointment of Officers.—The following officers are to be appointed to every prison:

A gaoler;

A chaplain, being a clergyman of the Established Church;

A surgeon, duly registered as such under the Act 21 & 22 Vict. c. 90 (*An Act to Regulate the Qualifications of Practitioners in Medicine and Surgery*);

Such subordinate officers as may be necessary; and, to every prison in which females are imprisoned, a matron and such subordinate female officers as may be necessary.

In a prison where females only are imprisoned, the matron is to be deemed to be the gaoler, and is, so far as is practicable, to perform all the duties and to be subject to all the obligations of a gaoler in relation to such prison (P. A., 1865, s. 10).

Tenure of Office and Salaries of Prison Officers.— Under The Prison Act, 1865, the officers of prisons were to be appointed by, and were to hold office during the pleasure of, the justices in sessions assembled, and were to receive such salary as the justices might direct, subject to the proviso, that in the case of a municipal borough the amount of the salary of every officer appointed under the Act should be approved by the council. But nothing contained in that Act was to affect any right vested by Act of Parliament or charter in the council of any municipal borough of appointing a gaoler, chaplain, or other officer to the prison of the borough (P. A., 1865, ss. 10, 14, 81). The Prison Act, 1877, declares, however, that the general power of appointing all officers of prisons shall, on its commencement, vest in the Secretary of State; although the Prison Commissioners are, subject to the approval of the Secretary of State, required to appoint all such officers of a prison as are by The Prison Act, 1865, declared to be subordinate officers of a prison, or in other words to appoint all officers of a prison except the gaoler, the chaplain, the surgeon, the matron, and any minister appointed under The Prison Ministers' Act, 1863, such appointments to be for the general prison service (P. A., 1877, ss. 5, 9). But The Prison Act, 1877, does not make any reservation of any right vested in the council of a municipal borough of appointing officers to the prison of the borough.

Position and Duties of existing Officers of Prisons.—The officers attached to prisons at the time of the commencement of The Prison Act, 1877, and who are termed by the Act " the existing officers of a prison," are, nevertheless, to hold their offices by the same tenure, and upon like terms and conditions, as if the Act had not passed, and they are to receive salaries of not less amount than those which they have hitherto received. Such existing officers may, however, be distributed amongst the several prisons to which the Act applies, in such manner as may be directed by the Secretary of State, and they are to perform such duties as he may require them to perform, so that those duties are the same as or analogous to those which they performed previously to the commencement of the Act; and, subject as thus provided, they are to perform the same duties, as nearly as may be, as they shall be performing at that time. An existing officer of a prison, who, at the commencement of the Act, is in receipt of military or naval pay, or who has commuted his pension under The Pensions Commutation Act, 1871, or who is in receipt of any pension payable out of public moneys, is not to be subject to any deduction from his salary, or to be deprived of any portion of his half-pay, or of his pension, by reason of his salary being thenceforward paid out of public moneys, or of his employment becoming a public employment, or an employment of profit under Her Majesty, within the meaning of the Acts of Parliament providing for such deduction of salary or deprivation of half-pay, nor is such officer to be disqualified from receiving such half-pay or pension by reason of his becoming, by virtue of The Prison Act, 1877, a civil servant of Her Majesty (P. A., 1877, s. 35).

Appointment of Chaplain to Two Prisons.—The same person may officiate as chaplain of any two prisons situate within a convenient distance from each other, if they are together calculated to receive not more than one hundred prisoners ; but the chaplain of more than one prison, or the chaplain of any prison in which the average number of prisoners confined at any one time during the three years next before his appointment has not been less than one hundred, is not, whilst holding his chaplaincy, to hold any benefice with cure of souls or any curacy (P. A., 1865, s. 11).

Assistant Chaplain and Deputy Gaoler.—The Prison Act, 1865, gives power to the justices in sessions assembled to appoint an assistant chaplain, being a clergyman of the Established Church, and a deputy gaoler, or either of such officers, to any prison which they may deem sufficiently large to require the appointment of such officers, or either of them (P. A., 1865, s. 12). This power will hereafter become vested in, and exerciseable by the Secretary of State (P. A. 1877, s. 5).

Notice to be sent to Bishop, as to Chaplains and Assistant Chaplains.—Within one month after the nomination of a chaplain or assistant chaplain to a prison, notice thereof is to be transmitted to the bishop of the diocese in which the prison is situate, and no chaplain or assistant chaplain is to officiate in any prison until he has obtained a licence for that purpose from such bishop, nor for any longer time than while the licence continues in force (P. A., 1865, s. 13).

Superannuation of Officers and Abolition of Office.—The Prison Act, 1865, provides for the granting, under certain conditions and restrictions, by the justices in sessions assembled, of superannuation allowances to prison officers ; but, inasmuch as the officers, who may be attached to prisons when The Prison Act, 1877, comes into operation, will thenceforth become civil servants of Her Majesty, and be subject to the provisions of that Act specially relating to the granting of superannuation allowances to them, it will be requisite in this place to notice only the last-mentioned provisions. The Prison Act, 1877, declares that if at any time after its commencement it shall appear to the Treasury that any existing officer of a prison (that is, an officer attached to a prison when the Act came into force) has been in the prison service (a term which is to mean, as respects the period before the commencement of the Act, service in a particular prison, or in the prisons of the same authority transferred to the Secretary of State, and as respects the period after the commencement of the Act, service in any such prison, or in any other prison transferred to the Secretary of State under the Act) for not less than twenty years, and is not less than sixty years of age, or that any such officer has become incapable, from confirmed sickness, age, or infirmity, or injury received in actual execution of his duty, of executing his office in person, and if such sickness, age, infirmity, or injury is certified by a medical certificate, and if there be also a report of the Prison Commissioners testifying to the good conduct of the officer during his period of service under them, and recommending a grant to be made to him, the Treasury may grant to him, having regard to his length of prison service, an annuity, by way of superannuation allowance, not exceeding two-thirds of his salary and emoluments, or a gratuity not exceeding the amount of his salary and emoluments for one year (P. A., 1877, s. 36).

Abolition of Office, or Retirement, or Removal of Officer.—If any office to which The Prison Act, 1877, applies is abolished, or if any officer retires or is removed, any existing officer of a prison who is in consequence deprived of any salary or emoluments, is to be dealt with in the manner provided by The Superannuation Act, 1869, with respect to a person retiring or removed from the public service in consequence of the abolition of his office or for the purpose of facilitating improvements in the organization of the department to which he belongs (P. A., 1877, s. 36).

Apportionment of Annuity.—Any annuity by way of superannuation allowance or gratuity granted in pursuance of the foregoing provisions is to be apportioned between the period of service before and the period of service after the commencement of The Prison Act, 1877; and so much of such annuity or allowance as is payable in respect of service before the commencement of the Act, regard being had to the amount of salary then paid, but without taking into account any number of years added to the officer's service on account of abolition of office, or for facilitating the organization of the department to which he belongs, is to be paid by the prison authority of the prison in which the officer was serving at the date of the commencement of the Act, out of rates which at or immediately before that date were applicable to the payment of the officer's salary, and the residue is to be paid out of moneys provided by Parliament (P. A., 1877, s. 36).

The provisions of The Prison Act, 1877, with respect to superannuation allowances and gratuities, are not, however, to entitle any existing officer of a prison to any such allowance or gratuity, the conditions of whose office would not have entitled him thereto under The Prison Act, 1865 (P. A., 1877, s. 53).

Removal of Prison Officers from Apartments.— The Prison Act, 1865, gives ample powers for obtaining possession of the house or apartments in which any officer of a prison who is suspended, or removed from, or who resigns his office, or who dies, has by virtue of his office resided (P. A., 1865, s. 16). These powers are exerciseable under that Act by or on behalf of the visiting justices or the prison authority, but they will hereafter be exerciseable by or on behalf of the Prison Commissioners under the provisions of The Prison Act, 1877 (P. A., 1877, s. 9).

JURISDICTION OVER PRISONS, AND COMMITMENT AND CLASSIFICATION OF PRISONERS.

Abolition of Distinction between Gaol and House of Correction.—Subject to the provisions of The Prison Act, 1865, with respect to the appropriation of prisons to particular classes of prisoners, every prison to which that Act applies is to be deemed to be a gaol and house of correction, but no class of prisoners that had not previously to the commencement of the Act been confined in any prison is to be confined there until the Secretary of State has certified that the prison is a fit place of confinement for that class of prisoners (P. A., 1865, s. 56).

Jurisdiction over Prison.—Every prison, wheresoever situate, is for all purposes to be deemed to be within the limits of the place for which it is used as a prison (P. A., 1865, s. 57). But the Secretary of State may from time to time, if he think it expedient so to do, for the purpose of any enactment, law, or custom, descriptive of or dependent on the circumstance of a prison being the prison of any county, riding, county of a city, county of a town, liberty, borough, or other place having a separate prison jurisdiction, by any general or special rule direct that, for such purpose, any prison locally situate within the county in which such riding, county of a city, county of a town, liberty, borough, or place is situate, or any prison which he may in pursuance of The Prison Act, 1877, have appointed as a prison to which prisoners may be committed, is to be considered to be the prison of any county or other place as above mentioned; but, subject to any such rule, and until the same be made, the transfer under that Act of the prisons to which it applies, and of the powers and jurisdiction of prison authorities, of justices in sessions assembled, and of visiting justices, is not to affect the jurisdiction of any sheriff or coroner, or, except as the Act provides, of any justice of the peace or other officer having at the commencement of the Act jurisdiction in, over, or in respect of such prison (P. A., 1877, s. 30).

Saving as to Commitment of Prisoners.—Subject to The Prison Act, 1877, and to any rules made in pursuance of it, prisoners may be committed to the same prison to which they might have been committed if that Act had not passed. The committal of a prisoner to or his imprisonment in a prison, if otherwise valid, is not to be illegal by reason only that such prisoner ought, according to the law for the time being in force, to have been committed to or imprisoned in some other prison; but any such prisoner as this provision refers to, is, on application being made on his behalf in a summary manner to any judge of the High Court of Justice, to be entitled to be removed at the public expense to such other prison (P. A., 1877, s. 27).

Confinement of Prisoners before and during Trial.—The Secretary of State may from time to time, by any general or special rule, appoint in any county a convenient prison or prisons in which prisoners are to be confined before and during trial, or at either of such times, and any prisoner who might, if The Prison Act, 1877, had not passed, have been lawfully confined in a prison situate within the area of such county, may be lawfully confined in any prison or prisons so appointed; and the Secretary of State may also, in like manner, appoint any convenient prison or prisons in any adjoining county to which prisoners may be committed for trial, safe custody, or otherwise, and any prisoners may be committed to such prison accordingly (P. A., 1877, s. 24).

Confinement of Prisoners after Conviction.—The Secretary of State may also from time to time, by any general or special rule appropriate either wholly or partially particular prisons within his jurisdiction to particular classes of convicted criminal prisoners, and may remove any convicted criminal prisoner from any one prison to any other prison for the purpose of his undergoing the whole or any portion of his punishment; but a prisoner who is confined in a prison situate beyond the limits of the county, borough, or place in which he was convicted of his offence is on his discharge to be taken back at the public expense to the county, borough, or place in which he was so convicted (P. A., 1877, s. 25).

Confinement of Debtors and Prisoners who are not Criminal Prisoners.—The Secretary of State may from time to time, by any general or special rule, appoint in any county a prison or prisons in which debtors and prisoners who are not criminal prisoners are to be confined during the period of their imprisonment, and any such debtor or prisoner may be confined in a prison so appointed, who might, if The Prison Act, 1877, had not passed, have been confined during such period in any prison situate within the area of the county (P. A., 1877, s. 26).

CUSTODY OF PRISONERS.

Legal Custody of Prisoners.—Every prisoner confined in a prison is to be deemed to be in the legal custody of the gaoler; but nothing contained in The Prison Act, 1865, is to affect the jurisdiction or responsibility of the sheriff in respect of prisoners under sentence of death, or his jurisdiction or control over the prison where such prisoners are confined, and the officers thereof, so far as may be necessary for the purpose of carrying into effect the sentence of death, or for any purpose relating thereto; and in any prison in which sentence of death is required to be carried into effect on any prisoner, whether such prison is or is not the common gaol of the county, the sheriff is, for the purpose of carrying that sentence into execution, to be deemed to have the same jurisdiction with respect to such prison as he has by law with respect to the common gaol of a county (P. A., 1865, s. 58). A prisoner is also to be deemed to be in legal custody whenever he is being taken to or from, or whenever he is confined in, any prison in which he may be lawfully confined, or whenever he is working outside or is otherwise beyond the walls of any such prison in the custody or under the control of a prison officer belonging to such prison; and any constable or other officer acting under the order of any justice of the peace or magistrate having power to commit a prisoner to prison may convey a prisoner to or from any prison to or from which he may be legally committed or removed, notwithstanding that the prison may be beyond the constablewick or other jurisdiction of such constable or officer, in the same manner and with the same incidents as if the prison were within such constablewick or other jurisdiction (P. A., 1877, s. 28).

Security to Sheriff.—The Prison Act, 1865, requires the gaoler of every prison in which debtors are confined to give security to the sheriff for their safe custody; but that Act, whilst it abolished the liability of the sheriff for the escape of a prisoner from imprisonment in other cases, continued that liability in the case of a debtor (P. A., 1865, ss. 59, 60). The Prison Act, 1877, however, declares that on and after its commencement the sheriff of any sheriffdom shall not be liable for the escape of any prisoner (P. A., 1877, s. 31). The liability of the sheriff even for the escape of a debtor from prison will clearly, therefore, cease at that period; and, such being the case, the obligation on the part of a gaoler to give security for the safe custody of debtors will likewise cease.

Prisoners under Sentence of Death.—The provisions of The Prison Act, 1877, are not, however, to affect the jurisdiction or responsibility of the sheriff in respect of prisoners under sentence of death, and confined in any prison within his jurisdiction, or his jurisdiction and control over the prison where such prisoners are confined, and the officers thereof, so far as may be necessary for the purpose of carrying into effect the sentence of death, or for any purpose relating thereto; and in any prison in which sentence of death is required or authorized to be carried into effect on any prisoner, the sheriff of the county in which the prison is situate, is, for the purposes of carrying that sentence into execution, to be deemed to have the same jurisdiction with respect to such prison as he would by law have had with respect to the common gaol of his county, if The Prison Act, 1877, had not passed, and such prison were the common gaol of his county (P. A., 1877, s. 32).

Description of Prison in Writ, &c.—Any writ, warrant, or other legal instrument addressed to the gaoler of a particular prison, describing the prison by its situation or other definite description, is to be valid, by whatever title such prison is usually known, or whatever be the description of the prison, whether gaol, house of correction, bridewell, penitentiary, or otherwise (P. A., 1865, s. 61).

Gaoler of Prison to deliver Calendar.—The gaoler of every prison is to deliver or to cause to be delivered to the judges of assize, and to the justices in quarter sessions, a calendar of all prisoners in custody for trial at such assizes or sessions, in the same way as the sheriff of a county has hitherto been required by law to deliver a calendar of such prisoners when committed to the common gaol of the county, and the sheriff is no longer to be required to deliver or to cause to be delivered such calendar (P. A., 1865, s. 62).

Custody and Trial of Prisoners in a Substituted Prison.—The Prison Act, 1865, made provision with respect to the commitment, trial, detention, and punishment of prisoners in cases where one prison authority had entered into a contract for the receiving and maintenance of its prisoners in the prison of another authority (P. A., 1865, s. 66). But, as all such contracts are to be deemed to be determined on and after the commencement of The Prison Act, 1877, it is unnecessary further to notice that provision in this place (P. A., 1877, s. 21).

Saving as to Commissions.—The validity of any commission of gaol delivery, commission of oyer and terminer, or other commission, precept, writ, warrant, or other document, is not to be affected by reason of its being addressed to or making mention of the sheriff of the county, &c., instead of being addressed to or making mention of the gaoler of a prison or prisons; and every such commission, &c., is to be obeyed by the gaoler, and is to take effect in the same manner as if he had been named therein instead of the sheriff (P. A., 1865, s. 82).

DISCIPLINE OF PRISONERS.

Separation of Prisoners.—The Prison Act, 1865, makes the following requisitions with regard to the separation of prisoners :
(1) In every prison separate cells are to be provided equal in number to the average of the greatest number of prisoners, not being convicts under sentence of penal servitude, who have been confined in the prison at any time during each of the preceding five years;

(2) In every prison punishment, cells are to be provided or appropriated for the confinement of prisoners for prison offences;
(3) In a prison containing female as well as male prisoners, the women are to be imprisoned in separate buildings or separate parts of the same buildings, in such manner as to prevent their seeing, conversing, or holding any intercourse with the men;
(4) In a prison where debtors are confined, means are to be provided for separating them altogether from the criminal prisoners;
(5) In a prison where criminal prisoners are confined, such prisoners are to be prevented from holding any communication with each other, either by every prisoner being kept in a separate cell by day and by night, except when he is at chapel or taking exercise, or by every prisoner being confined by night to his cell, and being subjected to such superintendence during the day as will, consistently with the provisions of the Act, prevent his communicating with any other prisoner (P. A., 1865, s. 17).

Cells to be Certified for Confinement of Prisoners.—No cell is to be used for the separate confinement of a prisoner, unless it is certified by one of Her Majesty's Inspectors of Prisons to be of such a size, and to be lighted, warmed, ventilated, and fitted up in such a manner as may be requisite for health, and to be furnished with the means of enabling the prisoner to communicate at any time with an officer of the prison; but a distinction may be made in respect of the use of cells for the separate confinement of prisoners during long and short periods of imprisonment, and in respect of the use of cells in which the prisoner is intended to be employed during the whole day, or for a long or short part thereof; and the certificates of the Inspector may be varied accordingly, so as to express the period of imprisonment for which each cell may be considered fit, and the number of hours in the day during which the prisoners may be employed therein. No punishment cell is to be used unless it is certified by an Inspector that it is furnished with the means of enabling the prisoner to communicate at any time with an officer of the prison, and that it can be used as a punishment cell without detriment to the prisoner's health, and the time for which it may be so used is to be stated in the certificate. Every certified cell is to be distinguished by a number or mark placed in a conspicuous position, and is to be referred to by its number or mark in the certificate of the Inspector, and if the number or mark of any certified cell is changed without the consent of the Inspector, the cell is to be deemed to be an uncertified cell, until a fresh certificate has been given. Any certificate given by an Inspector in respect of a cell may be withdrawn on such alteration taking place in such cell as to render the certificate, in his opinion, inapplicable thereto, and upon the certificate being withdrawn the cell is to cease to be a certified cell (P. A., 1865, s. 18).

Cells certified before The Prison Act, 1865.—All cells certified by an Inspector before the commencement of The Prison Act, 1865, as being fit to be used for the separate confinement of prisoners, are to be deemed to be cells certified for such purpose under that Act (P. A., 1865, s. 75).

Requisitions of The Prison Act, 1865, as to Hard Labour.—Hard labour is to be of two classes, consisting, 1st, of work at the tread-wheel, shot drill, crank, capstan, stone-breaking, or such other like description of hard bodily labour as may be appointed by the justices in sessions assembled, with the approval of the Secretary of State, which work is afterwards referred to in The Prison Act, 1865, as hard labour of the first class; 2nd, of such other description of bodily labour as may be appointed by the justices in sessions assembled, with the approval of the Secretary of State, which work is referred to as hard labour of the second class; and in every prison where prisoners sentenced to hard labour are confined, adequate means (having regard to the average number of such prisoners confined in that prison during the preceding five years) is to be provided for enforcing hard labour in accordance with the provisions of the Act; and no prison is to be deemed to be in conformity with the requisitions of the Act with respect to the enforcement of hard labour, unless such means have been provided therein, and prisoners sentenced to hard labour have been employed thereat in the manner provided by the Act; but employment in the necessary services of the prison may, in the case of a limited number of prisoners, to be selected by the visiting justices, as a reward for industry and good behaviour, be deemed to be hard labour of the second class (P. A., 1865, s. 19). The 34th regulation, as amended by the 37th section of The Prison Act, 1877, and the 35th, 36th, and 37th regulations contained in the first schedule of The Prison Act, 1865, prescribe under what circumstances and with reference to what prisoners each class of hard labour is to be carried into effect.

Misdemeanants of First Division.—In every prison to which The Prison Act, 1865, applies, prisoners convicted of misdemeanor, and not sentenced to hard labour, are to be divided into at least two divisions, one of which is to be called the first division, and whenever any person convicted of misdemeanor is sentenced to imprisonment without hard labour it is to be lawful for the court or judge before whom such person has been tried to order, if such court or judge think fit, that such person shall be treated as a misdemeanant of the first division, and a misdemeanant of that division is not to be deemed to be a criminal prisoner (P. A., 1865, s. 67).

Rules as to Treatment of Prisoners confined for Non-Payment of Sums in the Nature of Debts.—The Secretary of State may from time to time make rules and repeal, alter, or add to rules made by him, with respect to the classification and treatment of prisoners imprisoned for non-compliance with the order of a justice or justices to pay a sum of money or be imprisoned in respect of the default of a distress to satisfy a sum of money so adjudged to be paid, provided such rules are in mitigation and not in increase of the effect of such imprisonment as regulated by The Prison Act, 1865 (P. A., 1877, s. 38).

Special Rules as to Treatment of Unconvicted Prisoners and certain other Prisoners.—The Prison Act, 1877, after reciting that it is expedient that a clear difference should be made between the treatment of persons unconvicted of crime and in law presumably innocent during the period of their detention in prison for safe custody only, and the treatment of prisoners who have been convicted of crime during the period of their detention in prison for the purpose of punishment, and that there should, in order to secure the observance of the difference, be in force in every place in which prisoners are confined for safe custody only, special rules regulating their confinement in such manner as to make it as little as possible oppressive, due regard only being had to their safe custody, to the necessity of preserving order and good government in the place in which they are confined, and to the physical and moral well-being of the prisoners themselves, requires the

Secretary of State to make, and empowers him to repeal, alter, or add to when made, special rules with respect to the following subjects:

(1) The retention by a prisoner of the possession of any books, papers, or documents in his possession at the time of his arrest, and which may not be required for evidence against him, and are not reasonably suspected of forming part of property improperly acquired by him, or are not for some special reason required to be taken from him for the purposes of justice;

(2) Communications between a prisoner, his solicitor, and his friends, so as to secure to the prisoner as unrestricted and private communication between him and them as may be possible, having regard only to the necessity of preventing any tampering with evidence, and any plans for escape, and other like considerations; and

(3) Arrangements whereby prisoners may provide themselves with articles of diet, or may be furnished with a sufficient quantity of wholesome food, and may be protected from being called upon to perform any unaccustomed tasks or offices; and also with respect to any other matter which he may think conducive to the amelioration of the condition of a prisoner who has not been convicted of crime, regard being had to the matters already mentioned as being directed to be regarded (P. A., 1877, s. 39).

Treatment of Prisoners convicted of Sedition, &c.—The Prison Commissioners are required to see that any prisoner under sentence inflicted on a conviction for sedition or seditious libel shall be treated as a misdemeanant of the first division within the meaning of the 67th section of The Prison Act, 1865, notwithstanding any statute, provision, or rule to the contrary (P. A., 1877, s. 40).

Treatment of Persons committed for Contempt of Court.—Any person imprisoned under any rule, order, or attachment for contempt of any court is in like manner to be treated as a misdemeanant of the first division (P. A., 1877, s. 41).

Test of Malingering.—Where the prison medical officer considers it necessary to apply any painful test to a prisoner to detect malingering or otherwise, such test is only to be applied by authority of an order from the visiting committee of justices or a Prison Commissioner (P. A., 1877, s. 42).

Limitation of Time of Confinement in Punishment Cells.—It is not to be lawful for the gaoler to order any prisoner to be confined in a punishment cell for any term exceeding twenty-four hours; nor for the visiting committee of justices to order any prisoner to be punished by confinement in such a cell for any term exceeding fourteen days (P. A., 1877, s. 43). This provision has reference to the 37th and 38th Regulations contained in the first schedule of The Prison Act, 1865.

OFFENCES IN RELATION TO PRISONS.

Assisting Prisoners to Escape.—Every person who aids any prisoner in escaping or attempting to escape from any prison, or who, with intent to facilitate the escape of any prisoner, conveys or causes to be conveyed into any prison any mask, dress, or other disguise, or any letter, or any other article or thing, is to be guilty of felony, and on conviction to be sentenced to imprisonment with hard labour for a term not exceeding two years (P. A., 1865, s. 37).

Punishment for carrying Spirituous Liquors or Tobacco into Prison.—Every person who, contrary to the regulations of a prison, brings or attempts by any means whatever to introduce into it any spirituous or fermented liquor or tobacco, and every officer of a prison who suffers any such liquor or tobacco to be sold or used therein, contrary to such regulations, is on conviction to be sentenced to imprisonment for a term not exceeding six months, or to a penalty not exceeding twenty pounds, or, in the discretion of the Court, to both, and every officer of a prison convicted under this provision is, in addition to any other punishment, to forfeit his office and all arrears of salary due to him (P. A., 1865, s. 38).

Punishment for carrying Letters into and out of Prisons.—Every person who, contrary to the regulations of a prison, conveys or attempts to convey any letter or other document, or any article whatever not allowed by such regulations, into or out of the prison, is on conviction to incur a penalty not exceeding ten pounds, and if he be an officer of the prison, he is to forfeit his office and all arrears of salary due to him, but this provision is not to apply in cases where the offender is liable to a more severe punishment under either of the provisions before mentioned (P. A., 1865, s. 39).

Notice of Penalties to be placed outside of Prison.—A notice setting forth the penalties that will be incurred by persons committing any offence mentioned in the foregoing provisions, is to be affixed in a conspicuous place outside the prison (P. A., 1865, s. 40).

Recovery of Penalties.—Offences under The Prison Act, 1865, with the exception of felonies, and of offences for the mode of trial of which the Act makes express provision (see Sched. I., Regs. 56, 57, 58), are to be prosecuted summarily before two justices acting for the division or place where the matter requiring the cognizance of such justices arises, and in the manner directed by the Act 11 & 12 Vict. c. 43, or any Act amending that Act (P. A., 1865, s. 52).

REMOVAL OF PRISONERS FROM ONE PRISON OR PLACE OF CONFINEMENT TO ANOTHER.

Removal of Prisoners for Trial.—A prisoner may be brought up for trial, and may be removed by or under the direction of the gaoler from one prison to another, or from one place of confinement to another, to which he may be legally removed, for the purpose of being tried or undergoing his sentence, and no prisoner whilst in the custody of a gaoler is to be deemed to have escaped, although he may be taken into different jurisdictions or different places of confinement (P. A., 1865, s. 63).

Removal of Prisoners by Order of Her Majesty.—And Her Majesty may, by order under the hand of the Secretary of State, direct any person in prison in England and Wales under sentence of any court, or of any competent authority, for any offence committed by him, to be removed from the prison in which he is confined to any other of Her Majesty's prisons within England and Wales, there to be imprisoned during his term of imprisonment (P. A., 1865, s. 65).

Removal of Prisoners in other Cases.—Prisoners may also be removed from one prison to another prison or place of confinement, for the purpose of enabling any prison to be altered, enlarged, or rebuilt, or in case of any contagious or infectious disease breaking out in any prison, or for any other reasonable cause (P. A., 1865, s. 64). The Secretary of State is further empowered to remove any convicted criminal prisoner from any one prison to any other prison, for the purpose of his undergoing the whole or any portion of his punishment (P. A., 1877, s. 25).

Discharge of Prisoners.

When Term of Imprisonment Expires on Sunday, Prisoner to be Discharged on Preceding Day.—A prisoner, whose term of imprisonment would, according to his sentence, expire on a Sunday, is to be entitled to his discharge on the preceding Saturday, and the gaoler of every prison is authorised and required so to discharge any such prisoner (P. A., 1865, s. 41).

Allowance to Discharged Prisoners.—The Prison Act, 1865, provides for the payment, under an order of the visiting justices, either to a prisoner himself on his discharge from prison, or to the treasurer of a certified Prisoners' Aid Society, to be applied for his benefit, of a sum of money not exceeding £2 (P. A., 1865, s. 41). That provision will, however, become superseded on the commencement of The Prison Act, 1877, which enacts that, on the discharge of a prisoner from prison, the Prison Commissioners may, on the recommendation of the visiting committee, or otherwise, order a sum of money not exceeding £2 to be paid by the gaoler to the prisoner himself, or to the treasurer of a certified Prisoners' Aid Society, or Refuge, on the gaoler receiving from the society an undertaking in writing, signed by its secretary, to apply the money for the benefit of the prisoner (P. A., 1877, s. 29).

Discharged Prisoners to be provided with Means of returning to Place of Settlement.—The Prison Act, 1865, also provides that, on the discharge of a prisoner from prison, the visiting justices of the prison may provide the prisoner, out of any moneys under their control, and applicable to the payment of the expenses of the prison, with the means of returning to his home or place of settlement, by causing his fare to be paid by railway, or in any other convenient manner (P. A., 1865, s. 43). This power will, it would seem, on the commencement of The Prison Act, 1877, become exerciseable by the Prison Commissioners (P. A., 1877, s. 9).

And a convicted criminal prisoner who is confined in a prison situate beyond the limits of the county, city, borough, or place in which he was convicted of his offence, is, at the time of his discharge, to be taken back at the public expense to the county, borough, or place in which he was so convicted (P. A., 1877, s. 21).

Death of Prisoners in Prison.

Inquests on Prisoners.—It is the duty of the coroner having jurisdiction in the place to which a prison belongs, to hold an inquest on the body of every prisoner who may die within the prison. Where it is practicable, one clear day is to intervene between the day of the death and the day of the holding the inquest (P. A., 1865, s. 48).

Certain Persons not to be Jurors.—In no case where an inquest is to be held on the body of a prisoner, is any officer of the prison, or any prisoner confined in the prison (P. A., 1865, s. 48), or any person engaged in any sort of trade or dealing with the prison (P. A., 1877, s. 44), to be a juror on such inquest.

Regulations and Rules as to Government of Prisons.

Regulations as to Government of Prisons.—The regulations contained in the first schedule of The Prison Act, 1865, with respect to the government of prisons, are to be binding on all persons in the same manner as if they were enacted in the body of the Act (P. A., 1865, s. 20). Those regulations will be found, in their proper place, at pages 115 to 141 of this book.

Rules in Addition to Regulations in Schedule of Prison Act, 1865.—In addition to the regulations just referred to, the justices in sessions assembled are required by The Prison Act, 1865, to make rules for the supply to all prisoners confined in prisons within their jurisdiction of a sufficient quantity of plain and wholesome food, regard being had, so far as relates to convicted criminal prisoners, to the nature of the labour required from or performed by them, so that the allowance of food may be duly apportioned thereto, and to frame dietary tables for the purpose; and they are empowered to make rules in respect of any other matters relating to the government of such prisons, and from time to time to repeal or alter any rules made or dietary tables framed by them (P. A., 1865, s. 21).

The duty of making rules and dietary tables for the supply of food to prisoners, and the general power to make rules with regard to matters relating to the government of prisons thus created or conferred by The Prison Act, 1865, will, however, on the commencement of The Prison Act, 1877, be transferred to and become exerciseable by the Secretary of State (P. A., 1877, s. 5).

Rules in Force at Commencement of The Prison Act, 1865.—All rules in force in any prison which were inconsistent with The Prison Act, 1865, or with the regulations in its first schedule, were repealed by that Act, from its commencement, but the Act declared that all other rules, then in force, should continue, until altered in the manner provided by it (P. A., 1865, s. 80).

Proof of Rules of Secretary of State.—Any rule

made by a Secretary of State, in pursuance of The Prison Act, 1877, may be proved in the manner in which regulations made under the authority of a Secretary of State are capable of being proved in pursuance of The Documentary Evidence Act, 1868. (P. A., 1877, s. 51).

Rules, &c., to be laid before Parliament.—All rules and regulations made by virtue of The Prison Act, 1877, are to be forthwith laid in a complete form, after they have been settled and approved by the Secretary of State, before both Houses of Parliament, if Parliament be sitting, or if it be not then sitting, within three weeks after the beginning of the next ensuing session; and if any such rules or regulations are disapproved of by either House of Parliament within forty days after they have been so laid before Parliament, such rules or regulations, or the parts of them disapproved of, are to be void and of no effect; and no such rules or regulations are to come into force or operation until they have been so laid before Parliament for forty days (P. A., 1877, s. 51).

ACTIONS, ARBITRATION, AND ARRANGEMENT.

General Issue may be pleaded to Action.—If any suit or action is prosecuted against any person for anything done in pursuance of The Prison Act, 1865, such person may plead the general issue, and give that Act and the special matter in evidence at the trial, and that the same was done by the authority of the Act; and if a verdict passes for the defendant, or the plaintiff becomes nonsuited, or discontinues his action after issue joined, or if upon demurrer or otherwise, judgment be given against the plaintiff, the defendant is to recover double costs, and to have the like remedy for the same as any defendant has by law in other cases; and though a verdict be given for the plaintiff in any such action, he is not to have costs against the defendant, unless the judge before whom the trial takes place certifies his approbation of the action and of the verdict obtained thereupon (P. A., 1865, s. 49).

Venue and Commencement of Action.—All actions, suits, and prosecutions commenced against any person for anything done in pursuance of The Prison Act, 1865, are to be laid and tried in the county or place where the act complained of was committed, and are to be commenced within six calendar months after the committal thereof, and not otherwise (P. A., 1865, s. 50).

Arbitration.—Any difference authorised or directed by The Prison Act, 1865, to be settled by arbitration is to be referred to a barrister-at-law to be appointed in writing, on the application of any party to the difference, by any judge of assize of the last preceding or of the next succeeding circuit; and all the provisions of The Common Law Procedure Act, 1854, relating to compulsory references, are to be deemed to extend to any such arbitration, with the addition that it is to be obligatory on the arbitrator, at the request of any party to the difference, to state a special case for the opinion of a superior court (P. A., 1865, s. 51).

And the Secretary of State (with the assent of the Treasury, so far as any public moneys are concerned) on the one hand, and a prison authority on the other, may, with a view to carry into effect the provisions of The Prison Act, 1877, compromise any matter, or settle any difference, or refer to arbitration any matter or difference; and any such reference to arbitration is to be a single arbitrator, and the provisions of the Common Law Procedure Act, 1854, are to apply accordingly (P. A., 1877, s. 55).

Discontinuance of Certain Prisons.

Prohibition of Commitment to Certain Prisons.—The Prison Act, 1865, prohibited the committal, after its commencement, of any person to any of the prisons mentioned in the second schedule thereto. The prisons thus discontinued were the following:—

PRISON OF	LEGAL CHARACTER OF PRISON.	COUNTY.
Aberystwith	Borough prison	Cardigan.
Bradninch	Ditto	Devon.
Faversham	Ditto	Kent.
Helstone	Ditto	Cornwall.
King's Lynn	Ditto	Norfolk.
Lichfield	Ditto	Stafford.
Maldon	Ditto	Essex.
Newcastle-under-Lyme	Ditto	Stafford.
Penzance	Ditto	Cornwall.
Richmond	Ditto	York.
Romney Marsh	Liberty prison	Kent.
Rye	Borough prison	Sussex.
South Molton	Ditto	Devon.
Tenterden	Ditto	Kent.

All persons who, before the passing of the Act, might lawfully have been committed to any of the above-mentioned prisons are now to be committed to the prison of the county in which any such prison was situated; and the county prison is, for all purposes relating to or consequential on the committal, trial, detention, or punishment of prisoners committed or removed thereto in pursuance of this provision of the Act, to be regarded in law as if it were the discontinued prison (P. A., 1865, s. 68).

Removal of Prisoners from Discontinued Prisons.—The statute referred to also made provision for the removal from the above-mentioned prisons, as soon as conveniently might be after its commencement, of all the prisoners then confined in them, to the county prison (P. A., 1865, s. 69).

Expenses of Prisoners confined in County Prisons instead of in Discontinued Prisons.—The expenses incurred by any county in the conveyance, transport, maintenance, safe custody, and care of every prisoner confined in the county prison instead of in one of the discontinued prisons, including the expenses of the removal of the prisoners from one prison to another, are to be defrayed in the manner provided by law in cases where the prisoners committed for offences arising within any borough or other place that does not contribute to the county rate are sent to any prison of a county, and there is no special contract between such borough or other place and the county relative to such prisoners (P. A., 1865, s. 70).

Power to use aforesaid Discontinued Prisons as Lock-up Houses.—The prison authority of any prison discontinued as already mentioned was empowered to sell the prison in the manner provided by The Prison Act, 1865, for the sale of unnecessary prisons, or, with the sanction of the Secretary of State, to cause the prison to be used as a police station house or a lock-up house, and the money arising from any sale made in pursuance of the provisions of the Act in this respect was required to be applied in discharging any expenses that might be incurred by the prison authority in the maintenance of its prisoners, or otherwise in aid of the rate applicable to prison purposes (P. A., 1865, s. 71).

Power to allow Compensation to Persons deprived of Office.—Provision was also made for the granting by the justices in sessions assembled, and having jurisdiction over any discontinued prison, of such compensation or allowance as they might think fit to any person who was deprived of any salary or emoluments by reason of the discontinuance of the prison (P. A., 1865, s. 72).

Saving as to Rights of Creditors.—But, although the above-mentioned prisons were discontinued, it was expressly provided that nothing contained in the Act should affect the right of any creditor who might have advanced any moneys for building, repairing, or otherwise for the purposes of any such prison, or who might have advanced any money on any mortgage or other security; but that it should still be lawful for such a creditor to pursue any remedies for recovering the principal or interest on moneys due to him, and that he should still enjoy the benefit of any security possessed by him (P. A., 1865, s. 78). Similar provisions will be found to have been also made by The Prison Act, 1877, for saving the rights and for securing the payment of the debts or claims of creditors of prison authorities (P. A., 1877, ss. 20, 22, 23).

Sale of Unnecessary Prisons.—Any prison authority was empowered by The Prison Act, 1865, to sell under certain conditions any prison or land belonging to or held in trust for it as such prison authority, that might appear to it to be unnecessary by reason of its having provided for the accommodation of its prisoners; and the moneys arising from such a sale were to be applied in discharging any expenses that might have been or might thereafter be incurred by such authority in building, altering, enlarging, or rebuilding any prison within its jurisdiction, or otherwise in aid of the rate raiseable for the maintenance of its prison (P. A., 1865, ss. 46, 47).

Power of Secretary of State to Discontinue Prisons.—And it is now provided by The Prison Act, 1877, that the Secretary of State may by order from time to time discontinue any prison or prisons vested in him by that Act, provided that there remain one prison at least in every county, unless the Secretary of State shall otherwise order, for special reasons to be stated in his order; and any such order is to be laid before both Houses of Parliament forthwith, if Parliament be sitting at the time when it is made, or if not then sitting, within one month after the commencement of the then next session of Parliament (P. A., 1877, s. 33).

Effect of Discontinuance of Prison.—When a prison has been thus discontinued, the Secretary of State is to serve a notice on the prison authority to which the prison originally belonged, that he will, at any time within a period of not less than six months, which period he is to prescribe, from the date of the service of the notice, cause the prison, but without any furniture or effects belonging thereto, to be reconveyed to the authority on payment by the authority into the Exchequer, for the public use, of one hundred and twenty pounds in respect of each prisoner belonging to the authority for whom cell accommodation was provided in the discontinued prison at the time of the passing of the Act (12th of July, 1877), and also on repayment by the authority of any compensation it may have received in respect of its having provided a prison of its own more than adequate for the accommodation of the prisoners belonging to it.

A prison authority may sell or otherwise dispose of any prison so reconveyed to it in such manner as it may think fit. But if a prison authority declines to accept the offer of the reconveyance of a prison, or fail to pay or to secure, to the satisfaction of the Secretary of State, the payment of such sum as before mentioned into the Exchequer, the prison is to be sold by the Secretary of State, who, after paying the expenses of the sale, and paying into the Exchequer the sum required to be paid by the prison authority, is to render the overplus (if any) to that authority. Any sum so payable by a prison authority is to be deemed to be a debt due from that authority to the Crown, and may be recovered accordingly. A prison authority may borrow, and the Public Works Loan Commissioners may lend, at such rate per cent. of interest as the Treasury may determine, such sum of money as may be required for making the payment in question, but the whole amount so borrowed is to be repaid within thirty-five years. The Act, however, declares that the cell accommodation provided by a prison authority in all its prisons may be calculated, for the purpose of ascertaining the sum payable by the authority, and that if it appears from the calculation that sufficient accommodation has been provided by the authority in any one prison or prisons belonging to it, no sum shall be payable by the authority in respect of the discontinued prison, and that a proportionate deduction shall be made in the sum payable by such authority in the event of any partial accommodation in excess of the necessary accommodation having been provided in such other prisons belonging to the authority (P. A., 1877, s. 34).

REPEAL OF STATUTES AND PARTS OF STATUTES.

Repeal of Acts.—The several Acts specified in the third schedule of The Prison Act, 1865, were, to the extent therein mentioned, repealed from the commencement (1st of February, 1866) of that Act (P. A., 1865, s. 73).

Repeal not to affect any Order, &c., made, &c.—But no repeal thereby enacted was to affect:

(1) Any order made, sentence passed, or other act

or thing duly done under any Acts thereby repealed;
(2) Any right or privilege acquired, any security given, or other liability incurred under any Act thereby repealed;
(3) Any penalty, forfeiture, or other punishment incurred in respect of any offence against any Act thereby repealed;
(4) Any appointment to an office made under any Act thereby repealed, or any power of removing the holder of such office, or otherwise dealing with such office as respects the existing holder thereof in the manner provided by any Act thereby repealed;
(5) The power of committing prisoners to any prison, except in so far as the same was altered in pursuance of the powers given by the Act (P. A., 1865, s. 74).

Saving as to Repealed Provisions in other Acts.—Any unrepealed Act of Parliament in which reference is made to the provisions of any Act repealed by The Prison Act, 1865, is to be construed as if in such first-mentioned Act reference had been made to the corresponding provisions of The Prison Act, 1865 (P. A., 1865, s. 76).

Repeal of The Prison Act, 1865, ss. 53, 54, 55.—The fifty-third, fifty-fourth, and fifty-fifth sections of The Prison Act, 1865, relating to the appointment of visiting justices, to the regulation of their duties, and to visits to prisons by any justice of the peace, are repealed from the commencement (1st of April, 1878) of The Prison Act, 1877, and other provisions are substituted in their stead (P. A., 1877, ss. 13, 15).

Repeal of 5 & 6 W. IV. c. 38, s. 7, as to Appointment of Inspectors of Prisons.—The seventh section of the Act 5 & 6 W. IV. c. 38, relating to the appointment of inspectors of prisons by the Secretary of State, and to the duties to be discharged by them, is repealed from the commencement of The Prison Act, 1877, so far as respects England (P. A., 1877, s. 45).

Repeal of Enactments inconsistent with The Prison Act, 1877.—All enactments inconsistent with The Prison Act, 1877, are declared to be thereby repealed (P. A., 1877, s. 51).

THE PRISON ACT, 1865.

(28 & 29 VICT. C. 126.)

ARRANGEMENT OF SECTIONS.
Preliminary.

Sect.
1. Short title.
2. Commencement of Act.
3. Application of Act.
4. Definition of terms.
5. Description of "prison authorities."
6. Definition of "justices in sessions assembled."
7. Contracts, &c., by prison authority in counties.

PART I.

THE MAINTENANCE AND GOVERNMENT OF PRISONS.

Obligation to maintain Prisons.

8. Maintenance of prisons by separate prison jurisdiction.
9. Definition of separate prison jurisdiction.

Appointment of Officers.

10. Officers of prison.
11. Appointment of chaplain to two prisons.

Sect.
12. Assistant chaplains and deputy gaoler.
13. Notice to be sent to bishop as to chaplains and assistant chaplains.
14. Tenure of office and salaries of prison officers.
15. Superannuation of officers.
16. Removal of prison officers from apartments.

Discipline of Prisoners.

17. Requisitions of Act as to separation of prisoners.
18. Cells to be certified for confinement of prisoners.
19. Requisitions of Act as to hard labour.
20. Regulations as to government of prisons.
21. Rules in addition to regulations in schedule.
22. Inspector of prisons to leave a minute of observations.

Enlargement and Rebuilding of Prisons.

23. Power to build prisons.
24. Conditions as to building prisons.
25. Mode of obtaining sanction of Secretary of State to building of prisons.
26. Approval of Secretary of State.
27. Charge of borrowed moneys.
28. Certain clauses of 10 & 11 Vict. c. 16, as to borrowing money incorporated.
29. Public Works Loan Commissioners to lend money for building prisons.
30. Appointment of Surveyor-General of prisons.

Contracts for Maintenance of Prisoners and Appropriation of Prisons.

31. Contracts by prison authorities for maintenance of prisoners.
32. Expenses of contracts between prison authorities.

ARRANGEMENT OF SECTIONS.

Sect.
33. Appropriation of prisons for purposes of classification.
34. Public notice of prisons being appropriated to certain prisoners.

Penalty for inadequate Prisons.

35. Government allowance withheld from inadequate prisons.
36. Power of Secretary of State to close inadequate prisons.

Offences in relation to Prisons.

37. Assisting prisoners to escape.
38. Punishment for carrying spirituous liquors or tobacco into prisons.
39. Punishment for carrying letters into and out of prisons.
40. Notice of penalties to be placed outside of prisons.

Discharge of Prisoners.

41. When term of imprisonment expires on Sunday, prisoner to be discharged on preceding day.
42. Allowance to discharged prisoner.
43. Discharged prisoners provided with means of returning to place of settlement.

Purchase of Land.

44. Certain provisions of 8 & 9 Vict. c. 18 incorporated.
45. Confirmation of title to lands purchased for purpose of prison.

Disposal of unnecessary Prisons.

Sect.
46. Sale of unnecessary prisons.
47. Conditions of sale.

Miscellaneous.

48. Inquests on prisoners.
49. General issue may be pleaded to action.
50. Venue, where laid.
51. Provision as to arbitration.
52. Recovery of penalties.

Visiting Justices.

53. Appointment of visiting justices.
54. Power to make rules as to visiting justices.
55. Visits to prison by any justice.

PART II.

Law of Prisons.

56. Abolition of distinction between gaol and house of correction.
57. Jurisdiction over prison.
58. Custody of prisoners.
59. Security to sheriff.
60. Responsibility of sheriff.
61. Description of prison in writ.
62. Gaoler of prison to deliver calendar.
63. Removal of prisoners for trial.
64. Removal of prisoners in other cases.
65. Her Majesty may order prisoners to be removed from one prison to another.
66. Custody and trial of prisoners in a substituted prison.
67. Misdemeanants of first division.

PART III.

Discontinuance of certain Prisons.

Sect.
68. Prohibition of committals to prisons in second schedule.
69. Removal of prisoners in scheduled prisons.
70. Expenses of prisoners confined in county prisons under Act.
71. Power to use scheduled prisons as lock-up houses.
72. Power to allow compensation to persons deprived of office.

PART IV.

Repeal of Statutes, and Saving Clauses.

73. Acts and parts of Acts in third schedule repealed.
74. No repeal hereby enacted to affect any order made, &c.
75. Certificates as to cells.
76. Saving as to repealed provisions referred to in other Acts.
77. As to the meaning of Gaol Act, 25 & 26 Vict. c. 44.
78. Saving of rights of creditors.
79. Saving of superannuation allowances.
80. Saving as to rules.
81. Saving as to appointment of officers.
82. Saving as to commissions.

INDEX TO SCHEDULES.

SCHEDULES.

THE PRISON ACT, 1865.

(28 & 29 Vict. c. 126.)

An Act to consolidate and amend the Law relating to Prisons.

[6th of July, 1865.]

WHEREAS it is expedient to consolidate and amend the law relating to Prisons in *England:* (*a*) Be it enacted by the Queen's most Excellent Majesty, by and with the advice and consent of the Lords Spiritual and Temporal, and Commons, in this present Parliament assembled, and by the authority of the same, as follows:

(*a*) In all cases where England is named in any statute, Wales and the town of Berwick-upon-Tweed are to be deemed to be included (20 Geo. II. c. 42. s. 3).

PRELIMINARY.

Short Title.

1. This Act may be cited for all purposes as "The Prison Act, 1865."

Commencement of Act.

2. This Act shall come into operation on the first day of *February,* one thousand eight hundred and sixty-six, which day is hereinafter referred to as the commencement of the Act.

Application of Act.

3. This Act shall not extend to *Scotland* or *Ireland,*

and shall not apply to the prisons for convicts under the superintendence of the directors of convict prisons, or to any military or naval prison.

Definition of Terms.

1. In this Act,(*b*) and in any Act applied or incorporated by this Act, the expressions hereinafter mentioned shall have the meanings hereinafter attached to them, unless there is something in the tenor of the Act inconsistent with such meanings; that is to say,

"Municipal Borough" shall mean any place for the time being subject to The Municipal Corporation Act passed in the session of the fifth and sixth years of the reign of his late Majesty King *William* the Fourth, chapter seventy-six, and any Acts amending the same, and "Borough"(*c*) shall include "Municipal Borough:"

"Prison"(*d*) shall mean gaol, house of correction, bridewell, or penitentiary; it shall also include the airing grounds or other grounds or buildings occupied by prison officers for the use of the prison and contiguous thereto:

"Gaoler" shall mean governor, keeper, or other chief officer of a prison:

"Clerk of the Peace" shall include any officer performing similar duties to those of a clerk of the peace:

"Treasurer" shall include any officer performing duties similar to those of a treasurer:

"Quarter Sessions" shall include "general sessions:"

"Criminal Prisoner"(*e*) shall mean any prisoner charged with or convicted of a crime.

(*h*) All expressions defined in The Prison Act, 1865, are to have the same meaning also in The Prison Act, 1877, in addition to any more comprehensive meaning which may be given to any of them by that Act (P. A., 1877. s. 61. *post* p. 198).

(*c*) As to the meaning of the term "Borough" in The Prison Act, 1877, see s. 59 of that Act. *post* p. 197.

(*d*) The term "Prison" as used in The Prison Act, 1877, has a meaning in addition to that here given to it (P. A., 1877. s. 60. *post* p. 197).

(*e*) As to the meaning of the term "Criminal Prisoner," see also s. 67 of this Act, *post* p. 102.

Description of "Prison Authorities."

5. The persons hereinafter named shall be prison authorities for the purposes of this Act; (*f*) that is to say,

(1) As respects any prison belonging to any county, except as hereinafter mentioned, or to any riding, division, hundred, or liberty of a county, having a separate court of quarter sessions, the justices in quarter sessions assembled:

(2) As respects any prison belonging to a county divided into ridings or divisions, and maintained at the common expense of such ridings or divisions, the justices of the county assembled at a court of gaol sessions held in manner provided by the Act of the fifth year of King *George* the Fourth, chapter twelve: (*g*)

(3) As respects any prison belonging to the City of *London*, or the liberties thereof, the court of the Lord Mayor and Aldermen:

(4) As respects any prison belonging to a municipal borough, the council of the borough:

(5) As respects any prison belonging to any district, liberty, city, borough, or town having a separate prison jurisdiction, (*h*) and not hereinbefore mentioned, the justices, council, or other persons having power at law to build, enlarge, or repair such prison, assembled at any gaol session or other formal meeting of their body.

THE PRISON ACT, 1865.

(*f*) The expression "Prison Authorities" has the same meaning also in The Prison Act, 1877. See s. 61 of that Act, *post* p. 198.

(*g*) The Act 5 Geo. IV. c. 12 will be found in the Appendix. Sections 1, 4, and 5 of the Act provide for the holding of courts of gaol sessions.

(*h*) The term "separate prison jurisdiction" is defined by s. 9 of this Act. See *post* p. 66.

Definition of "Justices in Sessions assembled."

6. The expression "Justices in Sessions assembled" shall mean as follows ; (*i*) that is to say,

(1) As respects any prison belonging to any county, except as hereinafter mentioned, or to any riding, division, hundred, or liberty of a county, having a separate court of quarter sessions, the justices in quarter sessions assembled :

(2) As respects any prison belonging to any county divided into ridings or divisions, and maintained at the common expense of such ridings or divisions, the justices of the county assembled at gaol sessions : (*j*)

(3) As respects any prison belonging to the city of *London*, or the liberties thereof, the court of the Lord Mayor and Aldermen :

(4) As respects any prison belonging to any municipal borough, the justices of the borough assembled at sessions to be held by them at the usual time of holding quarterly sessions of the peace, or at such other time as they may appoint :

(5) As respects any prison belonging to any city, district, borough, or town having a separate prison jurisdiction, (*k*) and not hereinbefore mentioned, the justices or other persons having power at law to make rules for the government of such prison.

(*i*) This expression has the same meaning also in The Prison Act, 1877. See s. 61 of that Act, *post* p. 198.

(*j*) As to the holding of courts of gaol sessions in such counties, see the Act 5 Geo. IV. c. 12 ss. 1, 4, and 5. in the Appendix.

(*k*) The term "separate prison jurisdiction" is defined by s. 9 of this Act. See *post* p. 66.

Contracts, &c., by Prison Authority in Counties.

7. The provisions of the Act of the twenty-first and twenty-second years of the reign of her present Majesty, chapter ninety-two,(*l*) shall apply to all contracts, mortgages, or conveyances entered into or executed in pursuance of this Act by or on behalf of or with the justices of any county, riding, division, hundred, or liberty of a county in general or quarter sessions assembled; and in the construction of that Act the expression "justices in quarter sessions assembled" shall include the justices of the county in gaol sessions assembled, in pursuance of the Act of the fifth year of King George the Fourth, chapter twelve, and shall also include the bailiff and justices of the liberty of Romney Marsh assembled at any sessions or meeting. And all contracts, mortgages, or conveyances entered into or executed in pursuance of this Act by or on behalf of or with any other prison authority shall be entered into and executed in manner in which such instruments or deeds are usually entered into by such authority.

(*l*) The Act will be found in the Appendix.

PART I.

THE MAINTENANCE AND GOVERNMENT OF PRISONS.

OBLIGATION TO MAINTAIN PRISONS.

Maintenance of Prisons by separate Prison Jurisdiction.

8. There shall be provided, (*m*) at the expense of every county, riding, division, hundred, liberty, franchise, borough, town, or other place having a separate prison jurisdiction, (*n*) adequate accommodation for its prisoners in a prison or prisons constructed and regulated in such manner as to comply with the requisitions of this Act in respect of prisons.

All expenses incurred by a prison authority in carrying into effect the provisions of this Act shall be defrayed out of the county rate, or rate in the nature of a county rate, borough rate, or other rate leviable in the county, riding, division, hundred, liberty, franchise, borough, town, or other place having a separate prison jurisdiction, (*n*) and applicable to the maintenance of a prison, or out of any other property applicable to that purpose.

(*m*) On and after the commencement of The Prison Act, 1877 (1st of April, 1878) the obligation of any county, riding, division, hundred, liberty, franchise, borough, town, or place, having a separate prison jurisdiction, to maintain a prison or to provide prison accommodation for its prisoners, is to cease (P. A., 1877, s. 16, *post* p. 163); and all expenses incurred in respect of the maintenance of the prisons to which The Prison Act, 1865, and that Act apply, and of the maintenance of the prisoners confined in them, are thenceforth to be defrayed out of moneys provided by Parliament (P. A., 1877, s. 4, *post* p. 150). In other words, the expenditure in respect of those prisons will cease, at the period just mentioned, to be a local charge, and will become an imperial charge, and will be borne, not by the local rates, but by the Imperial Exchequer. The administration and general superintendence of the prisons in question, and the legal estate in them, will also be transferred, at the same time, from the various prison authorities or justices in sessions assembled to the Secretary of State for the Home

Department and to the Prison Commissioners, as constituted and appointed under the provisions of The Prison Act, 1877 (see ss. 5, 6, 9, 48 of the Act, *post* pp. 151, 153, 155, 191). That Act makes ample provision, however, for dealing with the contracts or obligations which may have been entered into by prison authorities, and with the expenditure which may have been incurred by one prison authority with regard to the reception into its prisons of prisoners belonging to some other prison authority, in providing a prison or prisons more than adequate for the accommodation of its own prisoners, or with regard to the construction of any building to be used as a prison, but which may not at the commencement of the Act be completed (see ss. 18, 19, 21, 22, 23, *post* pp. 164, 166, 168, 169); and also for making allowance to any prison authority for any sum of money which it may have contributed towards the construction by some other prison authority of cell accommodation for the use of the prisoners of such contributing authority, where the cell accommodation has been constructed accordingly (see s. 17 of the Act, *post* p. 163).

(*n*) See s. 9, *infra*.

Definition of "Separate Prison Jurisdiction."

9. For the purposes of this Act (*o*) every county, riding, division, hundred, liberty, franchise, borough, town, or other place shall be deemed to have a separate prison jurisdiction which maintains a separate prison, or would be liable at law to maintain a separate prison if accommodation were not provided for its prisoners in the prison of some other jurisdiction.

Where a county is divided into ridings or divisions, and a prison is maintained at the common expense of such ridings or divisions, that county shall, in relation to such prison, and for the purposes thereof, be deemed to have a separate prison jurisdiction, notwithstanding a separate county rate is not levied in such county at large.

(*o*) The term "separate prison jurisdiction" has the same meaning also in The Prison Act, 1877 (see s. 61 of that Act, *post* p. 198).

APPOINTMENT OF OFFICERS.
Officers of Prison.

10. There shall be appointed to every prison by the justices in sessions assembled, (*p*)

A gaoler;(*q*) a chaplain, being a clergyman of the
   Established Church;(*r*) a surgeon, duly registered as such, under the Act of the session of
   the twenty-first and twenty-second years of
   the reign of her present Majesty, chapter
   ninety;(*s*) and such subordinate officers(*t*) as
   may be necessary.
And to every prison in which females are confined,
A matron and such subordinate female officers (*t*) as
   may be necessary.
Provided, that in a prison where females only are imprisoned, the matron shall be deemed to be the gaoler,
and shall, so far as is practicable, perform all the duties
and be subject to all the obligations of a gaoler in relation to such prison.

(*p*) The 81st section of the Act (see *post* p. 109) provides that nothing contained in the Act shall affect any right vested by Act of Parliament or charter in the council of any municipal borough of appointing a gaoler, chaplain, or other officer of the prison of such borough ; a right which was also reserved to such councils by The Municipal Corporation Act (5 & 6 W. IV. c. 76). But on and after the commencement (1st of April, 1878) of The Prison Act, 1877, the appointment of the officers of all the prisons to which that Act and The Prison Act, 1865, apply, as well those of the prisons belonging to municipal boroughs, as those of other prisons, will become vested in the Secretary of State and, in some instances, in the Prison Commissioners (P. A., 1877, ss. 5, 9. *post* pp. 151, 155); inasmuch as that Act, whilst it transfers the appointment of all officers of such prisons to the Secretary of State and, as already specified, to the Prison Commissioners, in general terms, does not make any provision for reserving to town councils the right above mentioned.

(*q*) See s. 4, *ante* p. 61.

(*r*) So much of the 3rd section of The Prison Ministers' Act, 1863, (see the Act, *post* p. 222,) as is inconsistent with the provision of this Act is repealed (see Schedule III., *post* p. 144) so far as it relates to prisons to which this Act applies; but the provisions of that section which relate to the visiting of prisoners of a church or religious persuasion differing from that of the Established Church, by a minister of the church or persuasion to which they belong appear to be still in force (see also the 47th Prison Regulation in the 1st Schedule of this Act, *post* p. 125). As to the attendance of prisoners of a church or religious persuasion differing from that of the Established Church at Divine service performed by the chaplain of a prison, or at any religious instruction given by him, see the 46th Prison Regulation in the 1st Schedule of this Act (*post* p. 124).

(*s*) The Act 21 & 22 Vict. c. 90 (*An Act to Regulate the Qualifications of Practitioners in Medicine and Surgery*), as amended by the Act 23 Vict. c. 7 s. 3, provides (s. 36) that no person shall, after the 1st of January, 1861, hold any appointment as a physician, surgeon, or other medical officer, either in the military or naval service, etc., etc., or in any hospital, infirmary, etc., not supported wholly by voluntary contributions, or in any lunatic asylum, gaol, penitentiary, house of correction, house of industry, etc., or other public establishment, body, or institution, etc., unless he be registered under the former of those Acts. The Act also provides (s. 27) that the Registrar of the General Medical Council shall in every year cause to be printed, published, and sold, under the direction of the Council, a correct register of the names, in alphabetical order according to the surnames, with the respective residences, in the form set forth in Schedule D of the Act, or to the like effect, and medical titles, diplomas, and qualifications conferred by any corporation or university, or by doctorate of the Archbishop of Canterbury, with the dates thereof, of all persons appearing on the general register, as existing on the 1st of January in every year; and that such register shall be called the "Medical Register," and that a copy of such register for the time being, purporting to be printed and published in the manner above described, shall be evidence in all courts and before all justices of the peace and others, that the persons therein specified are registered according to the provisions of the Act; and that the absence of the name of any person from any such copy shall be evidence, until the contrary be made to appear, that such person is not registered according to the provisions of the Act: but that, in the case of any person whose name does not appear in such copy, a certified copy, under the hand of the Registrar of the General Medical Council, or of any branch Council, of the entry of the name of such person on the general or local register, shall be evidence that such person is registered under the provisions of the Act.

A book purporting to be a copy of the Medical Register, and professing to be "published and sold at the office of the General Council of Medical Education and Registration," has been held to be admissible as evidence, under the foregoing provision of the 21 & 22 Vict. c. 90 (Pedgrift *v.* Chevallier, 8 C. B. N. S. 246).

(*t*) The 10th Prison Regulation (see Schedule I. of this Act, *post* p. 141) declares that all officers of a prison shall be deemed to be subordinate officers, with the exception of the gaoler, the chaplain, the surgeon, the matron, and any minister appointed under The Prison Ministers' Act, 1863. As to the appointment of subordinate officers of a prison on or after the commencement of The Prison Act, 1877, see s. 9 of that Act, *post* p. 155.

Appointment of Chaplain to Two Prisons.

11. The same person may officiate as chaplain of any two prisons situate within a convenient distance from each other, if such prisons together are calculated to receive not more than one hundred prisoners; but the chaplain of more than one prison, and the chaplain of any prison in which the average number of prisoners confined at one time during the three years next before his appointment has not been less than one hundred, shall not, whilst holding his chaplaincy, hold any benefice with cure of souls or any curacy.

Assistant Chaplains and Deputy Gaoler.

12. The justices in sessions assembled (*u*) may appoint an assistant chaplain, being a clergyman of the Established Church, and a deputy gaoler, or either of such officers, to any prison which they deem sufficiently large to require the appointment of such officers, or either of them.

(*u*) See The Prison Act, 1877, s. 5, *post* p. 151, and s. 10 of this Act, Note (*p*), *ante* p. 67.

Notice to be sent to Bishop as to Chaplains and Assistant Chaplains.

13. Notice of the nomination of a chaplain or assistant chaplain to a prison shall, within one month after it has taken place, be transmitted to the bishop of the diocese in which the prison is situate, (*v*) and no chaplain or assistant chaplain shall officiate in any prison until he has obtained a licence for that purpose from the bishop of the diocese wherein the prison is situate, nor for any longer time than while such licence continues in force.

(*v*) The notice of the nomination must be sent to, and the licence to officiate must be obtained from, the bishop of the diocese in which the prison is actually situate, notwithstanding the provisions of the 57th section of this Act, which declares that every prison, wheresoever situate, shall for all purposes be deemed to be within the limits of the place for which it is used as a prison (see the section, *post* p. 98).

Tenure of Office and Salaries of Prison Officers.

14. Every officer of a prison appointed under this Act (*w*) shall hold his office during the pleasure of the justices in sessions assembled, and shall receive such salary as they may direct, subject to this proviso, that in the case of a municipal borough the amount of the salary of every prison officer appointed under this Act shall be approved by the council.

(*w*) As to the tenure of office, etc., of officers appointed before the commencement of this Act, see s. 79 of the Act, *post* p. 108; see also The Prison Act, 1877, s. 35, *post* p. 177.

Superannuation of Officers.

15. If any officer of a prison has been an officer of such prison for not less than twenty years, and is not less than sixty years of age, or becomes incapable, from confirmed sickness, age, or infirmity, or injury received in actual execution of his duty, of executing his office in person, and such sickness, age, infirmity, or injury is certified by a medical certificate, and there shall be a report of the visiting justices testifying to his good conduct during his period of service, and recommending a grant to be made to him (such report to be made at some sessions of the justices holden not less than two months before the sessions at which the grant is made), the justices in sessions assembled may grant to such officer, having regard to his length of service, an annuity, by way of superannuation allowance, not exceeding two-thirds of his salary and emoluments, or a gratuity not exceeding the amount of his salary and emoluments, for one year; any annuity or gratuity so fixed to be payable out of the rates lawfully applicable to the payment of the salaries of such officers. Where the power to levy the last-mentioned rates is vested in a different body from the justices, the consent of such last-mentioned body shall be obtained to the amount of superannuation allowed. (*x*)

(*x*) The provisions of this section do not apply to the superannuation allowance of an officer appointed prior to the commencement (1st of February, 1866) of the Act, and such an officer is to remain entitled to the same superannuation allowance as if the Act had not passed; but the superannuation allowance of such an officer may nevertheless, upon his own application, and with the consent of the justices in sessions assembled, be calculated upon the scale directed by this section (see s. 79, *post* p. 108). As to the granting of an annuity by way of superannuation allowance, or the granting of a gratuity on his superannuation, etc., to an officer attached to a prison at the time of the commencement of The Prison Act, 1877, and as to the granting of compensation to such an officer on the abolition of, or on his having retired from, his office, see ss. 36, 53 of that Act, *post* pp. 179, 194.

Removal of Prison Officers from Apartments.

16. Whenever any officer of a prison is suspended, removed from, or resigns his office, or departs this life, the officer so suspended, removed, or resigning, and his family, and the family of every such deceased officer, shall quit the possession of the house or apartments in which he or they have previously resided by virtue of such office, when required so to do by notice under the hand or hands of two or more visiting justice or justices of the peace; (*y*) and if he or they refuse or neglect to give such possession for forty-eight hours after such notice as aforesaid has been given to him or them, any two justices, upon proof made to them of such removal, resignation, or death, and of the service of such notice, and of such neglect or refusal to comply therewith, may, by warrant under their hands and seals, direct any constable, within a period therein named, to enter by force, if necessary, into such premises, and deliver possession thereof to the prison authority, (z) or to any person appointed by the visiting justices.

(y) As to the exercise by the Prison Commissioners, on and after the commencement of The Prison Act, 1877, of the powers now exerciseable by the visiting justices of a prison, see s. 9 of that Act, *post* p. 155.
(z) See The Prison Act, 1877, s. 5, *post* p. 151.

Discipline of Prisoners.

Requisitions of Act as to Separation of Prisoners.

17. The requisitions of this Act with respect to the separation of prisoners are as follows : (a)

(1) In every prison, separate cells shall be provided equal in number to the average of the greatest number of prisoners, not being convicts under sentence of penal servitude, who have been confined in such prison at any time during each of the preceding five years :

(2) In every prison, punishment cells (b) shall be provided or appropriated for the confinement of prisoners for prison offences :

(3) In a prison containing female prisoners as well as males, the women shall be imprisoned in separate buildings or separate parts of the same buildings, in such manner as to prevent their seeing, conversing, or holding any intercourse with the men :

(4) In a prison where debtors are confined, (c) means shall be provided for separating them altogether from the criminal prisoners :

(5) In a prison where criminal prisoners (d) are confined, such prisoners shall be prevented from holding any communication with each other, either by every prisoner being kept in a separate cell by day and by night, except when he is at chapel or taking exercise, or by every prisoner being confined by night to his

cell, and being subjected to such superintendence during the day as will, consistently with the provisions of this Act, prevent his communicating with any other prisoner.

(*a*) As to carrying these requisitions into effect, see ss. 33, 34 of the Act, *post* pp. 83, 84.

(*b*) As to the certifying of punishment cells by an Inspector of Prisons, see s. 18, *post* p. 73.

(*c*) The Prison Act, 1877, empowers the Secretary of State to appoint from time to time, by any general or special rule, in any county, a prison or prisons in which debtors and persons who are not criminal prisoners may be confined during the period of their imprisonment (see s. 26 of the Act, *post* p. 171). As to the making of rules by the Secretary of State with respect to the classification and treatment of prisoners confined for non-payment of sums in the nature of debts, see s. 38 of that Act, *post* p. 183.

(*d*) As to the meaning of the term "criminal prisoner," see s. 4 of this Act, *ante* p. 61, and s. 67, *post* p. 102.

Cells to be certified for Confinement of Prisoners.

18. No cell shall be used for the separate confinement of a prisoner unless it is certified (*e*) by one of Her Majesty's Inspectors of Prisons to be of such a size, and to be lighted, warmed, ventilated, and fitted up in such a manner as may be requisite for health, and furnished with the means of enabling the prisoner to communicate at any time with an officer of the prison; but a distinction may be made in respect of the use of cells for the separate confinement of prisoners during long and short periods of imprisonment, and in respect of the use of cells in which the prisoner is intended to be employed during the whole day, or for a long or short part thereof; and the certificates of the Inspector may be varied accordingly, so as to express the period of imprisonment for which each cell may be considered fit, and the number of hours in the day during which the prisoners may be employed therein.

No punishment cell shall be used unless it is certified by such Inspector that it is furnished with the means of enabling the prisoner to communicate at any time with an officer of the prison, and that it can be used as a punishment cell without detriment to the prisoner's health, and the time for which it may be so used shall be stated in the certificate.

Every certified cell shall be distinguished by a number or mark placed in a conspicuous position, and shall be referred to by its number or mark in the certificate of the Inspector; and if the number or mark of any certified cell is changed without the consent of the Inspector, such cell shall be deemed to be an uncertified cell until a fresh certificate has been given.

Any certificate given by an Inspector in respect of a cell may be withdrawn on such alteration taking place in such cell as to render the certificate, in his opinion, inapplicable thereto; and upon a certificate in respect of a cell being withdrawn, that cell shall cease to be a certified cell for the purposes of this Act.

If any prison authority feel aggrieved by the refusal of the Inspector to certify a cell for any of the purposes of this Act, it may appeal to one of Her Majesty's principal Secretaries of State, and his decision shall be final.

(*e*) All cells certified before the commencement (1st of February, 1866) of The Prison Act, 1865, by any Inspector of Prisons, as being fit to be used for the separate confinement of prisoners, are to be deemed to be cells certified for the purpose under that Act (P. A., 1865, s. 75, *post* p. 107).

Requisitions of Act as to Hard Labour.

19. Hard labour for the purposes of this Act shall be of two classes, (*f*) consisting, 1st, of work at the treadwheel, shot drill, crank, capstan, stone-breaking, or such other like description of hard bodily labour as may be appointed by the justices in sessions assembled, (*g*) with the approval of the Secretary of State, which work is hereinafter referred to as hard labour of the first class; 2ndly, of such other description of bodily labour as may be appointed by the justices in sessions assembled, (*g*) with the approval of the Secretary of State, which work is hereinafter referred to as hard labour of the second class; and in every prison where prisoners sentenced to hard labour are confined, adequate means (having regard to the average number of such prisoners confined in that prison during the preceding five years) shall be provided for enforcing hard labour in accordance with the regulations of this Act; and no prison shall be deemed to be in conformity with the requisitions of this Act with respect to the enforcement of hard labour, unless such means as aforesaid have been provided therein, and prisoners sentenced to hard labour have been employed thereat in manner provided by this Act: Provided, that employment in the necessary services of the prison may, in the case of a limited number of prisoners, to be selected by the visiting justices, (*h*) as a reward for industry and good behaviour, be deemed to be hard labour of the second class.

(*f*) The 34th, 35th, 36th, and 37th Prison Regulations in Schedule I. of this Act (*post* pp. 121, 122) direct under what circumstances and with reference to what prisoners each class of hard labour is to be enforced. With respect, however, to the 34th Regulation, which directs that a male prisoner of sixteen years and upwards, sentenced to hard labour, shall be kept to hard labour of the first class during the whole of his sentence, where it does not exceed three months, and during the first three months of his sentence, where it exceeds three months; an important amendment, for the purpose of relaxing its operation, is made by The Prison Act, 1877, which enacts (s. 37, *post* p. 183) that the Secretary of State may, in either of the cases just mentioned, substitute hard labour of the second class for hard labour of the first class during the last two of such three months, or any part of such last two months, and may make such substitution either by a general or special regulation, and either conditionally or unconditionally, and may from time to time vary any regulation so made. It is also provided by the section of the Act above referred to, that the Secretary of State shall, in making any such regulations, have regard to the previous convictions, the industry, and the conduct of the prisoners.

(*g*) On and after the commencement (1st of April, 1878) of The Prison Act, 1877, this power will be transferred to, vested in, and exerciseable by, the Secretary of State himself (P. A., 1877, s. 5, *post* p. 151).

(*h*) On and after the commencement of The Prison Act, 1877, this duty will devolve on the Prison Commissioners, or on such person or persons as the Secretary of State may appoint (P. A., 1877, s. 9, *post* p. 155).

Regulations as to Government of Prisons.

20. The regulations contained in the first schedule hereto, with respect to the government of prisons, shall be binding on all persons in the same manner as if they were enacted in the body of this Act. (*i*)

(*i*) The regulations will be found in their proper place, *post* pp. 115—141. All rules in force in any prison, which were inconsistent either with this Act or with the regulations contained in the first schedule thereto, were declared by the Act to be repealed from and after its commencement, but all other rules in force in any prison were to continue in force until altered in the manner provided in the next section (see s. 80, *post* p. 109). The general prison rules made by the Secretary of State in pursuance of The Prison Act, 1877, will be found in the Appendix, *post* pp. 279—293.

Rules in addition to Regulations in Schedule.

21. The justices in sessions assembled (*j*) shall make rules for the supply to all prisoners confined in prisons within their jurisdiction of a sufficient quantity of plain and wholesome food, regard being had, so far as relates to convicted criminal prisoners, to the nature of the labour required from or performed by such prisoners, so that the allowance of food may be duly apportioned thereto, and shall frame dietary tables for this purpose; and the said justices may make rules in respect of any other matters relating to the government of prisons within their jurisdiction, in addition to the regulations in the said first schedule, and may from time to time repeal or alter any rules made or dietary tables framed in pursuance of this section; but no rule or dietary table, or repeal or alteration of a rule or dietary table, shall be valid under this section until one of Her Majesty's principal Secretaries of State has certified his approval in writing under his hand; and when such approval has been certified, such rule or dietary table, or repeal or alteration of a rule or dietary table, shall be binding on all persons in the same manner as if it were enacted by this Act. If the justices in sessions assembled make default in making rules and dietary tables that may be approved by the said Secretary of State in respect of the supply of food to prisoners in any prison within their jurisdiction, there shall be in force in such prison such rules or dietary tables with respect to such supply as may from time to time be determined by the said Secretary of State in writing under his hand.

(*j*) The duty of making such rules will, on and after the commencement of The Prison Act, 1877, devolve upon the Secretary of State (see P. A., 1877, s. 5, *post* p. 151).

Inspector of Prisons to leave a Minute of Observations.

22. Upon visiting or inspecting a prison to which this Act applies, the Inspector shall, by letter addressed to the visiting justices, (*k*) call their attention to any irregularity he may have observed therein, or any complaint he may have to make against the buildings, the officers, or the discipline of the prison, and the visiting justices (*k*) shall enter a copy of such letter in their minute book.

(*k*) See The Prison Act, 1877, s. 9, *post* p. 155.

ENLARGEMENT AND REBUILDING OF PRISONS.
Power to Build Prisons.

23. Subject to the conditions hereinafter mentioned, any prison authority may (*l*) alter, enlarge, or rebuild any of its prisons, or may, if necessary, build other prisons in lieu of or in addition to any subsisting prisons, and may borrow money for the purpose of such alteration, enlargement, new building, or buildings. (*m*) (*l*) Many of the provisions of the several sections contained in this and in the two next succeeding divisions ("contracts for maintenance of prisoners and appropriation of prisons," and "penalty for inadequate prisons") of the Act, will, on the commencement of The Prison Act, 1877, cease to be operative so far as any new or further exercise of the various powers conferred by them is concerned ; but, inasmuch as contracts or other obligations at present in existence, or arrangements already made, may still be affected by them, it is considered desirable to retain them for the present in their place in the Act.

(*m*) As to the manner in which the money may be borrowed, as to the security to be given, and as to the time within which repayment is to be made, see ss. 27, 28, 29, and the notes thereto, *post* pp. 79, 80, 81.

Where at the time of the passing (12th of July, 1877) of The Prison Act, 1877, a prison authority may have contracted to construct a building to be used as a prison, but such building shall not at the commencement (1st of April, 1878) of that Act be completed or have become a prison within the meaning of the Act, the Secretary of State may, if he thinks fit so to do, allow the prison authority time to complete the building as a prison, and the building when so completed is to pass over to and vest in him as a prison completed at the commencement of the Act ; but if the Secretary of State does not think fit to allow time for the completion of such prison, he is nevertheless required, in assessing the amount of compensation payable by the prison authority (P. A., 1877, s. 17, *post* p. 163) in respect of cell accommodation, to make, with the consent of the Treasury, from the compensation so payable, such deduction as, having regard to all the circumstances of the case, may be agreed upon, or as may, in the event of disagreement between the Secretary of State and the prison authority, be determined by arbitration (P. A., 1877, s. 19, *post* p. 166).

Conditions as to Building Prisons.

24. The necessity for any alteration or enlargement, or for rebuilding of an existing prison, or for the building of a new prison, shall be proved, in the case of a municipal borough, by the certificate of the recorder, or chairman of quarter sessions where there is no recorder, and in any other case by a presentment of two or more of the visiting justices or other justices having jurisdiction within the district of the prison authority ; and the consideration of such certificate or presentment shall not be entertained by the prison authority, unless not less than three weeks' previous notice has been given in some one or more public newspaper or newspapers circulating within the district of the prison authority, of their intention to take the same into consideration at a time and place to be mentioned in such notice, and in every case the sanction of one of Her Majesty's Secretaries of State must be obtained to any such alteration, enlargement, rebuilding, or building.

Mode of obtaining Sanction of Secretary of State to Building of Prisons.

25. In order to obtain the sanction of the Secretary of State to the alteration, enlargement, or rebuilding of any prison, the prison authority shall forward to him a plan of the proposed alteration, enlargement, or new building, drawn on such scale and accompanied with such particulars as the said Secretary may determine, and shall add thereto an estimate of the expense proposed to be incurred by the prison authority, and the amount of money proposed to be borrowed; and wherever a new prison is built, or an old prison is altered, enlarged, or rebuilt, a chapel or suitable room shall be provided, easy of access to the prisoners, and shall be strictly set apart for religious worship, or for the religious and moral instruction of the prisoners, and shall not be employed for any other purpose.

Approval of Secretary of State.

26. The said Secretary of State may approve of the plans submitted to him with or without modification, or may disapprove of the same, and his approval or disapproval shall be certified in writing under his hand.

Charge of borrowed Moneys.

27. Any moneys borrowed by a prison authority may be charged by that authority on any county rate or rate in the nature of a county rate, borough rate, or other rate applicable to the maintenance of a prison, and leviable by that authority, or on any other property belonging to that authority, and applicable to the same purpose as the said rates, and shall be repaid, (*n*) together with the interest due thereon, out of such rates or other property.

(*n*) See s. 28 *infra*, and the note thereto.

Certain Clauses of 10 & 11 *Vict. c.* 16 *as to borrowing Money incorporated.*

28. The clauses of " The Commissioners' Clauses Act, 1847," with the exception of the eighty-fourth clause with respect to mortgages to be created by the Commissioners, shall form part of, and be incorporated with, this Act; and any mortgagee or assignee may enforce payment of his principal and interest by appointment of a receiver.

In the construction of the said clauses, " the Commissioners " shall mean " the prison authority."

Where a prison authority borrows any money for the alteration, enlargement, or rebuilding of any prison, or the building of any new prison, it shall charge the rates or property out of which the moneys borrowed are payable, not only with the interest of the moneys so borrowed, but also with the payment of such further sum as will ensure the repayment (*o*) of the whole sum borrowed within thirty years; or if the loan has been made by the Public Works Loan Commissioners, as defined by The Public Works Loan Act, 1853, within twenty years of the time of borrowing the same.

(*o*) Although the local obligation of counties, boroughs, and other places to maintain prisons, or to provide prison accommodation for their prisoners, will cease on the commencement (1st of April, 1878) of The Prison Act, 1877 (see s. 16 of that Act, *post* p. 163); and although the expenses incurred in respect of the maintenance of the prisons to which that Act applies, and of the prisoners in them, will at the same time cease to be a local charge, and become payable out of moneys to be provided by Parliament (see P. A., 1877, s. 4, *post* p. 150), it is expressly provided by the Act (s. 20, *post* p. 167) that its provisions shall not (except with respect to contracts and obligations between prison authorities themselves) affect any right or claim of any creditor of a prison authority under any contract legally made or in respect of any dealing legally had before its commencement, but that between such a creditor and the prison authority of which he is a creditor the contract may be enforced in the same manner in all respects as if the Act had not passed; and also (s. 22, *post* p. 169) that a prison authority shall still defray, in the same manner as if the Act had not passed, (1) All debts due and sums of money payable in respect of contracts performed, dealings completed, or any matter or thing done before the commencement of the Act; and (2) All mortgage debts (together with interest from time to time accruing thereon) contracted in respect of any prison. And it is declared that a mortgage debt shall, for the purposes of this provision, include any moneys, which, at the commencement of the Act, have been borrowed or contracted to be borrowed by a prison authority on the security of any prison, or on the security of any rate applicable to the payment of the expenses of a prison, and any debt or liability contracted before the same period, for the payment of which debt or liability money is authorised to be borrowed in pursuance of the 23rd section of this Act (see that section, *ante* p. 77). The Prison Act, 1877, provides, however (see s. 23, *post* p. 169), that where any contract or dealing, in which any prison authority is concerned is a continuous contract or dealing, to be performed partly before and partly after the commencement of the Act, and is not a contract or dealing which is declared by the Act to have determined, *i.e.* where the contract or dealing is not a contract or dealing, between two prison authorities (see s. 21 of the Act, *post* p. 168), and is not a mortgage debt, as above defined, such contract or dealing shall be deemed to be divisible; and as to so much of it as is performable before the commencement of the Act, it shall create a debt or obligation to be discharged or performed by the prison authority concerned in it, and as to so much of it as is performable after the commencement of the Act, it shall create a debt or obligation to be discharged or performed out of moneys provided by Parliament.

Public Works Loan Commissioners to lend Money for building Prisons.

29. The said Public Works Loan Commissioners as defined by The Public Works Loan Act, 1853, may advance to any prison authority, upon the security of any rate applicable to or chargeable with the maintenance of a prison, without any further security, for the purpose of altering, enlarging, or rebuilding any subsisting prison, or building any new prison in pursuance of this Act, such sums of money as may be recommended by one of Her Majesty's principal Secretaries of State.

Appointment of Surveyor-General of Prisons.

30. It shall be lawful for one of Her Majesty's principal Secretaries of State to appoint a proper person to be a Surveyor-General of prisons, for the purpose of advising prison authorities on the construction of prisons, and reporting to the Secretary of State on the several plans of prisons which may be sent to him for his report, and for the performance of such other duties connected with the construction of prisons as may be from time to time entrusted to him by the Secretary of State.

CONTRACTS FOR MAINTENANCE OF PRISONERS AND APPROPRIATION OF PRISONS.

Contracts by Prison Authorities for Maintenance of Prisoners.

31. Any prison authority may contract with any other prison authority having a prison in conformity with the requisitions of this Act, that the latter authority is to receive into and maintain in its prisons or one of its prisons all prisoners maintainable at the expense of the former authority, or any particular class or classes of such prisoners: Provided—

That no such contract shall be valid unless the prison of the latter authority is approved by one of Her Majesty's principal Secretaries of State as being a fit prison to receive the prisoners contracted to be received there. (*p*)

(*p*) As to the compensation to be made to any prison authority in respect of the accommodation which may have been provided by it for receiving the prisoners of some other authority, see The Prison Act, 1877, s. 18, *post* p. 164 ; and as to the determination of any contract made or obligation undertaken by any prison authority with any other prison authority for or in relation to the maintenance of any prison or prisoners, or any matter relating to such maintenance, see s. 21 of that Act, *post* p. 168.

Expenses of Contracts between Prison Authorities.

32. A contract entered into between prison authorities for the reception into and the maintenance in the prison of the one authority of the prisoners maintainable by the other authority may include the costs of conveying the prisoners to prison, and all other costs incurred in respect of such prisoners.

All moneys payable under the contract shall be raised in the same manner in which moneys for defraying the expenses of the prison for which a substitute is provided under the contract would be raiseable; and where such expenses are not by law wholly defrayable out of one fund, and a difference arises between the several persons interested in the several funds applicable to defraying such expenses, as to what proportion ought to be applied to paying the expenses arising under the contract, such difference shall be settled by arbitration, in manner hereinafter mentioned. (*q*)

(*q*) See s. 51, *post* p. 95.

Appropriation of Prisons for purposes of Classification.

33. Where two or more prisons are within the jurisdiction of the same prison authority, that authority may carry into effect the requisitions of this Act with respect to the separation of prisoners or the enforcement of hard labour (*r*) by appropriating particular prisons to particular classes of prisoners. (*s*)

(*r*) See ss. 17 and 18 of this Act, *ante* pp. 72, 73, as to the separation of prisoners, and s. 19, *ante* p. 74, as to the enforcement of hard labour.
(*s*) As to the appropriation by the Secretary of State of particular prisons to particular classes of prisoners, see The Prison Act, 1877, ss. 24, 25, and 26, *post* pp. 170, 171.

Public Notice of Prisons being appropriated to certain Prsioners.

34. Where a change has been made as to the prison to which prisoners committed within the jurisdiction of any prison authority may be sent by reason of such authority having appropriated any of its prisons to a particular class of prisoners, or having contracted with another prison authority for the reception of its prisoners, or from any other cause, notice of such change shall be published once at the least in each of two successive weeks in some newspaper or newspapers usually circulated within the jurisdiction of the said prison authority, and a copy thereof shall be served upon the gaoler of every prison within such jurisdiction.

Penalty for Inadequate Prisons.

Government Allowance withheld from inadequate Prisons.

35. Whenever it appears to one of Her Majesty's principal Secretaries of State that default has been made in any prison in complying with the requisitions of this Act in respect of the separation of prisoners, or of the enforcement of hard labour, or of providing a chapel or suitable room for religious worship, (*t*) it shall be lawful for the said Secretary of State to certify such non-compliance in writing under his hand to the Commissioners of Her Majesty's Treasury; and upon such certificate being given, no contribution shall thenceforth be paid out of moneys provided by Parliament towards the expenses of maintaining any prisoners in that prison until the said Secretary of State has revoked his certificate, upon being satisfied that the defaulting prison has been brought into conformity with the requisitions of this Act, and then only from the date of such revocation: Provided—

1st. That this section shall not affect the payment of any contribution payable on or before the thirty-first day of *December*, one thousand eight hundred and sixty-six:

2nd. That before the certificate of the said Secretary of State is given under this section with respect to any prison, a copy of the report of the Inspector of Prisons relating to that prison, and a statement of the grounds on which the said Secretary proposes to give his certificate, shall be sent to the prison authority; and it shall be lawful for such authority, upon receiving a copy of the said report and statement, to address any explanations or observations relating thereto to the said Secretary of State:

3rd. Whenever the certificate of the Secretary of State is given under this section in respect of a prison, a copy of the said statement of grounds, accompanied with any such explanations or observations as aforesaid, shall be laid before Parliament.

(*t*) As to the separation of prisoners, see ss. 17 and 18 of this Act, *ante* pp. 72, 73; as to the enforcement of hard labour, s. 19, *ante* p. 74; and as to providing a chapel or suitable room for religious worship, s. 25, *ante* p. 79.

Power of Secretary of State to close inadequate Prisons.

36. If at any time it appear to one of Her Majesty's principal Secretaries of State that a prison authority has, in respect of any prison within its jurisdiction, made default for four successive years in complying with the requisitions of this Act with respect to the separation of prisoners, or with respect to the enforcement of hard labour, or with respect to providing a chapel or suitable room for religious worship, (*u*) the said Secretary of State may, by notice under his hand, addressed to the authority of that prison, and forwarded by post in a prepaid letter to the gaoler of the prison, or otherwise delivered to him, require that authority, within a time specified in such notice, to bring such prison into conformity with the requisitions of this Act with respect to such matters as aforesaid, or to exercise the powers given to such authority by this Act of contracting for the removal of the whole or a number of its prisoners, proportioned to the inadequacy of its prison in respect of such separation or means of providing such hard labour, to some other prison where means exist for carrying into effect the requisitions of this Act with respect to the separation of prisoners or means of enforcing hard labour; and if any prison authority to whom such notice is given fail, within six months after the receipt thereof, to comply with the requirements thereby made, the said Secretary of State may order the said inadequate prison to be closed, (*v*) and direct the removal of the prisoners therein, and the committal of future prisoners to some other prison, the authority of which may be willing to receive them; and upon such order being made it shall be the duty of the gaoler of the said inadequate prison, without further warrant, to remove all the prisoners therein to the substituted prison named in the order of the Secretary of State, and such substituted prison shall thenceforth, and so long as such order is in force, for all purposes relating to the committal, detention, trial, and punishment of the prisoners so removed, and of the prisoners committed thereto in pursuance of this section, be deemed to be the prison of the defaulting authority, and that authority shall pay, out of any rates or moneys applicable to the support of the inadequate prison, all expenses incurred in and about the closing of that prison, and the removal of the prisoners therein to the substituted prison; and all expenses incurred by the authority of the substituted prison in respect of the prisoners committed to that prison in pursuance of this section shall be defrayed by the authority of the inadequate prison in the same manner in all respects as if that authority had contracted in pursuance of this Act with the authority of the substituted prison for the reception in the last-mentioned prison of prisoners belonging to the authority of the inadequate prison.

Notice of any order made by the said Secretary of State in pursuance of this section shall be published in the *London Gazette*, and once at least in two successive weeks in one of the newspapers usually circulating in the county, city, borough, or place in which the prison to which the order relates is situate, and a copy of the gazette or newspaper containing such order shall be conclusive evidence of its contents.

(*u*) See Note (*t*), *ante* p. 85.
(*v*) As to the power of the Secretary of State, under The Prison Act, 1877, to discontinue prisons, see ss. 33, 34 of that Act, *post* pp. 175, 176.

Offences in Relation to Prisons.

Assisting Prisoners to Escape.

37. Every person who aids any prisoner in escaping or attempting to escape from any prison, or who, with intent to facilitate the escape of any prisoner, conveys or causes to be conveyed into any prison any mask, dress, or other disguise, or any letter, or any other article or thing, (*w*) shall be guilty of felony, and on conviction be sentenced to imprisonment with hard labour for a term not exceeding two years.

(*w*) A crowbar has been held to be an " article or thing " within the meaning of this section, and a person who, with intent to facilitate the escape of a prisoner, conveyed such an instrument into a prison to be consequently guilty of felony (The Queen v. Payne, 35 L. J. Rep. (N. S.) M. C. 170; Law Rep. 1 C. C. R. 27).

Punishment for carrying Spirituous Liquors or Tobacco into Prison.

38. Every person who, contrary to the regulations

of the prison, brings or attempts by any means whatever to introduce into any prison any spirituous or fermented liquor or tobacco, and every officer of a prison who suffers any spirituous or fermented liquor or tobacco to be sold or used therein, contrary to the prison regulations, on conviction (*x*) shall be sentenced to imprisonment for a term not exceeding six months, (*y*) or to a penalty not exceeding twenty pounds, or both, in the discretion of the court; and every officer of a prison convicted under this section shall, in addition to any other punishment, forfeit his office and all arrears of salary due to him.

(*x*) As to the prosecution of offences and the recovery of penalties, see s. 52, *post* p. 95.

(*y*) That is, calendar months, 13 & 14 Vict. c. 21 s. 4.

Punishment for carrying Letters into and out of Prisons.

39. Every person who, contrary to the regulations of a prison, conveys or attempts to convey any letter or other document, or any article whatever not allowed by such regulations, into or out of any prison, shall on conviction incur a penalty not exceeding ten pounds; and if an officer of the prison, shall forfeit his office and all arrears of salary due to him; but this section shall not apply in cases where the offender is liable to a more severe punishment under any other provision of this Act. (*z*)

(*z*) As to the prosecution of offences and the recovery of penalties. see s. 52, *post* p. 95. The present section applies to cases where the act is done or attempted to be done contrary to the regulations of a prison merely, and where the "intent to facilitate the escape" of any prisoner is wanting. As to cases under other provisions of the Act, see s. 37, *ante* p. 87.

Notice of Penalties to be placed outside of Prison.

40. The visiting justices (*a*) shall cause to be affixed in a conspicuous place outside the prison a notice setting forth the penalties that will be incurred by persons committing any offence in contravention of the three preceding sections.

(a) See The Prison Act. 1877, s. 9, *post* p. 155.

Discharge of Prisoners.

When Term of Imprisonment expires on Sunday, Prisoner to be discharged on preceding Day.

41. Any prisoner confined in a prison, whose term of imprisonment would, according to his sentence, expire on any Lord's Day, shall be entitled to his discharge on the *Saturday* next preceding such Lord's Day; and every gaoler of every prison having the custody of any such prisoner as aforesaid is hereby required and authorized to discharge such prisoner on the *Saturday* next preceding any such Lord's Day.

Allowance to discharged Prisoner.

42. Where any prisoner is discharged from prison, c visiting justices may order a sum of money not exceeding two pounds to be paid out of any moneys under their control, and applicable to the payment of expenses of the prison, by the gaoler, to the prisoner himself, or to the treasurer of a certified Prisoners' Aid Society, (b) on his receiving from such Society an undertaking in writing, signed by the secretary thereof, to apply the same for the benefit of the prisoner, or, if that becomes impossible, to appropriate the whole or any unapplied part thereof for the benefit of such other prisoner or prisoners discharged from the said prison as the visiting justices may direct. (c)

(b) As to the manner in which a Prisoners' Aid Society may be certified, see the Act, 25 & 26 Vict. c. 44 s. 1, in the Appendix.
(c) The Prison Act, 1877, makes provision (s. 29, *post* p. 173) for the giving aid, after the commencement of that Act, to discharged prisoners by the Prison Commissioners.

Discharged Prisoners provided with Means of returning to Place of Settlement.

43. When a prisoner is discharged from prison, the visiting justices (*d*) of the prison may provide such prisoner out of any moneys under their control, and applicable to the payment of the expenses of the prison, with the means of returning to his home or place of settlement, by causing his fare to be paid by railway, or in any other convenient manner.

(*d*) See The Prison Act, 1877, s. 9, *post* p. 155.

PURCHASE OF LAND.

Certain Provisions of 8 & 9 Vict. c. 18 incorporated.

44. Any prison authority may purchase and hold such lands or easements relating to lands as they may require for the purposes of this Act; and to facilitate such purposes "The Lands Clauses Consolidation Act, 1845," and the Act amending the same, passed in the session of the twenty-third and twenty-fourth years of the reign of her present Majesty, chapter one hundred and six, shall be incorporated with this Act, with the exceptions and subject to the conditions hereinafter contained; that is to say,

1. There shall not be incorporated with this Act the sections and provisions of "The Lands Clauses Consolidation Act, 1845," hereinafter mentioned; that is to say, section sixteen, whereby it is provided that the capital is to be subscribed before the compulsory powers are to be put in force; section seventeen, whereby it is provided that the certificate of the justices shall be evidence that the capital has been subscribed; the provisions relating to the entry upon lands by the promoters of the

undertaking contained in sections eighty-four to ninety-one, both inclusive; section one hundred and twenty-three, whereby a limit of time for the compulsory purchase of land is imposed; or the provisions relating to access to the special Act:

2. In the construction of this Act and the said incorporated Acts this Act shall be deemed to be the special Act, and the prison authority shall be deemed to be the promoters of the undertaking, and the word "lands" shall include any easement in or out of lands:

3. The prison authority shall not, except in respect of lands contiguous to a prison, and required for the purpose of enlarging a prison, or rendering it more commodious or safe, put in force the provisions of the said incorporated Acts with respect to the purchase of land otherwise than by agreement.

Confirmation of Title to Lands purchased for Purpose of Prison.

45. When any lands have been purchased for the purposes of a prison in pursuance of this Act, such lands shall, at the expiration of five years from the date of a conveyance having been made to any person or body corporate on trust for such purposes, absolutely vest (*e*) in that person or body corporate for all the estate or interest purported to be conveyed, to be held on trust for the aforesaid purposes; and if before the expiration of the said term of five years any proceedings are taken on which judgment is obtained for the recovery of the possession of the said lands, then within two calendar months after judgment has been obtained there shall be paid to the person obtaining such judgment, instead of the delivery of possession of the lands, all costs incurred in obtaining such judgment, and compensation for the full value of his estate or interest in such lands, the amount of such compensation to be ascertained in manner provided by the said Lands Clauses Consolidation Act, 1845, in case of disputed compensation as to land, and to be calculated on the basis of the value of the land at the time of the purchase thereof.

(e) By The Prison Act, 1877, the term "prison" is declared (s. 60, *post* p. 197), in addition to the meaning attached to it by this Act (see s. 4, *ante* p. 61). to include any land or building bought, or contracted to be bought, before the commencement (1st of April, 1878) of the Act, by a prison authority, for the purpose of enlarging or altering any prison, or adding to the appurtenances of any prison. And the same Act also declares (s. 48, *post* p. 191) that the legal estate in every prison to which the Act applies, and in the site and land belonging thereto, shall, on and after the commencement of the Act, be deemed to be vested in the Prison Commissioners, and not in the Secretary of State, but shall from time to time be disposed of by the Commissioners in such mode as the Secretary of State, with the consent of the Treasury, may direct. But the 60th section of The Prison Act, 1877, above referred to contains a proviso that, if the Secretary of State is of opinion that any portion of the lands bought or contracted to be bought, as already mentioned, whether included or not within the walls of the prison, was not at the time of the passing of that Act (12th of July, 1877) necessary for the then subsisting purposes of the prison, he shall either direct that such portion shall be reconveyed to the prison authority, or retain such portion, or any part of such portion, on payment out of moneys provided by Parliament of such sum as may be agreed upon, or, in the event of difference, may be determined by arbitration in the manner provided by the Act.

Disposal of Unnecessary Prisons.
Sale of Unnecessary Prisons.

46. Any prison authority may sell any prison or land belonging to or held on trust for them as such prison authority that appears to them to be unnecessary *(f)* by reason of their having provided for the accommodation of their prisoners, and the moneys arising from such sale shall be applied in discharging any expenses that may have been or may hereafter be incurred by such authority in building, altering, enlarging, or rebuilding any prison within their jurisdiction, or otherwise in aid of the rate raiseable for the maintenance of their prison.

(*f*) As to the power of the Secretary of State, under The Prison Act, 1877, to discontinue prisons, and as to the power of a prison authority and of the said Secretary to sell any discontinued prison, see ss. 33, 34 of that Act, *post* pp. 175, 176.

Conditions of Sale.

47. No sale or purchase shall be made in pursuance of this Act by a prison authority, unless not less than three weeks' previous notice has been given in some one or more public newspaper or newspapers circulating within the district of the prison authority, of their intention to take into consideration the propriety of making such a sale or purchase at a time and place to be mentioned in such notice.

Any sale in pursuance of this Act may be made by private contract or public auction, and subject to any special conditions as to title or other matters the vendors may think expedient. No purchaser shall be required to examine into the propriety of the sale of any prison or land in pursuance of this Act, or into the appropriation of any moneys paid by him to the vendors; and any such sale shall, in the absence of actual fraud on his part, be valid so far as he is concerned, notwithstanding any omission to give such notice as aforesaid, or any other impropriety in the sale or misapplication of the purchase money.

MISCELLANEOUS.

Inquests on Prisoners.

48. It shall be the duty of the coroner having jurisdiction in the place to which the prison belongs to hold an inquest on the body of every prisoner who may die within the prison. Where it is practicable, one clear day shall intervene between the day of the death and the day of the holding the inquest; and in no case shall any officer of the prison, or any prisoner confined in the prison, be a juror on such inquest. (*g*)

(*g*) The Prison Act, 1877, further provides (s. 44, *post* p. 187) that in no case where an inquest is held on the body of a prisoner who dies within the prison, shall any person engaged in any sort of trade or dealing with the prison be a juror on the inquest. With regard to the time of holding an inquest upon the body of a prisoner who may die within a prison, it should be observed that The Capital Punishment Amendment Act, 1868 (31 Vict. c. 24), requires (s. 5) the coroner of the jurisdiction to which the prison belongs wherein judgment of death is executed on any offender, to hold an inquest on the body of the offender "within twenty-four hours after the execution." The Act also prohibits, in terms similar to those of the above section, any officer of or prisoner confined in the prison from being a juror on the inquest. The Act will be found in the Appendix.

General Issue may be pleaded to Action.

49. If any suit or action is prosecuted against any person for anything done in pursuance of this Act, such person may plead the general issue, and give this Act and the special matter in evidence, at any trial to be had thereupon, and that the same was done by authority of this Act; and if a verdict passes for the defendant, or the plaintiff becomes nonsuited, or discontinues his action after issue joined, or if, upon demurrer or otherwise, judgment be given against the plaintiff, the defendant shall recover double costs, and have the like remedy for the same as any defendant hath by law in other cases; and though a verdict be given for the plaintiff in any such action, such plaintiff shall not have costs against the defendant, unless the judge before whom the trial takes place certifies his approbation of the action and of the verdict obtained thereupon.

Venue where laid.

50. All actions, suits, and prosecutions commenced against any person for anything done in pursuance of this Act shall be laid and tried in the county or place where the Act complained of was committed, and shall be commenced within six calendar months after the committal thereof, and not otherwise.

Provision as to Arbitration.

51. Any difference authorized or directed by this Act to be settled by arbitration (*h*) shall be referred to the arbitration of a barrister-at-law to be appointed in writing, on the application of any party to the difference, by any judge of assize of the last preceding or of the next succeeding circuit; and all the provisions of "The Common Law Procedure Act, 1854," relating to compulsory references, shall be deemed to extend to any such arbitration, with this addition, that it shall be obligatory on the arbitrator, at the request of any party to the difference, to state a special case for the opinion of a superior court.

(*h*) As to the differences which may be settled by arbitration under the provisions of this Act, see s. 32, *ante* p. 83. The Prison Act, 1877, also makes provision (s. 55, *post* p. 194) for the reference to arbitration, under certain conditions, by the Secretary of State and prison authorities, of any matter or difference.

Recovery of Penalties.

52. Offences under this Act, with the exception of felonies, (*i*) and of offences for the mode of trial of which express provision is made by this Act, (*j*) shall be prosecuted summarily before two justices acting for the division or place where the matter requiring the cognizance of such justices arises, and in manner directed by the Act of the session holden in the eleventh and twelfth years of the reign of her present Majesty, chapter forty-three, and any Act amending the same.

(*i*) See s. 37, *ante* p. 87.
(*j*) See The Prison Regulations 56, 57, 58. in Schedule I. of this Act, *post* pp. 128, 198.

VISITING JUSTICES.

Appointment of Visiting Justices.

53. The justices within every prison jurisdiction, in sessions assembled, shall, (*k*) at their first sessions in each year, nominate two or more justices, with their consent, to be visitors of each prison within their jurisdiction, with power, if they think fit, to declare such nomination to be for the whole year, or to renew the same, or make a fresh nomination in each succeeding quarter of the year; and one or more of the visiting justices so appointed shall from time to time visit and inspect each prison, and shall examine into the state of the buildings, so as to form a judgment as to the repairs, additions, or alterations which may appear necessary, strict regard being had to the requisitions of this Act with respect to the separation of prisoners and enforcement of hard labour in prisons, and shall further examine into the conduct of the respective officers, and the treatment and conduct of the prisoners, the means of setting them to work, the amount of their earnings, and the expenses attending the prison, and shall inquire into all abuses within the prison, and shall take cognizance of matters of pressing necessity, and within the powers of their commission as justices, and regulate the same, and shall once at least in each quarter of a year make a report to the justices in sessions assembled.

(*k*) This section and the following section are both repealed by The Prison Act, 1877, s. 13 (see *post* p. 158), from the commencement (1st of April, 1878) of that Act, and provision, is therein made for the appointment for every prison of a "visiting committee," the members of which are to be justices of the peace, and which is, to some extent, to take the place of the visiting justices. Some of the duties of the visiting committee are pointed out by the 14th section of the Act just mentioned, but the Secretary of State is also required to make and publish rules with respect to the duties of the committee, and to those rules they are required to conform (see

P. A., 1877, ss. 13, 14, *post* pp. 158-160). The Act also declares (s. 14, *post* p. 160) that the visiting committee shall be deemed to be visiting justices for all the purposes of the regulations relating to the punishment of prisoners numbered 58 and 59 in Schedule I. of this Act (see *post* p. 129), or either of those regulations, and that any member of a visiting committee may exercise any power, or do any act, or receive any report which any one justice may exercise, do, or receive under those regulations or either of them. But no offender is to be punished, under those regulations or either of them, by personal correction, except in pursuance of the order of two justices of the peace, after such inquiry upon oath and determination concerning the matter reported to them as is mentioned in the said 58th regulation.

Power to make Rules as to Visiting Justices.

54. The justices in sessions assembled may make rules (*l*) with respect to the duties of visiting justices, and from time to time repeal or alter any rule so made, and make other rules in addition thereto or in substitution therefor, but no rules shall be valid which are inconsistent with any provision of this Act.

(*l*) See Note (*k*) to s. 53, *ante* p. 96.

Visits to Prison by any Justice.

55. Any justice of the peace having jurisdiction in the place to which a prison belongs may, (*m*) whenever he thinks fit, enter into and examine the condition of such prison, and of the prisoners therein, and he may enter any observations he may think fit to make in reference to the condition of the prison, or abuses therein, in the visitors'-book to be kept by the gaoler; and it shall be the duty of the gaoler to draw the attention of the visiting justices, at their next visit to the prison, to any entries made in the said book; but he shall not be entitled in pursuance of this section to visit any prisoners under sentence of death, or to communicate with any prisoner, except in reference to the treatment in prison of such prisoner, or to some complaint that such prisoner may make as to such treatment.

(*m*) This section is repealed by The Prison Act, 1877, s. 15, and the enactment continued in that section is to take effect instead (see the section, *post* p. 161).

PART II.
Law of Prisons.
Abolition of Distinction between Gaol and House of Correction.

56. Subject to the provisions of this Act with respect to the appropriation of prisons to particular classes of prisoners, (*n*) every prison to which this Act applies shall be deemed to be a gaol and house of correction, but no class of prisoners that have not previously to the commencement of this Act been confined in any prison shall be confined there until one of Her Majesty's principal Secretaries of State has certified that such prison is a fit place of confinement for that class of prisoners.

(*n*) See ss. 17, 18 of this Act, *ante* pp. 72, 73.

Jurisdiction over Prison.

57. Every prison, wheresoever situate, shall for all purposes be deemed to be within the limits of the place for which it is used as a prison.

Custody of Prisoners.

58. Every prisoner confined in a prison shall be deemed to be in the legal custody (*o*) of the gaoler, provided that nothing in this Act contained shall affect the jurisdiction or responsibility of the sheriff in respect of prisoners under sentence of death, or his jurisdiction or control over the prison where such prisoners are confined, and the officers thereof, so far as may be necessary for the purpose of carrying into effect the sentence of death, or for any purpose relating thereto ; and in any prison in which sentence of death is required to be carried into effect on any prisoner, whether such prison is or not the common gaol of the county, the sheriff shall, for the purposes of carrying that sentence into execution, be deemed to have the same jurisdiction with respect to such prison as he has by law with respect to the common gaol of a county, or would have had if this Act had not passed.

(*o*) As to the legal custody of a prisoner, see also The Prison Act, 1877, s. 28, *post* p. 172; and as to the jurisdiction or responsibility of the sheriff in respect of prisoners under sentence of death, see s. 32 of that Act, *post* p. 174.

Security to Sheriff.

59. The gaoler of any prison in which debtors are confined shall give security to the sheriff(*p*) for their safe custody to such amount as may be determined by agreement, or, in default of agreement, may be settled by the justices in sessions assembled; and any such security may be given to the sheriff and his successors in office, and shall be deemed to enure to the benefit of each succeeding sheriff in the same manner as if he were individually named therein.

(*p*) This Act, whilst it abolished the liability of the sheriff for the escape from prison of all other prisoners, continued that liability in the case of debtors (s. 60, *post* p. 100). Hence the requirement made in this section that the gaoler of a prison in which debtors are confined should give security to the sheriff for their safe custody to the amount and in the manner therein specified.

The Prison Act, 1877, expressly declares (s. 31, *post* p. 174), however, that on and after the commencement (1st of April, 1878) of that Act, the sheriff shall not be liable for the escape of any prisoner. At that date, therefore, the liability of the sheriff for the escape even of debtors will cease; and as he will be no longer liable for their escape, so the gaoler of any prison in which debtors are confined will be no longer required to give security to him for their safe custody.

Responsibility of Sheriff.

60. The sheriff shall not be liable for the escape from imprisonment of any prisoner other than a debtor.(*q*)

(*q*) On and after the commencement (1st of April. 1878) of The Prison Act, 1877, the sheriff is not (s. 31. *post* p. 174) to be liable for the escape of any prisoner. He will, therefore, at that date cease to be liable for the escape of even a debtor from prison.

Description of Prison in Writ.

61. Any writ, warrant, or other legal instrument addressed to the gaoler of a particular prison, describing the prison by its situation or other definite description, shall be valid, by whatever title such prison is usually known, or whatever be the description of the prison, whether gaol, house of correction, bridewell, penitentiary, or otherwise. (*r*)

(*r*) The distinction between a gaol and a house of correction is practically abolished by s. 56 of this Act (*ante* p. 98).

Gaoler of Prison to deliver Calendar.

62. The gaoler of every prison shall deliver or cause to be delivered to the judges of assize, and to the justices in quarter sessions, a calendar of all prisoners in custody for trial at such assizes or gaol* sessions, in the same way as the sheriff of a county has hitherto been required by law to deliver a calendar of such prisoners when committed to the common gaol of the county, and the sheriff shall no longer be required to deliver or cause to be delivered such calendar.

Removal of Prisoners for Trial.

63. A prisoner may be brought up for trial, and may be removed by or under the direction of the gaoler from one prison to another, or from one place

* *Sic.* in Stat.

of confinement to another, to which such prisoner may be legally removed, for the purpose of being tried or undergoing his sentence; and no prisoner whilst in the custody of a gaoler shall be deemed to have escaped, although he may be taken into different jurisdictions or different places of confinement. (*s*)

(*s*) As to the legal custody of prisoners whilst being taken to or from prison, see The Prison Act, 1877, s. 28, *post* p. 172.

Removal of Prisoners in other Cases.

64. Prisoners may be removed from one prison to another prison or place of confinement within the jurisdiction of the same prison authority, or to the prison of any other authority, with the consent of such last-mentioned authority, by order of the justices in sessions assembled, for the purpose of enabling any prison to be altered, enlarged, or rebuilt, or in case of a contagious or infectious disease breaking out in any prison, or for any other reasonable cause; and in case of emergency such removal may be made in pursuance of an order under the hands of the visiting justices; and any prisoners removed from a prison in pursuance of this section may, by order of the justices in sessions assembled, be taken back by the gaoler to the prison from whence they were removed, or be removed to any other place in which they can legally be imprisoned.

Her Majesty may order Prisoners to be removed from one Prison to another.

65. It shall be lawful for Her Majesty, by an order under the hand of one of Her Majesty's principal Secretaries of State, to direct any person in prison in England and Wales under sentence of any court, or of any competent authority, for any offence committed by him, to be removed from the prison in which he is confined to any other of Her Majesty's prisons within England and Wales, there to be imprisoned during his term of imprisonment. (*t*)

(*t*) See also The Prison Act, 1877, s. 25, *post* p. 171.

Custody and Trial of Prisoners in a substituted Prison.

66. Where a prison authority, in this section called the contracting authority, has contracted with any other prison authority, in this section called the receiving authority, that the receiving authority is to receive into and maintain in its prison any prisoners maintainable at the expense of the contracting authority, the prison of the receiving authority shall for all the purposes of and incidental to the commitment, trial, detention, and punishment of the prisoners of the contracting authority, or any of such purposes, according to the tenor of the contract, be deemed to be the prison of the contracting authority, except that the contracting authority shall have no right to interfere in the management of the prison of the receiving authority. (*u*)

(*u*) The 57th section of this Act (*ante* p. 98) declares that every prison shall, for all purposes, be deemed to be within the limits of the place for which it is used as a prison.

As to the power of prison authorities to contract for the purposes referred to in this section, see ss. 31 and 32 of this Act, *ante* pp. 82, 83.

As to the determination of contracts thus made between prison authorities, see The Prison Act, 1877, s. 21, *post* p. 168.

Misdemeanant of First Division.

67. In every prison to which this Act applies, prisoners convicted of misdemeanor, and not sentenced to hard labour, shall be divided into at least two divisions, one of which shall be called the first division; and whenever any person convicted of misdemeanor is sentenced to imprisonment without hard labour, it shall be lawful for the court or judge before whom such person has been tried to order, if such court or judge think fit, that such person shall be treated as a misdemeanant of the first division, and a misdemeanant of the first division shall not be deemed to be a criminal prisoner within the meaning of this Act (*v*).

(*v*) The meaning of the term "criminal prisoner" is defined in s. 4, *ante* p. 61. As to the power of the Secretary of State to appoint in any county a prison or prisons in which debtors and prisoners who are not criminal prisoners may be confined, see The Prison Act, 1877, s. 26, *post* p. 171.

Any prisoner under sentence inflicted on conviction for sedition or seditious libel, is to be treated as a misdemeanant of the first division within the meaning of this section, notwithstanding any statute, provision, or rule to the contrary (P. A., 1877, s. 40, *post* p. 186); and any person who shall be imprisoned under any rule, order, or attachment for contempt of any court is to be in like manner treated as a misdemeanant of the first division (P. A., 1877, s. 41, *post* p. 186). The special rules relating to misdemeanants of the 1st division, made in pursuance of the Prison Act, 1877, will be found in the Appendix, *post* p. 272.

PART III.

Discontinuance of certain Prisons.

Prohibition of Committals to Prisons in Second Schedule.

68. After the commencement of this Act no person shall be committed to any of the prisons mentioned in the second schedule hereto. (*w*)

All persons who before the passing of this Act might lawfully have been committed to any of the said scheduled prisons shall, after the passing thereof, be committed to the prison of the county in which the said scheduled prison is situated; and such county prison shall, for all purposes relating to or consequential on the committal, trial, detention, or punishment of prisoners committed or removed thereto in pursuance of this part of this Act, be regarded in law as if it were the said scheduled prison.

In this part of this Act, so far as it relates to the prison at *Richmond* in the said second schedule mentioned, " county " shall mean the north riding of *Yorkshire*, and so far as relates to the prison at *Rye* in the same schedule mentioned the county gaol of *Lewes* shall be deemed to be the prison of the county.

(*w*) See the schedule, *post* p. 142.

Removal of Prisoners in Scheduled Prisons.

69. As soon as conveniently may be after the commencement of this Act the gaoler of each of the said scheduled prisons shall, without writ of habeas corpus or other writ for that purpose, remove every prisoner under sentence or committed for trial in such prison to the prison of the county in which the said scheduled prison is situate, and deliver such prisoner into the custody of the gaoler of the said county prison, together with the writ and other process under which the prisoner was arrested or confined; and the gaoler of the said county prison shall be bound to receive such prisoner, and shall give a receipt to the gaoler of the said scheduled prison for every prisoner removed in pursuance of this section.

Expenses of Prisoners confined in County Prisons under Act.

70. The expenses which may be incurred by any county in the conveyance, transport, maintenance, safe custody, and care of every prisoner confined, in pursuance of this part of this Act, in the county prison instead of in one of the said scheduled prisons, including the expenses of the removal of the prisoners from one prison to another, shall be defrayed in manner provided by law in cases where the prisoners committed for offences arising within any borough or other place that does not contribute to the county rate are sent to any prison of a county, and there is no special contract between such borough or other place and the county relative to such prisoners. (*x*)

(*x*) The expenses incurred in respect of the maintenance of all prisons to which this Act and The Prison Act, 1877, apply, and of the prisoners in those prisons, are, on and after the commencement of the last-mentioned Act, to be defrayed out of moneys provided by Parliament. (See s. 4 of that Act, *post* p. 150.)

Power to use Scheduled Prisons as Lock-up Houses.

71. The prison authority of any of the said scheduled prisons may sell the same in manner provided by this Act (*y*) in case where a prison appears to a prison authority to be unnecessary by reason of its having provided for the accommodation of its prisoners in some other adequate prison, or may, with the sanction of the said Secretary of State, cause the same to be used as a police station house or a lock-up house, and the money arising from any sale made in pursuance of this section shall be applied in discharging any expenses that may be incurred by such authority in the maintenance of its prisoners, or otherwise in aid of the rate applicable to prison purposes.

(*y*) See ss. 46, 47, *ante* pp. 92, 93.

Power to allow Compensation to Persons deprived of Office.

72. The justices in sessions assembled having jurisdiction over each of the said scheduled prisons may allow such compensation or allowance as they think fit to any person who, by reason of the passing of this part of this Act, is deprived of any salary or emoluments, so that no such compensation or allowance exceeds the proportion of the salary and emolument, if any, which might be granted under similar circumstances to a person in the civil service under the Acts for regulating such compensations or allowances for the time being in force; and any compensation or allowance so allowed shall be paid out of any rates applicable to the payment of the salaries of such officers, subject to this proviso, that when the power to levy such rates is vested in a different body from the justices, the consent of such last-mentioned body shall be obtained to the amount allowed.

PART IV.

Repeal of Statutes, and Saving Clauses.

Acts and Parts of Acts in Third Schedule repealed.

73. After the commencement of this Act there shall be repealed the several Acts specified in the third schedule hereto to the extent in the said schedule mentioned. (*z*)

(*z*) See the Schedule, *post* pp. 142, 143, 144. Those portions of the statutes in question which are still unrepealed, and which apply to prisons, together with several other statutes and parts of statutes relating to the same subject, will be found in their proper chronological order in the Appendix.

No Repeal hereby enacted to affect any Order made, etc.

74. No repeal hereby enacted shall affect—
1. Any order made, sentence passed, or other Act or thing duly done under any Acts hereby repealed:
2. Any right or privilege acquired, any security given, or other liability incurred under any Act hereby repealed:
3. Any penalty, forfeiture, or other punishment incurred in respect of any offence against any Act hereby repealed:
4. Any appointment to an office made under any Act hereby repealed, or any power of removing

the holder of such office, or otherwise dealing with such office as respects the existing holder thereof in manner provided by any Act hereby repealed : (*a*)

5. The power of committing prisoners to any prison, except in so far as the same may be altered in pursuance of powers given by this Act.

(*a*) See also s. 79, *post* p. 108.

Certificates as to Cells.

75. All cells certified before the commencement of this Act by any Inspector of Prisons as being fit to be used for the separate confinement of prisoners shall be deemed to be cells certified for such purpose under this Act. (*b*)

(*b*) The Act came into operation on the 1st of February, 1866 (s. 2, *ante* p. 60). As to the certifying of cells for the separate confinement of prisoners under this Act, see s. 18, *ante* p. 73.

Saving as to repealed Provisions referred to in other Acts.

76. Any unrepealed Act of Parliament in which reference is made to the provisions of any Act hereby repealed shall be construed as if in such first-mentioned Act reference had been made to the corresponding provisions of this Act.

Saving as to meaning of Gaol Act, 25 & 26 Vict. c. 44.

77. In the construction of the Act of the twenty-fifth and twenty-sixth years of the reign of her present Majesty, chapter forty-four, (*c*) the expression "The Gaol Act" shall mean this Act instead of the Act therein referred to.

(*c*) The Act, 25 & 26 Vict. c. 44, will be found in the Appendix.

Saving of Rights of Creditors.

78. Nothing in this Act contained shall affect the right of any creditor who may have advanced any moneys for building, repairing, or otherwise for the purposes of any prison discontinued in pursuance of this Act, (*d*) or may have advanced any moneys on any mortgage or other security; and it shall be lawful for such creditor to pursue any remedies for recovering the principal or interest moneys due to him, and to enjoy the benefit of any security of which he may be possessed, in the same manner as if this Act had not passed, and as if the Acts hereby repealed had remained in full force.

(*d*) See s. 36. *ante* p. 85; s. 68, *ante* p. 103; and Schedule II. of this Act, *post* p. 141.

Saving of Superannuation Allowances.

79. Nothing in this Act (*e*) contained shall affect the tenure of office or salary or superannuation allowance of any officer of a prison, not being one of the said scheduled prisons, (*f*) appointed prior to the commencement of this Act, (*g*) but such officer shall remain entitled to the same tenure of office, salary, and superannuation allowance as if this Act had not passed: Provided that the superannuation allowance of any prison officer appointed before the commencement of this Act may, on the application of such officer, and with the consent of the justices in sessions assembled, be calculated on the same scale on which the superannuation allowances of officers appointed after the passing of this Act are directed to be calculated. (*h*)

(*e*) As to the tenure of office and salary of prison officers appointed under this Act, see s. 14, *ante* p. 70; and as to the superannuation allowances to be made to officers, see s. 15, *ante* p. 70.

(*f*) See s. 73, *ante* p. 105, and Schedule II. of this Act, *post* p. 142.

(*g*) The Act came into operation on the 1st of February, 1866 (s. 2, *ante* p. 60).

(*h*) See s. 15, *ante* p. 70.

Saving as to Rules.

80. All rules in force in any prison that are inconsistent with this Act, or the regulations in the schedule hereto, (*i*) shall be repealed from and after the commencement of this Act, but all other rules in force in any prison shall so continue until altered in manner in this Act provided. (*j*)

(*i*) See Schedule I. of the Act, *post* pp. 115—141.
(*j*) See s. 21, *ante* p. 76, and regulation 102 in Schedule I. of the Act, *post* p. 141.

Saving as to Appointment of Officers.

81. Nothing in this Act contained (*k*) shall affect the right vested by Act of Parliament or charter in any council of any municipal borough of appointing a gaoler, chaplain, or other officer to the prison of such borough.

(*k*) See ss. 10, 14, *ante* pp. 66, 70. On the commencement (1st of April, 1878) of The Prison Act. 1877, the power of appointing the officers of prisons is to be transferred to and vested in the Secretary of State, and in some cases, and subject to his control, in the Prison Commissioners (see ss. 5, 9 of that Act, *post* pp. 151, 155); but as the Act provides for the transfer of the power in question in terms which are perfectly general, and without making any reservation of any right hitherto vested in the council of any municipal borough of appointing the officers of the prison of the borough, it follows that at the period above mentioned any such right, so far as its exercise by a municipal council is concerned, will cease; and that the right will be transferred to and vested in the Secretary of State, or in the Prison Commissioners, as the case may be.

Saving as to Commissions.

82. Nothing in this Act contained relating to the custody of prisoners (*l*) shall affect the validity of any commission of gaol delivery, commission of oyer and terminer, or other commission, precept, writ, warrant, or other document, notwithstanding the same may be addressed to or make mention of the sheriff of any county, city, or place, instead of being addressed to or making mention of the gaoler of a prison or prisons; and every such commission, precept, writ, warrant, or other document shall be obeyed by the gaoler, and take effect in the same manner as if the gaoler had been named therein instead of the sheriff.

(*l*) As to the custody of prisoners, see s. 58, *ante* p. 98.

INDEX TO SCHEDULES.

Schedule I.

General.

No.
1. Cleanliness in prison.
2. Trees, etc., not allowed against walls.
3. Temperature of prison.
4. Visitors not to sleep within the prison.
5. Hours of locking and unlocking the prison.

Admission and Discharge of Prisoners.

6. Search of prisoners on admission.
7. Prisoner to be alone when searched.
8. Effects retained by gaoler.
9. Register of certain particulars relating to prisoner.
10. Removal and discharge of prisoners.
11. Separation of prisoners.
12. Female prisoners.

Food, Clothing, and Bedding of Prisoners.

13. Spirituous liquors.
14. Smoking.
15. Order of Surgeon as to spirituous liquors, etc.
16. Debtor may maintain himself.
17. Debtor not to sell provisions.
18. Prison allowance to debtors.
19. Prisoner before trial may maintain himself.
20. Dress of criminal prisoner before trial.
21. Prison allowance of food for convicted prisoner.
22. Convicted Prisoner restricted to prison allowances.
23. Dress of convicted criminal.
24. Return of clothing to discharged prisoner.

No.
25. Purification of clothing of prisoner.
26. Beds.
27. Bedding.

Personal Cleanliness.

28. Personal cleanliness of prisoners.
29. Hair-cutting.

Employment of Prisoners.

30. Prohibition of gaming.
31. Work and earnings of debtors.
32. Employment of criminal prisoners before trial.
33. Allowance out of earnings to acquitted prisoners.
34. Regulations as to hard labour of the first class.
35. Regulations as to hard labour of the second class.
36. Days of exemption from hard labour.
37. Examination by surgeon of prisoners at hard labour.
38. Employment of prisoners not sentenced to hard labour.

Health of Prisoners.

39. Exercise of debtors.
40. Of prisoners in separate confinement.
41. When prisoners to be reported to surgeon.
42. Entry of directions by surgeon.
43. Infirmaries.

Religious Instruction.

44. Room for use as chapel.
45. Prayers.
46. Performance of Divine service.
47. Ministers to visit prisoners under certain restrictions.
48. Books and printed papers.
49. Chaplain to communicate abuses to gaoler.
50. Assistant chaplain and chaplain's substitute.
51. Substitute for prison minister.
52. Substitute on death of chaplain or minister.

Instruction.

53. Instruction of prisoners.

INDEX TO SCHEDULES.

No. *Visits to and Communications with Prisoners.*
54. Communication with prisoners.
55. Power of gaoler as to visitors.

Prison Offences.
56. General regulation as to punishment.
57. Gaoler to punish for prison offences.
58. Punishment of prisoners by visiting justices.
59. Use of irons.
60. Corporal punishments.

Prisoners under Sentence of Death.
61. Prisoners under sentence of death.

Prison Officers.
62. Regulation as to employment of prisoners in prison offices.
63. Prison officers to be constables.
64. Officers not to sell or let to prisoners.
65. Officers not to contract with prisoners.
66. Officers not to take gratuities.
67. Females to be attended by female officers.

Gaoler.
68. Residence of gaoler.
69. Gaoler to conform to law and regulations of prison.
70. May suspend subordinate officers.
71. To inspect the prison daily.
72. To post up in cells abstract of certain regulations.
73. To report to surgeon prisoners disordered in mind.
74. To notify to chaplain and surgeon prisoners requiring their attention.
75. To give notice of death of prisoners.
76. To report to visiting justices insane prisoners.
77. To keep enumerated Books and Accounts.
78. To be responsible for safe custody of documents.
79. Not to be absent without leave.

No.
80. Power of deputy gaoler. Substitute of deputy gaoler.

Matron.

81. General duties.
82. To inspect daily female prison.
83. Not to be absent without leave.
84. To appoint deputy when absent.
85. To keep journal.

Surgeon.

86. When to visit prison.
87. To make daily record in respect to sick prisoners.
88. Occasionally to inspect every part of prison.
89. To report special cases.
90. To call in additional medical aid.
91. To make entries as to death of prisoner.
92. To appoint substitute when absent.

Prison Officers.

93. Officers to obey gaoler.
94. Not to be absent without leave.
95. Not to receive visitors without leave.
96. To examine cells, locks, etc.

Porter.

97. Duties of gate porter.

Reports.

98. Gaoler to transmit list of prisoners to Secretary of State.
99. Gaoler to attend sessions and make report.
100. Journals and reports of chaplain and surgeon.
101. Record of visits of chaplain and non-resident officers.

Construction and Application of Schedule.

102. Rules as to prisoners not debtors or criminals.
103. Construction of word "Regulation."
104. Definition of "subordinate officers."

SCHEDULE II.—List of discontinued prisons.
SCHEDULE III.—List of Acts repealed.

SCHEDULE I.

REGULATIONS FOR GOVERNMENT OF PRISONS.

GENERAL.

Cleanliness in Prison.

1. The prison shall be kept in a cleanly state, and the walls and ceilings of the wards, cells, rooms, and passages used by the prisoners throughout every prison shall either be painted with oil, or be limewashed, or partly painted and partly limewashed. Where painted with oil, the painting shall be washed with hot water and soap once at least in every six months. Where limewashed, the limewashing shall be renewed once at least in every year. The day rooms, work rooms, passages, and sleeping cells shall be washed or cleansed once a week, or oftener if requisite.

Trees, &c., not allowed against Walls.

2. Nothing shall be allowed to grow against the outer walls of the prison, nor any rubbish or other articles to be laid against them, nor shall any tools or implements of any kind likely to facilitate escape be left unnecessarily exposed.

Temperature of Prison.

3. Thermometers shall be placed in different parts of the prison.

Visitors not to Sleep within the Prison.

4. No person shall be permitted to sleep in the apartments of any subordinate officer of the prison without permission from the gaoler, such permission to be reported to a visiting justice.

Hours of locking and unlocking the Prison.

5. A report shall be made to the gaoler at ten o'clock each night, whether the officers resident in the prison are all present; and no ingress or egress shall be allowed into or out of the prison between the hours of ten o'clock at night and six o'clock in the morning, except to the gaoler and his family, the chaplain, or surgeon, or in special cases, which shall be entered in the journal of the gaoler.

ADMISSION AND DISCHARGE OF PRISONERS.

Search of Prisoners on Admission.

6. Prisoners on admission shall be searched, and all dangerous weapons, articles calculated to facilitate escape, and prohibited articles, shall be taken from them.

Prisoner to be alone when searched.

7. No prisoner shall be searched in the presence of any other prisoner.

Effects retained by Gaoler.

8. All money or other effects brought into the prison by any prisoner, or sent to the prison for his use, which he is not allowed to retain, shall be placed in the custody of the gaoler, who shall keep an inventory of them in a separate book.

Register of certain Particulars relating to Prisoner.

9. The name, age, height, weight, features, particular marks, and general appearance of a criminal prisoner shall, upon his admission, be noted in a nominal record of prisoners, to be kept by the gaoler. Every criminal prisoner shall also, as soon as possible, be examined by the surgeon, who shall enter in a book to be kept by the gaoler a record of the state of health of the prisoner, and any observations he may deem it expedient to add.

SCHEDULE I.—PRISON REGULATIONS.

Removal and Discharge of Prisoners.

10. All prisoners, previously to being removed to any other prison, or being discharged from prison, shall be examined by the surgeon; and no prisoner shall be removed to any other prison, unless the surgeon certifies, by an entry in the nominal record, that the prisoner is free from any illness that renders him unfit for removal; and no prisoner shall be discharged from prison if labouring under any acute or dangerous distemper, nor until, in the opinion of the surgeon, such discharge is safe, unless such prisoner require to be discharged.

Separation of Prisoners.

11. Prisoners before trial shall be kept apart from convicted prisoners.

Female Prisoners.

12. Female prisoners shall be searched on admission by female officers. In other respects the same course shall be pursued in reference to the admission, removal, or discharge of a female prisoner as in the case of a male prisoner, the matron performing the duties imposed on the gaoler in case of a male prisoner.

FOOD, CLOTHING, AND BEDDING OF PRISONERS.

Spirituous Liquors.

13. No tap shall be kept in any prison; nor shall spirituous liquors of any kind be admitted for the use of any of the prisoners therein, under any pretence whatever, unless by a written order of the surgeon, specifying the quantity to be admitted, and the name of the prisoner for whose use it is intended; but this regulation shall not apply to any stock of spirituous liquors kept in the prison for the use of the infirmary, and under the control of the surgeon.

Smoking.

14. No smoking shall be allowed, or tobacco introduced,

except with the consent and subject to the rules made by the visiting justices, or under a written order of the surgeon.

Order of Surgeon as to Spirituous Liquors, &c.

15. Any order by the surgeon for the admission of spirituous liquors or tobacco shall be entered by him in his journal.

Debtor may maintain himself.

16. A debtor shall be permitted to maintain himself, and to procure or receive at proper hours food, wine, malt liquor, clothing, bedding, or other necessaries, but subject to examination, and to such rules as may be approved by the visiting justices.

Debtor not to sell Provisions.

17. No part of any food, wine, malt liquor, clothing, bedding, or other necessaries belonging to any debtor shall be sold to any other prisoner; and any debtor transgressing this regulation shall lose the privilege of receiving or purchasing any wine or malt liquor for such a time as the visiting justices may deem proper.

Prison Allowance to Debtors.

18. A debtor, if unable to provide himself with sufficient food, clothing, bedding, or other necessaries, shall receive the allowance of food, clothing, bedding, or other necessaries allotted to debtors unable to maintain themselves by the prison rules for the time being in force.

Prisoner before Trial may maintain himself.

19. A criminal prisoner before trial may procure for himself, or receive at proper hours, food, and malt liquor, clothing, bedding, or other necessaries, subject to examination, and to such rules as may be approved by the visiting justices; and any articles so procured may be paid for out of the moneys belonging to such prisoner in the hands of the gaoler. No part of such food, malt liquor, bedding, clothing, or other necessaries shall be sold or transferred to

any other prisoner; and any prisoner transgressing this regulation shall be prohibited from procuring any food or other necessaries for such time as the visiting justices may deem proper. If a criminal prisoner before trial does not provide himself with food, he shall receive the allowance of food allotted to criminal prisoners before trial by the rules of the prison.

Dress of Criminal Prisoner before Trial.

20. Criminal prisoners before trial may, if they desire it, wear the prison dress, and they shall be required to do so if their own clothes are insufficient or unfit for use, or necessary to be preserved for the purposes of justice. The prison dress for prisoners before trial shall be of a different colour from that of convicted prisoners.

Prison Allowance of Food for convicted Prisoner.

21. Every convicted criminal prisoner shall be allowed a sufficient quantity of food according to the scale established by the rules of the prison. Prisoners under the care of the surgeon shall be allowed such diet as he may direct. Care shall be taken that all provisions supplied to the prisoners be of proper quality and weight. Scales and legal weights and measures shall be provided, open to the use of any prisoners, under such restrictions as may be made by the prison rules.

Convicted Prisoner restricted to Prison Allowances.

22. No convicted criminal prisoner shall be allowed any wine, beer, or other fermented liquor, except under a written order from the surgeon, to be entered in his journal, specifying the quantity, and the name of the prisoner for whose use it is intended, or shall receive any food, clothing, bedding, or necessaries other than the prison allowance, except under special circumstances, to be judged of by one or more of the visiting justices, and to be reported to the prison authority.

Dress of convicted Criminal.

23. A convicted criminal prisoner shall be provided with a complete prison dress, and shall be required to wear it.

Return of Clothing to discharged Prisoner.

24. On the discharge of a prisoner, his own clothes shall be returned to him, unless it has been found necessary to destroy them, in which case he shall be provided with clothing.

Purification of Clothing of Prisoner.

25. If necessary, the clothes of a prisoner shall be purified before he is allowed to wear them in the prison or to take them on his discharge.

Beds.

26. Every male prisoner shall sleep in a cell by himself, or under special circumstances in a separate bed placed in a cell containing not fewer than two other male prisoners, and sufficient bed clothes shall be provided for every prisoner. A convicted criminal prisoner may be required to sleep on a plank bed without a mattress during such time as may be determined by the rules of the prison. Epileptic prisoners, or prisoners labouring under diseases requiring assistance or supervision in the night, may at any time, notwithstanding this regulation, be placed by order of the surgeon with not fewer than two other male prisoners.

Bedding.

27. The bed clothes shall be aired, changed, and washed as often as the surgeon or the visiting justices may direct.

PERSONAL CLEANLINESS.

Personal Cleanliness of Prisoners.

28. Prisoners shall be required to keep themselves clean and decent in their persons, and to conform to such rules as may be laid down for that purpose.

Hair-cutting.

29. The hair of a female prisoner shall not be cut without her consent, except on account of vermin or dirt, or when the surgeon deems it requisite on the ground of health, and

SCHEDULE I.—PRISON REGULATIONS.

the hair of male criminal prisoners shall not be cut closer than may be necessary for purposes of health and cleanliness.

EMPLOYMENT OF PRISONERS.

Prohibition of Gaming.

30. No gaming shall be permitted in any prison, and the gaoler shall seize and destroy all dice, cards, or other instruments of gaming.

Work and Earnings of Debtors.

31. Debtors may be permitted to work and follow their respective trades and professions, provided their employment does not interfere with the regulations of the prison; and such debtors as find their own implements, and are not maintained at the expense of the prison, shall be allowed to receive the whole of their earnings; but the earnings of such as are furnished with implements, or are maintained at the expense of the prison, shall be subject to a deduction, to be determined by the visiting justices, for the use of implements and the cost of maintenance.

Employment of Criminal Prisoners before Trial.

32. Criminal prisoners before trial shall have the option of employment, but shall not be compelled to perform any hard labour.

Allowance out of Earnings to acquitted Prisoners.

33. On the acquittal of any criminal prisoner, or when no bill of indictment is found against him, such an allowance on account of his earnings, if any, shall be paid to such prisoner, on his discharge, as the visiting justices may think reasonable.

Regulations as to Hard Labour of the First Class.

34. Every male prisoner of sixteen years of age and upwards, sentenced to hard labour, shall, (*m*) during the whole of his sentence where it does not exceed three months, and during the first three months of his sentence where it exceeds three months, be kept at hard labour of the first class for such number of hours not more than ten or less than six

(exclusive of meals) as may be prescribed by the visiting justices, and during the remainder of his sentence shall be kept in like manner at hard labour of the first class, except where during such remainder of his sentence the visiting justices substitute hard labour of the second class for hard labour of the first class; provided that if the surgeon certifies any such prisoner to be unfit to be kept at hard labour of the first class during the whole or any part of the prescribed hours, such prisoner shall, during such whole or part of the prescribed hours, be kept at hard labour of the second class, unless the surgeon certifies that such prisoner is unfit to be kept at either class of hard labour during the whole or any part of such hours; provided that prisoners sentenced to hard labour for periods not exceeding fourteen days may, in pursuance of rules made by the justices in sessions, be kept in separate confinement at hard labour of the second class during the whole period of their sentences.

(*m*) As to the power of the Secretary of State to relax the requirements of this regulation, see The Prison Act, 1877, s. 37, *post* p. 183.

Regulations as to Hard Labour of the Second Class.

35. Every male prisoner under the age of sixteen years, sentenced to hard labour, and every female prisoner sentenced to hard labour, shall be kept at hard labour of the second class during such number of hours not more than ten or less than six (exclusive of meals) in each day as may be prescribed by the visiting justices, unless the surgeon certifies that he or she is unfit for hard labour.

Days of Exemption from Hard Labour.

36. No prisoner shall be employed at hard labour on Sundays, Christmas Day, Good Friday, and days appointed for public fasts or thanksgivings.

Examination by Surgeon of Prisoners at Hard Labour.

37. The surgeon shall from time to time examine the prisoners sentenced to hard labour during the time of their being so employed, and shall enter in his journal the name

of any prisoner whose health he thinks to be endangered by a continuance at hard labour of either class, and thereupon such prisoner shall not again be employed at such class of hard labour until the surgeon certifies that he is fit for such employment.

Employment of Prisoners not sentenced to Hard Labour.

38. Provision shall be made by the visiting justices for the employment of all convicted criminal prisoners not sentenced to hard labour. The visiting justices shall make rules as to the amount and nature of such employment, but no prisoner not sentenced to hard labour shall be punished for neglect of work, excepting by such alteration in the scale of diet as may be established by the rules of the prison in the case of neglect of work by such prisoners.

HEALTH OF PRISONERS.

Exercise of Debtors.

39. Debtors shall have the means of daily taking exercise in the open air.

Of Prisoners in Separate Confinement.

40. Criminal prisoners, if employed at work in their own cells, shall be permitted to take such exercise in the open air as the surgeon may deem necessary for their health.

When Prisoner to be reported to Surgeon.

41. The names of the prisoners who desire to see the surgeon, or appear out of health, shall be reported by the officer attending them to the gaoler, and by him without delay to the surgeon.

Entry of Directions by Surgeon.

42. All directions given by the surgeon in relation to any prisoner, with the exception of orders for the supply of medicines or directions in relation to such matters as are carried into effect by the surgeon himself or under his superintendence, shall be entered day by day in his journal,

which shall have a separate column in which entries are to be made by the gaoler, stating in respect of each direction the fact of its having been or not having been complied with, accompanied by such observations, if any, as the gaoler may think fit to make, and the date of the entry.

Infirmaries.

43. In every prison an infirmary or proper place for the reception of sick prisoners shall be provided.

Religious Instruction.
Room for use as Chapel.

44. In every prison where there is no chapel a suitable room shall be set apart for the purposes of the chapel.

Prayers.

45. Prayers to be selected by the chaplain from the liturgy of the Established Church shall be read daily by the chaplain, gaoler, or such other person as may be appointed by the visiting justices, and at such time or times as may be fixed by them, and portions of the Scriptures shall be read to the prisoners, when assembled for religious instruction, by the chaplain, or by such person, with the consent of the visiting justices, as he may appoint.

Performance of Divine Service.

46. The chaplain shall on every Sunday, and on Christmas Day and Good Friday, perform the appointed morning and evening services of the Established Church, and preach at such time or times as shall be fixed by him with the approval of the visiting justices. He shall give religious and moral instruction to the prisoners who are willing to receive it. He shall administer the Holy Sacrament of the Lord's Supper on suitable occasions to such prisoners as shall be desirous, and as he may deem to be in a proper frame of mind to receive the same. He shall frequently visit every room and cell of the prison occupied by prisoners, and shall direct such books to be distributed and read, and such lessons

to be taught in the prison, as he may deem proper for the religious instruction of the prisoners. Criminal prisoners shall attend Divine service on Sundays, and on other days when such service is performed, unless prevented by illness or other reasonable cause, to be allowed by the gaoler, or unless their attendance is dispensed with by the visiting justices: this regulation shall not apply to any prisoner who is attended or visited by a minister of a church or persuasion differing from the Established Church : and no prisoner shall be compelled to attend any religious service held or performed, or any religious instruction given, by the chaplain, minister, or religious instructor of a church or persuasion to which the prisoner does not belong.

Ministers to visit Prisoners under certain Restrictions.

47. If any prisoner is of a religious persuasion differing from that of the Established Church, and no minister has been appointed to attend at the prison on the prisoners of that persuasion, the visiting justices shall permit a minister of such persuasion to be approved by them to visit such prisoner at proper and reasonable times, under such restrictions as may be imposed by the visiting justices to guard against the introduction of improper persons and prevent improper communications, unless such prisoner expressly objects to see such minister.

Books and Printed Papers.

48. No books or printed papers shall be admitted into any prison for the use of the prisoners, except by permission of the visiting justices; and no books or printed papers intended for the religious instruction of prisoners belonging to the Established Church shall be admitted but those chosen by the chaplain; provided that in case there may be a difference of opinion between the chaplain and visiting justices with respect to books or papers proposed to be admitted for the religious instruction of a prisoner belonging to the Established Church, reference shall be had to the bishop of the diocese, whose decision shall be final; and, subject to such permission of the visiting justices as afore-

said, all books or printed papers admitted into any prison for the religious instruction of prisoners belonging to any other persuasion, and who are visited by a minister of such persuasion, shall be approved by such minister; and the gaoler shall keep a catalogue of all books and printed papers admitted into the prison.

Chaplain to communicate Abuses to Gaoler.

49. The chaplain shall communicate to the gaoler any abuse or impropriety in the prison which may come to his knowledge, and shall enter the same in his journal.

Assistant Chaplain and Chaplain's Substitute.

50. Where an assistant chaplain is appointed to a prison, he shall be competent to perform any duty required by law to be performed by the chaplain, and when either of them, the chaplain or assistant chaplain, is absent from the prison, the other shall take his duties. Where there is no assistant chaplain, or in case of the services of the assistant chaplain not being available by reason of sickness or other unavoidable cause, the chaplain shall, when absent from the prison on leave or from any unavoidable cause, appoint, with the consent of the visiting justices, a substitute, and insert his name and residence in his journal. In the event of any sudden cause preventing the chaplain, or, in the absence of the chaplain, the assistant chaplain, from performing his duties, he may accept the assistance of a clergyman of the Established Church in the performance of Divine service in the chapel, inserting the fact, and the name of such clergyman, in his journal.

Substitute for Prison Minister.

51. A minister appointed under The Prison Ministers' Act, 1863, may, when absent on leave, or from any unavoidable cause, appoint a substitute with the consent of the visiting justices.

Substitute on Death of Chaplain or Minister.

52. In the event of the death of any chaplain or assistant

SCHEDULE I.—PRISON REGULATIONS.

chaplain of a prison, or of a minister appointed under The Prison Ministers' Act, 1863, the visiting justices shall provide a substitute until the next meeting of the justices in sessions.

INSTRUCTION.

Instruction of Prisoners.

53. Provision shall be made in every prison for the instruction of prisoners in reading, writing, and arithmetic during such hours and to such extent as to the visiting justices may seem expedient, provided that such hours shall not be deducted from the hours prescribed for hard labour.

VISITS TO AND COMMUNICATIONS WITH PRISONERS.

Communication with Prisoners.

54. Due provision shall be made for the admission, at proper times and under proper restrictions, of persons with whom prisoners before trial may desire to communicate, care being taken that, so far as is consistent with the interests of justice, such prisoners shall see their legal advisers alone; such rules also shall be made by the justices in sessions assembled for the admission of the friends of convicted prisoners as they may deem expedient; the justices shall also impose such restrictions upon the communication and correspondence of prisoners with their friends as they judge necessary for the maintenance of good order and discipline in such prison.

Power of Gaoler as to Visitors.

55. The gaoler may demand the name and address of any visitor to a prisoner; and when he has any ground for suspicion, may search or cause to be searched male visitors, and may direct the matron or some other female officer to search female visitors, such search not to be in the presence of any prisoner or of another visitor; and in case of any visitor refusing to be searched, the gaoler may deny him or her admission; the grounds of such proceeding, with the particulars thereof, to be entered in his journal.

Prison Offences.

General Regulation as to Punishment.

56. No punishments or privations of any kind shall be awarded, except by the gaoler, or by a visiting or other justice.

Gaoler to punish for Prison Offences.

57. The gaoler shall have power to hear complaints respecting any of the offences following; that is to say,
  1. Disobedience of the regulations of the prison by any prisoner;
  2. Common assaults by one prisoner on another;
  3. Profane cursing and swearing by any prisoner;
  4. Indecent behaviour by any prisoner;
  5. Irreverent behaviour at chapel by any prisoner;
  6. Insulting or threatening language by any prisoner to any officer or prisoner;
  7. Absence from chapel without leave by any criminal prisoner;
  8. Idleness or negligence at work by any convicted criminal prisoner;
  9. Wilful mismanagement of work by any convicted criminal prisoner.

All the above acts are declared to be offences against prison discipline; and it shall be lawful for the gaoler to examine any person touching such offences, and to determine thereupon, and to punish such offences by ordering any offender, for any time not exceeding three days,(*n*) to close confinement, to be kept there upon bread and water. And the gaoler shall enter in a separate book called the punishment book a statement of the nature of any offence that he has punished in pursuance of this Regulation, with the addition of the name of the offender, the date of the offence, and the amount of punishment inflicted.

(*n*) The Prison Act, 1877, which will come into operation on the 1st of April, 1878, enacts (s. 43, *post* p. 186) that it shall not be lawful for the gaoler to order any prisoner to be confined in a punishment cell for any term exceeding twenty-four hours.

SCHEDULE I.—PRISON REGULATIONS.

Punishment of Prisoners by Visiting Justices.

58. If any criminal prisoner is guilty of repeated offences against prison discipline, or is guilty of any offence against prison discipline, which the gaoler is not by this Act empowered to punish, the gaoler shall report the same to the visiting justices, (*o*) or one of them; and any one of such justices, or any other justice having jurisdiction in the place to which the prison belongs, shall have power to inquire upon oath and to determine concerning any matter so reported to him, and to order the offender to be punished by confinement in a punishment cell for any term not exceeding one month,(*o*) or, in the case of prisoners convicted of felony or sentenced to hard labour, by personal correction.

(*o*) The Prison Act, 1877, enacts (s. 14. *post* p. 160) that the Visiting Committee of prisons, which after the commencement (1st of April, 1878) of that Act is to be appointed in the place of the visiting justices (P. A., 1877, s. 13, *post* p. 158), shall be deemed to be visiting justices for all the purposes of this and of the following regulation, or of either of those regulations, and that any member of a Visiting Committee may exercise any power, or do any act, or receive any report, which any one justice may exercise, do, or receive under those regulations or either of them; but the Act provides (s. 43. *post* p. 186) that it shall not be lawful for the Visiting Committee of justices to order any prisoner to be punished by confinement in a punishment cell for any term exceeding fourteen days; and also (s. 14, *post* p. 160) that an offender shall not be punished under the regulations referred to, or either of them, by personal correction, except in pursuance of the order of two justices of the peace, after such inquiry upon oath and determination concerning the matter reported to them, as is mentioned in the 58th regulation.

Use of Irons.

59. No prisoner shall be put in irons or under mechanical restraint by the gaoler of any prison, except in case of urgent necessity; and the particulars of every such case shall be forthwith entered in the gaoler's journal, and notice forthwith given thereof to one of the visiting justices;.(*o*) and no prisoner shall be kept in irons or under mechanical restraint for more than twenty-four hours without an order in writing from a visiting justice,(*o*) specifying the cause thereof, and

the time during which the prisoner is to be kept in irons or under mechanical restraint, which order shall be preserved by the gaoler as his warrant.

Corporal Punishments.

60. All corporal punishments within the prison shall be attended by the gaoler and the surgeon. The surgeon shall give such orders for preventing injury to health as he may deem necessary, and it shall be the duty of the gaoler to carry them into effect, and the gaoler shall enter in the punishment book the hour at which the punishment is inflicted, the number of lashes, and any orders which the surgeon may have given on the occasion.

PRISONERS UNDER SENTENCE OF DEATH.
Prisoners under Sentence of Death.

61. Every prisoner under warrant or order for execution shall, immediately on his arrival in the prison after sentence, be searched by or by the orders of the gaoler, and all articles shall be taken from him which the gaoler deems dangerous or inexpedient to leave in his possession. He shall be confined in a cell apart from all other prisoners, and shall be placed by day and by night under the constant charge of an officer. He shall be allowed such a dietary and amount of exercise as the gaoler, with the approval of the visiting justices, may direct. The chaplain shall have free access to every such prisoner, unless the prisoner be of a religious persuasion differing from that of the Established Church, and be visited by a minister of such persuasion, in which case the minister of such persuasion shall have free access to him. With the above exceptions, no person, not being a visiting justice or an officer of the prison, shall have access to the prisoner, except in pursuance of an order from a visiting justice.

During the preparation for an execution, and the time of the execution, no person shall enter the prison who is not legally entitled to do so, unless in pursuance of an order in writing from two or more visiting justices.

Prison Officers.

Regulation as to Employment of Prisoners in Prison Offices.

62. No prisoner shall be employed as turnkey, assistant turnkey, wardsman, yardsman, overseer, monitor, or schoolmaster, or in the discipline of the prison, or in the service of any officer thereof, or in the service or instruction of any other prisoner. But this regulation shall not be taken to prevent the employment of any debtor in that part of the prison in which he may be lawfully confined in any manner in which he may be willing to be employed, and which is consistent with his safe custody.

Prison Officers to be Constables.

63. Every prison officer, while acting as such, shall, by virtue of his appointment, and without being sworn in before any justice, be deemed to be a constable, and to have all such powers, authorities, protection, and privileges for the purpose of the execution of his duty as a prison officer as any constable duly appointed has within his constablewick by common law, statute, or custom.

Officers not to sell or let to Prisoners.

64. No officer of a prison shall sell or let to, nor shall any person in trust for or employed by him sell or let to, or derive any benefit from the selling or letting of any article to any prisoner.

Officers not to contract with Prisoners.

65. No officer of a prison shall, nor shall any person in trust for or employed by him, have any interest, direct or indirect, in any contract for the supply of the prison.

Officers not to take Gratuities.

66. No officer of a prison shall at any time receive money, fee, or gratuity of any kind for the admission of any visitors to the prison or to prisoners, or from or on behalf of any prisoner, on any pretext whatever.

THE PRISON ACT, 1865.

Females to be attended by Female Officers.

67. Female prisoners shall in all cases be attended by female officers.

GAOLER.

Residence of Gaoler.

68. The gaoler shall reside in the prison. He shall not be an under-sheriff or bailiff, or be concerned in any other employment.

Gaoler to conform to Law and Regulations of Prison.

69. The gaoler shall strictly conform to the law relating to prisons and to the prison regulations, and shall be responsible for the due observance of them by others. He shall observe the conduct of the prison officers, and enforce on each of them the due execution of his duties, and shall not permit any subordinate officer to be employed in any private capacity, either for any other officer of the prison, or for any prisoner.

May suspend Subordinate Officers.

70. The gaoler shall, in case of misconduct, have power to suspend any subordinate officer, and shall report the particulars without delay to a visiting justice.

To inspect the Prison daily.

71. The gaoler shall, as far as practicable, visit the whole of the prison, and see every male prisoner once at least in every twenty-four hours, and in default of such daily visits and inspections he shall state in his journal how far he has omitted them, and the cause thereof. He shall, at least once during the week, go through the prison at an uncertain hour of the night, which visit, with the hour and state of the prison at the time, he shall record in his journal. When visiting the females' prison, he shall be attended by the matron or some other female officer

To post up in Cells Abstract of certain Regulations.

72. The gaoler shall cause an abstract, to be approved by the Secretary of State, of the regulations relating to the treatment and conduct of prisoners, with a copy of the prison dietaries, (printed in legible characters,) to be posted in each cell, and shall read or cause the same to be read to every prisoner who cannot read within twenty-four hours after his admission.

To report to Surgeon Prisoners disordered in Mind.

73. The gaoler shall without delay call the attention of the surgeon to any prisoner whose state of mind or body appears to require attention, and shall carry into effect the written directions of the surgeon respecting alterations of the discipline or treatment of any such prisoner.

To notify to Chaplain and Surgeon Prisoners requiring their Attention.

74. The gaoler shall notify to the surgeon without delay the illness of any prisoner, and shall deliver to him daily a list of such prisoners as complain of illness, or are removed to the infirmary, or confined to their cells by illness, and he shall daily deliver to the chaplain and surgeon lists of such prisoners as are confined in punishment cells.

To give Notice of Death of Prisoners.

75. Upon the death of a prisoner the gaoler shall give immediate notice thereof to the coroner of the district to which the prison belongs, and to one of the visiting justices, as well as to the nearest relative of the deceased, where practicable.

To report to Visiting Justices Insane Prisoners.

76. The gaoler shall without delay report to the visiting justices any case of insanity or apparent insanity occurring among the prisoners.

To keep enumerated Books and Accounts.

77. The gaoler shall keep the following records and accounts :—

First, The register required by The Prison Ministers Act, 1863, to be kept of the church or religious persuasion to which each prisoner belongs.

Second, A journal in which he shall record all such matters as he is directed to record therein by this Act, and all other occurrences of importance within the prison.

Third, A nominal record of all prisoners committed to his charge, in such form as may be directed by the visiting justices.

Fourth, A punishment book for the entry of the punishments inflicted for prison offences.

Fifth, A visitors' book for the entry of any observations made by visitors to the prison.

Sixth, A record of articles taken from prisoners.

Seventh, A record of the employment of prisoners sentenced to hard labour, and the manner in which they have been so employed.

Eighth, A list of books and documents committed to his care.

Ninth, An inventory of all the furniture and moveable property belonging to the prison.

Tenth, An account of all prison receipts and disbursements.

To be responsible for safe Custody of Documents.

78. The gaoler shall be responsible for the safe custody of the journals, registers, books, commitments, and all other documents confided to his care.

Not to be Absent without Leave.

79. The gaoler shall not be absent from the prison for a night without permission in writing from a visiting justice; and his leave of absence, with the name of the visiting justice granting it, shall be entered in his journal; but if absent without leave for a night from unavoidable necessity, he shall state the fact and the cause of it in his journal.

SCHEDULE I.—PRISON REGULATIONS.

Power of Deputy Gaoler.

80. Where a deputy gaoler is appointed to a prison, he shall be legally competent to perform any duty required by law to be performed by the gaoler ; and when the gaoler is absent from the prison, the deputy gaoler shall perform all his duties. Where there is no deputy gaoler, or in case of his services not being available by reason of sickness or other unavoidable cause, the gaoler shall, when absent from the prison on leave, appoint, with the consent of the visiting justices, an officer of the prison to act as his substitute, and during such absence the substitute so appointed shall have all the powers and perform all the duties of the gaoler.

Substitute of Deputy Gaoler.

The deputy gaoler, when in charge of the prison as gaoler, shall, if absent from the prison from any unavoidable cause, or unable from sickness to perform his duties, appoint a substitute with the sanction of the visiting justices.

MATRON.

General Duties.

81. The matron shall reside in the prison. She shall have the care and superintendence of the whole female department. The wards, cells, and yards where females are confined shall be secured by locks different from those securing the wards, cells, and yards allotted to male prisoners, and the keys of those locks shall be kept in the custody of the matron.

To inspect daily Female Prison.

82. The matron shall, so far as practicable, visit and inspect every part of the prison occupied by females, and see every female prisoner once at least in every twenty-four hours, and in default of such daily visits and inspections she shall state in her journal how far she has omitted them, and the cause thereof. She shall, at least once during the week, go through such part of the prison at an uncertain hour of

the night, which visit, with the hour and state of such part of the prison at the time, shall be recorded in her journal.

Not to be Absent without Leave.

83. The matron shall not be absent from the prison for a night without permission in writing from a visiting justice, on the recommendation of the gaoler; and her leave of absence, with the name of the visiting justice granting it, shall be entered in her journal; but if absent without leave for a night from unavoidable necessity, she shall state the fact and the cause of it in her journal.

To appoint Deputy when Absent.

84. The matron shall, with the consent of the gaoler, and with the approval of the visiting justices, appoint a female officer of the prison to act as deputy matron whenever she is absent on leave from the prison, and during such absence the deputy matron shall have all the powers and duties of the matron. Before leaving the prison the matron shall personally give over the charge of the part of the prison occupied by females to the deputy matron.

To keep Journal.

85. The matron shall keep a journal in which she shall record all occurrences of importance within her department, and punishments of female prisoners, and lay the journal before the gaoler daily, and before the visiting justices at their ordinary meetings.

SURGEON.

When to visit Prison.

86. The surgeon shall visit the prison at least twice in every week, and oftener if necessary, and shall see every prisoner in the course of the week. He shall daily visit the prisoners, if any, confined in punishment cells, and he shall visit daily, and oftener if necessary, such of the prisoners as are sick, and, when necessary, shall direct any prisoner to be removed to the infirmary.

SCHEDULE I.—PRISON REGULATIONS.

To make daily Record respecting sick Prisoners.

87. The surgeon shall enter, in the English language, day by day, in his journal to be kept in the prison, an account of the state of every sick prisoner, the name of his disease, a description of the medicines and diet, and any other treatment which he may order for such prisoner.

Occasionally to inspect every part of Prison, &c.

88. The surgeon shall, once at least in every three months, inspect every part of the prison, and enter in his journal the result of each inspection, recording therein any observations he may think fit to make on any want of cleanliness, drainage, warmth, or ventilation; any bad quality of the provisions, any insufficiency of clothing or bedding, any deficiency in the quantity or defect in the quality of the water, or any other cause which may affect the health of the prisoners.

To report Special Cases.

89. Whenever the surgeon has reason to believe that the mind of a prisoner is or is likely to be injuriously affected by the discipline or treatment, he shall report the case in writing to the gaoler, together with such directions as he may think proper, and he shall call the attention of the chaplain to any prisoner who appears to require his special notice.

To call in additional Medical Aid.

90. The surgeon may, in any case of danger or difficulty which appears to him to require it, call in additional medical assistance; and no serious operation shall be performed without a previous consultation being held with another medical practitioner, except under circumstances not admitting of delay, such circumstances to be recorded in his journal.

To make Entries as to Death of Prisoner.

91. The surgeon shall forthwith, on the death of any prisoner, enter in his journal the following particulars; viz., at what time the deceased was taken ill, when the illness was

first communicated to the surgeon, the nature of the disease, when the prisoner died, and an account of the appearances after death (in cases where a post-mortem examination is made), together with any special remarks that appear to him to be required.

To appoint Substitute when Absent.

92. In case of sickness, necessary engagement, or leave of absence, to be given by the visiting justices, the surgeon shall appoint a substitute, approved of by the visiting justices. The name and residence of the substitute shall be entered in his journal.

PRISON OFFICERS.

Officers to obey Gaoler.

93. All officers of the prison shall obey the directions of the gaoler, subject to the regulations of this Act, and all subordinate officers shall perform such duties as may be directed by the gaoler, with the sanction of the visiting justices, and the duties of each subordinate officer shall be inserted in a book to be kept by him.

Not to be Absent without Leave.

94. Subordinate officers shall not be absent from the prison without leave from the gaoler, and before absenting themselves they shall leave their keys, instruction book, and report book in the gaoler's office.

Not to receive Visitors without Leave.

95. Subordinate officers shall not be permitted to receive any visitors within the prison without permission of the gaoler.

To examine Cells, Locks, etc.

96. All subordinate officers shall frequently examine the state of the cells, bedding, locks, bolts, etc., and shall seize all prohibited articles, and deliver them to the gaoler forthwith.

Porter.

Duties of Gate Porter.

97. The officer acting as gate porter may examine all articles carried in or out of the prison, and may stop any person suspected of bringing in spirits or other prohibited articles into the prison, or of carrying out any property belonging to the prison, giving immediate notice thereof to the gaoler.

Reports.

Gaoler to transmit List of Prisoners to Secretary of State.

98. Within one week after the termination of every assize or court of quarter sessions the gaoler shall transmit by post to one of Her Majesty's principal Secretaries of State a calendar containing the names, crimes, and sentences of every prisoner tried at such assize or court of quarter sessions, in such form and containing such particulars as may be required by the Secretary of State; and whenever such court adjourns for any longer time than one week, the day upon which the adjournment is made shall be deemed the termination of the session within the meaning of this regulation; and every adjourned session for the trial of prisoners shall, for the purposes of this Act, be deemed a separate session; and every gaoler who neglects or refuses to transmit such calendar, or wilfully transmits a calendar containing any false or imperfect statement, shall for every such offence forfeit a sum not exceeding twenty pounds, to be recovered summarily.

Gaoler to attend Session and make Report.

99. The visiting justices shall, once at least in each quarter of the year, carefully examine the following books kept by the gaoler of every prison, that is to say, the register kept in pursuance of The Prison Ministers Act, 1863, the journal, the nominal record, the punishment book, the visitors' book, the record of articles taken from prisoners, the record of the employment of prisoners, the list of books and documents committed to his care, the inventory and the account of

prison receipts and disbursements, and shall report to the justices in sessions assembled any special circumstances which call for notice in respect of such books. The gaoler shall also at such sessions answer, on oath if required, the inquiries of the justices with respect to the condition of the prison and of the prisoners, and with respect to any other matters relating thereto. He shall at the same time present a certificate, signed by himself, containing a declaration how far the requisitions of this Act with respect to the separation of prisoners and enforcement of hard labour have been complied with, and shall point out any deviation therefrom which has taken place since his last attendance at sessions.

Journals and Reports of Chaplain and Surgeon.

100. The journals of the chaplain and surgeon shall, once at least in each quarter of a year, be laid before the justices in sessions assembled at such time as they may appoint, and shall be signed by the chairman of the sessions in proof of the same having been there produced. The chaplain shall once in the year, and he may at any sessions, deliver to the justices in sessions assembled a statement of the condition of the prison to which he is attached, and his observations thereon; and the surgeon shall, once at least in each quarter of a year, report to the justices in sessions assembled the condition of the prison, and the state of health of the prisoners under his care.

Record of Visits of Chaplain and Non-resident Officers.

101. There shall be kept in every prison a book, to be called the non-resident officers' book, in which the chaplain and any other officer of the prison not residing within the prison, but attending on or required to attend on such prison, shall regularly enter the date of every visit made to the prison by such officer; and every entry shall be signed with the name and be in the handwriting of such officer, and such book shall, once at least in each quarter of a year, be laid before the justices in sessions assembled, at such time as they may appoint, and shall be signed by the chairman of the sessions in proof of the same having been produced. The

gaoler of every prison shall be responsible for the safe custody of such book, and shall at all times, when required so to do, produce it for inspection to the visiting justices, or to any justice of the peace for the county, riding, division, hundred, district, city, town, or place to which the prison belongs.

CONSTRUCTION AND APPLICATION OF SCHEDULE.

Rules as to Prisoners not Debtors or Criminals.

102. Subject to the provisions of this Act, the justices in sessions assembled shall make such rules as they think expedient with respect to the classification and treatment of prisoners who are not debtors and are not criminal prisoners within the meaning of this Act.

Construction of Word " Regulation."

103. Any rules made by the justices in sessions assembled, or by the visiting justices, and any dietary tables framed in pursuance of this Act, shall be deemed to be regulations of the prison within the meaning of this Act.

Definition of " Subordinate Officers."

104. All officers of a prison shall be deemed to be subordinate officers, with the exception of the gaoler, the chaplain, the surgeon, the matron, and any minister appointed under The Prison Ministers Act.

SCHEDULE II.

Prisons of	Legal Character of Prison.	County.
Aberystwith	Borough Prison.	Cardigan.
Bradninch	,,	Devon.
Faversham	,,	Kent.
Helstone	,,	Cornwall.
King's Lynn	,,	Norfolk.
Lichfield	,,	Stafford.
Maldon	,,	Essex.
Newcastle-under-Lyme	,,	Stafford.
Penzance	,,	Cornwall.
Richmond	,,	York.
Romney Marsh	Liberty.	Kent.
Rye	Borough.	Sussex.
South Molton	,,	Devon.
Tenterden	,,	Kent.

SCHEDULE III.

LIST OF ACTS REPEALED.

Date.	Title of Act.	Extent of Repeal.
4 Geo. IV. c. 64.	An Act for consolidating and amending the laws relating to the building, repairing, and regulating of certain gaols and houses of correction in England and Wales.	The whole Act.
5 Geo. IV. c. 85.	An Act for amending an Act of the last session of Parliament relating to the building, repairing, and enlarging of certain gaols and houses of correction, and for procuring information as to the state of all other gaols and houses of correction in England and Wales.	The whole Act.

SCHEDULE III. 143

Date.	Title of Act.	Extent of Repeal.
6 Geo. IV. c. 40.	An Act to enable justices of the peace in England in certain cases to borrow money on mortgage of the rate of the city, riding, or place for which such justices shall be then acting.	The whole Act.
7 Geo. IV. c. 18.	An Act to authorize the disposal of unnecessary prisons in England.	The whole Act.
5 & 6 W. IV. c. 38.	An Act for effecting greater uniformity of practice in the government of the several prisons in England and Wales, and for appointing inspectors of prisons in Great Britain.	Secs. 2, 5, 6, 11, and 12.
5 & 6 W. IV. c. 76.	An Act to provide for the regulation of municipal corporations in England and Wales.	Secs. 115 and 116.
6 & 7 W. IV. c. 105.	An Act for the better administration of justice in certain boroughs.	Secs. 1 and 2.
1 Vict. c. 78.	An Act to amend an Act for the regulation of municipal corporations in England and Wales.	Secs. 37 and 38.
2 & 3 Vict. c. 56.	An Act for the better ordering of prisons.	The whole Act, except Secs. 18, 19, 20, and 21, and except Secs. 22 and 23 so far as they relate to prisons or places of confinement to which this Act does not extend.
3 & 4 Vict. c. 25.	An Act to amend the Act for the better ordering of prisons.	The whole Act.
5 & 6 Vict. c. 53.	An Act to encourage the establishment of district prisons.	The whole Act.

Date.	Title of Act.	Extent of Repeal.
5 & 6 Vict. c. 98.	An Act to amend the law relating to prisons.	Secs. 1, 2, 4, 8, 9, 13, 25, and 30, so far as the said sections relate to prisons within the provisions of this Act.
7 & 8 Vict. c. 50.	An Act to extend the powers of the Act for encouraging the establishment of district courts and prisons.	The whole Act.
7 & 8 Vict. c. 93.	An Act to enable barristers to arbitrate between counties and boroughs, to submit a special case to the Superior Courts.	The whole Act.
11 & 12 Vict. c. 39.	An Act to facilitate the raising of money by corporate bodies for building or repairing prisons.	The whole Act.
16 & 17 Vict. c. 43.	An Act for enabling the justices of counties to contract in certain cases for the maintenance and confinement of convicted prisoners in the gaols of adjoining counties.	The whole Act.
25 & 26 Vict. c. 44.	An Act to amend the law relating to the giving of aid to discharged prisoners.	Secs. 2 and 3.
26 & 27 Vict. c. 79.	An Act for the amendment of the law relating to the religious instruction of prisoners in county and borough prisons in England and Scotland.	So much of Section 3 as is inconsistent with the provisions of this Act, and the whole of Section 5, but so far only as relates to prisons to which this Act applies.

THE PRISON ACT, 1877.

(40 & 41 Vict. c. 21.)

ARRANGEMENT OF SECTIONS.

Preliminary.

Section
1. Short title of Act.
2. Commencement of Act.
3. Application of Act.

PART I.

Transfer and Administration of Prisons.

Transfer of Prisons.

4. Maintenance of prisons and prisoners out of public funds.
5. Prisons to vest in Secretary of State.

Administration of Prisons.

Prison Commissioners.

6. Appointment of Prison Commissioners.
7. Appointment of inspectors, officers, and servants.
8. Salaries.
9. Duties of Prison Commissioners.
10. Reports by Prison Commissioners.
11. Report to contain information as to manufacturing processes in prison.

Section
12. Return of punishments and offences of prisoners to be made yearly.

Visiting Committee of Justices.

13. Repeal of 28 & 29 Vict. c. 126. ss. 53, 54. Appointment of visiting committee of prisons.
14. Duties of visiting committee.
15. Repeal of 28 & 29 Vict. c. 126. s. 55. Visits to prison by any justice.

PART II.

Supplemental Provisions.

As to Obligation to maintain Prisons.

16. Termination of local obligation to maintain prisons.
17. Compensation to be made in place of prison accommodation.
18. Compensation to be made to prison authority in respect of accommodation provided for prisoners of some other authority.
19. Allowance to be made to prison authority in respect of uncompleted prison.

As to Contracts and Debts.

20. General saving of rights of creditors.
21. Determination of contracts between prison authorities.
22. Existing debts to be defrayed by prison authorities.
23. Provision as to continuing contracts.

As to Classification and Commitment of Prisoners.

24. Confinement of prisoners before and during trial.

Section
25. Confinement of prisoners after conviction.
26. Confinement of debtors and prisoners who are not criminal prisoners.
27. Saving as to commitment of prisoners.
28. Legal custody of prisoner.
29. Allowance to discharged prisoners.

As to Jurisdiction.

30. Jurisdiction of sheriff, coroner, and other officers.
31. Sheriff not liable for escape.
32. Prisoners under sentence of death.

As to Discontinuance of Prisons.

33. Power of Secretary of State to discontinue prisons.
34. Effect of discontinuance of prison.

Status of Prison Officers.

35. Position and duties of existing officers of prisons.
36. Superannuation of officers and abolition of office.

As to Miscellaneous Matters.

37. Relaxation of the law relating to hard labour.
38. Rules as to treatment of prisoners confined for non-payment of sums in the nature of debts.
39. Special rules as to treatment of unconvicted prisoners and certain other prisoners.
40. Treatment of prisoners convicted of sedition, etc.
41. Treatment of persons committed for contempt of court.
42. Test of malingering.
43. Limitation of time of confinement in punishment cells.
44. As to inquests on the bodies of prisoners.
45. Transfer of duties of existing inspectors of prisons.

Section
46. Power of prison authority to borrow on rate.
47. Power of Public Works Loan Commissioners to lend.
48. Legal estate in prison.
49. Appropriation of court-houses situate within the precincts of a prison.
50. Protection of prisons in the nature of national monuments.
51. Rules of Secretary of State, and repeal of inconsistent enactments.
52. Saving clause as to reformatory and industrial schools.
53. Saving clause as to pensions.
54. Commutation of payment by University of Oxford to the city of Oxford.

Arrangement and Arbitration.

55. Power for Secretary of State and prison authority to compromise and refer to arbitration.

Definitions.

56. Definition of "furniture and effects belonging to a prison."
57. Definition of "prisoner" and "the maintenance of a prisoner." "Cell accommodation for a prisoner."
58. Definition of "county" and "riding."
59. Definition of "borough."
60. Definition of "prison."
61. Definition of "prison authorities," "justices in sessions assembled," "visiting justices."

THE PRISON ACT, 1877.

(40 & 41 VICT. C. 21.)

An Act to amend the Law relating to Prisons in England.

[12th of July, 1877.]

BE it enacted by the Queen's most Excellent Majesty, by and with the advice and consent of the Lords Spiritual and Temporal, and Commons, in this present Parliament assembled, and by the authority of the same, as follows:

PRELIMINARY.

Short Title of Act.

1. This Act may be cited for all purposes as The Prison Act, 1877.

Commencement of Act.

2. This Act shall, except as is hereinafter otherwise provided, (*p*) and except in so far as relates to the making of rules by the Secretary of State, in pursuance of any power transferred to or vested in the Secretary of State by this Act, which rules may be made at any time after the passing of this Act, (*q*) come into operation on the first day of April one thousand eight hundred and seventy-eight, which day is hereinafter referred to as the commencement of this Act.

(*p*) See ss. 6, 14, *post* pp. 153, 160.
(*q*) The 51st section of this Act (*post* p. 192) declares that all rules and regulations made under or in pursuance of the Act shall be forthwith laid in a complete form, after they have been settled and

approved by the Secretary of State, before both Houses of Parliament, if Parliament be sitting, or if not, then within three weeks after the beginning of the next ensuing session of Parliament; and that if any such rules or regulations shall be disapproved of by either House of Parliament within forty days after they have been so laid before Parliament, such rules or regulations, or such parts thereof as shall be disapproved of, shall be void and of no effect. The same section also declares that no rules or regulations so made by the Secretary of State shall come into force until they have been laid before Parliament, in accordance with its provisions, for forty days. Although the rules referred to in this section may be made by the Secretary of State at any time after the passing of the Act, they cannot therefore come into force until they have been laid before both Houses of Parliament for the period and in the manner provided by the 51st section. Any such rule may be proved in the manner in which regulations made under the authority of one of Her Majesty's principal Secretaries of State are capable of being proved in pursuance of The Documentary Evidence Act, 1868 (see s. 51, and note (*x*) thereto, *post* p. 192).

Application of Act.

3. This Act shall not extend to Scotland or Ireland, but shall apply to all prisons (*r*) belonging to any prison authority as defined by The Prison Act, 1865. (*s*)

(*r*) As to the meaning of the term "prison," see The Prison Act, 1865, s. 4. *ante* p. 61, and s. 60 of this Act, *post* p. 197.

(*s*) See s. 5 of that Act, *ante* p. 62.

PART I.

TRANSFER AND ADMINISTRATION OF PRISONS.

TRANSFER OF PRISONS.

Maintenance of Prisons and Prisoners out of Public Funds.

4. On and after the commencement of this Act all expenses incurred in respect of the maintenance of prisons to which this Act applies, and of the prisoners therein, shall be defrayed out of moneys provided by Parliament. (*t*)

(*t*) The Act will come fully into operation on the 1st of April, 1878 (see s. 2, *ante* p. 149). As to the prisons to which the Act applies, see s. 3, and the notes thereto. The term "maintenance of a prisoner" is defined by the 57th section of this Act, *post* p. 195. The Prison Act, 1865, required (s. 8, *ante* p. 65) that there should be provided at the expense of every county, riding, division, hundred, liberty, franchise, borough, town, or other place having a separate prison jurisdiction, adequate accommodation for its prisoners in a prison or prisons constructed and regulated in compliance with the requisitions of that Act; and declared that all expenses incurred by a prison authority in carrying into effect the provisions of the Act should be defrayed out of the county rate, or rate in the nature of a county rate, borough rate, or other rate leviable in the county, riding, division, hundred, liberty, franchise, borough, town, or other place having a separate prison jurisdiction, and applicable to the maintenance of a prison, or out of any other property applicable to the purpose. The effect of the provisions of the present section, in conjunction with those of the 16th section of this Act (see *post* p. 163), which abolishes, from the date above mentioned, the local obligation of any county, town, or other place as already named, to maintain a prison or to provide prison accommodation for its prisoners, will be entirely to relieve the local rates, after that date, from all expenses connected with the future maintenance of prisons to which the Act applies, and of the prisoners confined in them, and to transfer the burthen of those expenses to the Imperial Exchequer.

Prisons to vest in Secretary of State.

5. Subject as in this Act mentioned (*u*)—

1. The prisons to which this Act applies, and the furniture and effects belonging thereto; (*v*) also,
2. The appointment of all officers, (*w*) and the control and safe custody of the prisoners in the prisons to which this Act applies; also all powers and jurisdiction at common law or by Act of Parliament or by charter vested in or exerciseable by prison authorities or the justices in sessions assembled, (*x*) in relation to prisons or prisoners within their jurisdiction,

shall, on and after the commencement of this Act, (*y*) be transferred to, vested in, and exercised by one of Her Majesty's principal Secretaries of State, in this Act referred to as the Secretary of State.

(*u*) See ss. 6, 7, 9, 48, *post* pp. 153, 154, 155, 191, respectively.
(*v*) The Act applies to all prisons belonging to any prison authority

as defined by The Prison Act, 1865 (see s. 3, *ante* p. 150). As to the meaning of the term "prison," see The Prison Act, 1865, s. 4, *ante* p. 61, and s. 60 of this Act, *post* p. 197. The meaning of the term "furniture and effects belonging to a prison" is defined by s. 56 of this Act, *post* p. 195. Although this section declares that "the prisons to which the Act applies, and the furniture and effects belonging to them," shall, on and after the commencement (1st of April, 1878) of the Act, be transferred to and become vested in the Secretary of State, it is expressly declared by the 48th section of the Act (see *post* p. 191) that the "legal estate" in every such prison, and in the site and land belonging thereto, and in the furniture and effects, shall, on and after the date just mentioned, be deemed to be vested in the Prison Commissioners and "not in the Secretary of State," but it is further declared by the same section that they shall from time to time be disposed of by the Commissioners in such mode as the Secretary of State, with the consent of the Treasury, may direct.

(*w*) The officers heretofore required to be appointed for every prison will be found named in the 10th section of The Prison Act, 1865 (*ante* p. 66). The Prison Commissioners are, however, subject to the approval of the Secretary of State, to appoint (s. 9, *post* p. 155) all such officers of a prison as are by The Prison Act, 1865, declared (Regulation 104, Sched. I., *ante* p. 141) to be subordinate officers of a prison. The Commissioners are also to appoint, subject to approval, as above stated, all such officers and servants, with the exception of the inspectors of prisons, who are to be appointed by the Secretary of State himself, as may be required for assisting them in the performance of their duties, the number of those officers and servants being determined, with the sanction of the Treasury, by the Secretary of State (see s. 7, *post* p. 154). As to the tenure of office of officers attached to prisons at the time of the commencement of this Act, and as to their distribution amongst and employment in the prisons to which the Act applies, see s. 35, *post* p. 177.

(*x*) The terms "prison authorities" and "justices in sessions assembled" are (see s. 61, *post* p. 198) to have the same meaning in this Act, in relation to any prison, that they have (see ss. 5, 6 of the Act, *ante* pp. 62, 63 respectively) in The Prison Act, 1865. The provisions of this section, with respect to the transfer to and the exercise by the Secretary of State of the powers and jurisdiction of prison authorities, are not to affect the powers or jurisdiction of those authorities in relation to any reformatory school, or to any industrial school under The Reformatory Schools Act, 1866, or The Industrial Schools Act, 1866, or either of them, or any Act amending them or either of them (see s. 52 of this Act, *post* p. 193). The general rules for the government of prisons made by the Secretary of State, on the transfer to him under this Act of the powers hitherto exercised in relation to prisons by the justices in sessions assembled, will be found in the Appendix, *post* pp. 279—293.

(*y*) The 1st of April, 1878 (s. 2, *ante* p. 149).

ADMINISTRATION OF PRISONS.

PRISON COMMISSIONERS.

Appointment of Prison Commissioners.

6. For the purpose of aiding the Secretary of State in carrying into effect the provisions of this Act relating to prisons, Her Majesty may, on the recommendation of the Secretary of State, at any time and from time to time after the passing of this Act (z), by warrant under her sign manual, appoint any number of persons to be Commissioners during Her Majesty's pleasure, so that the whole number of Commissioners appointed do not at any one time exceed five, (a) and may, on the recommendation of the Secretary of State, on the occasion of any vacancy in the office of any Commissioner by death, resignation, or otherwise, by the like warrant appoint some other fit person to fill such vacancy. The Commissioners so appointed shall be a body corporate-with a common seal, with power to hold land without license in mortmain so far as may be necessary for the purposes of this Act, (b) and shall be styled "The Prison Commissioners."

The Secretary of State may from time to time appoint one of the Commissioners to be chairman.

Any act or thing required or authorised to be done by the Prison Commissioners may be done by any one or more of them as the Secretary of State may by general or special rule direct. (c)

(z) See s. 2. *ante* p. 149.
(a) The first appointment of Prison Commissioners under the Act was made on the 17th of July, 1877, when Lieutenant-Colonel Edmund Frederick Du Cane, C.B., R.E., Vice-Admiral William Windham Hornby. John Watlington Perry Watlington. Esq., and Walter James Stopford, Esq., were appointed to be such Commissioners. As to the salaries of the Commissioners, see s. 8, *post* p. 155.

(*b*) As to the vesting of the legal estate in prisons, etc., in the Prison Commissioners. see s. 48, *post* p. 191.

(*c*) The general duties of the Prison Commissioners are prescribed by s. 9 of this Act. *post* p. 155. As to their duties in making reports and returns to the Secretary of State or to Parliament, see ss. 10, 11, 12, *post* pp. 157, 158 respectively. The provisions of the Act with respect to the legal requisites of the rules of the Secretary of State will be found in s. 51, *post* p. 192.

Appointment of Inspectors, Officers, and Servants.

7. The Prison Commissioners shall be assisted in the performance of their duties by such number of inspectors, storekeepers, accountants, and other officers and servants as may, with the sanction of the Treasury as to number, be determined by the Secretary of State. The inspectors shall be appointed by the Secretary of State, (*d*) the other officers and servants of the Prison Commissioners by the Prison Commissioners themselves, subject to the approval of the Secretary of State.

(*d*) The inspectors of prisons have hitherto been appointed by the Secretary of State, under the provisions of the 7th section of the Act 5 & 6 W. IV. c. 38 (see that Act in the Appendix), but that section is, from and after the commencement (1st of April, 1878) of this Act, repealed (see s. 45, *post* p. 187) so far as respects England. The appointment of such inspectors will thenceforth, therefore, be made under the provisions of this Act. But on and after the commencement of this Act, any duties required by Act of Parliament or otherwise to be performed by an inspector of prisons appointed under the Act 5 & 6 W. IV. c. 38, may, subject to any directions to be given by the Secretary of State, be performed by any Prison Commissioner or inspector appointed under this Act. The inspectors holding office at that date, under the Act 5 & 6 W. IV. c. 38, are, however, to become inspectors under this Act, in the same manner, and liable to the performance of the same duties, as if they had been appointed under it, subject to the following qualifications:—

(1) That every such inspector shall hold his office by the same tenure, and upon like terms and conditions, as if this Act had not passed, and shall receive a salary of not less amount than that which he has hitherto received ; and

(2) That any duties such inspectors may be required to perform in pursuance of this Act shall be the same as or analogous to the duties which they performed previously to its commencement (s. 45, *post* p. 187).

As to the salaries of the new inspectors, see s. 8, *post* p. 155.

Salaries.

8. There may be paid, out of moneys provided by Parliament, to all or any one or more of the Prison Commissioners (*e*) such salary for their or his services as the Secretary of State may, with the consent of the Treasury, determine.

There shall be paid, out of moneys provided by Parliament, to the inspectors and other officers and servants (*f*) of the Prison Commissioners such salaries as the Secretary of State may, with the consent of the Treasury, determine.

(*e*) As to the appointment of the Prison Commissioners, see s. 6, *ante* p. 153.
(*f*) As to the appointment of the inspectors and other officers and servants of the Prison Commissioners, see s. 7, *ante* p. 154.

Duties of Prison Commissioners.

9. The general superintendence of prisons under this Act (*g*) shall be vested in the Prison Commissioners, subject to the control of the Secretary of State.

Subject as in this Act mentioned, (*h*) the Prison Commissioners shall appoint all such officers of a prison as are by The Prison Act, 1865, declared to be subordinate officers of a prison, (*i*) such appointments to be for general prison service. The Prison Commissioners shall also make contracts, (*j*) and do all other acts necessary for the maintenance of the prisons and prisoners within their jurisdiction.

Subject to the control of the Secretary of State, the Prison Commissioners, by themselves or their officers, shall visit and inspect the prisons within their jurisdiction, and shall examine into the state of the buildings, so as to form a judgment as to the repairs, additions, or alterations which may appear necessary, regard being had to the requisitions of The Prison Act,

1865, as amended by this Act, with respect to the separation of prisoners and enforcement of hard labour, (*k*) and shall further examine into the conduct of the respective officers, and the treatment and conduct of the prisoners, the means of setting them to work, the amount of their earnings, and the expenses attending the prison, and shall inquire into all abuses within the prison, and regulate all matters required to be regulated by them.

Subject to the control of the Secretary of State, the Prison Commissioners, or any one or more of them, may, in addition to any powers otherwise conferred on them by this Act, exercise in relation to any prison under this Act (*g*), and the prisoners therein, all powers and jurisdiction by any Act of Parliament or at common law, or by charter, exerciseable by visiting justices, or a visiting justice, of a prison. And any reports, acts, or things required to be made or done to or by or in relation to the visiting justices, or a visiting justice, of a prison, at common law, or by any Act of Parliament, or by charter, shall, except in so far as is otherwise provided by this Act, be made or done to or by or in relation to the Prison Commissioners, or any one or more of them, or to or by or in relation to such persons or person as the Secretary of State may from time to time appoint.

The Prison Commissioners shall, in the exercise of their powers and jurisdiction under this Act, conform to any directions which may from time to time be given to them by the Secretary of State.

(*g*) As to the prisons to which the Act applies, see s. 3, and the notes thereto, *ante* p. 150. As to the vesting of the legal estate in those prisons in the Prison Commissioners, see s. 48, *post* p. 191.

(*h*) That is, subject to the approval of the Secretary of State (s. 7, *ante* p. 154.

(*i*) By the 104th Prison Regulation (see P. A., 1865, Sched. I., *ante* p. 141), it is declared that all officers of a prison shall be deemed to be subordinate officers, with the exception of the gaoler, the chaplain, the surgeon, the matron, and any minister appointed under The Prison Ministers Act, 1863.

(*j*) By s. 6 (*ante* p. 153) the Prison Commissioners are declared to be a body corporate with a common seal.

(*k*) With regard to the separation of prisoners, see ss. 17, 18 of The Prison Act, 1865, *ante* pp. 72, 73, and ss. 24, 25, 26, 38, 40, 41 of this Act, *post* pp. 170, 171. 183, 186 respectively : and with regard to the enforcement of hard labour, see s. 19 of The Prison Act, 1865, *ante* p. 74, and the Prison Regulations 34 (amended by s. 37 of this Act, *post* p. 183), 35, 36, and 37, *ante* pp. 121, 122.

Reports by Prison Commissioners.

10. The Prison Commissioners shall, at such time or times as the Secretary of State may direct, make a report or reports to the Secretary of State of the condition of the prisons and prisoners within their jurisdiction, and an annual report (*l*) to be made by them with respect to every prison within their jurisdiction shall be laid before both Houses of Parliament.

(*l*) As to certain contents of the report, see the next section; and as to the yearly return of punishments and offences of prisoners to be made by the Prison Commissioners, see s. 12, *post* p. 158.

Report to contain Information as to Manufacturing Processes in Prison.

11. Whereas it is expedient that the expense of maintaining in prison prisoners who have been convicted of crime should in part be defrayed by their labour during the period of their imprisonment, and that, with a view to defraying such expenses, and also of teaching prisoners modes of gaining honest livelihoods, means should be taken in promoting in prison the exercise of and instruction in useful trades and manufactures, so far as may be consistent with a due regard on the one hand to the maintenance of the penal character of prison discipline, and on the other to the avoidance of undue pressure on or competition with any particular trade or industry : Be it enacted, that the annual report of the Prison Commissioners required by this Act (*m*) to be laid before both Houses of Parliament shall state the various manufacturing processes carried on in each of the prisons within their jurisdiction, and such statement shall contain such particulars as to the kind and quantities of, and as to the commercial value of the labour on the manufactures, as to the number of prisoners employed, and otherwise, as may, in the opinion of the Secretary of State, be best calculated to afford information to Parliament.

(*m*) See s. 10, *ante* p. 157.

Return of Punishments and Offences of Prisoners to be made Yearly.

12. The Prison Commissioners shall make a yearly return to Parliament of all punishments of any kind whatsoever which may have been inflicted within each prison, and the offences for which such punishments were inflicted.

Visiting Committee of Justices.

Repeal of 28 & 29 *Vict. c.* 126. *ss.* 53, 54.—*Appointment of Visiting Committee of Prisons.*

13. On and after the commencement of this Act (*n*) there shall be repealed the fifty-third and fifty-fourth sections of The Prison Act, 1865, relating to the appointment and duties of visiting justices. (*o*)

A Visiting Committee shall be annually appointed for every prison under this Act,(*p*)consisting of such number of persons being justices of the peace to be appointed at such time and by such court of quarter sessions or such bench or benches of magistrates as the Secretary of State, having regard to the locality of the prison, to the justices heretofore having jurisdiction over such prison, and to the class of prisoners to be confined in such prison, may from time to time by any general or special rule prescribe. (*q*) In the following manner ; namely,

The justices of any county, riding, or liberty of a county having a separate court of quarter sessions shall appoint members of a Visiting Committee when assembled at such general or quarter sessions as may be prescribed by the Secretary of State.

The justices of a borough shall hold special sessions, at such time as may be prescribed by the Secretary of State, for the purpose of appointing any members of a Visiting Committee they may be required to appoint.

Provided that, in the application of this Act to the Worcester Prison as constituted by The Worcester Prison Act, 1867, so long as the said prison is continued as a prison for the purposes of this Act, the appointment of such number of justices of the city of Worcester as the Secretary of State in pursuance of this section may prescribe to be appointed to serve on the Visiting Committee in respect of the said prison, shall be vested in the corporation acting by the council of the said city.

Nothing in this Act, or in any rules to be made under this Act, shall restrict any member of the Visiting Committee for any prison from visiting the prison at any time, and any such member shall at all times have free access to every part of the prison, and to every prisoner therein. (*r*)

(*n*) The 1st of April, 1878 (s. 2, *ante* p. 149).
(*o*) These sections will be found *ante* pp. 96, 97.
(*p*) See s. 3. *ante* p. 150.
(*q*) As to the legal requisites and the proof of such rules, see s. 51. *post* p. 192. The rules thus made will be found *post* pp. 250, 252, 262.
(*r*) The 15th section of this Act (see *post* p. 161), which repeals the fifty-fifth section of The Prison Act, 1865, relating to visits of any justice of the peace to a prison, enacts that any justice of the peace, having jurisdiction in the place in which a prison is situate, or in the place where the offence in respect of which any prisoner may be confined in prison was committed, may, when he thinks fit, enter into

and examine the condition of the prison and of the prisoners in it, but provides that the justice shall not be entitled to visit any prisoner under sentence of death, or to communicate with any prisoner, except in reference to the treatment of the prisoner in prison, or to some complaint that the prisoner may make as to such treatment. But as the present section expressly declares that nothing in the Act, nor in any rules to be made under it, shall restrict any member of the Visiting Committee for any prison from visiting the prison at any time, and also that any such member shall at all times have free access to every part of the prison and to every prisoner therein, it follows that any member of a Visiting Committee for a prison will be entitled to have access to the prison in the manner provided by the Act, and to visit all the prisoners confined in it, as well prisoners under sentence of death as other prisoners, and that he will not in communicating with them be restricted to communications in reference to their treatment in prison, or to complaints that they may have to make as to such treatment.

Duties of Visiting Committee.

14. The Secretary of State shall, on or before the commencement of this Act, (*s*) make and publish, and may hereafter from time to time repeal, alter, or add to, rules (*t*) with respect to the duties of a Visiting Committee, and such Committee shall conform to any rules so made and for the time being in force, but subject as aforesaid the members of such Committee shall from time to time and at frequent intervals visit the prison for which they are appointed, and hear any complaints which may be made to them by the prisoners, and if asked, privately. They shall report on any abuses within the prison, and also on any repairs which may be urgently required in the prison, and shall further take cognizance of any matters of pressing necessity and within the powers of their commission as justices, and do such acts and perform such duties in relation to a prison as they may be required to do or perform by the Secretary of State.

The Visiting Committee shall be deemed to be visiting justices for all the purposes of the regulations relating to the punishment of prisoners numbered 58 and 59 in the first schedule annexed to The Prison Act, 1865, (u) or either of such regulations, and any member of a Visiting Committee may exercise any power, or do any act, or receive any report which any one justice may exercise, do, or receive under the said regulations numbered 58 and 59, or either of them.

Provided that an offender shall not be punished under the said sections * 58 and 59, or either of them, by personal correction, except in pursuance of the order of two justices of the peace after such inquiry upon oath and determination concerning the matter reported to them as is mentioned in the said regulation numbered 58.

The Visiting Committee shall report to the Secretary of State any matters with respect to which they may consider it expedient, and shall report to the Secretary of State, as soon as may be, and in such manner as he may direct, any matter respecting which they may be required by him to report.

(s) The 1st of April, 1878 (s. 2. *ante* p. 149).
(t) As to the legal requisites and proof of such rules, see s. 51. *post* p. 192. The rules thus made will be found in the Appendix, *post* pp. 262—267.
(u) See the regulations in question, *ante* p. 129.

Repeal of 28 & 29 *Vict. c.* 126, *s.* 55.—*Visits to Prison by any Justice.*

15. Section fifty-five of "The Prison Act, 1865," is hereby repealed, (v) and instead thereof the following enactment shall take effect, viz.:

Any justice of the peace, having jurisdiction in the place in which a prison is situate, or having jurisdiction in the place where the offence in respect of which any prisoner may be confined in prison was committed, may, (w) when he thinks fit, enter into and examine the condition of such prison, and of the prisoners therein,

* *Sic.* in Stat.

and he may enter any observations he may think fit to make in reference to the condition of the prison or abuses therein in the visitors' book to be kept by the gaoler; and it shall be the duty of the gaoler to draw the attention of the Visiting Committee, at their next visit to the prison, to any entries made in the said book; but he shall not be entitled, in pursuance of this section, to visit any prisoner under sentence of death, or to communicate with any prisoner, except in reference to the treatment in prison of such prisoner, or to some complaint that such prisoner may make as to such treatment. (*x*)

(*v*) The section will be found *ante* p. 97.

(*w*) The 55th section of The Prison Act, 1865, restricted the right of visiting a prison conferred by it to justices of the peace having jurisdiction in the place to which the prison belonged; and the 66th section of the same Act (see *ante* p. 102). whilst it declared that where one prison authority, called the contracting authority, may have contracted with any other prison authority, called the receiving authority, that the receiving authority should receive into and maintain in its prison any prisoners maintainable at the expense of the contracting authority, the prison of the receiving authority should for all purposes of and incidental to the commitment, trial, detention, and punishment of the prisoners of the contracting authority, or any of such purposes, according to the tenor of the contract, be deemed to be the prison of the contracting authority, expressly provided that the contracting authority should have no right to interfere in the management of the prison. The present section, however, extends the right of visiting a prison to any justice of the peace having jurisdiction either in the place where the prison is situate, or in the place where the offence in respect of which any prisoner may be confined in prison was committed. A justice of the peace of one county may therefore visit and examine, in accordance with the powers conferred by this section, the prison of another county or the prison of a borough, when any prisoner is confined in such prison for an offence committed within his jurisdiction as a justice of the peace in his own county; and a justice of the peace for a borough may, in like manner, and under the same circumstances, visit either the prison of the county in which the borough is situate, or a prison in another county.

(*x*) These restrictions are not to affect the right of any member of a Visiting Committee for a prison; but any such member is at all times to have free access to every part of the prison, and to every prisoner therein (see s. 13, *ante* p. 158).

PART II.

SUPPLEMENTAL PROVISIONS.

As to Obligation to Maintain Prisons.

Termination of Local Obligation to Maintain Prisons.

16. On and after the commencement of this Act the obligation of any county, riding, division, hundred, liberty, franchise, borough, town, or other place having a separate prison jurisdiction, to maintain a prison or to provide prison accommodation for its prisoners shall cease. (*y*)

(*y*) The Act is to come into operation on the 1st of April, 1878 (s. 2. *ante* p. 149). and the 4th section of this Act (see *ante* p. 150) provides that from that date all expenses incurred in respect of the maintenance of prisons to which the Act applies, and of the prisoners confined in them, shall be defrayed out of moneys provided by Parliament ; a provision which will, in conjunction with this section, practically repeal, from the time specified, the 8th section of The Prison Act, 1865, and various other sections of the same Act relating to the provision and maintenance of prisons, and to the providing of prison accommodation for prisoners by the various prison authorities created by it.

Compensation to be made in place of Prison Accommodation.

17. Where at the time of the passing of this Act (*z*) any prison authority (*a*) has no prison of its own, or has not a prison or prisons of its own adequate to the accommodation of the prisoners belonging to such authority, it shall pay into the receipt of the Exchequer one hundred and twenty pounds in respect of each prisoner belonging to such prison authority for whom cell accommodation (*b*) has not at such time as last aforesaid been provided by such authority in a prison of its own.

Any sum payable by a prison authority in pursuance of this section shall be deemed to be a debt due from the prison authority to the Crown, and may be recovered accordingly.

Where one prison authority has contributed a sum of money towards the construction by some other prison authority of cell accommodation for the use of the prisoners of the contributing authority, and such cell accommodation has been constructed accordingly, then in assessing the sum payable into the Exchequer by the contributing authority under this section the contribution so made shall be taken into consideration, and a proportionate deduction be made accordingly.

For the purposes of this section a prison authority may borrow, and the Public Works Loan Commissioners may advance by way of loan, (c) to bear interest at such rate per cent. as the Treasury may determine to be sufficient to prevent any loss to the Exchequer, such sum as may be required, so that the whole amount so borrowed be discharged within a period not exceeding thirty-five years.

(z) The 12th of July, 1877.
(a). The term "prison authority" has the same meaning (see s. 61, post p. 198) in this Act as it has in The Prison Act, 1865 (see s. 5 of that Act, ante p. 62).
(b) "Cell accommodation" means a cell for the separate confinement of a prisoner certified in pursuance of The Prison Act, 1865 (see s. 51, post p. 192). As to the certifying of cells under The Prison Act, 1865, see ss. 18, 75 of that Act, ante pp. 73, 107.
(c) See further as to power of prison authorities to borrow, and as to the power of the Public Works Loan Commissioners to lend money, ss. 46, 47, post pp. 189, 190.

Compensation to be made to Prison Authority in respect of Accommodation provided for Prisoners of some other Authority.

18. Where before the first day of January one thousand eight hundred and seventy-seven any prison authority, having more than sufficient cell accommodation (d) for the number of prisoners belonging to such prison authority, and which prison authority is in this section called the receiving authority, has contracted (e) with any other prison authority, in this section called the sending authority, that the receiving authority is to receive into its prisons any prisoners belonging to such sending authority, and such receiving authority has in the performance of such contract provided cell accommodation for the prisoners of the sending authority, there shall be paid to the receiving authority, out of moneys provided by Parliament, any loss it may have so sustained in relation to such contract for cell accommodation by reason of the passing of this Act, so that the expense of providing cell accommodation for any one prisoner shall not in any case be held to have exceeded the sum of one hundred and twenty pounds.

For the purposes of this section any public department of State which has made contracts with respect to prisoners shall be included under the term "prison authority."

Where it appears that any contract under this section is intended to be renewed at the expiration of its subsisting term, the intention of renewal shall be taken into consideration in estimating the loss sustained by the receiving authority.

Where a prison authority has provided a prison or prisons of its own more than adequate for the accommodation of its prisoners, it shall be entitled to receive, out of moneys to be provided by Parliament, compensation to the extent of one hundred and twenty pounds in respect of each cell provided in such prison or prisons over and above the number of cells required for the average maximum number of prisoners maintained at the expense of such authority in its own prison or prisons during the five years immediately preceding the first day of January one thousand eight hundred and seventy-seven: Provided always, that in case the Prison Commissioners shall report to the Secretary of State that the prison accommodation is in excess of the probable requirements of such prison authority for its own prisoners, or that the buildings are dilapidated or unsuitable, it shall be lawful for the Secretary of State to decline to recommend to the Treasury to make such compensation, in whole or in part, as the circumstances of the case may demand.

Provided also, that no compensation shall be payable under such provision as last aforesaid in respect of any prison discontinued (*f*) within two years after the commencement of this Act.

A prison authority shall not be entitled to receive under this section more than one hundred and twenty pounds in the whole in respect of the same cell.

" Probable requirements " means the probable future requirements of a prison authority calculated as from the passing of this Act.

The average maximum number of prisoners of a prison authority maintained in any prison in any period of five years shall be calculated by finding the greatest number of such prisoners confined therein on the day on which such prison contained most of such prisoners as aforesaid in each of the said five years, and dividing the aggregate so found by five, excluding fractions.

(*d*) As to the meaning of this term, see s. 57, *post* p. 195.
(*e*) As to the power of prison authorities thus to contract, see ss. 31, 32 of The Prison Act, 1865, *ante* pp. 82, 83. As to the determination of contracts existing between prison authorities on the commencement of this Act, see s. 21, *post* p. 168.
(*f*) As to the power of the Secretary of State to discontinue prisons, and as to the effect of their discontinuance by him, see ss. 33, 34, *post* pp. 175, 176.

Allowance to be made to Prison Authority in respect of Uncompleted Prison.

19. Where at the time of the passing of this Act (*g*) a prison authority has contracted (*h*) to construct a building to be used as a prison, but such building has not at the commencement of this Act (*i*) been completed or become a prison within the meaning of this Act, the Secretary of State may, if he thinks fit so to do, allow the prison authority time to complete such building as a prison, and when so completed it shall pass over to and vest (*j*) in the Secretary of State as a prison completed at the commencement of this Act; but if the Secretary of State does not think fit to allow time for the completion of such prison as aforesaid, he shall nevertheless, in assessing the amount of compensation payable in respect of cell accommodation, (*k*) make, with the consent of the Treasury, from the compensation payable as aforesaid, such deduction as, having regard to all the circumstances of the case, may be agreed upon, or as may, in the event of disagreement between the Secretary of State and the prison authority, be determined by arbitration. (*l*)

(*g*) The 12th of July, 1877.
(*h*) As to the rights of creditors of prison authorities in respect of such contracts, and as to the payment of any debts due or sums of money payable under them, see s. 20 *infra*, and ss. 22, 23, *post* p. 169.
(*i*) The 1st of April, 1878 (s. 2, *ante* p. 149).
(*j*) See s. 5, *ante* p. 151.
(*k*) That is, in assessing the amount of compensation to be paid by the prison authority in respect of the prisoners belonging to it for whom it had not provided cell accommodation at the time of the passing (12th of July, 1877) of the Act (see s. 17, *ante* p. 163).
(*l*) As to the power under this Act of the Secretary of State and of a prison authority to refer any matter or difference to arbitration, and as to the mode of conducting the reference, see s. 55, *post* p. 194.

As to Contracts and Debts.

General Saving of Rights of Creditors.

20. Nothing in this Act contained (*m*) shall (save as in this Act mentioned with respect to contracts and obligations between prison authorities) (*n*) affect any right or claim of any creditor of a prison authority under any contract legally made (*o*) or in respect of any dealing legally had before the commencement of this Act, (*p*) and between such creditor and the prison authority of which he is a creditor such contract may be enforced in the same manner in all respects as if this Act had not passed.

(*m*) The local obligation of any county, borough, or other place as mentioned or referred to in this Act to maintain a prison or to provide prison accommodation for its prisoners, will, as we have already seen (s. 16, *ante* p. 163), cease on the commencement of the Act, and all expenses incurred in respect of the prisons to which the Act applies, and of the prisoners in them, will thenceforth be defrayed out of moneys provided by Parliament ; so that the powers of prison authorities, except in so far as special provision is made by this Act to the contrary, in respect of any such matters or expenses, will likewise cease. But, while the powers of prison authorities will thus terminate as regards the entering into any new contracts or dealings, this section expressly preserves the rights and claims of any creditor of a prison authority, not being also a prison authority, in respect of any contract legally made or in respect of any dealing legally had before the period above mentioned, and also preserves to him the same power and means of enforcing them which he would have if the Act had not passed. See also s. 23, *post* p. 169, as to continuing contracts.

(*n*) See s. 21, *infra*.

(*o*) As to the manner in which prison authorities may make contracts, see The Prison Act, 1865, s. 7, *ante* p. 64.

(*p*) The 1st of April, 1878.

Determination of Contracts between Prison Authorities.

21. Any contract made or obligation undertaken by any prison authority with any other prison authority for or in relation to the maintenance of any prison or prisoners, or any matter relating to such maintenance, (*q*) shall be deemed to be determined on and after the commencement of this Act, without prejudice nevertheless to any moneys which may have accrued due under or in respect of such contract or obligation at or before the commencement of this Act. (*r*)

(*q*) As to the power of prison authorities to make such contracts, see The Prison Act, 1865, s. 31, *ante* p. 82.

(*r*) The Act will come into operation on the 1st of April, 1878 (s. 2, *ante* p. 149). As to the manner in which any moneys payable under any contract to which this section applies are to be raised, see The Prison Act, 1865, ss. 8, 32, *ante* pp. 65, 83. See also s. 22, *infra*, as to the payment of existing debts by prison authorities.

Existing Debts to be defrayed by Prison Authorities.

22. There shall be defrayed by a prison authority, in the same manner as if this Act had not passed, (*s*)—

(1) All debts due and sums of money payable in respect of contracts performed, dealings completed, or any matter or thing done before the commencement of this Act ; and,

(2) All mortgage debts (together with interest from time to time accruing thereon) contracted in respect of any prison.

A mortgage debt in this section shall include any moneys which at the commencement of this Act have been borrowed or contracted to be borrowed by a prison authority on the security of any prison, or on the security of any rate applicable to the payment of the expenses of a prison, also any debt or liability contracted before the commencement of this Act, for the payment of which debt or liability money is authorised to be borrowed in pursuance of section twenty-three of The Prison Act, 1865. (*t*)

(*s*) See The Prison Act, 1865, ss. 8, 27, 32, *ante* pp. 65, 79, 83.

(*t*) That is to say, a debt or liability in respect of the alteration, enlargement, or rebuilding of a prison, or the building of a new prison (see the section in question, *ante* p. 77). As to the power of the Secretary of State to allow time to a prison authority to complete a prison contracted to be built at the time of the passing (12th of July, 1877) of this Act, and as to the allowance to be made to a prison authority in respect of an uncompleted prison, see s. 19, *ante* p. 166.

Provision as to continuing Contracts.

23. Where any contract or dealing, in which any prison authority is concerned, is a continuous contract or dealing, to be performed partly before and partly after the commencement of this Act, (*u*) and is not a contract or dealing which is declared by this Act to have determined, (*v*) and is not a mortgage debt as defined by the previous section, such contract or dealing shall be deemed to be divisible, and as to so much thereof as is performable before the commencement of this Act, shall create a debt or obligation to be discharged or performed by the prison authority concerned therein, (*w*) and as to so much thereof as is performable after the commencement of this Act, shall create a debt or obligation to be discharged or performed out of moneys provided by Parliament.

(*u*) The 1st of April, 1878 (s. 2, *ante* p. 149).
(*v*) That is to say, a contract or dealing between one prison authority and another prison authority (see s. 21, *ante* pp. 168).
(*w*) See ss. 20, 22, *ante* pp. 167, 169.

As to Classification and Commitment of Prisoners.

Confinement of Prisoners before and during Trial.

24. The Secretary of State may from time to time, by any general or special rule, (*x*) appoint in any county a convenient prison or prisons in which prisoners are to be confined before and during trial, or at either of such times, and any prisoner who might, if this Act had not passed, have been lawfully confined in a prison situate within the area of such county may be lawfully confined in any prison or prisons so appointed: Moreover, the Secretary of State may by any general or special rule (*x*) from time to time appoint any convenient prison or prisons in any adjoining county to which prisoners may be committed for trial, safe custody, or otherwise, and any prisoners may be committed to such prison accordingly.

(*x*) As to the legal requisites and proof of such rules, see s. 51, *post* p. 192. The rule thus made will be found *post* pp. 259, 260.

Confinement of Prisoners after Conviction.

25. The Secretary of State may from time to time, by any general or special rule,(*y*) appropriate either wholly or partially particular prisons within his jurisdiction to particular classes of convicted criminal prisoners,(*z*) and may remove any convicted criminal prisoner (*z*) from any one prison to any other prison within his jurisdiction for the purpose of his undergoing the whole or any portion of his punishment in such prison; provided that a prisoner who is confined in a prison situate beyond the limits of the county, borough, or place in which he was convicted of his offence shall, at the time of his discharge, be taken back at the public expense to the county, borough, or place in which he was so convicted.

(*y*) As to the legal requisites and proof of rules made by the Secretary of State, see s. 51, *post* p. 192.

(*z*) As to the meaning of the term "criminal prisoner," see The Prison Act, 1865, ss. 4, 67, *ante* pp. 61, 102, and s. 61 of this Act, *post* p. 198. Provision is made by s. 29, *post* p. 173, for the making of an allowance, not exceeding two pounds, to prisoners on their discharge from prison. See also The Prison Act, 1865, s. 43, *ante* p. 90, as to providing discharged prisoners with the means of returning to their place of settlement.

Confinement of Debtors and Prisoners who are not Criminal Prisoners.

26. The Secretary of State may from time to time, by any general or special rule,(*a*) appoint in any county a prison or prisons in which debtors and prisoners who are not criminal prisoners (*b*) are to be confined during the period of their imprisonment, and it shall be lawful to confine in any prison so appointed during the period of his imprisonment any debtor or prisoner who is not a criminal prisoner who might, if this Act had not passed, have been confined during such period in any prison situate within the area of the county.

(a) As to the legal requisites and proof of such rules, see s. 51, *pos* p. 192. The rule thus made will be found *post* p. 259.
(b) See ss. 4, 67 of The Prison Act, 1865, *ante* pp. 61, 102, and ss. 38, 40, 41 of this Act, *post* pp. 183, 186.

Saving as to Commitment of Prisoners.

27. Subject to this Act, and any rules made in pursuance thereof, prisoners may be committed to the same prison to which they might have been committed if this Act had not passed.

The committal or imprisonment of a prisoner to or in a prison, if otherwise valid, shall not be illegal by reason only that such prisoner ought, according to the law for the time being in force, to have been committed to or imprisoned in some other prison, but any such prisoner as is mentioned in this section shall, on application made on his behalf in a summary manner to any judge of the High Court of Justice, be entitled to be removed at the public expense to such other prison as aforesaid.

Legal Custody of Prisoner.

28. A prisoner shall be deemed to be in legal custody whenever he is being taken to or from, or whenever he is confined in, any prison in which he may be lawfully confined, or whenever he is working outside or is otherwise beyond the walls of any such prison in the custody or under the control of a prison officer belonging to such prison, and any constable or other officer acting under the order of any justice of the peace or magistrate having power to commit a prisoner to prison may convey a prisoner to or from any prison to or from which he may be legally committed or removed, notwithstanding such prison may be beyond the constablewick or other jurisdiction of such constable or officer, in the same manner and with the same incidents as if such prison were within such constablewick or other jurisdiction. (c)

(c) See also The Prison Act, 1865, ss. 58, 63, *ante* pp. 98, 100.

Allowance to Discharged Prisoners.

29. Where any prisoner is discharged from prison, (d) the Prison Commissioners may, (e) on the recommendation of the Visiting Committee or otherwise, order a sum of money, not exceeding two pounds, to be paid by the gaoler to the prisoner himself or to the treasurer of a certified Prisoners' Aid Society (f) or Refuge, on the gaoler receiving from such society an undertaking in writing, signed by the secretary thereof, to apply the same for the benefit of the prisoner.

(d) As to the discharge of a prisoner from prison, see The Prison Act, 1865, s. 41, *ante* p. 89.

(e) This section will, on the commencement of the Act, come into operation instead of s. 42 (see *ante*, p. 89) of The Prison Act, 1865, which confers a similar power upon the visiting justices. The mode of payment of such a gratuity is further provided for by the 10th of the Prison Rules, 1877. See *post*, p. 274. With regard to the provision of means to enable discharged prisoners to return to their place of settlement, see The Prison Act, 1865, s. 43, *ante* p. 90. See also s. 25 of this Act, *ante* p. 171, as to the taking back prisoners, at the public expense, to the county, borough, or place in which they were convicted of the offence for which they have been confined in a prison situate beyond the limits of such county, borough, or place.

(f) As to the mode in which a "Prisoners' Aid Society" may become certified, see the Act 25 & 26 Vict. c. 44, s. 1, in the Appendix.

As to Jurisdiction.

Jurisdiction of Sheriff, Coroner, and other Officers.

30. The Secretary of State may from time to time, if he think it expedient so to do, for the purpose of any enactment, law, or custom, descriptive of or dependent on the circumstance of a prison being the prison of any county, riding, county of a city, county of a town, liberty, borough, or other place having a separate prison jurisdiction, by any general or special rule (*g*) direct that for such purpose as aforesaid any prison locally situate within the county in which such riding, county of a city, county of a town, liberty, borough, or place is situate, or any prison which he may in pursuance of this Act (*h*) have appointed as a prison to which prisoners may be committed, is to be considered to be the prison of such county, riding, county of a city, county of a town, liberty, borough, or other place, but subject to any such rule as in this section mentioned, and until the same be made the transfer under this Act of the prisons to which this Act applies, and of the powers and jurisdiction of prison authorities, and of justices in sessions assembled, and of visiting justices, (*i*) shall not affect the jurisdiction of any sheriff or coroner, or, save as provided by this Act, of any justice of the peace or other officer having at the commencement of this Act jurisdiction in, over, or in respect of such prison.

(*g*) As to the legal requisites and proof of rules made by the Secretary of State, see s. 51, *post* p. 192.
(*h*) As to the power of the Secretary of State in this respect, see ss. 24, 25, 26, *ante* pp. 170, 171.
(*i*) See ss. 3, 5, 9, 13, *ante* pp. 150, 151, 155, 158.

Sheriff not Liable for Escape.

31. On and after the commencement of this Act the sheriff of any sheriffdom shall not be liable for the escape of any prisoner. (*j*)

(*j*) The Act will come into operation on the 1st of April, 1878 (s. 2, *ante* p. 149). The Prison Act, 1865, abolished (s. 60, *ante* p. 100) the liability of the sheriff for the escape of any prisoner other than a debtor; but under the terms of this section his liability in respect of the escape of any prisoner will cease at the period above named.

Prisoners under Sentence of Death.

32. Nothing in this Act contained shall affect the jurisdiction or responsibility of the sheriff in respect of prisoners under sentence of death, and confined in any prison within his jurisdiction, or his jurisdiction or control over the prison where such prisoners are confined, and the officers thereof, so far as may be necessary for the purpose of carrying into effect the sentence of death, or for any purpose relating thereto; and in any prison in which sentence of death is required or authorised to be carried into effect on any prisoner, the sheriff of the county in which the prison is situate shall, for the purposes of carrying that sentence into execution, be deemed to have the same jurisdiction with respect to such prison as he would by law have had with respect to the common gaol of his county if this Act had not passed, and such prison were the common gaol of his county.

As to Discontinuance of Prisons.

Power of Secretary of State to discontinue Prisons.

33. The Secretary of State may by order from time to time discontinue any prison or prisons which are vested in him by this Act, (*k*) provided that in every county there remain at least one prison, unless the Secretary of State otherwise order for special reasons to be stated in his order; and any order made by the Secretary of State in pursuance of this section shall be laid before both Houses of Parliament forthwith, if Parliament be sitting at the time of the order being made, or, if not then sitting, within one month after the commencement of the then next session of Parliament.

(*k*) As to the prisons vested in the Secretary of State by the Act, see ss. 3, 5, 19, *ante* pp. 150, 151, 166. The Prison Officers Compensation Act, 1868 (31 Vict. c. 21) makes provision for the payment of compensation to any person who, by reason of the discontinuance of any prison, other than the prisons specified in Schedule II. of that Act, since the date of the passing of The Prison Act, 1865, has been deprived of any salary or emolument. The Act will be found in the Appendix.

Effect of Discontinuance of Prison.

34. When a prison to which this Act applies (*l*) is discontinued, the Secretary of State shall serve notice on the prison authority to which such prison originally belonged, that he will, at any time within a period not less than six months, to be prescribed by the Secretary of State, from the date of the service of such notice, cause such prison, but without any furniture or effects belonging thereto, (*m*) to be reconveyed to such authority, on payment by such authority into the Exchequer, for the public use, of one hundred and twenty pounds in respect of each prisoner belonging to such prison authority for whom cell accommodation (*n*) was* provided in such discontinued prison at the time of the passing of this Act, (*o*) and on repayment by such authority of any compensation it may have received out of moneys provided by Parliament in respect of its having provided a prison of its own more than adequate for the accommodation of the prisoners belonging to such authority. (*p*)

A prison authority to whom a prison is reconveyed in pursuance of this section may sell or otherwise dispose of the same in such manner as it thinks fit.

If a prison authority decline to accept the offer of the reconveyance of the prison so made by the Secretary of State, or fail to pay or to secure to the satisfaction of the Secretary of State the payment of such sum into the Exchequer as is required to be paid by it in pursuance of this section, the prison shall be sold by the Secretary of State; and the Secretary of State, after paying the expenses of such sale, and paying into the Exchequer the amount so required to be paid as aforesaid, shall render the overplus (if any) to the prison authority to which the prison originally belonged.

Any sum payable by a prison authority in pursuance of this section shall be deemed to be a debt due from

* *Sic.* in Stat.

the prison authority to the Crown, and may be recovered accordingly.

For the purposes of this section a prison authority may borrow, and the Public Works Loan Commissioners may advance by way of loan, (q) to bear interest at such rate per cent. as the Treasury may determine to be sufficient to prevent any loss to the Exchequer, such sum as may be required, so that the whole amount so borrowed be discharged within a period not exceeding thirty-five years.

For the purposes of this section the cell accommodation (n) provided by a prison authority in all its prisons may be calculated; and if it appears from such calculation that sufficient accommodation (n) has been provided by such authority in any one prison or prisons belonging to such authority, no sum shall be payable under this section by such prison authority in respect of the discontinued prison, and a proportionate deduction shall be made in the sum payable under this section by a prison authority in the event of any partial accommodation in excess of the necessary accommodation having been provided in such other prisons belonging to that authority.

(l) As to the prisons to which the Act applies, see s. 3, *ante* p. 150.
(m) The meaning of the term " furniture and effects " is defined by s. 56, *post* p. 195.
(n) See s. 57, *post* p. 195, as to the meaning of the terms "cell accommodation" and " sufficient accommodation."
(o) The 12th of July, 1877.
(p) See s. 18, *ante* p. 164.
(q) See further as to the power of a prison authority to borrow, and of the Public Works Loan Commissioners to advance money by way of loan, ss. 46, 47, *post* pp. 189, 190.

Status of Prison Officers.

Position and Duties of existing Officers of Prisons.

35. The officers attached to prisons at the time of the commencement of this Act (r) (in this Act referred to as existing officers of a prison) shall hold their offices by the same tenure, and upon like terms and conditions, as if this Act had not passed, and shall receive salaries of not less amount than those which they have hitherto received. (*s*)

Such existing officers as aforesaid may be distributed amongst the several prisons to which this Act applies (*t*) in such manner as may be directed by the Secretary of State, and they shall perform such duties as they may be required to perform by the said Secretary of State, so that such duties are the same or analogous to those they performed previously to the commencement of this Act, (*r*) and, subject as aforesaid, they shall perform the same duties as nearly as may be as they are performing at the time of the commencement of this Act.

An existing officer of a prison who is at the commencement of this Act in the receipt of military or naval half-pay, or who has, at or before such commencement as aforesaid, commuted his pension in pursuance of The Pensions Commutation Act, 1871, (*u*) or is in receipt of any pension payable out of public moneys, shall not be subject to any deduction from his salary, or to be deprived of any portion of his half-pay, or of his pension, by reason of his salary being thenceforward paid out of public moneys, or of his employment becoming a public employment, or an employment of profit under Her Majesty, within the meaning of the Acts of Parliament providing for such deduction of salary or deprivation of half-pay, nor be disqualified from receiving such half-pay or pension by reason of his becoming by virtue of this Act a civil servant of Her Majesty.

(*r*) The 1st of April, 1878 (s. 2, *ante* p. 149).
(*s*) The officers attached to prisons at the time specified will probably consist of two classes; viz., those officers who were appointed previously to the commencement (the 1st of February, 1866) of The

Prison Act, 1865, and those officers who have been appointed under that Act.

As regards officers appointed previously to the commencement of The Prison Act, 1865, except the officers of the discontinued prisons named in Schedule II. of the Act, the 79th section of the Act (*ante* p. 108) declared that they should remain entitled to the same tenure of office, salary, and superannuation allowance as they would have been entitled to if that Act had not passed, subject to a proviso relative to their superannuation allowance; and with respect to officers of the second class (see s. 14 of the Act, *ante* p. 70), that they should hold their offices during the pleasure of the justices in sessions assembled, and should receive such salary as the justices may direct, subject to the proviso, that in the case of a municipal borough the amount of the salary of every prison officer appointed under the Act should be approved by the town council.

(*t*) See s. 3, *ante* p. 150.

(*u*) The Pensions Commutation Act, 1871, (34 & 35 Vict. c. 36) enables (ss. 3, 4) officers in Her Majesty's naval or land forces, and persons who may retire or who may be removed from public civil offices, in consequence of the abolition of their offices or for the purpose of facilitating improvements in the organization of the departments to which they belong, and to whom annual pensions have been granted by way of compensation for such retirement or removal, to make application to the Treasury, and, subject to such regulations as the Treasury may from time to time make, and to certain provisions contained in the Act, to commute their pensions for the payment of a capital sum of money, calculated according to the estimated duration of the life of the pension-holder.

The Act also declares (s. 2) that the term "pension" shall include half-pay, compensation allowance, superannuation, or retirement allowance, or other payment of the like nature; that "officer" shall mean commissioned and warrant officer in the army and navy, and subordinate officer in the navy; and that "public civil office" shall mean any office other than that of an officer in Her Majesty's naval or land forces, the holder of which is paid his remuneration out of moneys provided by Parliament for supply services.

Superannuation of Officers and Abolition of Office.

36. If at any time after the commencement of this Act (*w*) it appears to the Treasury that any exisitng officer of a prison (*x*) has been in the prison service for not less than twenty years, and is not less than sixty years of age, or that any existing officer of a prison has become incapable, from confirmed sickness, age, infirmity, or injury received in actual execution of his duty, of executing his office in person, and such sickness, age, infirmity, or injury is certified by a medical certificate, and there shall be a report of the Prison Commissioners testifying to his good conduct during his period of service under them, and recommending a grant to be made to him, the Treasury may grant to such officer, having regard to his length of prison service, an annuity, by way of superannuation allowance, not exceeding two-thirds of his salary and emoluments, or a gratuity not exceeding the amount of his salary and emoluments for one year. (*y*)

If any office in any prison to which this Act applies is abolished, or any officer is retired or removed, any existing officer of a prison who by reason of such abolition, retirement, or removal is deprived of any salary or emoluments shall be dealt with in manner provided by The Superannuation Act, 1859, with respect to a person retiring or removed from the public service in consequence of the abolition of his office, or for the purpose of facilitating improvements in the organization of the department to which he belongs. (*z*)

— "Prison service," for the purposes of this section, means, as respects the period before the commencement of this Act, service in a particular prison, or in the prisons of the same authority, transferred to the Secretary of State,(*a*) and as respects the period after the commencement of this Act, service in any such prison or in any other prison transferred to the Secretary of State under this Act.(*a*)

Any annuity by way of superannuation allowance, or gratuity granted under this section, shall be apportioned between the period of service before the commencement of this Act and the period of service after the commencement of this Act; and so much of such annuity or allowance as is payable in respect of service before the commencement of this Act, regard being had

THE PRISON ACT, 1877.   181

to the amount of salary then paid but without taking into account any number of years added to the officer's service on account of abolition of office or for facilitating the organization of the department shall be paid by the prison authority of the prison in which the officer to whom such annuity or allowance is granted was serving at the date of the commencement of this Act out of rates which at or immediately before the commencement of the Act were applicable to the payment of the salary of such officer,(*b*) and the residue shall be paid out of moneys provided by Parliament.

(*w*) The 1st of April, 1878 (s. 2, *ante* p. 149).

(*x*) See s. 35, *ante* p. 177, as to the meaning of the term "existing officer of a prison."

(*y*) But no existing officer of a prison is to be entitled (see s. 53, *post* p. 194) to any superannuation or other allowance under this Act, the conditions of whose office would not have entitled him to superannuation or other allowance under The Prison Act, 1865 ; and that Act directs (s. 79, *ante* p. 108) as to officers of prisons, except officers of the discontinued prisons named in Schedule II. (*ante* p. 142), appointed before its commencement (1st of February, 1866) that they shall remain entitled to the same superannuation allowance as if the Act had not passed ; provided that the superannuation allowance of any prison officer appointed before that date, may, on the application of such officer, and with the consent of the justices in sessions assembled, be calculated on the scale on which the superannuation allowances of officers appointed under the Act are appointed to be calculated. How the superannuation allowances of the last-mentioned officers are to be calculated is pointed out by s. 15 of The Prison Act, 1865, *ante* p. 70. As to the compensation to be allowed to persons who, by reason of the discontinuance of any prison, since the date of the passing of The Prison Act, 1865, other than the discontinued prisons specified in Schedule II. of that Act, have been deprived of any salary or emolument, see The Prison Officers Compensation Act, 1868, (31 Vict. c. 21,) in the Appendix.

(*z*) As to the prisons to which the Act applies, see s. 3, *ante* p. 150. An "existing officer" of a prison means an officer who may be attached to any prison to which the Act applies, at the time (1st of April, 1878) of its commencement (s. 35, *ante* p. 177). The Superannuation Act, 1859. (22 Vict. c. 26,) empowers (s. 7) the Commissioners of the Treasury to grant to any person retiring or removed from the public service in consequence of the abolition of his office, or for the purpose of facilitating improvements in the organization of the department to which he belongs, by which greater efficiency and economy can be effected, such special annual allowance by way of compensation, as on a full consideration of the circumstances of the case may seem to the said Commissioners to be a reasonable and just compensation for the loss of his office; but provides that, if the compensation shall exceed the amount to which such person would have been entitled under the scale of superannuation which the Act contains, if ten years were added to the number of years which he may have actually served, the allowance shall be granted by a special minute, stating the special grounds for granting it, which special minute must be laid before Parliament, and the Act further provides that no such allowance shall exceed two-thirds of the salary and emoluments of the office.

The Commissioners of the Treasury are, however, further empowered (s. 9) to grant to any person any superannuation, compensation, gratuity, or other allowance of greater amount than the amount which might be awarded to him under the foregoing provisions, when special services rendered by such person, and requiring special reward, shall appear to them to justify the increase, but so that such allowance shall in no case exceed the salary and emoluments enjoyed by the grantee at the time of his retirement, and the grounds of every such increase are to be stated in a minute of the Treasury, which is to be laid before Parliament; but the Commissioners may also, on the other hand, grant to any person any such allowance of less amount than otherwise would have been awarded to him, where his defaults or demerit in relation to the public service appear to them to justify such a diminution.

The scale fixed by The Superannuation Act, 1859, for granting superannuation allowances to persons who have served in an established capacity in the permanent Civil Service of the State, whether their remuneration be computed by day pay, weekly wages, or annual salary, is as follows:—

To any person who shall have served ten years and upwards, and under eleven years, an annual allowance of ten-sixtieths of the annual salary and emoluments of his office;

For eleven years, and under twelve years, an annual allowance of eleven-sixtieths of such salary and emoluments;

And in like manner a further addition to the annual allowance of one-sixtieth in respect of each additional year of such service, until the completion of a period of service of forty years, when the annual allowance of forty-sixtieths may be granted; but no addition is to be made in respect of any service beyond forty years (see, however, the provision as to allowances for special services, noticed above); and the Act provides that if any question shall arise in any department of the public service as to the claim of any person or class of persons for superannuation under this provision, it shall be referred to the Commissioners of the Treasury, whose decision is to be final. All orders, warrants, and minutes required by the Act to be laid before Parliament are (s. 13) to be laid before both Houses of Parliament within fourteen days after being made, if Parliament be sitting, and if Parliament be not sitting, then within fourteen days after its next meeting.

All superannuations, compensations, gratuities, and other allowances granted under the Act are to be paid (s. 16) to the persons entitled to receive them without any abatement or deduction in respect of any taxes or duties whatever, existing at the time of its passing (19th of April, 1859), except the tax upon property or income.

(*a*) As to the transfer of prisons to the Secretary of State, see s. 5, *ante* p. 151.

(*b*) See The Prison Act, 1865, s. 8, *ante* p. 65.

As to Miscellaneous Matters.

Relaxation of the Law relating to Hard Labour.

37. Whereas in pursuance of the 34th regulation of the first schedule annexed to The Prison Act, 1865, (*c*) a male person of sixteen years and upwards sentenced to hard labour is directed to be kept to hard labour of the first class during the whole of his sentence where it does not exceed three months, and during the first three months of his sentence where it exceeds three months; and whereas it is expedient to amend the said regulation: Be it enacted, that the Secretary of State may in either of such cases substitute hard labour of the second class for hard labour of the first class during the last two of such three months as aforesaid, or any part of such last two months, and he may make such substitution either by a general or special regulation, and either conditionally or unconditionally, and may from time to time vary any regulation so made. In making any regulations in pursuance of this section, the Secretary of State shall have regard to the previous convictions, the industry, and the conduct of the prisoners.

(*c*) The regulation referred to will be found in Schedule I. of The Prison Act, 1865, *ante* p. 121.

Rules as to Treatment of Prisoners confined for Non-payment of Sums in the nature of Debts.

38. The Secretary of State may from time to time make, and when made repeal, alter, or add to rules (*d*) with respect to the classification and treatment of prisoners imprisoned for non-compliance with the order of a justice or justices to pay a sum of money, or imprisoned in respect of the default of a distress to satisfy a sum of money adjudged to be paid by order of a justice or justices, so that such rules are in mitigation, and not in increase, of the effect of such imprisonment, as regulated by The Prison Act, 1865. (*e*)

(*d*) As to the legal requisites and proof of such rules, see s. 51, *post* p. 192. The rules made as to debtors, in pursuance of The Prison Act, 1877, are, except in certain cases, to apply to such prisoners. The rules will be found in the Appendix, *post* p. 276.

(*e*) See The Prison Act, 1865, s. 17, *ante* p. 72, and regulations 16, 17, 18, 31, 39, and 62, in Schedule I. of that Act, *ante* pp. 118, 121, 123, 131.

Special Rules as to Treatment of Unconvicted Prisoners and certain other Prisoners.

39. Whereas it is expedient that a clear difference shall be made between the treatment of persons unconvicted of crime and in law presumably innocent during the period of their detention in prison for safe custody only, and the treatment of prisoners who have been convicted of crime during the period of their detention in prison for the purpose of punishment, and that in order to secure the observance of such difference there shall be in force in every place in which prisoners are confined for safe custody only, special rules regulating their confinement in such manner as to make it as little as possible oppressive, due regard only being had to their safe custody, to the necessity of preserving order and good government in the place in which they are confined, and to the physical and moral well-being of the prisoners themselves: Therefore be it enacted, that the Secretary of State shall make, and when made may from time to time repeal, alter, or add to, special rules (*f*)—

(1) With respect to the retention by a prisoner of the possession of any books, papers, or docu-

ments in his possession at the time of his arrest, and which may not be required for evidence against him, and are not reasonably suspected of forming part of property improperly acquired by him, or are not for some special reason required to be taken from him for the purposes of justice ; (*g*)

(2) With respect to communications between a prisoner, his solicitor, and friends, so as to secure to such prisoner as unrestricted and private communication between him, his solicitor, and his friends as may be possible, having regard only to the necessity of preventing any tampering with evidence, and any plans for escape, or other like considerations ; (*h*) and,

(3) With respect to arrangements whereby prisoners may provide themselves with articles of diet, or may be furnished with a sufficient quantity of wholesome food, and may be protected from being called upon to perform any unaccustomed tasks or offices; (*i*) also any matter which the Secretary of State may think conducive to the amelioration of the condition of a prisoner who has not been convicted of crime, regard being had to such matters as are in this section directed to be regarded.

(*f*) As to the legal requisites and proof of such rules, see s. 51, *post* p. 192. The rules thus made will be found *post* pp. 268, 276.

(*g*) See regulations 6, 8, 48, in Schedule I. of The Prison Act, 1865, *ante* pp. 116, 125.

(*h*) See regulations 54, 55, in Schedule I. of The Prison Act, 1865, *ante* p. 127.

(*i*) See regulations 13, 15, 16, 17, 18, 19, 21, 22, in Schedule I. of The Prison Act, 1865, *ante* pp. 117, 118, 119, with regard to the right of prisoners to provide themselves with articles of diet, and as to their being furnished with a sufficient quantity of wholesome food. See also s. 21 of that Act (*ante* p. 76) with regard to the framing of **dietary** tables.

Treatment of Prisoners Convicted of Sedition, etc.

40. The Prison Commissioners shall see that any prisoner under sentence inflicted on conviction for sedition or seditious libel shall be treated as a misdemeanant of the first division within the meaning of section sixty-seven of "The Prisons Act, 1865," notwithstanding any statute, provision, or rule to the contrary. (*j*)

(*j*) See the section referred to, *ante* p. 102.

Treatment of Persons committed for Contempt of Court.

41. Any person who shall be imprisoned under any rule, order, or attachment for contempt of any court shall be in like manner treated as a misdemeanant of the first division within the meaning of the said section of the said Act. (*k*)

(*k*) Section 67 of The Prison Act, 1865. See *ante* p. 102.

Test of Malingering.

42. That where the prison medical officer considers it necessary to apply any painful test to a prisoner to detect malingering or otherwise, such test shall only be applied by authority of an order from the Visiting Committee of justices, or a Prison Commissioner.

Limitation of Time of Confinement in Punishment Cells.

43. It shall not be lawful for the gaoler to order any prisoner to be confined in a punishment cell for any term exceeding twenty-four hours ; (*l*) nor shall it be lawful for the Visiting Committee of justices to order any prisoner to be punished by confinement in a punishment cell for any term exceeding fourteen days. (*m*) (*l*) This provision applies to the 57th regulation in Schedule I. of The Prison Act, 1865 (*ante* p. 128) which empowers the gaoler to hear complaints respecting offences against prison discipline, and to punish such offences by ordering an offender to close confinement for any time not exceeding three days, and there to be kept upon bread and water.

(*m*) The 14th section of this Act declares (*ante* p. 160) that the Visiting Committee, a body created by the Act (s. 13, *ante* p. 158) in the place of the visiting justices, shall be deemed to be visiting justices for all the purposes of the regulations 58 and 59 in Schedule I. of The Prison Act, 1865, which relate to the punishment by the visiting justices of prisoners guilty of repeated offences against prison discipline, or of any offence against prison discipline which the gaoler is not empowered (regulation 57, *ante* p. 128) to punish; and the 58th regulation gave the justices power to order such an offender to be punished by confinement in a punishment cell for any term not exceeding one month, a period reduced by this section to any term not exceeding fourteen days.

As to Inquests on the Bodies of Prisoners.

44. In no case, where an inquest is held on the body of a prisoner who dies within the prison, shall any person engaged in any sort of trade or dealing with the prison be a juror on such inquest. (*n*)

(*n*) As to the holding an inquest on the body of a prisoner who dies within the prison, see The Prison Act, 1865, s. 48, *ante* p. 93, and regulation 75 in Schedule I. of that Act, *ante* p. 133. See also as to the holding of inquests on the body of a prisoner executed in a prison on the execution of judgment of death, The Capital Punishment Amendment Act, 1868 (31 Vict. c. 24 s. 5), in the Appendix.

Transfer of Duties of existing Inspectors of Prisons.

45. On and after the commencement of this Act, any duties required by Act of Parliament or otherwise to be performed by an inspector of prisons appointed in pursuance of the Act of the session of the fifth and sixth years of King William the Fourth, chapter thirty-eight, may, subject to any directions to be given by the Secretary of State, be performed by any Prison Commissioner or inspector appointed under this Act.(*o*)

The persons who at the commencement of this Act

hold the offices of inspectors of prisons, under such last-mentioned Act, shall become inspectors under this Act, in the same manner and liable to the performance of the same duties as if they had been appointed inspectors in pursuance of this Act, subject to the following qualifications, namely :—

(1) Every such inspector shall hold his office by the same tenure, and upon like terms and conditions, as if this Act had not passed, and shall receive a salary of not less amount than that which he has hitherto received ; and,

(2) Any duties they may be required to perform in pursuance of this Act shall be the same or analogous duties to those which they performed previously to the commencement of this Act.

The seventh section of the Act of the session of the fifth and sixth years of William the Fourth, chapter thirty-eight, shall be repealed from and after the commencement of this Act, in so far as respects England.

(*o*) The Act will come into operation on the 1st of April, 1878. The inspectors of prisons appointed under the 7th section of the Act 5 & 6 W. IV. c. 38, which section is, from the date just mentioned, repealed by the present section, in so far as respects England, are required by that Act to visit and inspect, either singly or together, every gaol, bridewell, house of correction, penitentiary. or other prison or place kept or used for the confinement of prisoners, in any part of the Kingdom of Great Britain ; and every such inspector is authorized to examine any person holding any office or receiving any salary or emolument in any such gaol, bridewell, house of correction, penitentiary, prison, or other place of confinement. and to call for and inspect all books and papers relating thereto, and to inquire into all matters touching and concerning such gaol, bridewell, house of correction, penitentiary, prison, or other place of confinement. Every such inspector is also required by the Act, on or before the 1st of February in every year, to make a separate and distinct report in writing of the state of every gaol, bridewell, house of correction, penitentiary, prison, or other place of confinement visited by him, and to transmit the same to one of the principal Secretaries of State. The Act also provides that a copy of every such report should be laid before both Houses of Parliament within fourteen days after the 1st of February in every year, if they should be then assembled ; or if

Parliament should not be then assembled, within fourteen days of its meeting after such 1st day of February. With regard to the reports relating to prisons, etc., which are after the commencement of The Prison Act, 1877, to be made by the Prison Commissioners to the Home Secretary and to Parliament, see ss. 10, 11, and 12, *ante* pp. 156, 157. As to the appointment of Prison Commissioners and inspectors under this Act, see ss. 6, 7, *ante* pp. 157, 158. The Act 5 & 6 W. IV. c. 38 provides (s. 8) for the punishment of persons knowingly and wilfully obstructing inspectors in the execution of any powers entrusted to them; and authorizes (s. 9) a justice of the peace, on any complaint being made to him against any person for any such offence, to issue his summons for the appearance of such person to answer the charge. The Act will be found in the Appendix.

Power of Prison Authority to Borrow on Rate.

46. A prison authority may borrow any moneys authorized to be borrowed by them under this Act, (*p*) as one loan, or as several loans in manner provided by The Local Loans Act, 1875, (*q*) on the security of any rate or property which would, if this Act had not passed, have been applicable to the maintenance of the prisons within the jurisdiction of such authority, and such prison authority may levy such rate or apply such property in the same manner in all respects as if this Act had not passed. (*r*)

The period for the discharge of a loan under this Act shall be deemed to begin at the date of the first advance of money made on account of any such loan or loans.

(*p*) See s. 17, *ante* p. 163; and s. 34, *ante* p. 176.

(*q*) The Local Loans Act, 1875, (38 & 39 Vict. c. 83,) empowers local authorities to borrow money (1) by the issue of debentures, (2) by the creation and issue of debenture stock, and (3) by the issue of annuity certificates, or partly in one way and partly in another. And the Act declares (s. 5) that a debenture under it shall be an instrument taking effect as a deed, and charging the local rate or property in such debenture specified with payment, as in the debenture mentioned, of the principal sum and interest therein specified. A debenture is not to be issued for less than the prescribed sum, or, where no sum is prescribed, for less than twenty pounds. A debenture stock may be created and issued (s. 6) by a local authority having power to raise a loan or any part thereof by the issue of debenture stock. Such stock is to be of nominal amount, not exceeding the amount of money authorized to be raised by such stock, and is, unless it be otherwise provided by the conditions of issue, to be redeemable at par at the option of the local authority, at such times and upon such conditions as that authority may declare at the time of issue. The title of any person to any share in debenture stock is to be evidenced by the entry in the register, which the Act requires (s. 23) to be kept, of the name of such person as owner. The stock is to bear such rate of interest, and the interest is to be payable at such times as the local authority may declare at the time of issue; and the debenture stock and the interest thereon are to be a charge on the local rate or property specified at the time of issue, in the same manner as if it were a principal sum and interest charged thereon by deed. An annuity certificate under the Act is to be (s. 7) an instrument taking effect as a deed, and charging the local rate or property specified in the certificate with payment, as in the certificate mentioned, of the annual sum therein specified. An annuity certificate is not to be issued for a less annual sum than the prescribed sum, or, where no sum is prescribed, for less than three pounds. Where a debenture or an annuity certificate charges property other than the local rate, and it is intended that, in default of payment of the principal sum, or of the interest due on such debenture, or of the annual sum secured by such annuity certificate or some part thereof, the property is to be sold, a statement to that effect is to be inserted in the debenture or annuity certificate as the case may be (ss. 5, 7); and similarly where debenture stock and the interest thereon is a charge on property other than the local rate, and it is intended that, in default of the payment of the interest, or for the purpose of raising the money required for the redemption of the stock, the property is to be sold, a declaration to that effect is to be made (s. 6) by the local authority at the time of the issue of the stock, and is to be deemed to form one of the conditions of the issue. The foregoing is an outline of some of the principal provisions of The Local Loans Act, 1875, with respect to the securities which may be created and issued under it; but for a full description of the nature of those securities, of the rights and liabilities which they may confer or impose, of the mode of negotiating them, and of the various other incidents belonging to them, the Act itself must be referred to.

(*r*) See The Prison Act, 1865, s. 8, *ante* p. 65.

Power of Public Works Loan Commissioners to Lend.

47. The Public Works Loan Commissioners may advance to any prison authority, on the security of such rate or property as aforesaid, (*s*) any moneys authorized to be borrowed by the prison authority for the purposes of this Act. (*t*)

The Public Works Loan Commissioners shall take, in respect of any loan advanced by them under this Act, in preference to any other securities, all or such one or more of the securities issuable under The Local Loans Act, 1875, (*u*) as they may prefer; and for the purposes of any loan so made, and so far as relates to the securities taken and to the recovery of the moneys due on such securities, The Local Loans Act, 1875, shall be deemed to be substituted for The Public Works Loans Act, 1875.

(*s*) See s. 46, *ante* p. 189 ; and The Prison Act, 1865, s. 8, *ante* p. 65.
(*t*) See ss. 17, 34, *ante* pp. 163, 176.
(*u*) The securities issuable under The Local Loans Act, 1875, are debentures, debenture stock, and annuity certificates (see Note (*g*) to s. 46, *ante* p. 189).

Legal Estate in Prison.

48. The legal estate in every "prison" to which this Act applies, and in the site and land belonging thereto, and in the furniture and effects, shall, on and after the commencement of this Act, be deemed to be vested in the Prison Commissioners, and not in the Secretary of State, but shall from time to time be disposed of by such Commissioners in such mode as the Secretary of State, with the consent of the Treasury, may direct. (*v*)

(*v*) As to the prisons to which the Act applies, see s. 3, *ante* p. 150. The meaning of the term "prison" is further defined than in The Prison Act, 1865, by s. 60 of this Act, *post* p. 197. As to the meaning of the term "furniture and effects," see s. 56, *post* p. 195. With respect to the vesting of the legal estate in the prisons to which the Act applies in the Prison Commissioners, and not in the Secretary of State, this section may be compared with s. 5, *ante* p. 151.

Appropriation of Court-Houses situated within the Precincts of a Prison.

49. Town halls, court-houses, or other rooms situate within the curtilage of a prison, or forming part of a prison as defined by this Act, (*w*) and which town halls, court-houses, or other rooms are used for the holding assizes or petty sessions, or for purposes other than those connected with the management of a prison, shall not be transferred to or vested in the Secretary of State under this Act, but it shall be lawful for the Secretary of State, with the consent of the Treasury, if he thinks it desirable, to purchase such town halls, court-houses, or other rooms so situate as aforesaid from the local authority to whom the same belong, and for the purposes of such purchase The Lands Clauses Consolidation Acts, 1845, 1860, and 1869, shall be incorporated with this section, and in the construction of the said incorporated Acts this Act shall be deemed to be the special Act, and the Secretary of State shall be deemed to be the promoter of the undertaking.

(*w*) As to the meaning of the term "prison" in this Act, see ss. 60, 61, *post* pp. 197, 198.

Protection of Prisons in the nature of National Monuments.

50. Any buildings which, being in the nature of national monuments, are, as to certain portions thereof, used as prisons, shall, as to the portions so used, during such time as they are used by the Secretary of State, be maintained in such manner as to prevent their being defaced or injured in their character of national monuments.

Rules of Secretary of State, and Repeal of Inconsistent Enactments.

51. Any rule made by a Secretary of State, in pursuance of this Act, may be proved in manner in which regulations made under the authority of one of Her Majesty's principal Secretaries of State are capable of being proved in pursuance of The Documentary Evidence Act, 1868, (*x*) and all enactments inconsistent

with this Act are hereby repealed : Provided always,
that all rules and regulations made under or in pursuance of this Act shall be forthwith laid in a complete
form, after the same shall have been settled and approved by such Secretary of State, before both Houses
of Parliament, if Parliament be sitting, or if not, then
within three weeks after the beginning of the next
ensuing session of Parliament ; and if any such rules or
regulations shall be disapproved by either House of
Parliament within forty days after the same shall have
been so laid before Parliament, such rules or regulations, or such parts thereof as shall be so disapproved
of, shall be void and of no effect : Provided also, that
no such rules or regulations shall come into force or
operation until the same shall have been so laid before
Parliament for forty days.

(x) The Documentary Evidence Act, 1868 (31 & 32 Vict. c. 37),
provides (s. 2) that *prima facie* evidence of any regulation made by
one of Her Majesty's principal Secretaries of State may be given in
all courts of justice and in all legal proceedings whatsoever, in all or
any of the following modes, so far as the provisions of that Act are
applicable to the rules in question, that is to say,—
  (1) By the production of a copy of *The London Gazette* purporting to contain such regulation ;
  (2) By the production of a copy of such regulation purporting to be printed by Her Majesty's printer ;
  (3) By the production of a copy of or extract from such regulation purporting to be certified to be true by any Secretary or Under-Secretary of State.
Any copy or extract made in pursuance of the Act may be in print
or in writing, or partly in print and partly in writing ; and no proof
is to be required of the handwriting or official position of any person
certifying to the truth of any copy of or extract from such regulation.
It is, however, declared by the Act (s. 6) that its provisions shall be
deemed to be in addition to, and not in derogation of, any powers
of proving documents given by any existing statute or existing at
common law.

Saving Clause as to Reformatory and Industrial Schools.

52. Nothing in this Act contained shall affect the
powers or jurisdiction of a prison authority in relation

to any reformatory school or to any industrial school under The Reformatory Schools Act, 1866, and The Industrial Schools Act, 1866, or either of such Acts, or any Act amending the said Acts, or either of them.

Saving Clause as to Pensions.

53. Nothing in this Act contained shall entitle any existing officer of a prison to any superannuation or other allowance, the conditions of whose office would not have entitled him to superannuation or other allowance under The Prison Act, 1865. (*y*)

(*y*) The provisions of this Act with regard to the superannuation or other allowance to be made to existing officers of a prison, or, in other words, to officers attached to prisons at the time of the commencement of this Act (1st of April, 1878), will be found in s. 36, *ante* p. 179. See also Notes (*y*) and (*z*) to that section, *ante* p. 181.

Commutation of Payment by University of Oxford to the City of Oxford.

54. The chancellor, masters, and scholars of the University of Oxford shall, in consideration of their being relieved from their obligation under The Oxford Police Act of 1868 to contribute to gaol expenses, pay to the mayor, aldermen, and citizens of the City of Oxford, on or before the first day of April, one thousand eight hundred and seventy-eight, the sum of four hundred pounds; and the said chancellor, masters, and scholars shall, from that date, be discharged from all liability under the said Act in respect of gaol expenses.

Power for Secretary of State and Prison Authority to Compromise and Refer to Arbitration.

55. The Secretary of State on the one hand (with the assent of the Treasury so far as any public moneys are concerned) and a prison authority on the other may, with a view to carry into effect the purposes of this Act, compromise any matter, or settle any difference, or refer to arbitration any matter or difference. (z)

A reference to arbitration under this Act shall be to a single arbitrator, and the provisions of The Common Law Procedure Act, 1854, shall apply accordingly.

(z) The Prison Act, 1865, also makes (s. 51, *ante* p. 95) provision for the reference of certain differences to arbitration. The terms of that Act differ, however, from those of this section, inasmuch as they are confined in their application to differences expressly directed by the Act to be settled in that manner; whereas the terms of this section are general, and authorize the reference of any matter or difference to arbitration, with a view to carry into effect the purposes of the Act.

Definition of " Furniture and Effects belonging to a Prison."

56. The expression "furniture and effects belonging to a prison" includes all furniture, beds, bedding, clothes, linen, implements, machinery, and stores, except goods manufactured for sale, and materials in store for the purposes of such manufacture, also all books, papers, registers, and documents whatsoever relating to such prison or to the prisoners therein, also all articles whatsoever, whether or not of the same kind as those previously described, belonging at the commencement of this Act to the prison authority of any prison for the purposes of such prison.

Definition of " Prisoner," " Maintenance of a Prisoner," and " Cell Accommodation for a Prisoner."

57. A "prisoner" for the purposes of this Act means any person committed to prison on remand or for trial, safe custody, punishment, or otherwise, and " the maintenance of a prisoner " includes all such necessary expenses incurred in respect of a prisoner for food, clothing, custody, safe conduct, and removal from one place of confinement to another, or otherwise, from the period of his committal to prison until his death or discharge from prison, as would if this Act had not passed have been payable by a prison authority; with this proviso, that nothing in this Act shall exempt a prisoner from payment of any costs or expenses in respect of his conveyance to prison (or otherwise) which he would have been liable to pay if this Act had not passed.

For the purposes of this Act, sufficient accommodation for the prisoners belonging to a prison authority shall, as nearly as can be ascertained, be deemed to be the average daily number of prisoners maintained at the expense of such authority, whether in its own prison or in a prison belonging to some other prison authority, during the five years immediately preceding the first day of January one thousand eight hundred and seventy-seven.

"Cell accommodation for a prisoner" means a cell for the separate confinement of such prisoner certified in pursuance of The Prison Act, 1865. (*a*)

^{*a*}) See ss. 18, 75 of that Act, *ante* pp. 73, 107.

Definition of "County" and "Riding."

58. In the construction of this Act, unless there is something inconsistent in the context,—

"County" means a county at large, inclusive of any riding, division, or parts of a county having a separate court of quarter sessions :

"Riding" means any riding, division, or parts of a county having a separate court of quarter sessions.

The City of London shall be deemed to be a county, and any prison belonging to the City of London to be situate within the limits of that city.

Save as aforesaid, all counties of cities, counties of towns, liberties and franchises of counties, shall be considered as forming part of the county by which they are surrounded, or if partly surrounded by two or more counties, then as forming part of that county with which they have the longest common boundary.

Definition of "Borough."

59. "Borough" means a place which is for the time being subject to the Act of the session of the fifth and sixth years of the reign of King William the Fourth (chapter seventy-six), "to provide for the regulation of municipal corporations in England and Wales," inclusive of any county of a city or county of a town.

Definition of "Prison."

60. "Prison," in addition to the meaning attached to it by The Prison Act, 1865, (*b*) includes any land or building bought or contracted to be bought before the commencement of this Act (*c*) by a prison authority, for the purpose of enlarging or altering any prison, or adding to the appurtenances of any prison; subject to this proviso, that if the Secretary of State is of opinion that any portion of the lands so bought or contracted to be bought, whether included or not within the walls of the prison, was not at the time of the passing (*d*) of this Act necessary for the then subsisting purposes of such prison, he shall either direct that such portion shall be reconveyed to the prison authority, or retain such portion, or any part of such portion, on payment out of moneys provided by Parliament of such sum as may be agreed upon, or, in the event of difference, may be determined by arbitration in manner provided by this Act, (*e*) on the transfer of any such prison to him, and the vesting thereof in him as by this Act provided.(*f*)

(*b*) See s. 4 of that Act. *ante* p. 61.
(*c*) The 1st of April. 1878 (s. 2, *ante* p. 149).
(*d*) The 12th of July, 1877.
(*e*) See s. 55, *ante* p. 194.
(*f*) See s. 5, *ante* p. 151, and s. 19, *ante* p. 166.

Definition of "Prison Authorities," "Justices in Sessions Assembled," "Visiting Justices."

61. In this Act the expressions "prison authorities," "justices in sessions assembled," and "visiting justices" shall respectively have the same meaning in relation to any prison as they have in The Prison Act, 1865, and expressions defined in that Act have the same meaning also in this Act. (*g*)

(*g*) The general definition of terms used in The Prison Act. 1865, will be found in s. 4 of that Act, *ante* p. 61. As to the meaning of the terms "prison authorities," "justices in sessions assembled," and "visiting justices," see ss. 5, 6, 53 respectively of the Act, *ante* pp. 62, 63, 96.

APPENDIX.

5 Geo. IV. c. 12.

An Act to facilitate in those Counties which are divided into Ridings or Divisions, the Execution of an Act of the last Session of Parliament, for Consolidating and Amending the Laws relating to the Building, Repairing, and Regulating of certain Gaols and Houses of Correction in England and Wales.—[23rd of March, 1824.]

Recital of 4 Geo. IV. c. 64 s. 2.—*In counties divided into ridings or divisions, a court of sessions for the gaol shall be held; and such court shall possess all the powers given by the former Act respecting the common gaol of such county.*—Whereas by an Act (h) passed in the fourth year of the reign of His present Majesty, intituled " An Act for consolidating and amending the Laws relating to the Building, Repairing, and Regulating of certain Gaols and Houses of Correction in England and Wales," it was (amongst other things) enacted, that there should be maintained at the expense of every county in England and Wales one common gaol, and that the regulations and provisions contained in the said Act should extend, in manner therein mentioned, to every such gaol : and whereas in certain counties in England there are distinct commissions of the peace for the several ridings and divisions into which such counties are divided, and distinct courts of sessions of the peace are holden for each of such ridings and divisions respectively, and in such counties there are no courts of general or quarter sessions holden for the whole county at large, in consequence whereof the provisions and regulations of the said Act cannot in such counties be carried into execution : for remedy thereof, and in order to extend to such counties all the benefits of the said Act ; be it therefore enacted by the King's most Excellent Majesty, by and with the advice and consent of the Lords Spiritual and Temporal, and Commons, in this present Parliament assembled, and by the authority of the same, that in every county divided into ridings or divisions, having distinct commissions of the peace, there shall be held from time to time a court of sessions for the gaol of such county, of which court all the justices of the peace of every riding and division of such county shall be members; and any two of such justices shall be able to hold such court; and such court shall possess and exercise all the powers and authorities respecting the common gaol of such county, and all matters relating thereto, which are in and by the said recited Act vested in the court of general or quarter sessions of the peace for any other county of England; and the justices of the peace for each of such ridings and divisions are hereby authorized as fully and effectually to perform and execute all the provisions and regulations of the said recited Act, with respect to such county gaol, as justices of the peace for the county are in any other county of England authorized to do with respect to the gaol of their respective counties; and the said court of gaol sessions is hereby empowered to transact and do, within the counties so divided, all such matters and things appertaining to the authority of justices of peace in sessions assembled, with respect to the county gaol, as are in other counties capable of being done by justices of the peace in their general or quarter sessions assembled; and where by the said Act any thing is ordered to be done at any general or quarter sessions, or at any adjournment thereof, or at any subsequent general or quarter sessions or adjournment thereof, respecting the county gaol, then such things may be done at such gaol sessions, or at any adjournment thereof, or at one or more subsequent gaol sessions, in such ways and with such public notices as in the said recited Act they are ordered or directed to be done by the general or quarter sessions or adjournment thereof.

(*h*) The Act, 4 Geo. IV. c. 64, was repealed by The Prison Act, 1865. See s. 73 of the Act, *ante* p. 100, and Schedule III., *ante* p. 142.

3. *Clerk of gaol sessions to continue in office till another is appointed, &c.*—And be it further enacted, that the clerk of the gaol sessions shall continue in his office until another shall be elected in his stead by the court of gaol sessions, and shall, with respect to the said recited Act and this Act, have and enjoy all the powers vested by the said recited Act in the clerk of the peace of any county.

4. *Courts of gaol sessions to be held, and notice thereof given, &c.*—And be it further enacted, that the clerk of the gaol sessions shall, on receiving a precept commanding him so to do, signed by any two justices of the peace acting for any of the ridings or divisions of the county, summon the justices to meet in a court of gaol sessions, by a notice to be published at least twice in some of the public newspapers most usually circulated in the county, which notice shall declare the day, hour, and place at which such court is to be held; and also that the said clerk, if

the court of gaol sessions shall be dissolved without adjournment, or shall adjourn for a longer time than three calendar months, shall by a like notice, to be issued of his proper authority, without any precept in that behalf, summon a court of gaol sessions to be held within three calendar months next after such dissolution or last adjournment.

5. *Place for holding sessions.*—And be it further enacted, that the sessions for the county gaols shall be held in some place in the gaol, or within one mile thereof, unless there shall be special reasons for the contrary, which shall be expressed in the precept to be directed to the said clerk as aforesaid ; and if it shall be held in the gaol, or within such distance thereof as aforesaid, all matters done thereat touching the county gaol shall be legal, though the sessions be held in some place not within the county.

6. *Appointment and duties of treasurer.—Salaries of clerk and treasurer.*—And be it further enacted, that the court of gaol sessions shall also elect a treasurer of the moneys applicable to the repair of the county gaol, who shall not be the clerk of the said court ; and the said treasurer shall receive and pay all moneys to be raised for the repair of the county gaol, or to be disbursed by order of the court, and shall give discharges for the moneys received, and apply the same as by such court shall be ordered, and shall keep a distinct account of such moneys received and paid, and shall from time to time, when called on by the said court, account upon oath, if required, for all moneys so by him received, and deliver in all vouchers respecting the same ; and the said court shall from time to time appoint such salaries to such clerk and treasurer respectively as they shall think fit, to be paid out of the moneys aforesaid ; and such treasurer shall give such security for the faithful performance of his duty as the court of gaol sessions shall direct.

7. *Proportions of county rates to be paid by each riding or division for expenses of gaol.*—And whereas it is expedient that all the expenses incurred respecting any county gaol, where the county is so divided as aforesaid, whether arising out of the provisions of the said recited Act or of this Act, or otherwise, should be discharged out of the county rates ; and it is necessary to fix the proportions in which the several ridings or divisions shall contribute to such expenses ; and it may also be necessary from time to time to vary the said proportions : Be it therefore further enacted, that where in any such county there are, at the time of passing this Act, any fixed proportions in which such expenses are or have been paid and borne, such proportions shall continue to be acted on, and the contributions shall be paid accordingly, till some alteration shall be made therein by the court of gaol sessions ; and that where there are now no such

fixed proportions, the said court shall forthwith fix the proportions in which the contribution is to be made; and the said court shall also have power and authority to alter the said proportions from time to time; provided that no such alteration shall be made, unless the intention of making such alteration shall be expressed in the notice whereby the court is summoned, and shall be published for one month at the least before the court shall be held.

8. *Proportions in which ridings or divisions are to contribute towards the expenses of the gaol, to be settled by arbitration in case of dispute.*—And be it further enacted, that when the court of gaol sessions shall order an alteration to be made in the proportions in which the ridings or divisions of the county are to contribute towards the expenses of the county gaol, or shall negative a proposition for making such alteration, and any riding or division shall be dissatisfied therewith, it shall be lawful for the clerk of the peace of such riding or division, being thereunto authorized by an order of the court of quarter or gaol sessions of such riding or division, to apply to the justices of assize of the last preceding circuit, or of the next succeeding circuit, or to one of such justices, who shall by writing under their or his hands or hand nominate a barrister-at-law, not having any interest in the question, to arbitrate between the ridings or divisions; and such arbitrator shall summons the several clerks of the peace of the ridings or divisions interested in the matter in dispute to appear before him, at a time to be by him appointed, and there to produce all information touching the matter in dispute; and such arbitrator may, if he shall see fit, adjourn the hearing from time to time, and require all such further information to be afforded by either of the parties as shall appear to him meet and necessary; and shall, by his award in writing, determine the proportions in which such ridings or divisions shall contribute towards the said expenses; and his award shall be final and conclusive between the parties for ten years, and until further order shall be made thereon by the court of gaol sessions; and such arbitrator shall also assess the costs of the arbitration, and shall direct by whom and out of what fund the same shall be paid.

9. *Order for payment of money shall be transmitted to treasurers of the several ridings, &c., who shall pay the proportionate sums charged on each riding, &c.*—And be it further enacted, that when and so often as the court of gaol sessions shall find it requisite to raise money for the purposes of the said recited Act or of this Act, they shall make an order accordingly, and their clerk shall forthwith transmit a copy of such order, signed by the chairman, together with the amount of the sum of money to be paid by

virtue of it, according to the then existing proportions, by each riding or division, to the treasurers of the several ridings or divisions of the county; which treasurers shall forthwith, out of the moneys in their hands, or if those moneys shall be insufficient, then so soon as sufficient moneys shall come to their hands, pay the sum required to the treasurer of the county gaol, and take his receipt for the same.

10. *Money may be raised by mortgage of all the rates of the county.*—And be it further enacted, that when the moneys necessary to be raised for the purposes of the said recited Act or of this Act shall exceed one-half of the ordinary aggregate amount of all the annual assessments for the rates of the several ridings or divisions of any such county, taken on an average of all such rates for the last seven years preceding, the court of gaol sessions may and is hereby authorized to mortgage all the rates of such county, by such instrument, and in such ways and means, and under such provisions of repayment, and with the same power of assignment, as in the said recited Act are enacted respecting the mortgage of any county rates therein mentioned.

11. *The rates on each riding, &c., to be charged in same manner as the whole rates on counties under recited Act.*—And be it further enacted, that the court of gaol sessions shall and is hereby required to charge all the rates upon the several ridings and divisions of the county, in the same manner and for the same purposes as in and by the said recited Act the justices in their general or quarter sessions are authorized and required to charge the rates of any county having one rate for the whole; and all the ways, means, and methods by the said recited Act directed and allowed, as to the repayment of moneys borrowed, and the interest thereof, and the accounts respecting the same, shall be kept and observed by the court of gaol sessions, respecting the moneys borrowed, on account of the gaol of any county so divided as aforesaid: provided that all the moneys to be raised on the several ridings or divisions of any such county, for repaying money borrowed, or the interest thereof, shall be raised in the same proportions as other moneys for the purposes of the said recited Act or of this Act shall be raised at the time of such money being so raised.

15. *Recovery of fines, &c., imposed by recited Act. Fines to be paid to treasurer of county gaol.*—And be it further enacted, that if any matter or thing be done within any county so divided as aforesaid, for which any fine, penalty, or forfeiture is by the said recited Act imposed and directed to be paid to the county treasurer, every conviction made in pursuance of the said recited Act for such matter or thing shall be made by one or more justices of the peace of the riding or division in which

the offence is committed; and all forfeitures, fines, and penalties thereon accruing shall be paid to the treasurer of the county gaol for the purposes of this Act.

16. *Common gaol of county to be deemed within each riding or division.*—And be it further enacted, that in the case of every county so divided as aforesaid, the common gaol of such county shall, for all purposes relative to the jurisdiction of justices of the peace, be deemed to be within and taken as part of each of the ridings and divisions of which such county is composed; and every justice of the peace for each of such ridings and divisions shall have like power and authority to execute all things appertaining to his office therein, as in any part of the riding or division to which his commission specially extends.

5 & 6 WILL. IV. c. 38.

An Act for effecting greater Uniformity of Practice in the Government of the several Prisons in England and Wales; and for appointing Inspectors of Prisons in Great Britain.—[25th *of August,* 1835.]

3. *Justices, &c., may commit offenders to any house of correction near the place where the assizes, &c., are to be held.*—Whereas great inconvenience and expense have been found to result from the practice of committing to the common gaol of the county persons charged with the offences intended to be tried at the assizes or sessions holden for such county where such assizes or sessions are holden at places distant from such common gaol, and it is expedient that the law should be altered and amended; for remedy thereof, be it enacted, that from and after the passing of this Act it shall be lawful for any justice of the peace or coroner, acting within their several jurisdictions in England and Wales, to commit for safe custody to any house of correction, (*i*) situate near to the place where such assizes and sessions are intended to be holden, any person or persons charged before them with any offence triable at such assizes or sessions; and that whenever any such persons shall be committed to any such house of correction for trial at such assizes or sessions, the keeper of such house of correction shall deliver to the judges of assize or justices at sessions a calendar of all prisoners in his custody for trial at such assizes or sessions respectively, in the same way that the sheriff of the county would be by law required to do if such prisoners had been committed to the common gaol of the county.

(*i*) The distinction between a gaol and a house of correction was practically abolished by The Prison Act, 1865. See s. 56 of that Act, *ante* p. 98.

4. *Commitment, &c., of persons convicted of offences for which they are liable to death, &c.*—And be it further enacted, that whenever any person shall be convicted at any assizes or sessions of any offence for which he or she shall be liable either to the punishment of death, transportation, or imprisonment, it shall be lawful for the court (if it shall so think fit) to commit such person to any house of correction for such county, in execution of his or her judgment; and in case of the commitment of any person sentenced to death, execution of such judgment shall and may be had and done by the sheriff of the county; and in case of the commitment of any person either sentenced to transportation, or pardoned for any capital offence on condition of transportation, all the powers, provisions, and authorities for the removal of offenders sentenced to transportation, given or granted by any former Act or Acts of Parliament to sheriffs or gaolers, shall be and the same are hereby extended and given to the keepers of houses of correction in whose custody such last-mentioned offenders shall be.

7. *Power to appoint inspectors of prisons.*—And be it enacted, (*j*) that it shall be lawful for one of His Majesty's principal Secretaries of State to nominate and appoint a sufficient number of fit and proper persons, not exceeding five, to visit and inspect, either singly or together, every gaol, bridewell, house of correction, penitentiary, or other prison or place kept or used for the confinement of prisoners, in any part of the kingdom of Great Britain; and every person so appointed shall have authority to examine any person holding any office or receiving any salary or emolument in any such gaol, bridewell, house of correction, penitentiary, prison, or other place of confinement as aforesaid, and to call for and inspect all books and papers relating thereto, and to inquire into all matters touching and concerning such gaol, bridewell, house of correction, penitentiary, prison, or other place of confinement; and every such person so appointed shall, on or before the first day of February in every year, make a separate and distinct report in writing of the state of every gaol, bridewell, house of correction, penitentiary, prison, or other place of confinement visited by him, and shall transmit the same to one of His Majesty's principal Secretaries of State; and a copy of every such report shall be laid before both Houses of Parliament within fourteen days after such first day of February, if they shall then be assembled; or if Parliament shall not be then assembled, within fourteen days after the meeting thereof after such first day of February.

(*j*) This section is repealed from and after the commencement (1st of April, 1878) of The Prison Act, 1877, in so far as respects England. See s. 45 of that Act, *ante* p. 188.

8. *Penalty on obstructing inspectors.*—And be it further enacted, that if any person shall knowingly and wilfully obstruct any person so appointed in the execution of any of the powers intrusted to him by this Act, such person shall, on conviction before a justice of the peace, forfeit and pay for each and every such offence any sum not exceeding twenty pounds, and in default of payment of any penalty so adjudged, immediately, or within such time as the said justice shall appoint, shall be committed to prison for any period not exceeding one calendar month.

9. *A justice may summon offenders on complaint being made.*—And be it further enacted, that it shall be lawful for a justice of the peace, on any complaint made to him against any person for any such offence, to issue his summons for the appearance of such person.

10. *Secretary of State may visit or authorize persons to visit prisons.*—And be it enacted, that it shall be lawful for any one of His Majesty's principal Secretaries of State to visit and inspect, or to authorize in writing any person or persons to visit and inspect, any prison or prisons or any penitentiary or other place of confinement for prisoners in Great Britain upon any occasion which such Secretary of State may think expedient.

5 & 6 WILL. IV. c. 76.

An Act to provide for the Regulation of Municipal Corporations in England and Wales.—[9th of September, 1835.]

113. 7 *Geo. IV. c.* 64 *s.* 25.—*Sums in respect of offences committed in boroughs having a court of quarter sessions shall be paid out of the borough fund.*—And whereas, by an Act made in the seventh year of His late Majesty George IV., intituled "An Act for improving the Administration of Criminal Justice in England and Wales," it was enacted, that all sums directed to be paid by virtue of that Act in respect of felonies and misdemeanors therein enumerated, committed in liberties, franchises, cities, towns, and places which do not contribute to the payment of any county rate, should be paid as therein is directed : Be it therefore enacted, that all sums directed to be paid by virtue of the last-recited Act in respect of felonies and such misdemeanors as aforesaid, committed or supposed to have been committed in any borough in which a separate court of quarter sessions of the peace shall be holden, shall be paid out of the borough fund of such borough, anything in the said Act contained notwithstanding ; and the order of court shall in every such case be directed

to the treasurer of such borough instead of the treasurer of the county.

114. *Treasurers of counties to keep an account of expenses of prosecution, &c., of offenders sent from such boroughs for trial at the assizes, and make order on the council for payment thereof.— In case of difference respecting such account, the same to be referred to arbitration, as provided in 5 Geo. IV. c. 85, &c.*—And be it enacted, that the treasurer of every county in England and Wales shall keep an account of all costs arising out of the prosecution, maintenance, and punishment, conveyance, and transport of all offenders committed for trial to the assizes in such county from any borough in which a separate court of quarter sessions of the peace shall be holden; and the treasurer of every such county shall, not more than twice in every year, send a copy of the said account to the council of each of the said boroughs, and shall make an order for payment of the same on the council of such borough; and the council of every such borough shall forthwith order the same, with all reasonable charges of making and sending such account, to be paid to the treasurer of such county out of the borough fund; and in case any difference shall arise concerning the said account, it shall be decided by the arbitration of a barrister to be named, as is provided in the case of differences with respect to the payment of moneys under contracts made by authority of an Act made in the fifth year of His late Majesty King George IV., intituled "An Act for amending an Act of the last Session of Parliament, relating to the Building, Repairing, and Enlarging of certain Gaols and Houses of Correction, and for procuring Information as to the State of all other Gaols and Houses of Correction in England and Wales:" provided that nothing herein contained shall be construed to alter or restrain the powers given by the last-mentioned Act of contracting with the justices of the peace having authority or jurisdiction in and over any gaol or house of correction of the county wherein or where such borough is situated, or whereto it is adjacent, for the conveyance, support, and maintenance in such last-mentioned gaol or house of correction of prisoners committed thereto from such borough, save only that all such powers shall, after the first day of May, one thousand eight hundred and thirty-six, be vested in the council of such borough in the name of the body corporate whose council they are, and none other; and for the purpose of making such contracts as aforesaid, the council of such borough, and none other, shall have power to make the orders required by the said last-mentioned Act to be made by the justices of the borough at the borough sessions.

7 WILL. IV. & 1 VICT. c. 78.

An Act to amend an Act for the Regulation of Municipal Corporations in England and Wales.—[17th of July, 1837.]

39. *Mayor, &c., not to be interested in any contract for building, &c., gaols, &c.*—And be it enacted, that it shall not be lawful for any mayor, alderman, councilman, or other officer of a corporation to be interested or concerned or employed, directly or indirectly, as an architect, builder, artist, mechanic, workman, merchant, trader, or otherwise howsoever in any part of the work to be done or materials to be supplied at any such gaol or house of correction, or in any contract (*k*) whatever relating thereto; and if any one holding such office shall be so interested, concerned, or employed in such work or contract as aforesaid, he shall thenceforward be disqualified from continuing to hold such office, and also from being thereafter elected or appointed to fill any corporate office within any such city or borough.

(*k*) The Act, 5 & 6 Vict. c. 104, explains (s. 1) the meaning of the word "contract" as used in this section, and in the Act 5 & 6 Will. IV., c. 76, s. 28, and declares that the word, in the said respective enactments, shall not extend or be construed to extend to any lease, sale, or purchase of any lands, tenements, or hereditaments, or to any agreement for any such lease, sale, or purchase, or for the loan of money, or to any security for the payment of money only.

40. *Borough gaol may be built beyond the limits of the borough.*—And be it enacted, that it shall be lawful for the mayor, aldermen, and burgesses of any borough, by their council, to contract for the purchase of, and to have and hold to them and their successors, any lands not exceeding in the whole five acres, either within or beyond the limits of the borough, and to build thereon a town hall, council house, police office, gaol, or house of correction for the borough; and any such gaol or house of correction, although built beyond the limits of the borough, may be declared by a resolution of the council, and upon such resolution shall be taken to be, the gaol or house of correction of the borough, and shall be within the same jurisdiction, and shall be governed and regulated in like manner as if within the limits of the borough.

41. *Gaols, &c., under county jurisdiction previous to 6 & 7 Will. IV. c. 103, excluded from the provisions of that Act.*—And whereas by the extension of the boundaries of certain boroughs, cities, and places, the county gaols, court houses, depôts for militia arms, and other public edifices and offices of counties

have been included within the boundaries of those cities or boroughs, and are thereby subject to the jurisdiction of such cities or boroughs, and of the sheriffs and other municipal authorities thereof; in remedy whereof be it enacted, that all county gaols, courts, depôts for arms, and all lands, buildings, easements, and appurtenances thereunto belonging, which before the passing of the Act passed in the last session of Parliament to make temporary provisions for the boundaries of certain boroughs, or the authorized extension of the boundaries of any borough since the passing of that Act, were in, of, or belonging to any county, shall be taken to be, and considered, and shall remain part and parcel of such county, and under the exclusive jurisdiction of the authorities of such county, as if the said last-mentioned Act had not passed.

42. *Certain borough debtors and prisoners in contempt may be removed to the county gaol.*—And be it enacted, that in every case in which by virtue of any contract made between the council of any borough and the justices of any county, riding, parts, or divisions of a county, liberty, or jurisdiction, according to the provisions of the said Act for regulating corporations, the gaol belonging to such county, riding, parts, or division of a county, liberty, or jurisdiction shall be used as the gaol of such borough, prisoners for debt or in contempt arrested in any such borough under any process from any court may be taken and removed from such borough and confined in that part of such gaol which is appropriated to debtors, and such removal shall not be taken to be an escape : provided always, that every such prisoner shall still be taken to be within the legal custody of the person or persons in whose custody he would have been if imprisoned within the borough gaol, and the sheriff of such county, riding, parts, or division of a county, liberty, or jurisdiction shall not be answerable for the safe custody of any such prisoner : provided also, that it shall be lawful for the person or persons in whose custody such prisoner would have been if imprisoned within the borough gaol to take such security from the gaoler or keeper of the gaol to which any such prisoner shall be so removed, for the safe custody of all such prisoners, as shall be agreed on between the council and justices aforesaid.

5 & 6 Vict. c. 98.

An Act to amend the Laws concerning Prisons.—
[10th August, 1842.]

3. *Borough councils under 5 & 6 W. IV. c. 76 may borrow money for building prisons, &c.*—And be it enacted, that in every borough in which there is or shall be a body corporate of mayor, aldermen, and burgesses, under the provisions of an Act passed in the sixth year of the reign of His late Majesty, intituled "An Act to provide for the Regulation of Municipal Corporations in England and Wales," or of any charter granted in pursuance of that or any subsequent Act, and in which there shall be a separate court of sessions of the peace, it shall be lawful for the mayor, aldermen, and burgesses, by their council, from time to time to take up and borrow any sum of money, not exceeding the amount of the estimate or estimates approved by the council, for building or rebuilding, repairing or enlarging the prison, court-house, and other necessary buildings to be used with the prison for such borough, according to any plan approved by one of Her Majesty's principal Secretaries of State, and for the purchase of land for the purposes of any such prison, court-house, and other necessary buildings as aforesaid, or for repaying any moneys which may have been borrowed for any of the said purposes before the passing of this Act: provided always, that the whole of the sum borrowed under this Act, and the interest accruing due from time to time, shall be repaid within thirty years from the time of borrowing the same.

5. *Borough councils may secure repayment of loans by bonds or mortgages, or make gaol rates, &c.*—And be it enacted, that for securing repayment of the money so advanced, it shall be lawful for the council to grant bonds under the common seal of the mayor, aldermen, and burgesses of the borough, or instead of issuing such bonds to mortgage, with the consent of three or more Commissioners of Her Majesty's Treasury, any part of the lands, tenements, and hereditaments of the said body corporate, the issues, rents, and profits of which, by any law now in force, are or may be applied towards erecting or maintaining a gaol or house of correction in their borough, and to repay the money borrowed, and the interest accruing due thereon, or so much thereof as the council shall think fit to charge thereupon, out of the borough fund or borough rate, but subject and without prejudice to any prior claim upon such borough fund, or instead or in aid thereof it shall be lawful for the council to make gaol rates, and to secure the repayment of any money so advanced, with the interest accruing due, or so much as shall be charged

thereupon, by mortgage of the borough rates or gaol rates, so that all the money borrowed, with the interest due thereon, shall be repaid within the said term of thirty years, or in case the money shall have been advanced by the Commissioners of Exchequer Bills, within twenty years; and every such mortgage may be by instrument in the form contained in the schedule annexed to this Act, or in any other suitable form.

6. *Gaol rate to be made and raised in the same manner as borough rate.*—And be it enacted, that every gaol rate made for the purpose of repaying any money advanced by any person or body corporate for any of the purposes aforesaid, shall be made, levied, and raised in like manner as the borough rate may be made, levied, and raised; and all powers and authorities now vested in the council, or in overseers of the poor, or persons appointed by the council to act as such overseers, relating to the making, levying, and collecting the borough rate, shall be in full force and effect in relation to the making, levying, and collecting any such gaol rate.

10. *Extending the period for repayment of loans in counties.*—And be it enacted, that when the justices of any county shall have borrowed any money for building, rebuilding, repairing, or enlarging any prison, they shall charge the rate to be raised upon such county, not only with the interest of the money so borrowed, but also with the payment of such further sum as will insure the payment of the whole sum borrowed within thirty years, or if the loan shall have been made by the Commissioners appointed for the execution of the Acts authorizing the issue of Exchequer Bills, within twenty years from the time of borrowing the same.

15. *Gaol and house of correction to be provided for every borough having separate courts of sessions of the peace, except where there is a contract for support of prisoners in another prison.*—And be it enacted, that in every such borough as aforesaid to which a separate court of sessions of the peace hath been or shall hereafter be granted, there shall be one common gaol and at least one house of correction, (*k*) excepting those boroughs in which the mayor, aldermen, and burgesses, by their council, shall have contracted with the justices of the peace having authority or jurisdiction in or over any gaol or house of correction of the county, riding, or division wherein such borough is situated, or whereunto it is adjacent, or with the mayor, aldermen, and burgesses of some other borough in which there is a gaol or house of correction, or with the committee of a district prison, for the support and maintenance in such last-mentioned gaol or house of correction, or district prison, respectively, of any prisoners committed thereunto from such borough; and during

the continuance of any such contract, but no longer, the first-mentioned mayor, aldermen, and burgesses shall not be bound to maintain any other gaol or house of correction for their borough; and it shall be lawful for the mayor, aldermen, and burgesses of any such borough, by their council, to enter into such contracts as aforesaid, although at the time of entering into such contract there may be no gaol or house of correction belonging to such borough; and all enactments with respect to such contracts shall apply as well to those contracts where at the time of entering into the same there was or is a gaol or house of correction belonging to the borough, as to those contracts where there was or is no gaol or house of correction belonging to the borough at the time of entering into the same.

(*k*) The obligation of any such borough to maintain a prison or house of correction, or to provide prison accommodation for its prisoners, will cease on the commencement of The Prison Act, 1877 (see s. 16 of that Act, *ante* p. 163).

18. *Expense of borough prisoners in county prisons to be paid by the borough.*—And be it enacted, that in every borough to which a separate court of sessions of the peace hath been or shall hereafter be granted or purported to be granted, and where the persons committed for offences arising within such borough have been or shall hereafter be sent to any prison of the county in which such borough is situated, and that no special contract shall be subsisting between such borough and county relative to the said prisoners, the council of such borough shall pay or cause to be paid to the treasurer of such prison, or other person appointed by the justices of the peace, in general or quarter sessions assembled, for the county in which such prison is situated, the actual expenses heretofore incurred, or hereafter to be incurred, in the conveyance, transport, maintenance, safe custody, and care of every such prisoner, (*l*) according to the time for which each such prisoner shall have been or shall remain in custody there, at the average daily cost of each prisoner, according to the whole number of prisoners confined in the said prison, such average to be taken yearly, half-yearly, quarterly, or at such other intervals as the visiting justices of the prison shall from time to time determine, including in such expenses all salaries of officers, all expenses of repairs, alterations, additions, and improvements in or to the said prison, all sums paid to prisoners under any Act of Parliament on their discharge or otherwise, and any other charge whatsoever on account of the prisoners confined in such prison; subject nevertheless to a proportional share of all deductions on account of the earnings of prisoners in the said prison, and of

all sums of money received in aid of the rates levied for the maintenance of the said prison.

(*l*) With regard to the manner in which these expenses are to be paid on and after the commencement of The Prison Act, 1877, see s. 4 of that Act, *ante* p. 150, and s. 57, *ante* p. 195.

19. *Expenses of prosecution of such prisoners, how to be defrayed,* —5 & 6 *W. IV.* c. 76, s. 113.—And be it enacted, that the expenses heretofore incurred or hereafter to be incurred in the prosecution of such prisoners as aforesaid at the general or quarter sessions of the peace of the county wherein such borough is situated shall be defrayed by the treasurer of such borough in such manner as is directed for the payment of the costs of prosecutions by an Act passed in the sixth year of the reign of His late Majesty, intituled "An Act to provide for the Regulation of Municipal Corporations in England and Wales," out of a rate to be made, levied, and recovered within the said borough in the same manner as the rate hereinafter mentioned.

20. *Expenses of conveyance and maintenance of such prisoners, how to be paid.*—5 *Geo. IV.* c. 85.—And be it enacted, that the expense heretofore incurred or hereafter to be incurred in the conveyance, transport, maintenance, safe custody, and care of such prisoners as aforesaid, shall be paid out of a rate to be made and levied for that purpose by the council of such borough in the nature of a borough rate; and any such rate may be made and recovered in the same manner as any borough rate may be made or recovered; and the amount of all such expenses of conveyance, transport, maintenance, safe custody, and care of prisoners as aforesaid shall, in case of dispute, be settled by such barrister-at-law as shall be determined upon in writing between the visiting justices of such prison and the council of such borough; and in case no appointment of such barrister be agreed upon by the said parties within the space of fourteen days next after such dispute shall have arisen, such dispute shall be decided by the arbitration of a barrister, to be named as provided in the case of differences with respect to the payment of moneys under contracts made by authority of an Act passed in the fifth year of the reign of King George IV., intituled "An Act for amending an Act of the last Session of Parliament, relating to the Building and Enlarging of certain Gaols and Houses of Correction, and for procuring Information as to the State of all other Gaols and Houses of Correction in England and Wales."

21. *An account of such expenses to be rendered to town clerks of boroughs.*—And be it enacted, that an account in writing of the expenses due and payable, or claimed to be due and payable, in

respect of the conveyance, transport, maintenance, safe custody, and care of such prisoners as aforesaid, shall be made out from time to time, and signed by the clerk to the visiting justices of the prison to which such prisoners shall be committed, and delivered to the town clerk of the borough within which the offences shall have been committed, and such account shall be conclusive against such borough, unless some objection thereto shall be made in writing, and signed by the town clerk of such borough, and delivered to the clerk of the said visiting justices within one calendar month next after such account shall have been delivered to such town clerk.

22. *Such boroughs to be freed from county rate in respect of such expenses.*—And be it enacted, that every such borough as aforesaid shall be freed from contributing to any rate in the nature of a county rate made for the county in which such borough is situated, in respect of the prosecution, conveyance and transport, maintenance, and safe custody, and care of such prisoners as aforesaid, so long as such expenses shall be defrayed under the provisions of this Act.

23. *Invalidity of grant of sessions of the peace not to alter liability until next county quarter sessions.*—And be it enacted, that in case any grant of a separate court of sessions of the peace, heretofore or hereafter to be made, or purported to be made, to any such borough as aforesaid, shall be quashed, vacated, or adjudged to be invalid, such borough shall, notwithstanding, continue to be freed from the payment of rates in the nature of county rates for such county, and liable to the payment of the costs of the prosecution, conveyance and transport, maintenance, safe custody, and care of such prisoners as aforesaid, in the manner herein-before provided, up to the time at which such grant shall have been quashed, vacated, or adjudged to be invalid, and thenceforth to the time of holding the general or quarter sessions of the peace at which the next rate in the nature of a county rate shall be made in respect of the prosecution, conveyance and transport, maintenance, safe custody, and care of prisoners for offences arising within the county within which such borough is situated, and no longer.

24. *Act not to affect the validity of charters, &c.*—And be it enacted, that nothing in this Act contained shall be deemed to affect any question which has arisen or may hereafter arise touching the validity of any charter of incorporation or grant of a separate court of sessions of the peace; but every rate to be made or levied as last herein-before provided, and every other proceeding under the authority of this Act, shall be valid, whether any such charter or grant is valid or invalid.

31. *Sheriffs, &c., to be liable in damages only for escapes of*

debtors, and not to receive poundage, &c.—7 W. IV. & 1 Vict. c. 55.
—And be it enacted, that if any debtor in execution shall escape out of legal custody after the passing of this Act, the sheriff, (*m*) bailiff, or other person having the custody of such debtor shall be liable only to an action upon the case for damages sustained by the person or persons at whose suit such debtor was taken or imprisoned, and shall not be liable to any action of debt in consequence of such escape; and that after the first day of March in the year one thousand eight hundred and forty-three, no poundage shall be payable to sheriffs, bailiffs, and others, for taking the body of any person in execution, but there shall be payable to the sheriff or other person having the return of writs, upon every such execution against the body, such fees only as shall be allowed to be taken by sheriffs or other officers concerned in the execution of process under the sanction and authority of the judges of the courts of common law at Westminster, pursuant to the statute passed in the first year of the reign of Her Majesty, intituled "An Act for better regulating the Fees payable to Sheriffs upon the Execution of Civil Process."

(*m*) The Prison Act, 1877, declares (s. 31, *ante* p. 174) that on and after the commencement of that Act (1st of April, 1878), the sheriff shall not be liable for the escape of any prisoner.

32. *Interpretation of Act.*—And be it enacted, that in this Act the word "county" shall be taken to mean also riding, parts, division, or hundred; and the word "prison" shall be taken to mean also gaol or house of correction.

33. *Act to extend to England only.*—And be it enacted, that this Act shall not extend to Scotland or Ireland.

SCHEDULE to which the foregoing Act refers.

Form of mortgage and charge upon the borough rates or gaol rates for securing money borrowed by the mayor, aldermen, and burgesses of any borough.

The mayor, aldermen, and burgesses of the borough [town or city] of   by their council, at a special meeting of the said council, holden on the   day of   in pursuance of the powers given by an Act passed in the sixth year of the reign of Her Majesty Queen Victoria, intituled [*insert the title of this Act*], do hereby mortgage and charge all the rates to be raised within the said borough [town or city] under the description of borough [*or* gaol] rates, with the payment of   which *G. H.* of   hath agreed to lend, and hath now actually paid towards defraying the expenses of building [*or* rebuilding, repairing, or enlarging, *as the case may be*], the gaol [*or* house of correction, court house. *or other necessary buildings, as the case may be*], for the said borough [town *or* city] : and do hereby, by the council aforesaid, confirm the same unto the said *G. H.*, his executors, administrators, and assigns, for securing payment of   and interest for the same, after the yearly rate of   by the hundred; and do order the treasurer for the said borough [town *or* city] to pay the interest of the said half-yearly as the same shall become due, until the principal shall be discharged, pursuant to the directions of the said Act.

Given under the common seal of the borough [town *or* city] this   day of   in the year   .

17 & 18 VICT. c. 115.

An Act to amend the Law relative to the Removal of Prisoners in Custody.—[11th August, 1854.]

WHEREAS by the several Acts of Parliament made and passed for regulating gaols and houses of correction in England, Wales, and Ireland, and for the better ordering of prisoners, provision is made for the custody and treatment of debtors as one of the classes of prisoners to be confined therein : and whereas in some counties prisoners for debt and for contempt of court are confined in separate prisons, not being gaols within the meaning of the said Acts for regulating gaols and houses of correction, and for better ordering of prisons, and doubts have arisen whether such prisoners for debt and contempt of court may be lawfully removed to and confined in such last-mentioned gaols, and it is expedient that such doubts should be removed, and that the power given by law for the removal of prisoners in custody should be enlarged and rendered more generally applicable : Be it therefore enacted by the Queen's most Excellent Majesty, by and with the advice and consent of the Lords Spiritual and Temporal, and Commons, in this present Parliament assembled, and by the authority of the same, as follows :

1. *If common gaol be adapted for reception of debtors as a class, they may be removed thereto.*—From and after the passing of this Act, when the common gaol for any county in England, Wales, or Ireland shall be adapted for debtors as a class of prisoners to be confined therein, it shall be lawful for the sheriff of such county, or any other person having custody of persons for debt within any county, to remove to such common gaol all prisoners in his custody for debt or contempt of court from any prison in which they may be confined, and such common gaol shall be deemed the legal place of custody for such debtors, and no such removal shall be deemed or taken to be an escape.

2. *No such removal to take place till after certificate by inspector of prisons.*—Provided always, that no such removal shall take place until one of Her Majesty's Inspectors of Prisons,

acting for the county in which such common gaol is situate, on the application of Her Majesty's justices of the peace for such county in quarter sessions assembled, shall have signed and transmitted to the clerk of the peace of the said county a certificate in the form or to the effect in the schedule to this Act annexed, nor until one of Her Majesty's principal Secretaries of State or the chief Secretary for Ireland shall, by warrant under his hand, direct and authorize such removal.

3. *After such removal debtors may be sent to such gaol.*— From and after such removal as aforesaid, it shall be lawful for the sheriff of the county to send to and confine in such common gaol all future prisoners for debt or for contempt of court, which common gaol shall be deemed the legal place for their confinement, any local Act or usage to the contrary notwithstanding.

4. *Where governor of common gaol appointed by other authority than sheriff, it shall be lawful for him to give security.*— And whereas in some counties in England and Wales the keeper or governor of the common gaol is by usage or under some legal authority appointed by the justices in quarter sessions assembled, and in Ireland by boards of superintendence, and not by the sheriff: Be it enacted, that in all cases in which the keeper of any common gaol (in which debtors are or under this Act may be confined) shall be appointed by any authority other than that of the sheriff, it shall and may be lawful for the keeper so appointed to give security by bond or otherwise to the sheriff for the time being for the safe keeping of all such debtors as may be placed in his custody, and such bond or other security may be made and given to such sheriff for the time being, and shall and may be prosecuted by such sheriff in case of default of such keeper.

5. *Sheriff not relieved from present obligations.*—Provided nevertheless, that, except as aforesaid, nothing herein contained shall tend to relieve the sheriff of any county from the duty of keeping the common gaol in the same manner as is now by law required from him.

6. *Present powers for disposing of unnecessary prisons not disturbed.*—All the powers and provisions of the several Acts of Parliament in force authorizing the disposal of unnecessary prisons shall and may be exercised and applied for the sale and disposition of any prison rendered unnecessary by this Act having been carried into effect in any county, in the same manner as if such last-mentioned prison were a gaol or prison within the words or meaning of the said several Acts of Parliament, or any of them.

7. *Allowances to keepers of gaols to be continued where superseded by this Act.*—Whereas by the Act 55 Geo. III. c. 50, s. 2, the

justices of the peace in quarter sessions are authorized to make allowances to certain gaolers by way of compensation for fees abolished by that Act : and whereas by the Act 7 & 8 Vict. c. 96, s. 70, it is enacted, that every keeper or other officer of any debtors' prison whose emoluments should be diminished by that Act might make claim for compensation, and the Commissioners of Her Majesty's Treasury were thereby authorized to award a gross or yearly sum in respect thereof : Be it enacted, that the justices of the peace assembled in quarter sessions may order and direct that the allowance (or such part thereof as they may think fit) hitherto made to the keeper of any gaol which may become unnecessary by virtue of the provisions of this Act may be continued for and during the life of such keeper, and the Commissioners of Her Majesty's Treasury may continue the allowance (or such part thereof as they may think fit) hitherto made to the keeper of any such gaol for and during the life of such keeper.

SCHEDULE.

Form of Certificate.

I hereby certify, that I have inspected the new common gaol [*or* the alterations and additions made to the common gaol] of the county of   and particularly that portion of the building which it is proposed to appropriate for the custody of debtors ; and I further certify that the same is in a fit and proper state for the reception of such prisoners as are or may be confined in prison for debt or contempt of court within the jurisdiction of the sheriff of the said county.

21 & 22 Vict. c. 92.

An Act to provide for the Conveyance of County Property to the Clerk of the Peace of the County.—[*2nd August,* 1858.]

WHEREAS by divers Acts of Parliament Her Majesty's justices of the peace for the several counties in England and Wales, in general or quarter sessions assembled, are authorized and empowered to purchase and hire lands, tenements, and hereditaments for certain public works and purposes within such counties, and they are also authorized and empowered to make and enter into contracts in relation to such public works and purposes, and for other purposes within their jurisdiction as justices of the peace ; but no provision is made for the manner in which such purchases, hirings, and contracts are to be carried into effect : for remedy whereof be it enacted by the Queen's most Excellent Majesty, by and with the advice and consent of the Lords Spiritual and Temporal, and Commons, in this present Parliament assembled, and by the authority of the same, as follows :

1. *Justices of the peace may order conveyances or grants of land, &c., to be made to the clerk of the peace, &c.*—In all cases where by any Act or Acts of Parliament justices of the peace of any county or division of a county now are or may be hereafter authorized to purchase or to take on hire, for any of the public uses or purposes of such county, any lands, tenements, and hereditaments, it shall be lawful for such justices of the peace, if they shall think fit, to order and direct that the conveyance or grant thereof shall and may be made and taken to and in the name of the clerk of the peace for the time being of such county, and his successors upon trust for such public uses and purposes ; and such conveyance or grant, when so made, shall be valid and effectual in the law, and shall vest such lands, tenements, and hereditaments in such clerk of the peace and his successors, upon trust for the purposes for which the same were purchased and granted and conveyed, and be by him and them held for the public uses and purposes aforesaid, or otherwise be by him and them sold, conveyed, and disposed of in such manner as the justices of the peace for the time being of such county or division of a county in general or quarter sessions assembled may from time to time order and direct.

2. *Contracts and agreements may be entered into in the name of the clerk of the peace, &c.*—Except where otherwise specially provided for by any Act or Acts of Parliament, all contracts and agreements to be made and entered into by the justices of the peace of any county or division of county for any of the public uses or purposes of such county shall and may, by the order of such justices, if they shall think fit, be made and entered into on their behalf by and in the name of the clerk of the peace for the time being of such county or division of county ; and all such contracts and agreements shall and may be enforced and sued upon by or against the clerk of the peace for the time being of such county or division of county ; and no action, suit, or proceeding shall abate or be discontinued by the death, resignation, or removal of such clerk of the peace, but the clerk of the peace for the time being shall always be deemed the plaintiff or defendant, as the case may be ; and all costs, charges, damages, and expenses which such clerk of the peace may incur or pay, or be liable to pay by reason of such action, suit, or proceeding, shall be reimbursed to him or paid, by order of the said justices of the peace, by the treasurer of the county or division of the county out of the county rates raised or to be raised within such county or division of county.

3. *Lands, &c., to be vested in the clerk of the peace, &c.*—Except where otherwise specially provided by any Act or Acts of Parliament, on the resolution of the general or general quarter sessions

to that effect, all lands, tenements, and hereditaments which shall have been heretofore purchased or hired by the justices of the peace of any county or division of a county under the authority of any Act or Acts of Parliament, for any of the public uses and purposes of such county or division of county, and granted or conveyed to any person or persons in trust for or on behalf of the said justices, and which now remain applicable to such uses and purposes, shall, from and immediately after the passing of this Act, notwithstanding such grant or conveyance, become and be absolutely vested in the clerk of the peace for such county or division of county and his successors upon the trusts and for the uses and purposes in the grant or conveyance thereof respectively declared; and the same lands, tenements, and hereditaments shall be at all times hereafter held, used, and managed, or, when so ordered by the said justices, sold, conveyed, and disposed of, by the clerk of the peace for the time being of such county or division of county, according to the orders and directions of the said justices of the peace from time to time in general or quarter sessions assembled; and every sale and conveyance so made and executed by the clerk of the peace for the time being shall be valid in the law, and effectually vest the lands and hereditaments thereby conveyed in the purchaser or purchasers thereof.

4. *Grants and conveyances to be valid, though not enrolled.*—All grants and conveyances of any lands, tenements, and hereditaments heretofore made or hereafter to be made, under any of the Acts herein-before referred to, to or in trust for the said justices, for any of the public uses and purposes of such counties or divisions of counties, shall be valid and effectual to all intents and purposes, notwithstanding the same grants and conveyances may not have been or be enrolled, any law, statute, or usage to the contrary notwithstanding.

25 & 26 Vict. c. 44.

An Act to Amend the Law relating to the giving of Aid to Discharged Prisoners.—[17th July, 1862.]

4 *Geo. IV.* c. 64 (1823).—Whereas by the thirty-ninth section of an Act passed in the session holden in the fourth year of King George IV., chapter sixty-four, (*n*) intituled " An Act for consolidating and amending the Laws relating to the Building, Repairing, and Regulating of certain Gaols and Houses of Correction in England and Wales," and hereinafter referred to as the Gaol Act, it is provided that it should be lawful for any one or more of the visiting justices of any prison to which

that Act extended, from whence any prisoner should be discharged, to direct that such moderate sum of money should be given and paid to any and every such prisoner so discharged, who should not have the means of returning to his or her family or place of settlement, or resorting to any place of employment or honest occupation, as in the judgment of such justice or justices should be requisite and necessary for such purpose, under all the circumstances attending the case of any such prisoner; and that such sum of money should be paid by the keeper of such prison, to or for the use of such prisoner for the purpose aforesaid, and that all such sums should be provided for, either out of such bequests or benefactions as therein mentioned, or in such manner as is by the Gaol Act directed with respect to the expense of the support and maintenance of the prisoners in the prisons to which such Act extends: and whereas divers societies, hereinafter referred to as Discharged Prisoners Aid Societies, have been formed in divers parts of England, by persons subscribing voluntarily, for the purpose of finding employment for discharged prisoners, and enabling them by loans and grants of money to live by honest labour: and whereas it is expedient that power should be given to the visiting justices of prisons to give aid under the said Act to discharged prisoners through the medium of a Discharged Prisoners Aid Society, in cases where such society has been previously certified by the justices having jurisdiction over such gaol or house of correction, at some court of general or quarter sessions, or at some quarterly sessions held by them, to be a society approved of by them: Be it enacted by the Queen's most Excellent Majesty, by and with the advice and consent of the Lords Spiritual and Temporal, and Commons, in this present Parliament assembled, and by the authority of the same, as follows:

1. *Power to justices to grant certificates of approval of Prisoners Aid Societies; and to revoke or suspend the same.*—The justices having jurisdiction over any gaol or house of correction to which the Gaol Act (*o*) extends may, at any court of general or quarter sessions, or at any quarterly sessions, upon the application of any one or more member or members of a Prisoners Aid Society, and after examining the rules of such society, and receiving such evidence as they think fit as to the condition of such society, issue a certificate under the hand of their chairman, to the effect that such society is approved of by them for the purposes of this Act; and they may, at any future court of general or quarter sessions, or at any future quarterly sessions, upon due cause shown, by a writing under the hand of their chairman, revoke or suspend such certificate; and any society in respect of

which such certificate as aforesaid has been granted and remains in force shall be deemed to be a certified Prisoners Aid Society, and to be entitled to such privileges as are hereinafter mentioned.

(n) The Act, 4 Geo. IV. c. 64, was repealed by The Prison Act, 1865. See s. 73 of that Act, *ante* p. 100, and Schedule III., *ante* p. 142. As to the giving of aid to discharged prisoners, see now, The Prison Act, 1865, ss. 42, 43, *ante* pp. 89, 90, and The Prison Act, 1877, s. 29, *ante* p. 173.

(o) The expression the "Gaol Act" is now to mean The Prison Act, 1865. See s. 77 of that Act, *ante* p. 107.

26 & 27 VICT. c. 79.

An Act for the Amendment of the Law relating to the Religious Instruction of Prisoners in County and Borough Prisons in England and Scotland.—[28th *July*, 1863.]

WHEREAS it is expedient to amend the law relating to prisons in England and Scotland with respect to the religious instruction of the prisoners confined therein: Be it enacted by the Queen's most Excellent Majesty, by and with the advice and consent of the Lords Spiritual and Temporal, and Commons, in this present Parliament assembled, and by the authority of the same, as follows:

1. *Short title.*—This Act may be cited for all purposes as "The Prison Ministers Act, 1863."

2. *Act to apply to all gaols, &c.*—This Act shall apply in England to all gaols, prisons, and houses of correction (hereinafter included under the term "prisons") that are maintained at the expense of any county, riding, division, or liberty of a county, or of any county of a city, county of a town or borough; and in Scotland to all local prisons as defined by "The Prisons (Scotland) Administration Act, 1860."

3. *Power to appoint additional ministers to prisons* (p).—Where the number of prisoners confined in any prison to which this Act applies, and belonging to some Church or religious persuasion differing, if in England, from the Church of England, and if in Scotland, from the Church of Scotland, is so great as, in the opinion of the justices, county board, or other persons having the appointment of chaplain in the said prison, to require the ministrations of a minister of their own Church or persuasion, the said justices, county board, or other persons may appoint a minister of such last-mentioned Church or persuasion to attend at the said prison on the prisoners of his own Church or persuasion, and they may, if they think fit, award to him a reasonable sum as a recompence for his services, such sum to be deemed a part of the expenses of the prison to which he is

appointed, and to be paid out of the funds legally applicable to the payment of such expenses.

Regulation as to admission of ministers.—The visiting justices of any prison may, if they think fit, without a special request being made by, but not against the will of, any prisoner of a Church or religious persuasion differing from that of the Established Church, permit a minister of the Church or persuasion to which such prisoner belongs (if no appointment of such minister has been made under this Act) to visit such prisoner at proper and reasonable times, under such restrictions imposed by them as may guard against the introduction of improper persons, and may prevent improper communications; provided that any prisoner shall, on request, be allowed, subject to the rules of the gaol, to attend the chapel or to be visited by the chaplain of the gaol. Every minister appointed or permitted to visit prisoners under this Act shall hold his appointment or permission to visit during the pleasure of the authority by whom he was appointed or permitted to visit, and shall conform in all respects to the regulations of the prison which he attends. No minister shall be appointed under this Act for any prison in which there is not a chaplain of the Established Church.

(*p*) So much of this section as is inconsistent with the provisions of The Prison Act, 1865, is repealed by that Act, so far as relates to prisons to which the Act applies. See s. 73, *ante* p. 106, and Schedule III., *ante* p. 144. As to the giving religious instruction to prisoners of a religious persuasion differing from that of the Established Church, see the 46th and 47th Prison Regulations, *ante* pp. 124, 125.

4. *Keepers of prisons to register religion of prisoners.*—The keeper or other person performing the duties of keeper of a prison on receiving into his custody any prisoner shall enter his name in a book to be provided for the purpose, with the addition of the Church or religious persuasion to which the prisoner shall declare himself to belong, and the said keeper or other person shall from time to time give to any minister appointed or permitted to visit prisoners in the prison a list of the prisoners so declared to belong to the Church or persuasion of such minister, and no such minister shall be permitted to attend or visit any prisoner belonging to any religious persuasion differing from that to which such minister belongs.

29 & 30 VICT. c. 100.

An Act for the Amendment of the Laws relating to Prisons.— [10*th August*, 1866.]

WHEREAS, in pursuance of the Act passed in the session holden in the third and fourth years of the reign of His late Majesty

King William IV., chapter seventy-one, intituled "An Act for the Appointment of convenient Places for the holding of Assizes in England and Wales," orders of Her Majesty in Council have been made changing the places at which assizes may be held, and with a view to such changes requiring the prisoners of certain prison authorities to be removed to prisons beyond the jurisdiction of such authorities: and whereas difficulties have arisen in relation to the maintenance of the prisoners so removed: be it enacted by the Queen's Most Excellent Majesty, by and with the advice and consent of the Lords Spiritual and Temporal, and Commons, in this present Parliament assembled, and by the authority of the same, as follows:

1. *As to maintenance of prisoners removed out of the jurisdiction of the authorities liable to maintain them.*—Where, in pursuance of any orders of Her Majesty in Council, prisoners committed for offences arising within the jurisdiction of one prison authority hereinafter referred to as "the sending authority" may hereafter be committed or sent to the prison of another prison authority hereinafter referred to as "the receiving authority," then, if and so long as no contract with respect to the maintenance of such prisoners exists, all expenses that may hereafter be incurred by the receiving authority in the conveyance, maintenance, or care of the prisoners of the sending authority, or otherwise by reason of such prisoners having been committed or sent to the prison of the receiving authority, ncluding a due proportion of the salaries of officers, and the expense of repairing, adding to, or altering the prison, shall be deemed to be a debt due from the sending authority to the receiving authority, and shall be payable out of the same rate or funds out of which the expenses of maintaining the prisoners of the sending authority are by law payable.

2. *Dispute as to amount to be determined by arbitration.*—Any dispute as to the amount of expenses payable by the sending authority to the receiving authority in pursuance of this Act shall be deemed to be a difference authorized by The Prisons Act, 1865, to be settled by arbitration, and the provisions of the said Act shall apply accordingly.

3. *Time of payment of expenses by Sending Authority to Receiving Authority.*—Payment by the sending authority to the receiving authority of any expenses incurred after the passing of this Act shall be made half-yearly, or at such other times as may be determined by the said authorities: and any moneys not paid at the time appointed for the payment thereof shall bear interest at the rate of four *per centum per annum* from such time until the time of the payment thereof.

4. *As to custody of prisoners in custody of Receiving Authority.*

The prison of the receiving authority shall, for all the purposes of and incidental to the commitment, trial, detention, and punishment of the prisoners of the sending authority, be deemed to have been and to be the prison of the sending authority, except that the sending authority shall have no right to interfere in the management of the prison of the receiving authority, and that the prisoners of the sending authority shall be in the legal custody of the gaoler of the prison of the receiving authority, and shall, as respects prison discipline, be in all respects subject to the jurisdiction of the receiving authority.

5. *Construction of Act.*—This Act may be cited for all purposes as The Prisons Act, 1866, and shall, so far as is consistent with the tenor thereof, be construed as one with The Prisons Act, 1865.

31 VICT. C. 21.

An Act to provide Compensation to Officers of certain discontinued Prisons.—[29th of May 1868.]

WHEREAS by The Prison Act, 1865, certain prisons mentioned in the second schedule to the said Act are directed to be discontinued : and whereas by the seventy-second section of the said Act the justices in sessions assembled are empowered to award compensation to any person deprived of any salary or emolument by the discontinuance of any of the said prisons : and whereas it is expedient to extend the power of awarding compensation to all cases in which prisons are discontinued : Be it enacted by the Queen's most Excellent Majesty, by and with the advice and consent of the Lords Spiritual and Temporal, and Commons, in this present Parliament assembled, and by the authority of the same, as follows :

1. *Short title.*—This Act may be cited for all purposes as The Prison Officers Compensation Act, 1868.

2. *Construction of Act.*—This Act shall be construed as one with The Prisons Act, 1865.

3. *Compensation to officers of all discontinued prisons.*—The justices in sessions assembled having jurisdiction over any such discontinued prison as is hereinafter mentioned may allow such compensation or superannuation allowance as they think fit to any person who, by reason of the discontinuance of such prison, is deprived of any salary or emolument, so that no such compensation or superannuation allowance exceed the proportion of the salary or emolument which might be granted under similar circumstances to a person in the civil service under the Acts for regulating such compensations or superannuation allowances for the time being in force ; and any compensation or superannua-

tion allowance so allowed shall be paid out of any rates or property applicable to the payment of the salaries of the officers of such prison before the discontinuance thereof, subject to this proviso, that when the power to levy such rates or such property is vested in a different body from the justices, the consent of such last-mentioned body shall be obtained to the amount of compensation or superannuation allowance allowed.

"Discontinued Prison" shall for the purposes of this section mean any prison other than the prisons specified in the second schedule to the said Prisons Act which has ceased to be used as a prison since the date of the passing of the said Prisons Act, 1865, or which may hereafter cease to be used as a prison.

4. *As to expression "justices in sessions assembled."*—The expression "justices in sessions assembled" shall in this Act mean as follows; that is to say,

1. As respects any prison belonging to any county, except as hereinafter mentioned, or to any riding, division, hundred, or liberty of a county, having a separate court of quarter sessions, the justices in quarter sessions assembled:
2. As respects any prison belonging to any county divided into ridings or divisions, and maintained at the common expense of such ridings or divisions, the justices of the county assembled at gaol sessions:
3. As respects any prison belonging to the city of London, or the liberties thereof, the court of the Lord Mayor and aldermen:
4. As respects any prison belonging to any municipal borough, the justices of the borough assembled at sessions to be held by them at the usual time of holding quarterly sessions of the peace, or at such other time as they may appoint:
5. As respects any prison belonging to any city, district, borough, or town having a separate prison jurisdiction, and not herein-before mentioned, the justices or other persons having power at law to make rules for the government of such prison.

31 Vict. c. 24.

An Act to provide for carrying out of Capital Punishment within Prisons.—[29th *of May,* 1868.]

WHEREAS it is expedient that capital punishments should be carried into effect within prisons: Be it enacted by the Queen's most Excellent Majesty, by and with the advice and consent of the Lords Spiritual and Temporal, and Commons, in this present

Parliament assembled, and by the authority of the same, as follows :

1. *Short title.*—This Act may be cited for all purposes as "The Capital Punishment Amendment Act, 1868."

2. *Judgment of death to be executed within walls of prison.*—Judgment of death to be executed on any prisoner sentenced after the passing of this Act on any indictment or inquisition for murder shall be carried into effect within the walls of the prison in which the offender is confined at the time of execution.

3. *Sheriff, &c., to be present.*—The sheriff charged with the execution, and the gaoler, chaplain, and surgeon of the prison, and such other officers of the prison as the sheriff requires, shall be present at the execution.

Any justice of the peace for the county, borough, or other jurisdiction to which the prison belongs, and such relatives of the prisoner or other persons as it seems to the sheriff or the visiting justices of the prison proper to admit within the prison for the purpose, may also be present at the execution.

4. *Surgeon to certify death; and declaration to be signed by sheriff, &c.*—As soon as may be after judgment of death has been executed on the offender, the surgeon of the prison shall examine the body of the offender, and shall ascertain the fact of death, and shall sign a certificate thereof, and deliver the same to the sheriff.

The sheriff and the gaoler and chaplain of the prison, and such justices and other persons present (if any) as the sheriff requires or allows, shall also sign a declaration to the effect that judgment of death has been executed on the offender.

5. *Coroner's inquest on body.*—The coroner of the jurisdiction to which the prison belongs wherein judgment of death is executed on any offender shall within twenty-four hours after the execution hold an inquest on the body of the offender, and the jury at the inquest shall inquire into and ascertain the identity of the body, and whether judgment of death was duly executed on the offender; and the inquisition shall be in duplicate, and one of the originals shall be delivered to the sheriff.

No officer of the prison or prisoner confined therein shall in any case be a juror on the inquest.

6. *Burial of body.*—The body of every offender executed shall be buried within the walls of the prison within which judgment of death is executed on him: provided that if one of Her Majesty's principal Secretaries of State is satisfied, on the representation of the visiting justices of a prison, that there is not convenient space within the walls thereof for the burial of offenders executed therein, he may, by writing under his hand,

appoint some other fit place for that purpose, and the same shall be used accordingly.

7. *Power to Secretary of State to make rules, &c., to be observed on execution of judgment of death.*—One of Her Majesty's principal Secretaries of State shall from time to time make such rules and regulations to be observed on the execution of judgment of death in every prison as he may from time to time deem expedient for the purpose, as well of guarding against any abuse in such execution, as also of giving greater solemnity to the same, and of making known without the prison walls the fact that such execution is taking place.(*q*)

(*q*) The following are the rules made by the Secretary of State, in pursuance of the provisions of this section, for regulating the execution of capital sentences :—
1. For the sake of uniformity it is recommended that executions should take place at the hour of 8 a.m. on the first Monday after the intervention of three Sundays from the day on which sentence is passed.
2. The mode of execution, and the ceremonial attending it, to be the same as heretofore in use.
3. A black flag to be hoisted at the moment of execution, upon a staff placed on an elevated and conspicuous part of the prison, and to remain displayed for one hour.
4. The bell of the prison, or if arrangements can be made for that purpose, the bell of the parish or other neighbouring church, to be tolled for fifteen minutes before and fifteen minutes after the execution.

8. *Such rules to be laid before Parliament.*—All such rules and regulations shall be laid upon the tables of both Houses of Parliament within six weeks after the making thereof, or if Parliament be not then sitting, within fourteen days after the next meeting thereof.

9. *Penalty for signing false certificate, &c.*—If any person knowingly and wilfully signs any false certificate or declaration required by this Act, he shall be guilty of a misdemeanor, and on conviction thereof shall be liable, at the discretion of the court, to imprisonment for any term not exceeding two years, with or without hard labour, and with or without solitary confinement.

10. *Certificate, &c., to be sent to Secretary of State, and exhibited on or near entrance to prison.*—Every certificate and declaration and the duplicate of the inquisition required by this Act shall in each case be sent with all convenient speed by the sheriff to one of Her Majesty's principal Secretaries of State, and printed copies of the same several instruments shall as soon as possible be exhibited and shall for twenty-four hours at least

be kept exhibited on or near the principal entrance of the prison within which judgment of death is executed.

11. *Provisions as to duties and powers of Sheriff, &c., extended.*—The duties and powers by this Act imposed on or vested in the sheriff may be performed by and shall be vested in his under-sheriff or other lawful deputy acting in his absence and with his authority, and any other officer charged in any case with the execution of judgment of death.

The duties and powers by this Act imposed on or vested in the gaoler of the prison may be performed by and shall be vested in the deputy gaoler (if any) acting in his absence and with his authority, and (if there is no officer of the prison called the gaoler) by the governor, keeper, or other chief officer of the prison and his deputy (if any) acting as aforesaid.

The duties and powers by this Act imposed on or vested in the surgeon may be performed by and shall be vested in the chief medical officer of the prison (if there is no officer of the prison called the surgeon).

The duties by this Act imposed on the chaplain may, in the event of the absence of the chaplain, be performed by the assistant-chaplain or other person acting in place of the chaplain.

12. *Forms in Schedule.*—The forms given in the schedule to this Act, with such variations or additions as circumstances require, shall be used for the respective purposes in that schedule indicated, and according to the directions therein contained.

⁎ Sections 13 and 14 are omitted here, as applying, respectively, to Scotland and Ireland only.

15. *Saving clause as to legality of execution.*—The omission to comply with any provision of this Act shall not make the execution of judgment of death illegal in any case where such execution would otherwise have been legal.

16. *General saving.*—Except in so far as is hereby otherwise provided, judgment of death shall be carried into effect in the same manner as if this Act had not passed.

THE SCHEDULE.

Certificate of Surgeon.

I, *A.B.*, the surgeon [*or as the case may be*] of the [*describe Prison*], hereby certify that I this day examined the body of *C.D.*, on whom judgment of death was this day executed in the [*describe same Prison*]; and that on that examination I found that the said *C.D.* was dead.

Dated this   Day of   .

(Signed)   *A.B.*

Declaration of Sheriff and others.

We, the undersigned, hereby declare that judgment of death was this day executed on *C.D.* in the [*describe Prison*] in our presence.

    Dated this   Day of
        (Signed)   *E.F.*, Sheriff of
                      L.M., Justice of the Peace for
                      G.H., Gaoler of
                      J.K., Chaplain of
                      &c.   *&c.*

32 & 33 VICT. c. 71.

An Act to consolidate and amend the Law of Bankruptcy.—
[9th of August, 1869.]

77. *Commitment to prison.*—Where any Court having jurisdiction in bankruptcy under this Act commits any person to prison, the commitment may be to such convenient prison as the Court thinks expedient; and if the gaoler of any prison refuses to receive any prisoner so committed, he shall be liable for every such refusal to a penalty not exceeding one hundred pounds.

34 & 35 VICT. c. 112.

An Act for the more effectual Prevention of Crime.—
[21st of August, 1871.]

WHEREAS it is expedient to make further provision for the effectual prevention of crime: Be it enacted by the Queen's most Excellent Majesty, by and with the advice and consent of the Lords Spiritual and Temporal, and Commons, in this present Parliament assembled, and by the authority of the same, as follows:

PRELIMINARY.

1. *Short title.*—This Act may be cited as "The Prevention of Crimes Act, 1871."

2. *Commencement of Act.*—This Act shall not come into operation until the second day of November one thousand eight hundred and seventy-one.

6. *Register and photographing of criminals.*—The following enactments shall be made with a view to facilitate the identification of criminals:

    1. Registers of all persons convicted of crime (*r*) in the United Kingdom shall be kept in such form and containing such particulars as may from time to time be prescribed, in Great Britain by one of Her Majesty's principal Secretaries of State, (*s*) and in Ireland by the Lord Lieutenant:

2. The register for England shall be kept in London under the management of the commissioner of police of the metropolis, or such other person as the Secretary of State may appoint:
3. The register for Scotland shall be kept in Edinburgh under the management of the secretary to the managers of the General Prison at Perth, or such other person as the Secretary of State may appoint:
4. The register for Ireland shall be kept in Dublin under the management of the commissioners of police for the police district of Dublin metropolis, or such other person as the Lord Lieutenant may from time to time appoint:
5. In every prison, the gaoler or other governor of the prison shall make returns of the persons convicted of crime and coming within his custody; and such returns shall be in such form or forms and contain such particulars in Great Britain as the Secretary of State, and in Ireland as the said Lord Lieutenant, may require; and every gaoler or other governor of a prison who refuses or neglects to transmit such returns, or wilfully transmits a return containing any false or imperfect statement, shall for every such offence forfeit a sum not exceeding twenty pounds, to be recovered summarily:
6. In Great Britain the Secretary of State, and in Ireland the said Lord Lieutenant, may make regulations(s) as to the photographing of all prisoners convicted of crime who may for the time being be confined in any prison in Great Britain or Ireland, and may in such regulations prescribe the time or times at which and the manner and dress in which such prisoners are to be taken, and the number of photographs of each prisoner to be printed, and the persons to whom such photographs are to be sent:
7. Any regulations made by the Secretary of State as to the photographing of prisoners in any prison in England shall be deemed to be regulations for the government of that prison, and binding on all persons, in the same manner as if they were contained in the first schedule annexed to The Prison Act, 1865:
8. Any regulations made by the Secretary of State as to the photographing of prisoners in any prison in Scotland shall be deemed to be rules for prisons in Scotland, and as such shall be binding on all whom they may concern, in the same manner as if the same were made under and in virtue of the powers contained in "The Prisons (Scotland) Administration Act, 1860:"

9. Any regulations made by the Lord Lieutenant as to the photographing of prisoners in any prison in Ireland shall be deemed to be byelaws duly made by the Lord Lieutenant, and shall be binding on all persons, in the same manner as if the same were made under the authority of the Act passed in the session holden in the nineteenth and twentieth years of the reign of Her present Majesty, chapter sixty-eight:

10. Any prisoner refusing to obey any regulations made in pursuance of this section shall be deemed guilty of an offence against prison discipline, in England within the meaning of the fifty-seventh regulation in the first schedule annexed to the said Prison Act, 1865, in Scotland within the meaning of the rules for prisons in Scotland, certified under the hand of one of Her Majesty's principal Secretaries of State, under and by virtue of "The Prisons (Scotland) Administration Act, 1860," and in Ireland within the meaning of the fifteenth regulation contained in section one hundred and nine of the Act passed in the seventh year of the reign of His late Majesty King George the Fourth, chapter seventy-four:

11. Any authority having power to make regulations in pursuance of this section may from time to time modify, repeal, or add to any regulations so made:

12. Any expenses incurred in pursuance of this section shall be defrayed as follows; (that is to say,)

    The expense of keeping the register in London, Edinburgh, and Dublin shall, to such amount as may be sanctioned by the Treasury, be paid out of moneys provided by Parliament:

    The expenses incurred in photographing the prisoners in any prison shall be deemed to be part of the expenses incurred in the maintenance of the prison, and shall be defrayed accordingly.

This section shall not apply to the prisons for convicts under the superintendence of the directors of convict prisons or to any military or naval prison.

(r) The provisions of this Act with regard to the registering and photographing of criminals have been amended by the Act 39 & 40 Vict. c. 23, see *post*, p. 233. The 20th section of the Act declares that the expression "crime" shall mean, in England, any felony, or the offence of uttering false or counterfeit coin, or of possessing counterfeit gold or silver coin, or the offence of obtaining goods or money by false pretences, or the offence of conspiracy to defraud, or any misdemeanor under the 58th section of the Act 24 & 25 Vict. c. 96, which declares that "whosoever shall be found by night armed with any dangerous or offensive weapon or instrument whatsoever, with intent to break or enter into any dwelling-house or other building whatsoever, and to commit any felony therein, or shall be found by night having in his possession without lawful excuse (the proof of which excuse shall lie on such person) any picklock, key, crow. jack, bit, or other implement of housebreaking, or shall be found by night having his face blackened or otherwise disguised with intent to commit any felony, or shall be found by night in any dwellinghouse or other building whatsoever with intent to commit any felony therein, shall be guilty of a misdemeanour;" and that the expression "offence" shall mean any act or omission which is not a crime as defined by the Act, and is punishable on indictment or summary conviction.

(s) The regulations made by the Secretary of State with regard to registering and photographing criminals will be found in Note (t), below.

39 & 40 Vict. c. 23.

An Act to amend the Prevention of Crimes Act, 1871.— [13th of July, 1876.]

WHEREAS by the Prevention of Crimes Act, 1871, all persons convicted of crime in the United Kingdom are required to be registered and photographed, and unnecessary expense is thereby incurred : Be it therefore enacted by the Queen's most Excellent Majesty, by and with the advice and consent of the Lords Spiritual and Temporal, and Commons, in this present Parliament assembled, and by the authority of the same, as follows :

1. *Short title of Act.*—This Act may be cited for all purposes as the Prevention of Crimes Amendment Act, 1876.

2. *Restriction on obligation to register and photograph criminals.*—In Great Britain the Secretary of State, and in Ireland the Lord Lieutenant, may from time to time by order(t) prescribe the class or classes of prisoners to which the enactments of The Prevention of Crimes Act, 1871, relating to registry and photographing are for the time being to apply ; and such enactments shall, so long as any such orders are in force, be deemed to apply to the prescribed class or classes of prisoners only, and not to all persons convicted of crime.

(t) The following regulations were made on the 15th of March, 1877, by the Secretary of State, in pursuance of the provisions of this Act and of The Prevention of Crimes Act, 1871 :—
1. The regulations, dated 28th October, 1871, as to periodical returns to be made by the governors of gaols to the registrar of criminals, and as to the photographing of persons convicted of crime, and also the Supplementary Regulations as regards the photographing of prisoners of the 15th of March, 1872, are cancelled from the 1st of April, 1877.
2. The governor of each prison is every Saturday to forward to the Registrar of Habitual Criminals, Home Office, Whitehall, a separate

return of every habitual criminal about to be liberated from the prison in the following week. By "habitual criminal" is meant a person who, within the meaning of the Prevention of Crimes Act (see ss. 7, 20), is "convicted on indictment of a crime, a previous conviction of a crime being proved against him." The return is to be made on form as annexed, or such form as may from time to time be issued by the Registrar of Habitual Criminals.

3. In addition, there are to be forwarded at the same time returns of any habitual criminals liberated during the current week, which for any reason have been omitted to be sent on the previous Saturday.

4. A photograph, made in accordance with the directions given in circular of 3rd of July, 1872, is to be sent with each form of return.

5. The name of the prisoner and the date are to be marked, reversed, on the negative, so as to appear in a conspicuous position on the background of the portrait.

6. When such prisoner is going, on discharge, to reside in Scotland or Ireland, an additional return on a like form, with photograph attached, is also to be sent to the Registry of Criminals in Edinburgh or Dublin respectively.

7. As directed in the circular dated 1st June, 1876, when any habitual criminal who has been sentenced to police supervision is about to be discharged, information to that effect, accompanied by a photograph, is to be forwarded to the police authorities of the district in which he is going to reside, seven days before he will be due for release. Forms for this purpose will be furnished by the Registrar of Habitual Criminals.

8. In order to secure accuracy and uniformity in the returns, instructions will from time to time be issued from the Habitual Criminals Registry, which are to be carefully followed.

The circular issued from the Home Office, concurrently with the issue of the foregoing regulations, to the Visiting Justices of the various prisons, explained that they were made in consequence of the experience gained since the first establishment of the Registry of Criminals having suggested various changes in the system on which it was carried on.

Up to that time all persons convicted of "crime" as defined by the statute applying to the subject (now The Prevention of Crimes Act, but formerly The Habitual Criminals Act, 1869,) had been registered and photographed, and a large number of names of criminals had thus been accumulated, respecting the majority of whom the information which the registry was intended to furnish was not likely to be required, and the usefulness of the registry, as a means of identification, had become much impeded by the difficulty and loss of time involved in searching among so large a mass of names and descriptions.

For the future, therefore, the register will include only the following:—

1. Every "habitual criminal," that is, every person who, within s. 7 of The Prevention of Crimes Act, is convicted on indictment of a crime, a previous conviction of a crime being proved against him:

2. Every person who, having been convicted of a "crime," is discharged from a sentence of penal servitude.

With a view, however, to making the work already done as useful as possible to local authorities, and avoiding the loss of time occasioned by referring to a central registry, the names and descriptions of all such persons returned previously to the making of the revised regulations have been extracted from the register, placed in alphabetical order, and printed and circulated to all police and prison authorities; and, as this list contains information as to the prisons in which the offenders have been confined, application can be made direct to such prisons in all cases where photographs or witnesses to identify may be required.

The 7th section of The Prevention of Crimes Act, 1871, above referred to, provides that, "where any person is convicted on indictment of a crime, and a previous conviction of a crime is proved against him, he shall, at any time within seven years immediately after the expiration of the sentence passed on him for the last of such crimes, be guilty of an offence against this Act, and be liable to imprisonment, with or without hard labour, for a term not exceeding one year, under the following circumstances or any of them:

First. If, on his being charged by a constable with getting his livelihood by dishonest means, and being brought before a court of summary jurisdiction, it appears to such court that there are reasonable grounds for believing that the person so charged is getting his livelihood by dishonest means: or,

Secondly. If, on being charged with any offence punishable on indictment or summary conviction, and on being required by a court of summary jurisdiction to give his name and address, he refuses to do so, or gives a false name or a false address: or,

Thirdly. If he is found in any place, whether public or private, under such circumstances as to satisfy the court before whom he is brought that he was about to commit or to aid in the commission of any offence punishable on indictment or summary conviction, or was waiting for an opportunity to commit or aid in the commission of any offence punishable on indictment or summary conviction: or,

Fourthly. If he is found in or upon any dwelling-house, or any building, yard, or premises, being parcel of or attached to such dwelling-house, or in or upon any shop, warehouse, counting-house, or other place of business, or in any garden, orchard, pleasure ground, or nursery ground, or in any building or erection in any garden, orchard, pleasure ground, or nursery ground, without being able to account to the satisfaction of the court before whom he is brought for his being found on such premises.

The provisions of the 20th section of The Prevention of Crimes Act, 1871, will be found in Note (r), *ante* p. 232. The directions with regard to the photographing of prisoners given in the circular of the 3rd of July, 1872, which is referred to in the 4th regulation, state that, as the whole success of the system of photographing criminals depends on the correctness of the likeness, and as an incorrect likeness may be even worse than useless, it is required that every photograph shall be inspected and passed by the Governor (or Lady Superintendent), or Deputy Governor, and initialed, as a certificate that it gives a correct idea of the man or woman it professes to represent. The directions also state that care must be taken that the photographs shall be properly "fixed;" that only likenesses which are passed as above mentioned should be paid for; that prisoners about to be discharged should be photographed in liberty clothing; that the photograph should be an album portrait $3\frac{1}{4}$ in. long and $2\frac{1}{2}$ in. wide, showing the hands, and the figure nearly to the knees; and that the measurement of the head must be 1 in. long. The directions likewise contain elaborate and minute instructions for performing the operation of photographing prisoners.

40 VICT. c. 7.

An Act for punishing Mutiny and Desertion, and for the better payment of the Army and their Quarters.—[24th of April, 1877.]

*** The Mutiny Act continues in force in England and Wales for one year only, and is passed annually by Parliament; but, inasmuch as the principal provisions are always re-enacted, it has been considered desirable to insert here those provisions which relate to prisons.

30. *As to the custody of military offenders under sentence of court-martial and in other cases.*—Every governor, provost marshal, gaoler, or keeper of any public prison or of any gaol or house of correction in any part of Her Majesty's dominions shall receive into his custody any military offender, whether of the regular, reserve, or auxiliary forces, under sentence of imprisonment (*u*) by a court-martial, upon delivery to him of an order in writing in that behalf from the general commanding in chief, or the adjutant general, or the officer who confirmed the proceedings of the court, or the officer commanding the regiment or corps to which the offender belongs or is attached, which order shall specify the offence of which he shall have been convicted, and the sentence of the court, and the period of imprisonment which he is to undergo, and the day and hour of the day on which he is to be released; and such governor, provost marshal, gaoler, or keeper shall keep such offender in a proper place of confinement, with or without hard labour, and with or without solitary confinement, according to the sentence of the court and during the time specified in the said order, or until he be discharged or delivered over to other custody before the expiration of that time under an order duly made for that purpose; and every governor, provost marshal, gaoler, or keeper of any public prison, gaol, house of correction, lock-up house, or other place of confinement, shall receive into his custody any soldier, whether of the regular, reserve, or auxiliary forces, for a period not exceeding seven days, upon delivery to him of an order in writing on that behalf from the officer commanding the regiment, corps, or body of troops to which such soldier shall belong.

(*u*) In all cases where the punishment of death shall have been awarded by a general court-martial or detachment general court-martial, Her Majesty may (s. 16) commute the sentence, and order the offender to be kept in penal servitude for any term not less than five years, or to suffer such term of imprisonment, with or without hard labour, and with or without solitary confinement, as shall seem meet to Her Majesty: provided that the imprisonment shall not exceed two years, and that the solitary confinement shall not exceed seven days at a time, with intervals of not less than seven days between the periods of solitary confinement; and that if the imprisonment exceeds eighty-four days, the solitary confinement shall not exceed seven days in any twenty-eight days of the imprisonment.

In any case where a sentence of penal servitude shall have been awarded by a general or detachment general court-martial, Her Majesty may (s. 20) commute the sentence, and order that the offender be imprisoned, with or without hard labour, and with or without solitary confinement, for such term not exceeding two years as shall seem meet to Her Majesty: provided that the solitary confinement shall not exceed seven days at a time, with intervals of not less than seven days between the periods of solitary confinement; and that if the imprisonment exceeds eighty-four days, the solitary confinement shall not exceed seven days in any twenty-eight days of the imprisonment.

No court-martial is (s. 22) for any offence whatever committed under the Act during the time of peace within the Queen's dominions to have power to sentence any soldier to corporal punishment; but, it is provided that any court-martial may sentence any soldier to corporal punishment while on active service in the field, or on board any ship not in commission, for mutiny, insubordination, desertion, drunkenness on duty or on the line of march, disgraceful conduct, or any breach of the Articles of War. No sentence of corporal punishment is, however, to exceed fifty lashes.

Any general, district, or garrison court-martial may (s. 23), in addition to any sentence of corporal punishment, award imprisonment, with or without hard labour, and with or without solitary confinement, but such confinement must not exceed the periods prescribed by the Articles of War.

In all cases in which corporal punishment forms the whole or part of the sentence awarded by any court martial, Her Majesty, or the general or other officer authorized to confirm the sentences of courts-martial, may commute such corporal punishment to imprisonment for any period not exceeding forty-two days, with or without hard labour, and with or without solitary confinement, or may mitigate such sentence, or instead of such sentence may award imprisonment for any period not exceeding twenty days, with or without hard labour, and with or without solitary confinement and corporal punishment, to be inflicted in the prison, not exceeding twenty-five lashes; solitary confinement is not in any but such case to exceed seven days at a time, with intervals of not less than seven days between each period of such confinement.

31. *As to the removal or discharge of prisoners in certain cases.*—In the case of a prisoner undergoing imprisonment under the sentence of a court-martial in any public prison other than the military prisons set apart by the authority of this Act, or in any gaol or house of correction in any part of the United Kingdom, it shall be lawful for the general commanding in chief, or the adjutant general, or the officer who confirmed the proceedings of the court, or the officer commanding the district or garrison in which such prisoner may be, to give, as often as occasion may arise, an order in writing directing that the prisoner be discharged, or be delivered over to military custody, whether

for the purpose of being removed to some other prison or place in the United Kingdom, there to undergo the remainder or any part of his sentence, or for the purpose of being brought before a court-martial either as a witness or for trial ; and in the case of a prisoner undergoing imprisonment or penal servitude under the sentence of a court-martial in any public prison other than such military prison as aforesaid, or in any gaol or house of correction in any part of Her Majesty's dominions other than the United Kingdom, it shall be lawful for the general commanding in chief or the adjutant general of Her Majesty's forces in the case of any such prisoner, and for the Commander-in-Chief in India in the case of any prisoner so confined in any part of Her Majesty's Indian dominions, and for the general commanding in chief in any presidency in India in the case of a prisoner so therein confined, and for the officer commanding in chief or the officer who confirmed the proceedings of the court at any foreign station in the case of a prisoner so there confined, to give, as often as occasion may arise, an order in writing directing that the prisoner be discharged or be delivered over to military custody, whether for the purpose of being removed to some other prison or place in any part of Her Majesty's dominions, there to undergo the remainder or any part of his sentence, or for the purpose of being brought before a court-martial either as a witness or for trial ; and in the case of any prisoner who shall be removed by any such order from any such prison, gaol, or house of correction either within the United Kingdom or elsewhere to some other prison or place either in the United Kingdom or elsewhere, the officer who gave such order shall also give an order in writing directing the governor, provost marshal, gaoler, or keeper of such other prison or place to receive such prisoner into his custody, and specifying the offence of which such prisoner shall have been convicted, and the sentence of the court, and the period of imprisonment which he is to undergo, and the day and the hour on which he is to be released ; and such governor, provost marshal, gaoler, or keeper shall keep such offender in a proper place of confinement, with or without hard labour, and with or without solitary confinement, according to the sentence of the court, and during the time specified in the said order, or until he be duly discharged or delivered over to other custody before the expiration of that time under an order duly made for that purpose ; and in the case of a prisoner undergoing imprisonment or penal servitude under the sentence of a court-martial in any military prison in any part of Her Majesty's dominions, the Secretary of State for the War Department, or the general officer commanding the district or station in which the prison may be situated, shall have the like powers in regard to the discharge and delivery over of such prisoners to military custody as may be lawfully exercised by any of the military authorities above mentioned in respect of any prisoners undergoing confinement as aforesaid in any public prison other than a military prison, or in any gaol or house of correction in any part of Her Majesty's dominions; and such prisoner in any of the cases herein-before mentioned shall accordingly, on the production of any such order as is herein-before mentioned, be discharged or delivered over, as the case may be: Provided always, that the time during which any prisoner under sentence of imprisonment by a court-martial shall be detained in such military custody under such order as aforesaid shall be reckoned as imprisonment under the sentence, for whatever purpose such detention shall take place; and such prisoner may during such time, either when on board ship or otherwise, be subjected to such restraint as is necessary for his detention and removal.

32. *Provision for subsistence.*—The gaoler or keeper of any public prison, gaol, house of correction, lock-up house, or other place of confinement in any part of Her Majesty's dominions shall diet and supply every soldier imprisoned therein under the sentence of a court-martial or as a deserter with fuel and other necessaries according to the regulations of such place of confinement, and shall receive on account of every soldier, out of the subsistence of such soldier during the period of his imprisonment, in Great Britain and Ireland, one shilling per diem, and in other parts of Her Majesty's dominions such sum as the Secretary of State may order: In all cases where such soldier is sentenced to be discharged or is ordered by the military authorities to be discharged from the army on the completion of his term of imprisonment, the Secretary of State for the War Department may cause to be issued out of army votes, upon application in writing, signed by any justice within whose jurisdiction such place of confinement shall be locally situated, together with a copy of the order of commitment, a further sum not exceeding sixpence per diem, and all of which said sums shall be carried to the credit of the fund from which the expense of such place of confinement is defrayed. A sentence of imprisonment or of penal servitude passed either by a court-martial or by any court of criminal jurisdiction upon any person subject to this Act, shall be in no respect affected by such person ceasing to be subject to this Act by discharge or otherwise at any time: provided, that for each person so ceasing to be subject to this Act, the Secretary of State for the War Department may cause to be issued out of army votes, upon application in writing, signed by any justice as aforesaid, together with a copy

of the order of commitment, a sum not exceeding one shilling and sixpence per diem, which said sum shall be carried to the credit of the fund from which the expense of such place of confinement is defrayed.

*　　*　　*　　*　　*

33. *Expiration of imprisonment of soldiers in common gaols.*—Every gaoler or keeper of any public prison, gaol, house of correction, or other place of confinement, to whom any notice shall have been given, or who shall have reason to know or believe, that any person in his custody for any offence, civil or military, is a soldier liable to serve Her Majesty on the expiration of his imprisonment, shall forthwith, or as soon as may be, give, if in Great Britain, to the Secretary of State for the War Department, and if in Ireland to the general commanding Her Majesty's forces in Ireland, or if in India to the adjutant general of the army, or to the nearest military authority with whom it may be convenient to communicate, notice of the day and hour on which the imprisonment of such person will expire; and every such gaoler or keeper is hereby required to use his best endeavours to ascertain and report in all cases where practicable the particular regiment or corps, battalion of a regiment or battery of artillery, to which such soldier belongs, and also whether he belongs to the depot or the head-quarters of his regiment; and in the event of his being a recruit who has not joined, that it may be so stated in his report, together with the name of the place where the man enlisted. In all cases where the soldier in custody is under sentence to be discharged from the service on the completion of his term of imprisonment, and the discharge document is in the hands of the gaoler, such gaoler shall not be required to make any report thereof to the Secretary of State for War, or to the military authorities hereinbefore referred to.

34. *Apprehension of deserters. Transfer of deserters.*—Upon reasonable suspicion that a person is a deserter, it shall be lawful for any constable or other person to apprehend him, and forthwith bring him before a justice acting for any county, district, city, borough, or place wherein or near to which the place in which he was apprehended is situate; and the justice shall deal with the suspected deserter as if he were brought before him by warrant in accordance with the provisions of an Act passed in the eleventh and twelfth years of Her present Majesty, chapter forty-two, section twenty-one; and upon its appearing to the justice by the testimony of one or more witnesses taken upon oath, or by the confession of such suspected deserter, that the accused is a deserter, he shall cause him to be conveyed to the head-quarters

of the regiment or depôt to which he may appear to belong, or to the nearest or most convenient military or police station, or other place legally provided for the confinement of persons in custody, or delivered up to a party of soldiers in charge of a non-commissioned officer, as to the justice may seem most expedient, having regard to the safe custody of such suspected deserter; and the justice shall make a report to the Secretary of State of the persons through whom or by whose means the deserter was apprehended or secured; and for such information, commitment, and report the gaoler or other person into whose custody the accused is committed shall pay at the time of commitment to the clerk to the justice the sum of two shillings; and the Secretary of State, upon receipt of a report of the same, together with a copy of the commitment, shall cause such sum to be repaid to such gaoler or other person so entitled; and upon the report of a justice, as aforesaid, the Secretary of State shall cause to be paid to the person or persons by whom or through whose means it shall appear to his satisfaction that the deserter was apprehended and secured, a sum not exceeding forty shillings; and the justice shall in every case transmit, if in the United Kingdom, to the Secretary of State, and if elsewhere, to the general or other officer commanding, a descriptive return in the form prescribed in the schedule to this Act annexed; and a return purporting to be so made shall be evidence of the facts and matters therein stated: provided always, that any such person so committed as a deserter in any part of Her Majesty's dominions shall, subject to the provisions hereinafter contained, be liable to be transferred by order of the general or other officer commanding to serve in any regiment or corps or depôt nearest to the place where he shall have been apprehended, or to any other regiment or corps to which it may be desirable that he should be transferred, and shall also be liable after such transfer of service to be tried and punished as a deserter.

35. *As to the temporary custody of deserters in gaols.*—Every gaoler or keeper of any public prison, gaol, house of correction, lock-up house, or other place of confinement in any part of Her Majesty's dominions is hereby required to receive and confine therein every deserter who shall be delivered into his custody by any soldier or other person conveying such deserter under lawful authority, on production of the warrant of the justice of the peace on which such deserter shall have been taken, or some order from the office of the Secretary of State for the War Department, which order shall continue in force until the deserter shall have arrived at his destination; and such gaoler or keeper shall be entitled to one shilling for the safe custody of the said deserter while halted on the march, and to such sub-

sistence for his maintenance as shall be directed by Her Majesty's regulations.

36. *Penalty on keepers of prisons for refusing to confine, &c., military offenders.*—Any governor, provost marshal, gaoler, or keeper of any public prison, gaol, house of correction, lock-up house, or other place of confinement, who shall refuse to receive and to confine, or to discharge or deliver over, any military offender in the manner herein-before prescribed, shall forfeit for every such offence the sum of one hundred pounds.(*v*)

(*v*) All penalties and forfeitures imposed by the Act, exceeding twenty pounds. must, in accordance with the provisions of the Act (s. 90) be recovered by action in the High Court of Justice, and the defendant may, in addition to the penalty or forfeiture. be adjudged to pay the cost of the proceedings. One moiety of every penalty in the Act (s. 91) is to go to the person who informs or sues for the same, and the remainder of the penalty, or. where the offence is proved by the person who informs, the whole of the penalty. is to be paid to the paymaster of the London recruiting district, St. George's Barracks, London, to be at the disposal of the Secretary of State for the War Department, anything in The Municipal Corporation Act, 5 & 6 W. IV. c. 76, or in any other Act or Acts, to the contrary notwithstanding ; and the division of the High Court adjudging the penalty is required to report the same immediately to the Secretary of State.

40 VICT. C. 8.

An Act for the Regulation of Her Majesty's Royal Marine Forces while on shore.—[24th *of April,* 1877.]

₊ The Marine Mutiny Act continues in force in England and Wales for one year only. and is passed annually by Parliament ; but, inasmuch as the principal provisions are always re-enacted, it has been considered desirable to insert here those provisions which relate to prisoners.

42. *Custody of prisoners under military sentence in common gaols.*—Every governor, provost marshal, gaoler, or keeper of any public prison, or of any gaol or house of correction, in any part of Her Majesty's dominions, shall receive (*w*) into his custody any military offender under sentence of imprisonment (*x*) by a general or other court-martial, upon delivery to him of an order in writing in that behalf from the Lord High Admiral, or the Commissioners for executing the office of Lord High Admiral, or from the officer commanding the division or detachment to which the offender belongs or did last belong or is attached, which order shall specify the period of imprisonment or remainder of imprisonment which the offender is to undergo, and the day and hour of the day on which he is to be released or be otherwise disposed of ; and such governor, provost marshal, gaoler, or keeper shall keep such offender in a proper place of

confinement, with or without hard labour, and with or without solitary confinement, according to the sentence of the court, and during the time specified in the said order, or until he be discharged or delivered over to other custody before the expiration of that time, under an order duly made for that purpose; (*y*) and every governor, provost marshal, gaoler, or keeper of any public prison, gaol, house of correction, lock-up house, or other place of confinement, shall receive into his custody any marine for a period not exceeding seven days, upon delivery to him of an order in writing in that behalf from the officer commanding such marine.

(*w*) This Act, it may be observed, does not contain any provision similar to that made (s. 84) by the annual Mutiny Act, for the infliction of a penalty on the governor, etc., of a prison who may refuse to receive, to discharge, or to deliver over, any offender in accordance with its requirements.

(*x*) In all cases where the punishment of death shall have been awarded by a general court-martial or by a detachment general court-martial, Her Majesty may (s. 21) commute the sentence, and order the offender to be kept to penal servitude for any term not less than five years, or to suffer such term of imprisonment, with or without hard labour, and with or without solitary confinement, as shall seem meet to Her Majesty : provided that the imprisonment shall not exceed two years, and that the solitary confinement shall not exceed seven days at a time, with intervals of not less than seven days between the periods of solitary confinement ; and that if the imprisonment exceeds eighty-four days, the solitary confinement shall not exceed seven days in any twenty-eight days of the imprisonment.

In any case where a sentence of penal servitude shall have been awarded by a general or detachment general court-martial, Her Majesty may (s. 25) commute the sentence, and order that the offender be imprisoned, with or without hard labour, and with or without solitary confinement, for such term not exceeding two years as shall seem meet to Her Majesty : provided that the solitary confinement shall not exceed seven days at a time, with intervals of not less than seven days between the periods of solitary confinement ; and that if the imprisonment exceeds eighty-four days, the solitary confinement shall not exceed seven days in any twenty-eight days of the imprisonment.

When any sentence of death is commuted for penal servitude, or when any marine is adjudged by court-martial to penal servitude as authorized by the Act, the commanding officer of the division to which such marine shall have belonged or may belong may (s. 27) cause him to be detained and conveyed to any gaol or prison, there to remain in safe custody until he shall be removed therefrom by due authority under an order for his penal servitude to be made by some judge of the High Court of Justice provided by the Act : and a certificate of his sentence, after the same shall have been approved by the Lord High Admiral, or the Commissioners for executing the office of Lord High Admiral, (such certificate to be signed by the commanding officer of the division from which he shall be sent,) is to be a sufficient order, requisition, and authority to the governor, keeper, or superintendent of the gaol or prison to receive and detain him : provided always, that in case of any such offender being so conveyed to gaol or prison the usual allowance of sixpence per diem, or such other sum as the said Lord High Admiral or the said Commissioners may at any time or times direct, shall be made to the keeper of the gaol or prison for the subsistence of such offender during his detention therein, which allowance is to be paid by the paymaster of the division, upon production to him, by the said governor, keeper, or superintendent, of a declaration, to be made by him before one of Her Majesty's justices of the peace of such county, of the number of days during which the offender shall have been so detained and subsisted in such gaol or prison.

No court-martial is, for any offence whatever committed in time of peace within the Queen's dominions, to have power to sentence any marine to corporal punishment : provided that any court-martial may sentence any marine to corporal punishment while on active service in the field, or on board any ship not in commission, for mutiny, insubordination, desertion, drunkenness on duty or on the line of march. No sentence of corporal punishment is, however, to exceed fifty lashes.

Any general, district, or garrison court-martial may (s. 29) award imprisonment, with or without hard labour, and with or without solitary confinement, such confinement not exceeding the periods prescribed in the provisions of the Act noticed below or by the Articles of War; and in case of a marine, in addition, to corporal punishment.

In all cases in which corporal punishment shall form the whole or part of the sentence awarded by any court-martial, the Lord High Admiral of the United Kingdom of Great Britain and Ireland, or the Commissioners for executing the office of Lord High Admiral of the United Kingdom of Great Britain and Ireland, or the officer authorized to confirm the sentences of courts-martial, may (s. 30) commute such corporal punishment to imprisonment for any period not exceeding forty-two days, with or without hard labour, and with or without solitary confinement, or may mitigate such sentence, or instead of such sentence may award imprisonment for any period not exceeding twenty days, with or without hard labour, and with or without solitary confinement, and corporal punishment, to be inflicted in the prison, not exceeding twenty-five lashes, and the solitary confinement before mentioned is not in any case to exceed seven days at a time, with intervals of not less than seven days between each period of such confinement : provided always, that the lashes shall not be administered by any instrument save one of a pattern approved by the Admiralty.

A general or district or garrison court-martial may (s. 37) sentence any marine to imprisonment, with or without hard labour, and may also direct that such offender shall be kept in solitary confinement for any portion or portions of such imprisonment, in no case exceeding fourteen days at a time, nor eighty-four days in any one year, with intervals between the periods of solitary confinement of not less duration than such periods ; and when the imprisonment awarded shall exceed three months, the court-martial is required to imperatively order that the solitary confinement shall not exceed seven days in any one month of the whole imprisonment awarded, with intervals between the periods of solitary confinement of not less duration than such periods.

Any divisional or detatchment court-martial may (s. 38) sentence any marine to imprisonment, with or without hard labour, for any period not exceeding forty-two days, and may also direct that such marine be kept in solitary confinement for any portion or portions of such imprisonment, not exceeding fourteen days at a time, with intervals between them of not less duration than such periods of solitary confinement : provided always, that when any court-martial, whether general, garrison, or district, or divisional, or detachment, shall direct that the imprisonment shall be solitary confinement only, or when any sentence of corporal punishment shall have been commuted to imprisonment only, the period of such solitary confinement shall in no case exceed fourteen days.

Except as the Act specially provides, every term of penal servitude or imprisonment under the sentence of a court-martial, whether original or revised, shall be reckoned as commencing on the day on which the original sentence and proceedings shall be signed by the president; and the place of imprisonment under the sentences of courts-martial shall be appointed by the court or the Lord High Admiral, or the Commissioners for executing the office of Lord High Admiral, or the commanding officer of the division to which the offender belongs or is attached, or the officer commanding the district, garrison, island, or colony.

(*y*) The Act provides (s. 41) that "in the case of a prisoner undergoing imprisonment under sentence of a court-martial, or as part of commuted punishment, in any public prison other than a military prison, or in any gaol or house of correction or elsewhere, in any part of the United Kingdom, it shall be lawful for the said Lord High Admiral, or the Commissioners for executing the office of Lord High Admiral, for the time being, in all cases, or for the officer who confirmed the proceedings of the court, or the officer commanding the division or the district or garrison in which such prisoner may be, to give, as often as occasion may arise, an order in writing directing that the prisoner be discharged, or be delivered over to military custody, whether for the purpose of being removed to some other prison or place in the United Kingdom, there to undergo the remainder or any part of his sentence, or for the purpose of being brought before a court-martial either as a witness or for trial; and in the case of a prisoner undergoing imprisonment under the sentence of a court-martial in any public prison other than a military prison, or in any gaol or house of correction, in any part of Her Majesty's dominions other than the United Kingdom, it shall be lawful for the said Lord High Admiral or the said Commissioners, or for the officer commanding the Royal Marines there serving, in the case of any such prisoner, to give as often as occasion may arise an order in writing directing that the prisoner be discharged, or be delivered over to military or other custody, whether for the purpose of being removed to some other prison or place in any part of Her Majesty's dominions, there to undergo the remainder or any part of his sentence, or for the purpose of being brought before a court-martial either as a witness or for trial; and in the case of any prisoner who shall be removed by any such order from any such prison, gaol, or house of correction, either within the United Kingdom or elsewhere, to some other prison or place, either in the United Kingdom or elsewhere, the officer or authorities who gave such order shall also give an order in writing directing the governor, provost marshal, gaoler, or keeper of such other prison or place to receive such prisoner into his custody, and specifying the offence of which such prisoner shall have been convicted, and the sentence of the court, and the period of imprisonment which he is to undergo, and the day and the hour on which he is to be released; and such governor, provost marshal, gaoler, or keeper shall keep such offender in a proper place of confinement, with or without hard labour, and with or without solitary confinement, according to the sentence of the court, and during the time specified in the said order, or until he be duly discharged or delivered over to other custody before the expiration of that time, under an order duly made for that purpose; and in the case of a prisoner undergoing imprisonment under the sentence of a court-martial in any military prison in any part of Her Majesty's dominions, the Secretary of State for War, or the general officer commanding the district or station in which the prison may be situated, shall have the like powers in regard to the discharge and delivery over of such prisoners to military or other custody as may be lawfully exercised by any of the authorities above mentioned in respect of any prisoners undergoing confinement as aforesaid in any public prison other than a military prison, or in any gaol or house of correction in any part of Her Majesty's dominions ; and such prisoner in any of the cases herein-before mentioned shall accordingly, on the production of any such order as is herein-before mentioned, be discharged or delivered over, as the case may be : provided always, that the time during which any prisoner under sentence of imprisonment by a court-martial shall be detained in such military or other custody under such order as aforesaid shall be reckoned as imprisonment under the sentence, for whatever purpose such detention shall take place, and such prisoner may during such time, either when on board ship or otherwise, be subjected to such restraint as is necessary for his detention and removal."

43. *Subsistence of prisoners in common gaols.*—The gaoler or keeper of any public prison, gaol, house of correction, lock-up house, or other place of confinement in any part of Her Majesty's dominions shall diet and supply every marine imprisoned therein under the sentence of a court-martial or as a deserter with fuel and other necessaries according to the regulations of such place of confinement, and shall receive on account of every marine during the period of his imprisonment one shilling per diem, or such other sum as the said Lord High Admiral or the said Commissioners may at any time or times direct, which the Secretary of the Admiralty shall cause to be issued out of the subsistence of such marine, upon application in writing signed by any justice within whose jurisdiction such place of confinement shall be locally situated, together with a copy of the order of commitment ; and which sum of one shilling per diem, or such other sum as aforesaid, shall be carried to the credit of the fund from which the expense of such place of confinement is defrayed. A sentence of imprisonment or of penal servitude passed either by a court-martial or by any court of criminal jurisdiction upon any person subject to this Act shall be in no respect affected by such person ceasing to be subject to this Act by discharge or otherwise at any time after the passing of such sentence ; but the discharge of such person shall not be deemed in any manner to affect the provisions for the cost of his maintenance while undergoing a sentence of imprisonment or penal servitude, as otherwise enacted.

44. *Notice to be given of expiration of imprisonment in common gaols.*—Every gaoler or keeper of any public prison, gaol, house of correction, or other place of confinement, to whom any notice

shall have been given, or who shall have reason to know or believe that any person in his custody for any debt or contempt, or upon any charge or for any offence, civil, criminal, or military, is a marine, shall on receiving him into custody give notice thereof to the Secretary of the Admiralty, and also, previous to the expiration of the period of the confinement or imprisonment of such marine, give to the Secretary of the Admiralty one month's notice of the period of such expiration of confinement or imprisonment; or if there shall not be sufficient time for a month's notice, then the longest practicable notice thereof, specifying the day and hour of the day on and at which he is to be released; and for every default of giving either or any of such notices such gaoler or person shall forfeit the sum of twenty pounds; and moreover every gaoler or other person having such immediate inspection as aforesaid shall, as soon as any such marine shall be entitled to be discharged out of custody, with all convenient speed, safely and securely conduct and convey, and safely and securely deliver, every such marine either unto the officer commanding at the nearest head-quarters of the Royal Marines or to the officer commanding Her Majesty's ship to which any such marine may happen to belong, unless the said Commissioners shall, by writing under the hand of the Secretary of the Admiralty, or the officer commanding at the nearest head-quarters of the Royal Marines, or the officer commanding Her Majesty's ship to which any such marine may belong, shall, by writing under his hand, direct that such marine be delivered to some other officer or person, in which case he shall be delivered to such other officer or person accordingly, and the officer or person to whom such marine shall be so delivered in accordance with this Act shall thereupon give to such gaoler or person delivering up such marine a certificate, directed to the Secretary of the Admiralty, specifying the receipt of such marine, and, if such gaoler or other person as aforesaid has conducted or conveyed any such marine, specifying the place from and to which he shall have been conducted and conveyed as aforesaid; and such gaoler or person who shall have so conducted, conveyed, and delivered any such marine shall, upon the production of such certificate, be entitled to receive of and from the Accountant-General of Her Majesty's Navy the sum of one shilling per mile, and no more, for conducting, conveying, and delivering any such marine as aforesaid; and every such gaoler or other person having such immediate inspection as aforesaid, who shall not safely and securely conduct, convey, or deliver any such marine as aforesaid, shall for every such misconduct or offence forfeit and pay the sum of one hundred pounds. In all cases where the marine in custody is under sentence to be discharged from the service on the completion of his term of imprisonment, and the discharge document is in the hands of the gaoler, such gaoler shall not be required to make any report thereof to the Secretary of the Admiralty or to the Deputy Adjutant-General of Marines.

49. *Apprehension of deserters.—Transfer of deserters.*—Upon reasonable suspicion that a person is a deserter, it shall be lawful for any constable or other person to apprehend him, and forthwith bring him before a justice acting for any county, district, city, borough, or place within or near to which the place in which he was apprehended is situate; and the justice shall deal with the suspected deserter as if he were brought before him by warrant in accordance with the provisions of an Act passed in the eleventh and twelfth years of Her present Majesty, chapter forty-two, section twenty-one; and upon its appearing to the justice by the testimony of one or more witnesses taken upon oath, or by the confession of such suspected person, that the accused is a deserter, he shall cause him to be conveyed to the head-quarters of the division or depôt to which he may appear to belong, or to the nearest or most convenient military or police station, or other place legally provided for the confinement of persons in custody, or delivered up to a party of marines in charge of a non-commissioned officer, as to the justice may seem most expedient, having regard to the safe custody of such suspected deserter; and the justice shall make a report to the Secretary of the Admiralty of the persons through whom or by whose means the deserter was apprehended or secured; and for such information, commitment, and report the gaoler or other person into whose custody the accused is committed shall pay at the time of commitment to the clerk to the justice the sum of two shillings; and the Secretary of the Admiralty, upon receipt of a report of the same, together with a copy of the commitment, shall cause such sum to be repaid to such gaoler or other person so entitled; and upon the report of a justice as aforesaid the Secretary of the Admiralty shall cause to be paid to the person or persons by whom or through whose means it shall appear to his satisfaction that the deserter was apprehended and secured a sum not exceeding forty shillings; and the justice shall in every case transmit to the Secretary of the Admiralty a descriptive return in the form prescribed in the schedule to this Act annexed; and a return purporting to be so made shall be evidence of the facts and matters therein stated: provided always, that any such person so committed as a deserter in any part of Her Majesty's dominions shall, subject to the provisions hereinafter contained, be liable to be transferred, by order of the colonel

commandant or other officer commanding, to serve in any division, corps, detachment, or party nearest to the place where he shall have been apprehended, or to any other division corps, detachment, or party to which the Lord High Admiral or the Commissioners for executing the office of Lord High Admiral may deem it desirable that he should be transferred, and shall also be liable after such transfer of service to be tried and punished as a deserter.

50. *Temporary custody of deserters in gaols.*—Every gaoler or keeper of any public prison, gaol, house of correction, lock-up house, or other place of confinement in any part of Her Majesty's dominions is hereby required to receive and confine therein every deserter who shall be delivered into his custody by any marine or other person conveying such deserter under lawful authority, on production of the warrant of the justice of the peace on which such deserter shall have been taken, or some order from the Admiralty, which order shall continue in force until the deserter shall have arrived at his destination ; and such gaoler or keeper shall be entitled to one shilling for the safe custody of the said deserter while halted on the march, and to such subsistence for his maintenance as shall be directed by the said Lord High Admiral or the said Commissioners.

RULES SETTLED AND APPROVED BY THE SECRETARY OF STATE,

UNDER

THE PRISON ACT, 1877.

IN pursuance of The Prison Act, 1877, I hereby make the following rules, which shall apply exclusively to the first appointment of Visiting Committees under the said Act.

1. Such members of a Visiting Committee as are to be appointed by Quarter Sessions shall be appointed at the next Quarter Sessions to be held after the date of this order, or at some adjourned meeting thereof, to be held in the first whole week after the 31st day of March next; provided that such members of a Visiting Committee as are to be appointed at the sessions specified in the first column of the subjoined table shall be appointed respectively as mentioned in the second column of the same table:—

Gaol Sessions for the County of York.	At Gaol Sessions to be held in the first whole week after the 31st day of March next.
Gaol Sessions for the County of Lincoln.	Ditto ditto.
Annual General Sessions for the County of Kent.	At Annual General Sessions to be held in the first whole week after the 31st day of March next.
Annual General Sessions for the County of Lancaster.	Ditto ditto.
Adjourned Quarter Sessions for the whole County of Herts.	At the Easter Adjourned Session to be held for the whole county in the first whole week after the 31st day of March next, within the liberty of St. Alban's Division.

2. Such members of a Visiting Committee as are to be appointed by the justices of a borough shall be appointed at Special Sessions to be held for that purpose on some day in the first whole week after the 31st day of March next.

3. Such members of the Visiting Committee for the Worcester Prison as are to be appointed by the Town Council of the city of Worcester shall be appointed at a meeting to be held for that purpose on some day in the first whole week after the 31st day of March next.

4. The first meeting of a Visiting Committee for a prison shall be held at the prison on Monday, the 15th of April, at noon.

5. In the interval between the 1st and the 15th days of April next, such of the reports, acts, or things which, previous to the passing of The Prison Act, 1877, were required to be made or done to or by or in relation to the Visiting Justices or a Visiting Justice of a prison at common law, or by any Act of Parliament or by charter, as by any rules bearing date this 19th day of February, 1878, are required to be made or done to or by or in relation to a Visiting Committee to be appointed under The Prison Act, 1877, shall (except in so far as is otherwise provided by The Prison Act, 1877) be made or done to or by or in relation to the persons who, immediately before the 1st day of April, were the Visiting Justices of that prison, or any of them.

Settled and approved this 19th day of February, 1878,

RICH^D. ASSHETON CROSS,

One of her Majesty's principal Secretaries of State.

THE PRISON RULES, 1878.

IN pursuance of The Prison Act, 1877, I hereby make the following rule as to the appointment of Visiting Committees.

The Visiting Committees for the prisons specified in the first column of the subjoined table shall be constituted as set forth for the same prisons respectively in the two sub-columns of the second column of the same table.

TABLE.

NAME OF PRISON.	Constitution of Visiting Committee.	
	Sessions to Appoint Visiting Committees.	Number of Justices to be Appointed.
BEDFORDSHIRE: Bedford County	Bedfordshire Quarter	12
BERKSHIRE: Reading County	Berkshire Quarter	7
BUCKINGHAMSHIRE: Aylesbury County	Bucks Quarter	6
CAMBRIDGESHIRE: Chesterton County	{ Cambridgeshire Quarter { Cambridge Borough Special { Isle of Ely Quarter	3 3 3 — 9
CHESHIRE: Knutsford County Chester County	Cheshire Quarter Cheshire Quarter	12 12
CORNWALL: Bodmin County	{ Cornwall Quarter { Devonport Borough Special { Plymouth Borough Special	10 1 1 — 12
CUMBERLAND: Carlisle County	{ Cumberland Quarter { Carlisle City Special	6 2 — 8
DERBYSHIRE: Derby County	Derbyshire Quarter	8
DEVONSHIRE: Exeter County	{ Devonshire Quarter { Barnstaple Borough Special { Tiverton Borough Special	10 1 1 — 12

THE PRISON RULES, 1878.

TABLE—(*continued*).

NAME OF PRISON.	Constitution of Visiting Committee.	
	Sessions to Appoint Visiting Committees.	Number of Justices to be Appointed.
Plymouth Borough	Devonport Borough Special - Devonshire Quarter - Plymouth Borough Special -	2 2 2 —— 6
DORSETSHIRE: Dorchester County	Dorsetshire Quarter - Poole Borough Special -	11 1 —— 12
DURHAM: Durham County -	Durham Quarter -	— 9
ESSEX: Springfield County	Essex Quarter -	— 12
GLOUCESTERSHIRE: Gloucestershire County Bristol City Common -	Gloucestershire Quarter - Bristol City Special -	— 12 — 5
HEREFORDSHIRE: Hereford County -	Herefordshire Quarter - Hereford City Special - Radnorshire Quarter -	6 2 2 —— 10
HERTFORDSHIRE: St. Alban's County	Adjourned Quarter Sessions for the whole county of Herts -	— 12
HUNTINGDONSHIRE: Great Stukeley County	Huntingdonshire Quarter -	— 7
KENT: Maidstone County	Kent General Annual -	— 12
Canterbury County	Kent General Annual - Dover Borough Special - Sandwich Borough Special -	4 2 2 —— 8
LANCASHIRE: Lancaster County Kirkdale County - Preston County -	Lancashire General Annual - Lancashire General Annual - Lancashire General Annual -	— 12 — 12 — 12

THE PRISON RULES, 1878.

TABLE—*(continued).*

NAME OF PRISON.	Constitution of Visiting Committee.		
	Sessions to Appoint Visiting Committees.		Number of Justices to be Appointed.
Salford County	Lancashire Quarter Sessions, to be held in the hundred of Salford	—	12
Liverpool Borough	Liverpool Borough Special	—	12
Manchester City	Manchester Borough Special	—	12
LEICESTERSHIRE:			
Leicester County	{ Leicestershire Quarter	6	
	{ Leicester Borough Special	6	
			12
Leicester Borough	{ Leicestershire Quarter	6	
	{ Leicester Borough Special	6	12
LINCOLNSHIRE:			
	⎧ Parts of Lindsey Quarter	5	
	⎪ Parts of Kesteven Quarter	2	
Lindsey County	⎨ Parts of Holland Quarter	2	
	⎪ Lincoln City Special	1	
	⎪ Grantham Borough Special	1	
	⎩ Stamford Borough Special	1	
			12
	⎧ Parts of Lindsey Quarter	5	
	⎪ Parts of Kesteven Quarter	2	
Spalding County	⎨ Parts of Holland Quarter	2	
	⎪ Lincoln City Special	1	
	⎪ Grantham Borough Special	1	
	⎩ Stamford Borough Special	1	
			12
NEWGATE, CITY	City of London Special	—	12
MIDDLESEX:			
Clerkenwell County	Middlesex Quarter	—	12
Westminster County	Middlesex Quarter	—	12
Holloway, City	City of London Special	—	12
Cold Bath Fields County	Middlesex Quarter	—	12
MONMOUTHSHIRE:			
Usk County	Monmouthshire Quarter	—	12

TABLE—(continued).

NAME OF PRISON.	Constitution of Visiting Committee.	
	Sessions to Appoint Visiting Committees.	Number of Justices to be Appointed.
NORFOLK: Norwich County	Norfolk Quarter Norwich City	9 3 — 12
NORTHAMPTONSHIRE: Northampton County	Northamptonshire Quarter Liberty of Peterborough Quarter Northampton Borough Special	8 2 2 — 12
Northampton Borough	Northamptonshire Quarter Liberty of Peterborough Quarter Northampton Borough Special	8 2 2 — 12
NORTHUMBERLAND: Newcastle Borough	Newcastle City Special Berwick Borough Special	11 1 — 12
Morpeth County	Northumberland Quarter	— 12
NOTTINGHAMSHIRE: Nottingham Borough	Nottingham Borough Special Nottinghamshire Quarter	6 2 — 8
Southwell	Nottinghamshire Quarter	— 6
OXFORDSHIRE: Oxford County	Oxfordshire Quarter Oxford City Special	8 4 — 12
RUTLANDSHIRE: Oakham County	Rutlandshire Quarter	— 12
SHROPSHIRE: Shrewsbury County	Shropshire Quarter Montgomeryshire Quarter	5 1 — 6

TABLE—*(continued).*

NAME OF PRISON.	Constitution of Visiting Committee.		
	Sessions to Appoint Visiting Committees.	\multicolumn{2}{c}{Number of Justices to be Appointed.}

NAME OF PRISON.	Sessions to Appoint Visiting Committees.		Number of Justices to be Appointed.
SOMERSETSHIRE:			
Taunton County	Somersetshire Quarter	—	6
Shepton Mallet County	Somersetshire Quarter	—	9
Bath City	Bath City Special	—	4
SOUTHAMPTON:			
Winchester County	Hants Quarter	6	
	Portsmouth Borough Special	3	
			9
Southampton Borough	Hants Quarter	3	
	Southampton Borough Special	3	
			6
STAFFORDSHIRE:			
Stafford County	Staffordshire Quarter	—	12
SUFFOLK:			
Ipswich County	Suffolk Quarter, Eastern Division	5	
	Suffolk Quarter, Western Division	5	
Ipswich Borough	Ipswich Borough Special	2	
			12
SURREY:			
Newington County	Surrey Quarter	—	12
Wandsworth County	Surrey Quarter	—	12
SUSSEX:			
Lewes County	Sussex Quarter, Eastern Division	6	
	Sussex Quarter, Western Division	6	
			12
Petworth	Sussex Quarter, Eastern Division	6	
	Sussex Quarter, Western Division	6	
			12
WARWICKSHIRE:			
Warwick County	Warwickshire Quarter	—	12
Birmingham Borough	Birmingham Borough Special	—	8

THE PRISON RULES, 1878.

TABLE—*(continued)*.

NAME OF PRISON.	Constitution of Visiting Committee.	
	Sessions to Appoint Visiting Committees.	Number of Justices to be Appointed.
WESTMORELAND: Kendal County	Westmoreland Quarter	12
WILTSHIRE: Devizes County	Wiltshire Quarter	12
WORCESTERSHIRE: Worcester County	{ Worcestershire Quarter — 9 City of Worcester Town Council — 3	12
YORKSHIRE: Northallerton County	{ North Riding Quarter — 9 Liberty of Ripon Quarter — 1	10
Wakefield County.	{ West Riding Quarter — 11 East Riding Quarter — 1	12
Kingston-on-Hull Borough	{ Kingston-on-Hull Borough Special — 10 Scarborough Borough Special — 2	12
Leeds Borough	Leeds Borough Special	12
York County	County of York Gaol	8
BRECONSHIRE: Brecon County	Breconshire Quarter	12
CARMARTHENSHIRE: Carmarthen County	{ Carmarthenshire Quarter — 5 Cardiganshire Quarter — 2 Pembrokeshire Quarter — 5	12
CARNARVONSHIRE: Carnarvon County	{ Carnarvonshire Quarter — 4 Anglesea Quarter — 4	8
DENBIGHSHIRE: Ruthin County	{ Denbighshire Quarter — 5 Flintshire Quarter — 5 Merionethshire Quarter — 2	12
GLAMORGANSHIRE: Cardiff County	Glamorganshire Quarter	12
Swansea County	Glamorganshire Quarter	12

17

NAME OF PRISON.	Constitution of Visiting Committee.	
	Sessions to Appoint Visiting Committees.	Number of Justices to be Appointed.
Buckingham Borough	Buckingham Borough Special	6
Cambridge Borough	Cambridge Borough Special	6
Ely, Isle of Ely	Isle of Ely Quarter	6
Wisbeach, Isle of Ely	Isle of Ely Quarter	6
Barnstaple Borough	Barnstaple Borough Special	6
Tiverton Borough	Tiverton Borough Special	6
Devonport Borough	Devonport Borough Special	6
Poole Borough	Poole Borough Special	6
Bristol City Bridewell	Bristol City Special	6
Ilford County	Essex Quarter	6
Hereford City	Hereford City Special	6
Hertford County	Adjourned Quarter Sessions for the whole County of Herts	6
Dover Borough	Dover Borough Special	6
Sandwich Borough	Sandwich Borough Special	6
Lincoln County	Lincoln County Gaol	6
Falkingham County	Parts of Kesteven Quarter	6
Lincoln City	Lincoln City Special	6
Grantham Borough	Grantham Borough Special	6
Stamford Borough	Stamford Borough Special	6
Norwich City	Norwich City Special	6
Wymondham County	Norfolk Quarter	6
Peterborough Liberty	Peterborough Liberty Quarter	6
Berwick-upon-Tweed Borough	Berwick-upon-Tweed Special	6
Nottingham County	Nottinghamshire Quarter	6
Oxford City	Oxford City Special	6
Portsmouth Borough	Portsmouth Borough Special	6
Bury St. Edmunds County	Suffolk Quarter	6
Appleby County	Westmoreland Quarter	6
Beverley County	East Riding Quarter	6
Ripon Liberty	Ripon Liberty Quarter	6
Scarborough Borough	Scarborough Borough Special	6
Beaumaris County	Anglesea Quarter	6
Cardigan County	Cardigan Quarter	6
Mold County	Flint Quarter	6
Dolgelly County	Merioneth Quarter	6
Montgomery County	Montgomery Quarter	6
Haverfordwest County	Pembroke Quarter	6
Presteign County	Radnor Quarter	6

Settled and approved this 19th day of February, 1878,

RICHD. ASSHETON CROSS,

One of Her Majesty's principal Secretaries of State.

THE PRISON RULES, 1878.

In pursuance of The Prison Act, 1877, I hereby appoint that upon an order being made for the discontinuance of any prison specified in the first column of the subjoined table, then as from the date of such order such prison or prisons in the same county as is or are specified in the third column shall be a prison or prisons in which prisoners may be confined before and during trial, or at either of such times, and in which debtors and prisoners who are not criminal prisoners may be confined during the period of their imprisonment; and that on and after the same date, any prisoner who might, if the Act had not passed, have been lawfully confined in any prison situate within the area of any one of the said counties, may be lawfully confined in any of the prisons hereby appointed for the same county.

TABLE.

Prisons to be Discontinued.	County in which discontinued Prison is situated.	Prison Appointed.
Buckingham Borough	Buckingham	Aylesbury County
Cambridge Borough	Cambridge	Cambridge County.
Ely, Isle of Ely	ditto	ditto.
Wisbeach, Isle of Ely	ditto	ditto.
Barnstaple Borough	Devon	Exeter County.
Tiverton Borough	ditto	ditto.
Devonport Borough	ditto	Exeter County and Plymouth Borough.
Poole Borough	Dorset	Dorchester County.
Bristol City Bridewell	Gloucestershire	Gloucester County.
Ilford County	Essex	Springfield County.
Hereford City	Hereford	Hereford County.
Hertford County	Hertford	St. Alban's Conty.
Dover Borough	Kent	{ Maidstone County and Canterbury County.
Sandwich Borough	ditto	ditto.
Lincoln County	Lincoln	Lindsey County.
Falkingham County	ditto	Lindsey County, and Spalding County.
Lincoln City	ditto	Lincoln County.
Grantham Borough	ditto	ditto.
Stamford Borough	ditto	Lincoln County, and Spalding County.
Norwich City	Norfolk	Norwich County.
Wymondham County	ditto	ditto.

TABLE—(*continued*).

Prisons to be Discontinued.	County in which discontinued Prison is situated.	Prison Appointed.
Peterborough Liberty	Northampton	Northampton County.
Berwick-upon-Tweed Borough	Northumberland	Newcastle-on-Tyne City.
Nottingham County	Nottingham	Nottingham Borough and Southwell County.
Oxford City	Oxford	Oxford County.
Portsmouth Borough	Southampton	Winchester County.
Bury St. Edmunds County	Suffolk	Ipswich County and Ipswich City.
Appleby County	Westmoreland	Kendal County.
Beverley County	York	Wakefield County, Leeds Borough, and York County.
Ripon Liberty	ditto	Northallerton County, Wakefield County, Leeds Borough, and York County.
Scarborough Borough	ditto	Kingston-on-Hull Borough and York County.

Settled and approved this 19th day of February, 1878,

RICH^D. ASSHETON CROSS,

One of Her Majesty's principal Secretaries of State.

IN pursuance of The Prison Act, 1877, I hereby appoint that after the 1st day of April, 1878, any prisoner, who, in respect of a matter arising within such county or part of a county as is specified in the first column of the subjoined table, might, if the said Act had not passed, have been lawfully confined in the prison situated in the same county, and specified in that behalf in the second column, may be committed for trial, safe custody, or otherwise to such prison in the adjoining county as is specified in that behalf in the third column.

TABLE.

County or part of County within which matter arises.	Prison in which, if Prison Act, 1877, had not passed, Prisoners might have been confined.	Prison in adjoining County to which Prisoners may be committed.
Such part of the County of Essex as is within the Petty Sessional Division of Ilford.	Ilford County Prison	Clerkenwell County Prison and Holloway Prison in County of Middlesex.
Such part of the County of Kent as is within the Districts assigned to the Metropolitan Police Courts of Woolwich and Greenwich.	Maidstone County Prison	Clerkerkenwell County Prison in County of Middlesex, Newington County Prison, and Wandsworth County Prison, in County of Surrey.
County of Anglesea	Beaumaris County Prison	Carnarvon County Prison in County of Carnarvon.
County of Cardigan	Cardigan County Prison	Carmarthen County Prison in County of Carmarthen.
County of Flint	Mold County Prison	Ruthin County Prison in County of Denbigh.
County of Merioneth	Dolgelly County Prison	Ruthin County Prison in County of Denbigh.
County of Montgomery	Montgomery County Prison	Shrewsbury County Prison in County of of Salop.
County of Pembroke	Haverfordwest County Prison	Carmarthen County Prison in County of Carmarthen.
County of Radnor	Presteign County Prison	Hereford County Prison in County of Hereford.

Settled and approved this 19th day of February, 1878,

RICHD. ASSHETON CROSS,

One of Her Majesty's principal Secretaries of State.

Rules for the Visiting Committee.

In pursuance of The Prison Act, 1877, I hereby make the following rules with respect to Visiting Committees :—

1. The following provisions shall apply with respect to the time of appointments of Visiting Committees other than the first appointments in the year 1878 :

(*a.*) Such members of a Visiting Committee as are to be appointed by Quarter Sessions shall be appointed at the Quarter Sessions held in the first week after the 28th day of December; provided that such members of a Visiting Committee as are to be appointed at the sessions specified in the first column of the subjoined table shall be appointed respectively as mentioned in the second column of the same table :—

Gaol Sessions for the County of York	At Gaol Sessions, to be held in the first whole week after the 28th of December.
Gaol Sessions for the County of Lincoln	ditto ditto
Annual General Sessions, County of Kent	At Annual General Sessions, to be held in the first whole week after the 28th of December.
Annual General Sessions, County of Lancaster	ditto ditto
Adjourned Quarter Sessions for the whole County of Herts	At an Epiphany Adjourned Session for the whole county, held within the Hertford Division in the first whole week after the 28th of December.

(*b.*) Such members of a Visiting Committee as are to be appointed by the justices of a borough shall be appointed at Special Sessions to be held for that purpose in the first whole week after the 28th of December.

(*c.*) Such members of a Visiting Committee for the Worcester Prison as are to be appointed by the Town Council of the city of Worcester, shall be appointed at a meeting to be held for that purpose in the first whole week after the 28th of December.

(d.) The first meeting of a Visiting Committee for a prison shall be held at the prison at noon, on the Monday in the second whole week after the 28th of December.

2. The Visiting Committee shall continue to hold office until their successors shall have met and taken over their duties.

3. They shall, at their first meeting, appoint a chairman, and make rules as regards their attendance at the prison for the purpose of carrying out the duties assigned to them.

4. The chairman of the Visiting Committee shall report to the Secretary of State the names and addresses of the members of the Visiting Committee.

5. No member of the Visiting Committee shall have any interest in any contract made in respect of any prison of which he is on the Visiting Committee.

6. The members of the Visiting Committee shall be treated with the utmost respect and courtesy by every prison officer. Any infringement of this rule will render the offender liable to severe punishment.

7. They shall co-operate with the Commissioners in promoting the efficiency of the service, and shall make inquiry into any matter specially referred to them by the Secretary of State or the Commissioners, and report their opinion thereon.

8. Should any abuses in connection with the prison come to the knowledge of the Visiting Committee, or any of them, they shall take care that such abuses are brought to the notice of the Commissioners immediately; and in case of urgent necessity, they may suspend any officer of the prison until the decision of the Commissioners is made known.

9. They shall keep a book of minutes of their proceedings, in which all minutes shall be recorded.

10. They shall hear and adjudicate on any report made by the governor of the misconduct or idleness of any prisoner.

11. If the governor shall represent to them that he has, in case of urgent necessity, put a prisoner in irons or under mechanical restraint, and that it is necessary that such

prisoner should be kept in irons or under mechanical restraint for more than 24 hours, they may authorize such detention by order in writing, which shall specify the cause thereof and the time during which the prisoner is to be kept in irons or under mechanical restraint.

12. They shall furnish such information with respect to the offences reported to them, and the punishments they award, as may from time to time be required.

13. They shall hear any complaint which any prisoner may desire to make to them; and, if necessary, report the same, with their opinion, to the Commissioners, or take such steps with regard to the matter as they may from time to time be directed to take.

14. They shall attend to any report in writing which they may receive as to the mind or body of any prisoner being likely to be injured by the discipline or treatment to which he is subjected, and shall communicate their opinion to the Commissioners; if the case be urgent, they shall give such directions thereon as they may deem expedient, communicating the same to the Commissioners.

15. They shall frequently inspect the diets of the prisoners, and if they shall find that the quality of any article does not fulfil the terms of the contract, they shall report the circumstances to the Commissioners and note the same in their minute book, and the governor shall thereupon take such steps as may be immediately necessary to provide the prisoners with suitable food.

16. They may inspect any of the books of the prison.

17. They shall report to the Secretary of State any matter with respect to which they may consider it expedient.

18. They may, on application from any non-criminal prisoner, dispense with his attendance at Divine service on Sundays and other days.

19. They shall, before granting any permission which, by the following rules, they are authorized or required to grant, satisfy themselves that it can be granted without interfering with the security, good order, and government of the prison and prisoners therein; and if, after it has been granted, its continuance seems likely to cause any such interference, or the prisoner has abused such permission, or has been guilty

of any misconduct, they shall have power to suspend or withdraw such permission.

20. They shall, on the application of any prisoner awaiting trial, if, having regard to his ordinary habits and condition of life, they think such special provision should be made in respect to him, permit any such prisoner—

 (1.) To occupy, on payment of a small sum fixed by the Commissioners, a suitable room or cell specially fitted for such prisoners, and furnished with suitable bedding and other articles in addition to or different from those furnished for ordinary cells;

 (2.) To exercise separately or with selected untried prisoners, if the arrangements and construction of the prison permit it;

 (3.) To have, at his own cost, the use of private furniture and utensils suitable to his ordinary habits, to be approved by the governor;

 (4.) To have, on payment of a small sum fixed by the Commissioners, the assistance of some person to be appointed by the governor, relieving him from the performance of any unaccustomed tasks or offices.

21. They may also permit the governor to modify the routine of the prison in regard to any prisoner awaiting trial, so far as to dispense with any practice which is, in the opinion of the governor, clearly unnecessary in the case of that particular prisoner.

22. They shall permit prisoners awaiting trial and misdemeanants of the first division to have supplied to them, at their own expense, such books, newspapers, or other means of occupation, other than those furnished by the prison, as are not, in their opinion, or in their absence, pending their approval, in the opinion of the governor, of an objectionable kind.

23. They shall, on the application of any misdemeanant of the first division, permit him to wear his own clothing, provided that it is sufficient and is fit for use, and to supply his own food under the restrictions made in respect thereto; also if, having regard to his ordinary habits and condition of life, they think such special provision should be made in respect to him, they shall permit any such prisoner—

(1.) To occupy, on payment of a small sum fixed by the Commissioners, a room or cell specially fitted for such prisoners, and furnished with suitable bedding and other articles, in addition to or different from those furnished for ordinary cells.

(2.) To have, at his own cost, the use of private furniture and utensils suitable to his ordinary habits, to be approved by the governor.

(3.) To have, on payment of a small sum fixed by the Commissioners, the assistance of some person, to be appointed by the governor, relieving him from the performance of any unaccustomed tasks or offices.

24. They may, by permission, in any special case, for special reasons, prolong the period of the visit allowed to any prisoner. Further, they may, for special reasons in each case, permit any prisoner to have an extension of the privileges of communicating with his friends, either by visit or writing, provided such extension is in conformity with the rules relating to the class to which the prisoner belongs.

25. A person shall not, without an order from a member of the Visiting Committee, be permitted to visit a prisoner under order for execution, except as authorized in pursuance of The Prison Acts, 1865 and 1877; and if such prisoner applies to the governor to be allowed to be visited by any person, the name of such person shall be forthwith submitted to the Visiting Committee.

26. The Visiting Committee are requested to give such assistance as may be in their power towards securing the proper disposal of any gratuities which may be earned by prisoners, especially in places where there is no Discharged Prisoners' Aid Society, according to such instructions as may from time to time be issued.

27. When any youthful offender imprisoned in the prison has been sentenced to be sent to a reformatory school, and the particular school to which he is to be sent is not named at the time of his sentence being passed, or within seven days thereafter, by the court, justices, or magistrate who sentenced him, then any member of the Visiting Committee may, at any time before the expiration of the term of im-

prisonment, name the school to which he is to be sent, provided that he shall endeavour to ascertain the religious persuasion to which the youthful offender belongs, and, so far as is possible, select a school conducted in accordance with such religious persuasion, and shall specify such persuasion in his order.

28. If the parent, step-parent, or guardian, or if there be no parent, step-parent, or guardian, then the God-parent or nearest adult relative of any youthful offender who has been sent, or is about to be sent, to a certified reformatory school which is not conducted in accordance with the religious persuasion to which the offender belongs, shall apply to a member of the Visiting Committee of the prison to which the offender was committed, to send or to remove such offender to a certified reformatory school, conducted in accordance with the offender's religious persuasion, such member of the Visiting Committee shall, upon proof of such offender's religious persuasion, comply with the request of the applicant, provided—

(1.) That the application be made before the offender has been sent to a certified reformatory school, or within thirty days after his arrival at such school.

(2.) That the applicant show, to the satisfaction of such member of the Visiting Committee, that the managers of the school named by him are willing to receive the offender.

29. The Visiting Committee shall also discharge such other duties as are assigned to them in the Special Rules for special classes of prisoners and in the General Rules for the government of prisons.

30. The foregoing rules shall come into operation on the 15th of April, 1878.

Settled and approved this 19th day of February, 1878,

RICH^D. ASSHETON CROSS,

One of Her Majesty's principal Secretaries of State.

SPECIAL RULES FOR PRISONERS AWAITING TRIAL.

In pursuance of The Prison Act, 1877, I hereby make the following special rules with respect to prisoners awaiting trial :—

Admission, Discharge, and Removal.

1. Such prisoner shall not be required to take a bath on reception, if, on the application of the prisoner, the governor shall decide that it is unnecessary, or the surgeon shall state that it is for medical reasons unadvisable.

2. In order to prevent such prisoners from being contaminated by each other, or endeavouring to defeat the ends of justice, they shall be kept separate, and shall not be permitted to communicate together.

3. Such prisoners while attending chapel and at other times shall, if possible, be placed so that they may not be in view of the convicted prisoners.

4. The Visiting Committee or governor, before granting any permission which by the following rules they are authorized or required to grant, shall satisfy themselves that it can be granted without interfering with the security, good order, and government of the prison and prisoners therein; and if after it has been granted its continuance seems likely to cause any such interference, or the prisoner has abused such permission or been guilty of any misconduct, the Visiting Committee shall have power to suspend or withdraw such permission, and in the like circumstances the governor may suspend or withdraw the same when it has been granted by himself, or suspend it when it has been granted by the Visiting Committee, if the case is urgent, provided that he report the case within 24 hours to them.

5. The Visiting Committee shall, on the application of any such prisoner, if, having regard to his ordinary habits and condition of life, they think such special provision should be made in respect to him, permit any such prisoner—

    (1.) To occupy, on payment of a small sum fixed by the Commissioners, a suitable room or cell specially fitted for such prisoners, and furnished with suitable bedding and other articles in addition to or different from those furnished for ordinary cells.

(2.) To exercise separately or with selected untried prisoners, if the arrangements and construction of the prison permit it.

(3.) To have at his own cost the use of private furniture and utensils suitable to his ordinary habits, to be approved by the governor.

(4.) To have, on payment of a small sum fixed by the Commissioners, the assistance of some person to be appointed by the governor, relieving him from the performance of any unaccustomed tasks or offices.

6. Any money in the hands of the governor belonging to any such prisoner may be applied to the purpose of making special provision for him in cases where the prisoner is, by these rules, required to make any payment in respect of such special provision.

7. The Visiting Committee may also permit the governor to modify the routine of the prison in regard to any such prisoner, so far as to dispense with any practice which in the opinion of the governor is clearly unnecessary in the case of that particular prisoner.

8. The governor shall, on the application of any such prisoner, permit him to have any books or papers, such as are referred to in Section 39, Sub-section 1, of The Prison Act, 1877.

Food, Clothing, and Bedding.

9. Any such prisoner who prefers to provide his own food for any meal shall give notice thereof beforehand at the time required, but the governor shall not permit any such prisoner to receive any prison allowance of food for the meal for which he procures or receives food at his own expense.

10. Articles of food shall be received only at such hours as may be laid down from time to time. They shall be inspected by the officers of the prison, and shall be subject to such restrictions as may be necessary to prevent luxury or waste.

11. Any such prisoner shall not during the 24 hours

receive or purchase more than one pint of malt liquor, fermented liquor, or cider, or, if an adult, half a pint (8 ozs.) of wine.

12. No such prisoner shall be allowed to sell or transfer any article whatsoever allowed to be introduced for his use to any other person.

Personal Cleanliness.

13. Such prisoner shall not be compelled either to have his hair cut or (if he usually wears his beard, etc.) to shave, except on account of vermin or dirt, or when the surgeon deems it necessary on the ground of health and cleanliness, and the hair of such prisoner shall not be cut closer than may be necessary for the purpose of health and cleanliness.

14. The beds of such prisoners shall be made, and the rooms and yards in their occupation shall be swept and cleaned, every morning. The furniture and utensils appropriated to their use shall be kept clean and neatly arranged. Should any such prisoner object to perform any of these duties, they may be performed for him as provided in Rule 5, Sub-section 4.

Health.

15. If any such prisoner who is out of health shall desire the attendance of his usual medical man, the Visiting Committee shall, if they are satisfied that the application is *bona fide*, permit him to be visited by such medical man at his own expense, and to be supplied with medicine by him, proper precautions being in all cases observed to prevent abuse of these privileges.

Instruction.

16. Such prisoner shall be permitted to have supplied to him, at his own expense, such books, newspapers, or other means of occupation, other than those furnished by the prison, as are not, in the opinion of the Visiting Committee, or in their absence, and pending their approval, in the opinion of the governor, of an objectionable kind.

Visits to and Communications with Prisoners.

17. So far as prison arrangements may admit, facilities

shall be given to such prisoners to work and follow their respective trades and employments, and all earnings of such prisoner, after payment thereout of such sum as the Commissioners may determine on account of the cost of his maintenance in the prison, or on account of the use of implements lent to him, shall belong to such prisoner.

18. Each such prisoner shall be permitted to be visited by one person, or (if circumstances permit) by two persons at the same time, for a quarter of an hour on any week-day, during such hours as may from time to time be appointed.

19. The Visiting Committee may, by permission in any special case for special reasons, prolong the period of the visit allowed to any such prisoner, or allow him to be visited by more than two persons at the same time.

20. Every endeavour shall be made to provide that such prisoners shall not, when being visited, be exposed to the view of the friends of other prisoners; and to prevent the friends of one prisoner from coming in contact with the friends of another while in the prison.

21. Such prisoner shall at his request be allowed to see his legal adviser (by which is to be understood a certificated solicitor or his clerk, if such clerk is furnished by his principal with written authority) on any week-day, at any reasonable hour, and, if required, in private, but (if necessary) in the view of an officer of the prison.

22. Any such prisoner who is in prison in default of bail shall be permitted to see any of his friends, on any weekday, at any reasonable hour, for the *bonâ fide* purpose of providing bail.

23. Paper and all other writing materials to such extent as may appear reasonable to the governor shall be furnished to any such prisoner who requires to be so supplied for the purposes of communicating with friends or preparing a defence. Any confidential written communication prepared as instructions for a solicitor may be delivered personally to him or his authorized clerk, without being previously examined by any officer of the prison; but all other written communications are to be considered as letters, and are not to be sent out of the prison without being previously inspected by the governor.

24. No such prisoner who is attended or visited by a minister of a church or persuasion differing from the Established Church shall be compelled to attend any religious services except those of the said church or persuasion; but, subject to the foregoing provisions, such prisoners shall attend Divine service on Sundays and on other days when such service is performed, unless prevented by illness or excused by the governor or Visiting Committee for any other reason.

25.. Prisoners awaiting trial shall also be subject to any general rules made by the Secretary of State for the government of prisons, except so far as the same are inconsistent with the special rules relating to such prisoners.

26. The foregoing rules relating to prisoners awaiting trial shall apply to any person committed to prison for safe custody in any of the following circumstances:—

(*a.*) On his commitment for trial for any indictable offence.
(*b.*) Pending the preliminary hearing before justices of a charge against him of an indictable offence, or pending the hearing of an information or complaint against him.
(*c.*) On default in entering into recognizances or finding surety or sureties.

27. The foregoing rules shall come into operation on the 15th of April, 1878.

Settled and approved this 19th day of February, 1878,

RICH^D. ASSHETON CROSS,

One of Her Majesty's principal Secretaries of State.

SPECIAL RULES FOR MISDEMEANANTS OF THE FIRST DIVISION.

In pursuance of The Prison Act, 1877, I hereby make the following special rules with respect to prisoners who are misdemeanants of the first division:—

Admission, Discharge, and Removal.

1. No person shall be placed in this division except as provided by statute or by order of the judge or court before whom he is tried.

2. Such prisoner shall not be required to take a bath on reception, if, on the application of the prisoner, the governor shall decide that it is unnecessary, or the surgeon shall state that it is, for medical reasons, unadvisable.

3. Every such prisoner shall be searched only by an officer specially appointed for the purpose.

4. He shall be placed as soon as possible after reception in a cell appropriated to prisoners of his class, unless there is reason to believe that he is suffering from some infectious disease, in which case he shall be detained in a reception cell till he can be seen by the surgeon.

5. He shall at all times, except when at chapel or exercise, occupy the room or cell assigned to him.

6. He shall not be placed in association or at exercise with criminal prisoners.

7. The Visiting Committee or governor, before granting any permission which by the following rules they are authorized or required to grant, shall satisfy themselves that it can be granted without interfering with the security, good order, and government of the prison and prisoners therein; and if, after it has been granted, its continuance seems likely to cause any such interference, or the prisoner has abused such permission, or been guilty of any misconduct, the Visiting Committee shall have power to suspend or withdraw such permission, and in the like circumstances the governor may suspend or withdraw the same when it has been granted by himself, or suspend it when it has been granted by the Visiting Committee, if the case is urgent, provided that he report the case within 24 hours to them.

8. The Visiting Committee shall, on the application of any such prisoner, if, having regard to his ordinary habits and condition of life, they think such special provision should be made in respect to him, permit any such prisoner—

    (1.) To occupy, on payment of a small sum fixed by the Commissioners, a room or cell specially fitted for such prisoners, and furnished with suitable bedding and other articles in addition to or different from those furnished for ordinary cells.

(2.) To have at his own cost the use of private furniture and utensils suitable to his ordinary habits, to be approved by the governor.

(3.) To have, on payment of a small sum fixed by the Commissioners, the assistance of some person to be appointed by the governor, relieving him from the performance of any unaccustomed tasks or offices.

9. Any money in the hands of the governor, belonging to any such prisoner, may be applied to the purpose of making special provision for him, in cases where the prisoner is by these rules required to make any payment in respect of such special provision.

Food, Clothing, and Bedding.

10. He shall be permitted by the Visiting Committee to supply his own food, on giving due notice beforehand, at the time required; but the governor shall not permit such prisoner to receive any prison allowance of food at any meal for which he procures or receives food at his own expense.

11. Articles of food shall be received only at such hours as may be laid down from time to time. They shall be inspected by the officers of the prison, and shall be subject to such restrictions as may be necessary to prevent luxury or waste.

12. Any such prisoner shall not during the 24 hours receive or purchase more than one pint of malt liquor, fermented liquor, or cider, or, if an adult, half a pint (8 ozs.) of wine.

13. He shall be permitted by the Visiting Committee to wear his own clothing, provided that it is sufficient and is fit for use.

14. No such prisoner shall be allowed to sell or transfer any article whatsoever allowed to be introduced for his use to any other person.

Personal Cleanliness.

15. Such prisoner shall not be compelled either to have his hair cut, or (if he usually wears his beard, etc.) to shave, except on account of vermin or dirt, or when the surgeons deem it necessary on the ground of health and cleanliness, and the hair of such prisoner shall not be cut closer than may be necessary for the purposes of health and cleanliness.

16. The beds of such prisoners shall be made, and the rooms and yards in their occupation shall be swept and cleaned, every morning. The furniture and utensils appropriated to their use shall be kept clean and neatly arranged. Should any such prisoner object to perform any of these duties, they may be performed for him, as provided in Rule 8.

Instruction.

17. Such prisoner shall be permitted to have supplied to him, at his own expense, such books, newspapers, or other means of occupation other than those furnished by the prison, as are not, in the opinion of the Visiting Committee, or in their absence, and pending their approval, in the opinion of the governor, of an objectionable kind.

Employment.

18. Such prisoners may be permitted to work, and may follow their respective trades and professions. Such prisoners as find their own implements, and are not maintained at the expense of the prison, shall be allowed to receive the whole of their earnings; but the earnings of such as are furnished with implements, or are maintained at the expense of the prison, shall be subject to a deduction, to be determined by the Commissioners, for the use of implements and the cost of maintenance.

Visits to and Communications with Prisoners.

19. The Visiting Committee may, by permission in any special case for special reasons, prolong the period of the visit allowed to any such prisoner, or accord additional visits or letters to such reasonable extent as they may deem advisable.

20. The place in which such prisoners receive their visits shall not be the same as that in which criminal prisoners receive their visits, if any other suitable place can conveniently be provided.

21. No such prisoner who is attended or visited by a minister of a church or persuasion differing from the Established Church shall be compelled to attend any religious services, except those of the said church or persuasion; but, subject to the foregoing provisions, such prisoner shall attend Divine service on Sundays and on other days when such service is performed, unless prevented by illness or excused by the governor or Visiting Committee for any other reason.

22. No other privileges than the foregoing shall be allowed to such prisoners.

23. Misdemeanants of the first division shall also be subject to any general rules made by the Secretary of State for the government of prisons, except so far as the same are inconsistent with the special rules relating to such misdemeanants.

24. The foregoing rules relating to misdemeanants of the first division shall (to the exclusion of any other rules applicable exclusively to any particular class of prisoners) apply also to—

(a.) Any prisoner committed under any rule, order, or attachment for contempt of court.

(b.) Any prisoner sentenced to imprisonment on conviction for sedition or seditious libel.

26. The foregoing rules shall come into operation on the 15th of April, 1878.

Settled and approved this 19th day of February, 1878,

Rich^{D.} Assheton Cross,

One of Her Majesty's principal Secretaries of State.

Special Rules for Debtors.

In pursuance of The Prison Act, 1877, I hereby make the

following special rules with respect to prisoners who are debtors:—

Admission, Discharge, and Removal.

1. Such prisoner shall not be required to take a bath on reception, if, on the application of the prisoner, the governor shall decide that it is unnecessary, or the surgeon shall state that it is, for medical reasons, unadvisable.

2. He shall at all times, except when at chapel or exercise, occupy the cell or room assigned to him.

Food, Clothing, and Bedding.

3. Any such prisoner who prefers to provide his own food shall give notice thereof beforehand at the time required, but the governor shall not permit such prisoner to receive any prison allowance of food at any meal for which he procures or receives food at his own expense.

4. Articles of food shall be received only at such hours as may be laid down from time to time. They shall be inspected by the officers of the prison, and shall be subject to such restrictions as may be necessary to prevent luxury or waste.

5. Any such prisoner shall not, during the 24 hours, receive or purchase more than one pint of malt liquor, fermented liquor, or cider, or, if an adult, half a pint (8 ozs.) of wine.

6. No such prisoner shall be allowed to sell or transfer any article whatsoever allowed to be introduced for his use to any other person.

Personal Cleanliness.

7. Such prisoner shall not be compelled either to have his hair cut or (if he usually wears his beard, etc.) to shave, except on account of vermin or dirt, or when the surgeon deems it necessary on the ground of health and cleanliness; and the hair of such prisoner shall not be cut closer than may be necessary for the purpose of health and cleanliness.

8. The beds of such prisoners shall be made, and the rooms and yards in their occupation shall be swept and cleaned by them, every morning. The furniture and utensils appropriated to their use shall be kept clean and neatly arranged by them.

Religious Instruction.

9. No such prisoner who is attended or visited by a minister of a church or persuasion differing from the Established Church, shall be compelled to attend any religious services except those of the said church or persuasion; but, subject to the foregoing provisions, such prisoner shall attend Divine service on Sundays and on other days when such service is performed, unless prevented by illness or excused by the Visiting Committee or governor for any other reason.

Visits to and Communications with Prisoners.

10. The Visiting Committee or governor, before granting any permission, which by the following rules they are authorized or required to grant, shall satisfy themselves that it can be granted without interfering with the security, good order, and government of the prison and prisoners therein; and if, after it has been granted, its continuance seems likely to cause any such interference, or the prisoner has abused such permission, or been guilty of any misconduct, the Visiting Committee shall have power to suspend or withdraw such permission, and in the like circumstances the governor may suspend or withdraw the same if it has been granted by himself, or, if the case is urgent, suspend it if it has been granted by the Visiting Committee, provided that he report the case within 24 hours to them.

11. The place in which such prisoners receive their visits shall not be the same as that in which criminal prisoners receive their visits, if any other suitable place can conveniently be provided.

12. Each such prisoner shall be permitted to be visited by one friend or relation, or (if circumstances permit) by two such persons at the same time once a month, for a period of a quarter of an hour, during such hours as may from time to time be appointed. They shall also be allowed to write one letter and to receive one letter in each month.

13. The Visiting Committee may, by permission in any special case, for special reasons, prolong the period of the visit allowed to any such prisoner, or allow him to be visited by more than two persons at the same time.

THE PRISON RULES, 1878. 279

14. Debtors shall also be subject to any general rules made by the Secretary of State for the government of prisons, except so far as the same are inconsistent with the special rules relating to debtors.

1_5_. The foregoing rules relating to debtors shall apply to any person committed to prison for default in payment of any debt, or instalment of any debt, or any_sum of _money, due from or payable by such person in_pursuance of any order or judgment of any county court or other competent court, or any order of a justice or justices, unless, by_the terms of the warrant of commitment,_the imprisonment is to be with hard labour.

16. The foregoing rules shall come into operation on the 15th of April, 1878.

Settled and approved this 19th day of February, 1878,

Rich^{D.} Assheton Cross,

One of Her Majesty's principal Secretaries of State.

General Rules for Government of Prisons.

In pursuance of The Prison Act, 1877, I hereby make the following general rules for the government of prisons:—

Admission, Discharge, and Removal of Prisoners.

1. Every prisoner shall take a bath on reception, unless it shall be otherwise directed in any particular case by the governor or medical officer, or as provided in the rules.

2. Every prisoner shall on admission be examined by the surgeon separately.

3. If any prisoner is found to have any cutaneous disease, or to be infested with vermin, means shall be taken effectually to eradicate and destroy the same.

4. Every prisoner shall be weighed on reception, and subsequently at such periods as the Commissioners may order or the surgeon may require, and the result shall be recorded by the surgeon.

5. Every prisoner may, if required for purposes of justice, be photographed on reception and subsequently; but no

copy of such photograph shall be given to any persons except those officially authorized to receive it for the purposes of identification.

6. Such of the clothing, linen, and other articles belonging to prisoners as may be retained in the prison shall, if necessary, be washed, cleaned, or disinfected as soon as possible after they are received.

7. After prisoners are received at the prison, the abstract of the rules relating to the conduct and treatment of prisoners shall be read over to them, and proper means shall afterwards be taken by the governor for making them acquainted with the purport and effect of such rules.

8. If the divisions and cells appropriated to any class of prisoners should be full, while other wards and cells are unoccupied, the governor may use such spare room for prisoners of another class, provided the prisoners of different classes are prevented from exercising together.

9. Prisoners shall be exposed to public view as little as possible while being removed from or to prison. In order to avoid such exposure while passing through the public streets, they shall, if necessary, be conveyed in a cab or other closed vehicle.

10. The gratuity granted to a prisoner may be paid to him through a Prisoners' Aid Society, or in such manner as the Commissioners may direct, for the purpose of preventing its being misapplied by the prisoner, and he may be required to take the value of it in whole or in part in some article which will be useful to him.

11. Before a prisoner under the age of 16 years is discharged, the governor shall inform his relatives and friends on what day and at what time he will be discharged, that they may have the opportunity of attending to receive him; but if such relatives or friends are known to be bringing such young prisoner up in evil courses, then the governor may, with the consent of the Visiting Committee, abstain from informing his relatives, if some other respectable person, to be approved by the Visiting Committee, is willing to take care of him, and the prisoner consents.

12. The child of a female prisoner may be received into prison with its mother, provided it is at the breast; in all

such cases an authority from the committing magistrate for the child's admission should accompany the prisoner on reception.

13. Any such child so admitted shall not be taken from its mother until the surgeon of the prison certifies that it is in a fit condition to be removed.

14. When any such child has attained the age of nine months, the surgeon shall report whether it is desirable or necessary that it should be any longer retained; but except under special circumstances, no such child shall be kept in prison after it has arrived at the age of 12 months.

15. Any such child so retained may be supplied with clothing at the public expense.

16. Previous to the discharge of any such child, the governor shall ascertain from the relations whether they are willing and in a position to receive it; in the event of their being unable to do so, he shall cause it to be sent to the union or workhouse of the parish in which the mother was apprehended, having previously communicated thereon with the workhouse authorities.

Food, Clothing, and Bedding of Prisoners.

17. A prisoner who has any complaint to make regarding the diet furnished to him, or wishes his diet to be weighed to ascertain whether he is supplied with the authorized quantity, must make his request as soon as possible after the diet is handed to him, and it will be weighed in his presence and in that of the officer deputed for that purpose. Should, however, repeated complaints of a groundless nature be made by any prisoner under colour of this rule, with the evident purpose of giving annoyance or trouble, it shall be treated as a breach of prison discipline, and the offender will be liable to punishment accordingly.

18. Such additional clothing and bedding may be issued during severe weather, or in special cases, as the surgeon may deem requisite.

19. A convicted criminal prisoner shall, during the whole of his sentence when it does not exceed one month, and during one month of his sentence when it exceeds one month, be required to sleep on a plank bed. The prisoner shall be

allowed the opportunity of earning by industry the gradual remission of this requirement after the expiration of one month; but after he has earned such remission, he shall be liable to forfeit the same on account of idleness, inattention to instruction, or misconduct.

Personal Cleanliness.

20. Prisoners shall obey such regulations as regards washing, bathing, hair cutting, and shaving as may be from time to time established with a view to a proper maintenance of health and cleanliness.

21. They shall be allowed a proper supply of clean linen, towels, etc.

22. No prisoner shall be stripped or bathed in the presence of any other prisoner.

23. Prisoners shall keep their cells, utensils, clothing, and bedding clean and neatly arranged, and shall clean and sweep the yards, passages, and other parts of the prison as may be directed, unless provision for the performance of these duties is otherwise made in accordance with the rules.

Employment of Prisoners.

24. A male prisoner above 16 years of age, who has been committed to prison to be imprisoned with hard labour, shall, during the whole of his sentence when it does not exceed one month, and during one month of his sentence when it exceeds one month, be kept to hard labour of the first class. Moreover he shall for the rest of his term of imprisonment be kept to hard labour of the first class, unless he avail himself of the opportunity which shall be duly given to him of earning, by industry, the privilege of remission to hard labour of the second class; and after he has earned such privilege, he shall be liable to forfeit the same on account of idleness, inattention to instruction, or misconduct.

25. No prisoner who is a Jew shall be compelled to labour on his Sabbath.

Religious Instruction.

26. Each prisoner who can read shall be furnished with a Bible and prayer book, such as is approved for the denomination to which he belongs.

27. The chaplain shall, as soon as possible after the 31st December, send to the Prison Commissioners a report with reference to the year on the religious and moral condition of the prisoners, the result of the instruction given in the schools, and such other matters belonging to his department as he may from time to time be desired to report on.

28. He shall report periodically, and from time to time, for the information of the Commissioners, on such points connected with his department as he may think it desirable to bring before them, or as they may from time to time direct.

29. He shall attend the prison daily, recording in his journal the times of his arrival and departure, as well as of his presence in the chapel, and the duties he performed.

30. He shall notify the times of the administration of the Holy Sacrament, and that prisoners desiring to become communicants must signify their wish to him before the time appointed, in order that he may confer with them thereon.

31. He shall see and admonish the prisoners on admission and discharge; he shall also occasionally see each prisoner separately.

32. He shall daily visit the infirmary and sick and the prisoners under punishment in the punishment cells, and attend at all reasonable times any prisoners who may require spiritual advice and assistance.

33. He shall pay particular attention to a prisoner under orders for execution or committed on a charge punishable with death.

34. A prison minister shall be made acquainted with the names of all prisoners of his persuasion, and with such other particulars respecting them as may be necessary for the performance of his duties.

35. Such prison minister shall have access to such prisoners at the usual hours for the purpose of affording to them religious instruction; but he shall not hold communication with any prisoners other than those of his own persuasion.

36. Such prison minister shall perform Divine service at such times as may be appointed, if it should appear to the

Commissioners that there is a substantial number of prisoners to attend, and the circumstances of the prison admit of the necessary arrangements for the purpose being made.

37. Such prison minister shall, so far as may be practicable, see and admonish every prisoner of his persuasion, both on admission and on discharge, and he shall visit any prisoners of his persuasion who may require spiritual advice and assistance.

38. Such prison minister shall visit the sick prisoners of his persuasion as the exigencies of each case may require.

39. Such prison minister shall pay particular attention to a prisoner of his persuasion under order for execution or committed on a charge punishable with death.

40. Such prison minister shall have access to the catalogue of books to be issued to prisoners, and no book to which he makes objection shall be issued to any prisoner of his persuasion.

41. Such prison minister shall, in carrying out his duties, be careful not to interfere with the established rules and regulations of the prison or the routine of discipline and labour. He shall confer with the governor on all points connected with his duty; and he shall co-operate with him and with the other officials of the prison in promoting the good order of the establishment so far as concerns the duties of his office.

Instruction.

42. A library shall be provided in each prison, consisting of such books as may from time to time be sanctioned by the Commissioners, which may be furnished to the prisoners under the conditions laid down from time to time; and except as provided in the rules, no newspapers or books, other than those supplied to the prison library, shall be permitted for the use of prisoners.

43. The school shall be under the superintendence of the governor or the chaplain, as may be directed.

44. Prisoners who do not do their best to profit by the instruction afforded them may be deprived of any advantages which might be accorded to them, in the same way as if they had been idle or negligent at labour.

Visits to and Communications with Prisoners.

45. A convicted prisoner, after three months of the term of his sentence have expired, shall, provided his conduct and industry have been satisfactory, be allowed to communicate with his relatives and respectable friends by letter, and to be visited by them in the prison; and subsequently he shall be allowed the same privilege at intervals, to be determined according to his good conduct and industry.

No other person shall be allowed to communicate with a prisoner except by special authority. These privileges may be forfeited at any time for misconduct or breach of regulations of the prison.

46. No visitor shall be admitted until he has given his name and address, and relationship to or connection with the prisoner, if any, and these particulars shall be duly recorded.

47. If a member of the Visiting Committee shall have issued an order that any particular person shall not be allowed to visit a prisoner, or if the governor shall know any sufficient cause why any visitor should not be admitted, the governor shall refuse admission to such person, duly recording the circumstances in his journal, and reporting the same to the Visiting Committee.

48. Visitors to prisoners shall be admitted only to the place appropriated for the purpose, except in special cases under the authority of the Commissioners of Prisons; and in the case of prisoners reported by the surgeon to be seriously ill, who may be visited elsewhere by any near relative or friend, by a written order of the governor.

49. Male prisoners shall be visited in the presence of a male officer; female prisoners in the presence of a female officer.

50. The Visiting Committee may, in any special case, for special reasons, extend the period of the visit allowed to any prisoner.

51. No person shall be allowed to visit a prisoner on a Sunday, except in cases of emergency.

52. Officers of police may visit prisoners for the purpose of identification, on production of an order from the proper police or magisterial authority.

53. If there are reasonable grounds for suspecting that any person, who is admitted within the prison for the purpose of seeing a prisoner, brings in or takes out any articles for an improper purpose, or contrary to the regulations of the prison, the governor is authorized to suspend the visit of such person, duly recording the fact in his journal, and reporting it to the Visiting Committee.

54. If any person is committed to prison in default of the payment of any sum which in pursuance of any conviction or order he is required to pay, such person shall be allowed to communicate by letter with and to see any of his friends at any reasonable time, for the *bonâ fide* purpose of providing for the payment which would procure his release from prison.

Prison Offences.

55. No prisoner shall be punished until he has had an opportunity of hearing the charges and evidence against him, and of making his defence.

56. No dietary punishment shall be inflicted, on any prisoner, nor shall he be placed in a punishment cell, nor shall corporal punishment be inflicted, unless the surgeon shall certify that such prisoner is in a fit condition of health to undergo such punishment.

57. The following offences committed by male prisoners convicted of felony, or sentenced to hard labour, will render them liable to corporal punishment :—

1st. Mutiny, or open incitement to mutiny, in the prison; personal violence to any officer of the prison; aggravated or repeated assault on a fellow-prisoner; repetition of insulting or threatening language to any officer or prisoner.

2nd. Wilfully and maliciously breaking the prison windows, or otherwise destroying the prison property.

3rd. When under punishment, wilfully making a disturbance tending to interrupt the order and discipline of the prison, and any other act of gross misconduct or insubordination requiring to be suppressed by extraordinary means.

58. Corporal punishment, in the case of prisoners over 18 years of age, shall be inflicted with a "cat" or birch rod; and in the case of prisoners under 18 years of age, with a birch rod; the instruments, in both instances, shall be of a pattern approved by the Secretary of State.

59. The number of lashes inflicted on a prisoner over 18 years of age shall not exceed 36; or on a prisoner under 18 years of age, 18.

60. The order for the punishment shall be duly entered in the appointed manner, and the number of lashes, and the instrument with which they are to be inflicted, shall, in all cases, be stated in such order.

61. No irons or other means of restraint shall be made use of except those of such patterns as have been approved by the Secretary of State.

Prisoners under Sentence of Death.

62. A prisoner under sentence of death may be visited by such of his relations, friends, and legal advisers as he may desire to see, by an order in writing from a member of the Visiting Committee.

63. If any person make it appear to a member of the Visiting Committee that he has important business to transact with the convict, such member may grant permission, in writing, to such person to have a conference with the prisoner.

Prison Officers.

64. It is the duty of all officers to treat the prisoners with kindness and humanity, to listen patiently to and report their complaints or grievances, being firm at the same time in maintaining order and discipline, and enforcing complete observance of the rules and regulations of the prison.

65. Officers shall duly inform the governor of any prisoner who desires to see him, or to make any complaint or prefer any request to him or to any superior authority. Any neglect in carrying out this instruction will be most severely dealt with.

66. It shall be the duty of every officer to direct the attention of the governor to any prisoner who may appear

to him not in health, although he may not complain; or whose state of mind may appear to him deserving of special notice and care, in order that the opinion and instructions of the medical officer may be taken on the case.

67. No officer shall strike a prisoner, unless compelled to do so in self-defence.

68. No subordinate officer, on any pretence whatever, through favour, or mistaken notions of kindness, shall fail to make an immediate report to the governor, or other his superior officer, of any misconduct or wilful disobedience of the prison regulations.

69. No subordinate officer shall unnecessarily converse with a prisoner, nor allow any familiarity on the part of prisoners towards himself or any other officer of the prison; nor shall he on any account speak of his duties, or of any matters of discipline or prison arrangement, within the hearing of the prisoners.

70. No officer shall have any pecuniary dealing whatsoever with any prisoner, or employ any prisoner on his private account, nor shall he correspond with or hold any intercourse with the friends or relatives of any prisoner, unless expressly authorized by the governor; nor shall he make any unauthorized communications concerning the prison or prisoners to any person whatever.

71. All officers shall be careful not to allow any prisoners under their charge to be employed, directly or indirectly, for the private benefit or advantage of any person or persons, or in any way not in conformity to the established rules of the prison.

72. All officers will be held responsible for being fully acquainted with the rules and orders relating to their respective duties. They shall strictly conform to and obey the orders of the governor in every respect. They shall assist him in maintaining order and discipline among the prisoners. For this end, punishment for prison offences must sometimes be resorted to by the governor, upon their report; but good temper and good example on the part of the officers will have great influence in preventing the frequent recurrence of offences, and the necessity for such punishments.

73. Every officer shall treat members of the Visiting

Committee with the greatest courtesy and respect. Any infringement of this rule will render the offender liable to severe punishment.

74. Any officer desiring to appeal against any decision which affects him, or wishing to bring any matter before superior authority, will state his complaint for the consideration of the Commissioners.

75. No officer shall use tobacco or spirituous liquors within the prison walls, except under such restrictions as to time and place as may be laid down by the governor and approved by the Commissioners.

76. Every officer who shall, contrary to orders, bring in or carry out, or endeavour to bring in or carry out, or knowingly allow to be brought in or carried out to or for any prisoner, any money, clothing, provisions, tobacco, letters, papers, or other articles whatsoever, shall be forthwith suspended from his office by the governor of the prison, who shall report the offence to the Commissioners.

77. Officers may, if the terms of the contract permit it, purchase provisions for the use of themselves and their families at the contract rates.

78. All reports, etc., by officers ordered by The Prison Act, 1865, shall be made to the Commissioners.

Gaoler or Governor.

79. The governor may, if the terms of the contract permit it, purchase provisions for the use of his family at the contract rate; but with this exception, he shall not have for his own use, or that of any other person, any dealings with any tradesmen supplying the prison.

80. He shall take care that the labour of all the prisoners is made use of in such a way as to be to the best advantage to the public service, and shall not employ or allow to be employed any prisoner in any private work whatever, for himself or for any other officer of the prison.

81. All orders or communications having reference to any department of a prison shall be addressed to the governor as the responsible head of the establishment, whose duty it shall be to communicate them as the orders of superior authority to all officers of the department concerned, and they shall be

obeyed in the same manner as if addressed to those officers themselves.

82. He shall bring to the notice of the Visiting Committee the case of any child of tender years who may be sentenced to imprisonment in the prison, in order that they may, if they think fit, report the case to the Secretary of State.

83. He shall use his best endeavours to assist in the identification of prisoners, and with that object shall furnish to the governors of other prisons and to the police any information in his power.

84. He shall not allow any person to view the prison, except as provided by statute, or with an order from the Commissioners, or by persons authorized according to instructions which may be issued from time to time, and shall be careful that no visitor holds any communication with any prisoner unless duly authorized to do so.

85. He shall notify to the chaplain or the visiting minister of the religious denomination to which a prisoner belongs, any case in which the life of such prisoner appears to be in danger.

86. He shall carry into effect the written directions of the medical officer for the supply of any additional articles which the medical officer may deem necessary in any particular case.

87. He shall pay attention to the ventilation, drainage, and sanitary condition of the prison, and take such measures as may be necessary for their being maintained in perfect order.

88. The governor and medical officer shall frequently examine and see that the washing places, baths, fumigating ovens, and other provision for like purposes are in efficient working order; and it shall be the duty of any officer to report at once any defect by which these arrangements do not effect their proper object.

89. He shall hear the reports every day at such hour as shall be most convenient.

90. He shall take care that every prisoner having a complaint to make or request to prefer to him should have ample facilities for doing so, and he shall redress any grievance or take such steps as may seem necessary, recording the same in the appointed manner.

91. He shall forward to the Commissioners without delay any report or complaint which any officer of the prison may desire to make to them, and shall on no account suppress it, but he may offer any explanation with it which it may seem to require.

92. He shall inform the Visiting Committee of any prisoner who desires to see them.

93. He shall enforce the observance of silence throughout the prison, and prevent all intercourse or communication between the prisoners, so far as the conduct of the business of the prison or the labour of the prisoners will permit, and shall take care that all necessary and unavoidable intercourse or communication between them be conducted in such manner only as he shall from time to time direct.

94. He shall, at least once in each day, visit every cell in which a prisoner is located in solitary confinement, and shall see that every prisoner in a punishment cell shall be visited during the day at intervals of not greater than three hours by the appointed officer.

95. He shall take care that no prisoner is subjected to any punishment which the medical officer is not satisfied he is capable of undergoing.

96. In case he shall put a prisoner in irons or under mechanical restraint, he shall give notice thereof forthwith to the Visiting Committee, and he shall not keep a prisoner in irons or under mechanical restaint for more than 24 hours without an order in writing from the Visiting Committee, specifying the cause thereof and the time during which the prisoner is to be kept in irons or under mechanical restraint, which order shall be preserved by the governor as his warrant.

97. Upon the death of any prisoner the governor shall give immediate notice thereof to one of the Visiting Committee.

98. The governor, before granting any permission for any purpose to any prisoner by authority of the rules applicable to the class to which such prisoner belongs, shall satisfy himself that it can be granted without interfering with the security, good order, and government of the prison and the prisoners therein; and if after it has been granted its con-

tinuance seems likely to cause any such interference, or the prisoner has abused such permission, or has been guilty of any misconduct, he shall have power to suspend or withdraw such permission. Further, where such permission has been granted by the Visiting Committee, he shall, in the like circumstances, have power to suspend it, if the case is urgent, provided that he report the same, within 24 hours, to them.

99. He shall enter in his journal all cases, together with the reasons, where such permission as is mentioned in the foregoing rule has been granted, suspended, or withdrawn, whether by himself or by the Visiting Committee.

100. He shall, if any doubt arises as to which class of rules is applicable to any prisoner, report the case forthwith to the Commissioners for reference to the Secretary of State, whose decision thereon shall be final.

Matron.

101. The matron shall take care that no male officer or visitor enters the division of the prison allotted to females, unless accompanied by herself or some other female officer.

Surgeon.

102. The surgeon shall medically examine every prisoner on reception, and shall record his state of health and such other facts connected therewith as may be directed.

103. He shall inform the governor of any particular point which he may become aware of in regard to the prisoner's person, which might assist in identifying him.

104. He shall report to the governor the case of any prisoner to which he may think it necessary on medical grounds to draw attention; and whenever he shall be of opinion that the life of any prisoner is endangered by his continuance in prison, he shall state such opinion and the grounds thereof in writing to the governor, who shall duly report the circumstance to the Commissioners.

105. He shall examine every prisoner sentenced to hard labour, and shall report if he is unfit to be kept at hard labour of either the first or second class or at any particular kind of labour, and shall assist when called on in assigning

the task of labour according to the physical capacity of a prisoner. He shall from time to time examine the prisoners during the time of their being employed at hard labour, and shall report and enter in his journal the name of any prisoner whose health he thinks to be endangered by a continuance at hard labour of any particular kind, and report the same to the governor; and thereupon such prisoner shall not again be employed at such labour until the surgeon certifies that he is fit for such employment.

106. He shall report to the governor any case in which the discipline or treatment seems likely to injure the health of any prisoner, and the governor shall issue such directions as the circumstances may require.

107. He shall examine any prisoner before corporal punishment is inflicted on him, and certify whether or not such prisoner is fit for corporal punishment.

108. He shall keep such statistical records of the health of the prisoners as may be directed.

109. He shall report periodically, and from time to time as may be directed, on the general health and sanitary condition of the establishment, the health of the officers, their capability for performing their duties, the health of the prisoners, and in reference to any other point upon which he may be directed to report.

110. No article, whether of food, bedding, clothing, or of any other kind, shall be received into the prison until it has been examined to ascertain that it contains nothing contrary to the rules of the prison, and the admission of any article which appears likely to be used for an improper purpose may be refused by order of the governor.

111. The foregoing rules shall come into force in each prison on the 15th day of April, 1878.

Settled and approved this 19th day of February, 1878.

RICH^D. ASSHETON CROSS,

One of Her Majesty's principal Secretaries of State.

INDEX.

Aberystwith:
borough prison of, to be discontinued, 48, 103.

Abolition:
of office of prison officers, provisions as to, 27, 179, 180.
of distinction between gaol and house of correction, 29, 98.
of local obligation to maintain prisons, 8, 163.

Abstract of Regulations, &c.:
to be posted up in every cell, 133.
duties of gaoler as to, 133, 280.

Abuses in Prisons:
chaplain to communicate to gaoler, 126.
to enter in his journal, 126.
entries as to, by justice of the peace, in visitor's book, 23, 162.
Prison Commissioners to inquire into, 18, 156.
Visiting Committee to report on, 22, 160.
Visiting Committee to bring to notice of the Commissioners, 263.

Accommodation: (See Cell Accommodation).

Accountants:
appointment of, 16, 154.

Accounts:
what to be kept by gaoler, 134.

Act:
short title of, (1865), 1, 60; (1877), 1, 149.
commencement of (1865), 1, 60; (1877), 1, 149.
application of (1865), 1, 60; (1877), 1, 150.
Gaol, meaning of term, 5, 107.

Action:
for anything done under P. A., 1865, provisions as to, 46, 94.
as to costs in, 46, 94.
venue and commencement of, 47, 94.
recovery of penalties by, under Mutiny Act, 242.

Acts:
named in Schedule III. of P. A., 1865, repeal of, 52, 106.

Acts (continued)—
  saving clauses as to repeal of, 52, 53, 106.
  saving clause as to repealed provisions referred to in certain, 53, 107.
  inconsistent with the P. A., 1877, repealed, 54, 192.

Aid Society, Prisoners': (See Prisoners' Aid Society).

Airing Grounds:
  included in term "prison," 2, 61.

Alderman:
  not to be interested in any contract relating to borough gaol, 208.
  penalty for being so interested, 208.

Allowance:
  to prisoners, on their discharge from prison, 43, 89, 173, 280.
  to prison authority, in respect of uncompleted prison, 11, 166.
  out of earnings, to debtors, 121.
    to acquitted prisoners, &c., 121.
    to prisoners awaiting trial, 271.
    to misdemeanants of first division, 275.

Annuity:
  to prison officers by way of superannuation, 27, 70. 108. 180. 194.
  of prison officers, apportionment and payment of, 28, 180.

Apartments:
  removal of prison officers from, 28. 71.
  when visitors not to sleep in, of subordinate officers, 115.

Application:
  of P. A., 1865, 1, 60.
  of P. A., 1877. 1, 150.
  summary, to a judge for removal of prisoner, 30, 172.

Appointment:
  of prison officers, to vest in Secretary of State, 14, 151.
        general provisions as to, 23, 24, 66, 109.
  of Prison Commissioners, 15, 153.
  of Inspectors, officers, and servants, provisions as to. 16, 154.
  of subordinate officers, 18, 155.
  of Visiting Justices, 20, 96.
  repeal of provisions as to, of Visiting Justices. 20, 158.
  of Visiting Committee of prisons, 21, 158.
  rules as to first, of Visiting Committee, 250, 251.
  of Visiting Committee, by what sessions to be made, 252—258.
  rules as to, of Visiting Committee, after the year 1878, 262.
  of chaplain to two prisons, 26, 69.
  of assistant-chaplain and deputy gaoler, 26. 69.
  of Inspectors, repeal of 5 & 6 Will. IV., c. 38, s. 7, as to. 53, 188.
  of Surveyor-General of prisons, 82.

Apportionment:
  of annuity granted to prison officers, 28, 180.

Appropriation:
of prisons for purposes of classification, 30. 31. 83, 170, 171.
of court houses, &c., within the curtilage of a prison, 14, 191.

Arbitration:
certain differences may be referred to under P. A. 1865, 47. 95.
power of Secretary of State and of prison authority to refer any matter to, under P. A.. 1877, 47, 194.
of dispute respecting contract for maintenance of prisoners, 83.
difference as regards amount payable in respect of lands included in term "prison," under P. A., 1877, may be referred to, 197.
of disputes, as to contribution by ridings, &c., to gaol expenses, 202.
of disputes, respecting payment of costs of certain prosecutions, 207.

Arithmetic:
prisoners to be taught, 127.

Assignee:
power of, to obtain payment of loan made to a prison authority, under P. A.. 1865. 80.

Assistant-Chaplain: (See also Chaplain).
when he may be appointed. 26, 69.
to be a clergyman of the Established Church, 26. 69.
notice of appointment of, to be sent to bishop. 26 69.
not to officiate until licensed by the bishop, 26, 69.
powers and duties of, 126.
substitute to be provided on death of, 126.
when he may accept assistance in performance of Divine service, 126.
may perform chaplain's duties on execution of capital sentences, 229.

Assisting Prisoners to Escape:
offence of, and punishment for, 40, 87.

Bankruptcy:
to what prison, court having jurisdiction in, may commit, 230.
penalty for refusal by gaoler to receive persons committed, 230.

Bedding:
criminal prisoner may procure or receive before trial. 118.
of criminal prisoner not to be sold, &c., to other prisoners. 118.
convicted criminal prisoners to have prison allowance of, 119.
sufficient, to be provided for every prisoner, 120,
to be aired, changed, &c., as often as surgeon, &c., may direct, 120.
debtor may provide himself with, 118.
    not to sell to other prisoners, 118.
allowance of, to debtor, if unable to provide himself with, 118.
included in term "furniture and effects," 5, 195.
duty of surgeon respecting insufficiency of, 137.
when additional may be issued to prisoners, 281.
articles of, not to be received into prisons until examined, 293.
when gaoler may refuse admission of articles of, 293.

Beds:
of prisoners, and regulation as to sleeping, 120, 270, 275, 277, 281.

Beer:
prisoners awaiting trial, and debtors, may provide themselves with, 118, 269, 270, 277.
what quantity of, they may receive or buy, 270, 277.
quantity of, for misdemeanants of first division, 274.
not to be sold to other prisoners, 118, 270, 274, 277.
allowance of, to convicted criminal prisoners, 119.

Benefice:
not to be held by prison chaplain in certain cases, 26, 69.

Bishop:
notice of appointment of chaplain and of assistant-chaplain to be sent to, 26, 69.
chaplain and assistant-chaplain to obtain licence from, 26, 69.
reference to be made to, to decide difference of opinion between chaplain and visiting justices respecting books for religious instruction, 125.

Books:
special rules to be made as to retention of, by unconvicted prisoners, 39, 184.
provisions as to retention of, by unconvicted prisoners, 269.
when chaplain to direct what shall be distributed, &c., in prison for religious instruction, 125.
when prison minister to approve those intended for religious instruction, 126.
difference of opinion respecting, between chaplain and visiting justices, to be referred to the bishop, 125.
catalogue of, to be kept by gaoler, 126.
prison minister to have access to catalogue of, 284.
included in term "furniture and effects," 5, 195.
gaoler to be responsible for safe custody of, 134.
what to be kept by gaoler, 134.
of prison, Visiting Committee may inspect, 264.
supply of, to prisoners awaiting trial and to misdemeanants of the first division, 265, 270, 275.
power of prison minister to object to issue of certain, 284.
of what, prison library is to consist, 284.
what may be issued to prisoners, 284.

Borough: (See Municipal Borough).

Borough Gaol: (See also Prisons).
mayor, &c., not to be interested in any contract relating to, 208.
penalty for being so interested, 208.
may be built beyond the limits of the borough, 208.

Borough Rate:
how far expenses of prisons to be charged upon, 7, 65.

Borough Rate (continued)—
money borrowed for prisons to be charged upon, 79.
power of prison authority to borrow on security of, and to levy as if P. A., 1877, had not passed, 189.
Public Works Loan Commissioners may lend on security of, 190.
how far loan for prison purposes may be repaid out of, 210.
gaol rate to be made in the same manner as, 211.

Bradninch:
borough prison of, to be discontinued, 48, 103.

Bridewell: (See Prisons).
included in term "prison," 2, 61.

Buildings:
when included in term "prison," 2, 61, 197.

Calendar of Prisoners:
to be delivered by gaoler, to judges of assize and justices at Quarter Sessions, 33, 100.
sheriff no longer to be liable to deliver, 33, 100.
to be transmitted by gaoler to Secretary of State, 139.

Capital Punishment Amendment Act, 1868:
provisions of, 227, 228, 229.

Catalogue: (See also Inventory).
of all books, &c., admitted into prison to be kept by gaoler, 126.
of books issued to prisoners, prison minister to have access to, 284.

Cell Accommodation:
for a prisoner, definition of, 8, 196.
"sufficient accommodation," for prisoners, defined, 6, 196.
provision of, 7, 65.
termination of local obligation to provide, 8, 163.
when compensation to be made by prison authority in respect of unprovided, 8, 163.
how to be calculated, for certain purposes, on discontinuance of a prison, 52, 177.
compensation to be made to prison authority in respect of, when provided for prisoners of another authority, 9, 164.
compensation to prison authority in respect of, when more than adequate for its own prisoners, 10, 165.

Cells:
separate, to be provided in prisons, 34, 72.
to be certified for confinement of prisoners, 35, 73.
to be furnished with means of communication with officers, 35, 73.
when certified, to be distinguished by number, &c., 36, 74.
certified before P. A., 1865, to be deemed to be certified under, 36, 107.
abstract of certain regulations, &c., to be posted up in, 133.
of females, to be secured by locks different from those of males, 135.

INDEX. 299

Cells (continued)—
  to be examined frequently by subordinate officers, 138.
  punishment, to be provided and certified, 35, 36, 72, 73.
      limitation of time of confinement in, 40, 186.
      daily list of prisoners confined in, to be delivered to chaplain and surgeon, 133.
      prisoners confined in, to be visited daily by surgeon, 136.
      prisoners confined in, to be visited daily by chaplain, 283.
      prisoners not to be placed in, without surgeon's certificate, 286.
      how often prisoners in, to be visited by appointed officer, 291.
  when prisoners awaiting trial and misdemeanants of the first division may occupy specially fitted, 265, 266, 268, 273.
  in what, misdemeanants of first division are to be placed on admission, 273.
  misdemeanants of first division and debtors to occupy those assigned to them, 273, 277.
  when, for one class of prisoners, may be used for another, 280.
  duty of prisoners in keeping clean, 282.
  how often prisoners in solitary confinement in, to be visited, 291.

Certificate:
  of Inspector of Prisons, as to fitness of cells for prisoners, 35, 36, 73.
      may be varied or withdrawn, 36, 73, 74.
  of surgeon, to be given before removal, &c., of prisoners, 117.
      as to unfitness of prisoners for hard labour, 122.
      as to unfitness of female prisoner for hard labour, 122.
      as to due execution of judgment of death, 227.
      required for infliction of certain punishments, 286.
      as to fitness of prisoner for hard labour, 293.
  as to execution of judgment of death, penalty for signing a false, 228.
  printed copy of, to be exhibited near entrance of the prison, 228.
  medical, with respect to superannuation of prison officers, 27, 70, 180.

Chairman:
  of Prison Commissioners, Secretary of State may appoint, 15, 153.
  of Visiting Committee, to be appointed by Committee, 263.
  of Visiting Committee, to report names, &c., of members to Secretary of State, 263.

Chapel:
  when to be provided for prison, 79.
  when room to be used as, 124.
  to be used only for religious worship, or for religious and moral instruction of prisoners, 79.

Chaplain: (See also Assistant-Chaplain).
  to be appointed for every prison, 24, 67.

Chaplain (continued)—
    to be a clergyman of the Established Church, 24, 67
    appointment of, to two prisons, 26, 69.
    may not hold benefice or curacy in certain cases, 26, 69.
    notice of appointment of, to be sent to bishop, 26, 69.
    not to officiate, unless licensed by bishop, 26, 69.
    to read prayers daily, 124.
    to read portions of Scripture when giving religious instruction, 124.
    when to preach, 124.
    when to give religious and moral instruction to prisoners, 124.
    when to administer the Holy Sacrament, 124.
    to give notice as to administration of the Holy Sacrament, 283.
    frequently to visit every room and cell of the prison, 124.
    to direct what books shall be read and lessons taught, 124.
    books, &c., for religious instruction to be chosen by, 125.
    to communicate abuses in prison to gaoler, 126.
    to enter abuses in prison in his journal, 126.
    to take assistant-chaplain's duties in his absence, 126.
    when, and in what manner, substitute may be appointed by, 126.
    when he may accept help for performance of Divine service, 126.
    on death of, substitute to be appointed, 126.
    to have free access to prisoners under sentence of death, 130.
    daily list to be delivered to, of prisoners in punishment cells, 133.
    surgeon to call attention of, to prisoners appearing to require his special notice, 137.
    when to make entry of his visits in non-resident officers' book, 140.
    to be present at execution of capital sentences, 227.
    to sign a declaration of the due execution of capital sentences, 227.
    penalty for signing false declaration, &c., 228.
    duties of, as regards execution of capital sentences, may be performed by assistant-chaplain or other person acting as chaplain, 229.
    to send to Commissioners a yearly report on the religious condition, &c., of prisoners, 283.
    upon what matters, to report periodically, 283.
    duty of, in attending prison and making entries in his journal, 283.
    duty of, in seeing and admonishing prisoners, 283.
    to visit daily infirmary, prisoners in punishment cells, &c., 283.
    duty of, in attending to prisoners under orders for execution, &c., 283.
    when school to be under superintendence of, 284.
    gaoler to notify to, case of life of prisoner in danger, 290.

Chief Officer: (See Gaoler—Matron).
    of prison, included in term gaoler, 3, 61.

Child:
    when to be received into prison with female prisoner, 280.
    retention and clothing of, when received, 281.

INDEX. 301

Child (continued)—
    discharge of, from prison, 281.
    of tender years in prison, gaoler to report case of, to Visiting Committee, 290.

Christmas Day:
    prisoners not to be put to hard labour on, 122.
    chaplain to perform Divine service on, 124.

Cider:
    what quantity of, prisoners awaiting trial may procure, 270.
        misdemeanants of first division may procure, 274.
        debtors may procure, 277.
    not to be sold to other prisoners, 270, 274, 277.

City:
    county of a, of what county to be considered a part, 6, 197.

Civil Servants:
    existing officers of prisons in receipt of military or naval half-pay or pension, not to be subject to deduction from salary, on becoming, under P. A., 1877, 25, 178.

Cleanliness:
    in prisons, regulations as to, 115, 270, 275, 277, 282.
    personal, of prisoners, 120, 270, 275, 277, 282.
    cutting hair of prisoners for purposes of, 120, 121, 270, 275, 277, 282.
    power and duty of surgeon as to, on inspecting prison, 137.

Clerk of Gaol Sessions:
    to be elected by court of gaol sessions, 200.
    powers of, 200.
    duties of, in giving notice of holding of gaol sessions, 200, 201.
    not to be treasurer, 201.
    salary of, 201.
    duty of, as to transmitting orders for payment of gaol expenses, 202.

Clerk of the Peace:
    definition of, 3, 61.
    clerk of gaol sessions to have powers of, as regard such sessions, 200.
    power of, as to arbitration of dispute respecting gaol expenses, 202.
    conveyances, &c., of land, &c., may be made in the name of, 219.
    contracts, &c., may be entered into in the name of, 219.
    lands, &c., to be vested in, 219, 220.

Clothing: (See also Dress).
    debtor may procure for himself or receive, 118.
        not to sell to other prisoners, 118, 277.
        to receive prison allowance of, if unable to provide it, 118.
    criminal prisoner may procure or receive, before trial, 118.
        not to sell, &c., to other prisoners, 118.
    included in term "furniture and effects," 5, 195.
    return of, to discharged prisoners, 120.

Clothing (continued)—
  provision of, for discharged prisoners, 120.
  purification and disinfection of, 120, 280.
  duty of surgeon respecting insufficiency of, 137.
  provision of, for children of female prisoners, in prisons, 281.
  when additional, may be issued to prisoners, 281.
  when misdemeanants of first division to wear their own, 265, 274.
  suspension of officers, for carrying into or out of prison, contrary to orders, 289.
  articles of, not to be received into prisons until examined, 293.
  when gaoler may refuse admission of articles of, 293.

Commencement:
  of P. A., 1865, 1, 60; of P. A., 1877, 1, 149.
  of action, suit, &c., for anything done under P. A., 1865, 47, 94.

Commissioners: (See Public Works Loan Commissioners—Prison Commissioners).

Commissions:
  of Gaol Delivery, &c., saving as to, 34, 109.

Commissioners Clauses Act, 1847:
  incorporation of certain clauses of, with P. A., 1865, 80.

Commitment of Prisoners:
  to what prison it may be, 30, 172.
  for matter arising in one county, to prison in adjoining, 30, 170, 260.
  saving as to validity of, in certain cases, 30, 172.
  prohibition of, to certain prisons, 48, 103.
  of prisoners for trial at assizes or sessions, to what house of correction it may be, 204.
  of persons convicted of capital offences, 205.
  of persons by court having jurisdiction in bankruptcy, 230.

Committee: (See Visiting Committee of Prisons).

Common Law Procedure Act, 1854:
  certain provisions of, to apply to arbitration, under P. A., 1865, and P. A., 1877, 47, 95, 195.

Communication: (See also Letters—Visits).
  criminal prisoners to be prevented from holding, 35, 72.
  between unconvicted prisoners, their solicitors and friends, special rules to be made as to, 39, 184, 185.
  with prisoners by friends, &c., regulations as to, 127, 271, 275, 278, 285, 286.
  supply of paper, &c., to prisoners awaiting trial for purposes of, with friends, 271.
  confidential written, of prisoner awaiting trial to his solicitor, to be exempt from examination, 271.
  written, what to be considered as a letter, and inspected, 271.
  unauthorised, not to be made by officers as to prison, &c., 288.

Communication (continued)—
   unauthorised, between visitors and prisoners to be prevented, 290.
   between prisoners, duties of gaoler as to, 291.

Compensation:
   by a prison authority in place of prison accommodation, 8, 163.
   when deduction may be made from amount of, 9, 164.
   Public Works Loan Commissioners may lend money for payment of, 9, 164.
   to a prison authority in respect of accommodation provided for prisoners of another authority, 9, 164.
   in respect of accommodation more than adequate for prisoners of an authority, 10, 165.
   not to be paid in respect of certain discontinued prisons, 10, 166.
   when Secretary of State may decline to recommend payment of, 10, 166.
   to persons deprived of office by closing of prisons scheduled in P. A., 1865, 49, 105.
   power of justices in sessions assembled to allow, to officers of certain discontinued prisons, 225, 226.

Complaints:
   against officers, by inspector of prisons, to be reported, 17, 77.
   duty of Visiting Committee as to, 22, 160, 264.
   power of a Justice of the Peace as to, 23, 162.
   of prisoners as to food, when to be made, 281.
   when complaints of prisoners as to food may be punished, 281.
   made by prisoners, prison officers to report, 287.
   by prisoners, gaoler's duty in hearing, &c., 290.
   by prison officers, when gaoler to send to Commissioners, 291.

Confinement:
   of prisoners, before and during trial, 30, 170, 259.
         after conviction, 31, 171.
   limitation of time of, in punishment cells, 40, 186.
   of debtors, and non-criminal prisoners, 31, 35, 72, 171, 259.

Constable:
   power of, to convey a prisoner to or from prison, 32, 172.
   every prison officer to be a, 131.

Contempt of Court:
   treatment of persons imprisoned for, 40, 186, 267.
   commitment of prisoners in, from borough to county gaol, 209.

Contracts:
   by prison authority, how to be made, 11, 64.
   by prison authority for maintenance, &c., of prisoners, 8, 82.
   how expenses of, to be defrayed, 83.
   determination of, between prison authorities, 12, 168.
   provision as to, when intended to be renewed, 10, 165.
   power of Prison Commissioners to make, 18, 155.

Contracts (continued)—
    all debts due in respect of, to be paid by prison authority, 13, 169.
    continuing, provision as to, 13, 169.
    for supply of prison, officers not to have any interest in, 131.
    when they may be entered into in name of Clerk of the Peace, 219.
    mayor, &c., not to be interested in, relating to borough gaols. 208.
    prison, members of Visiting Committee not to be interested in, 263.
    prison, when prison officers may purchase provisions under, 289.
    prison, when gaoler may purchase provisions under, 289.

Conveyance:
    by or to prison authority, how to be executed, 11, 64.
    of land, &c., may be made to Clerk of the Peace in counties, 219.
    to be valid, although not enrolled, 220.

Convict Prisons:
    P. A., 1865, and P. A., 1877, not to apply to, 1, 61, 150.
    provisions of The Prevention of Crimes Act, 1871, as to registering and photographing criminals, not to apply to, 232.

Coroner:
    jurisdiction of, how far affected by transfer of prisons, 30, 174.
    duty of, as to holding inquests on prisoners dying in prison, 44, 93.
    death of a prisoner in prison to be reported to, 133.
    to what house of correction he may commit prisoners for trial, 204.
    duty of, as to holding inquests on bodies of executed criminals, 227.

Corporal Punishment of Prisoners:
    order of two justices required for, 22, 161.
    to be attended by gaoler and surgeon, 130.
    duty of surgeon in giving directions on infliction of, 130.
    gaoler to carry into effect surgeon's directions respecting, 130.
    particulars of, to be entered by gaoler in punishment book, 130.
    of military offenders, 237.
    of marine offenders, 244.
    surgeon's certificate required for infliction of, 286.
    what offences to render certain male prisoners liable to, 286.
    how to be inflicted, 287.
    of what number of lashes to consist, 287.
    order for, to specify number of lashes, &c., and to be entered 287.
    surgeon to examine prisoners, and certify their fitness for, 293.

Councilman:
    not to be interested in any contract relating to borough gaol, 208.
    penalty for being so interested, 208.

County:
    definition of, 6, 196.
    of a city, or of a town, to be included in term ' borough," in P. A., 1877, 2, 197.

INDEX. 305

County (*continued*)—
    city of London to be deemed to be a, 6, 196.
    of what, certain counties of cities, &c., to be deemed part. 6, 197.
    how far liable to maintain prison, 7, 65.
    termination of obligation of a, to maintain a prison, &c., 8 163.
    certain gaols still to be deemed part of, although within limits of a municipal borough, &c., 208, 209.
    one prison, at least, to be continued in every, except, &c., 51, 175.

County Gaol : (See also Prisons).
    when to remain part of the county, although within limits of a municipal borough. 208, 209.
    when certain borough debtors, &c., may be committed to, 209.
    expenses of borough prisoners in, how to be defrayed. 212.
    expenses of conveyance, &c., of borough prisoners to, 213.
    confinement of debtors in, when adapted for them as a class, 216.

County Rate :
    how far liable for prison accommodation, 7, 8, 65.
    money borrowed for prisons to be charged upon, 79.
    prison authority may borrow on security of, and levy, as if P. A., 1877, had not passed, 189.
    Public Works Loan Commissioners may lend on security of, 190.
    when municipal borough to be free from, 214.
    mortgage of, by court of gaol sessions in ridings or divisions, 203.
    proportions of, for gaol expenses in ridings or divisions. 204
    how repayment of loans for prison purposes to be charged upon, 211.

Court Houses :
    appropriation of, situate within precincts of a prison, 14, 191.
    may be bought by Secretary of State, 14, 192.

Creditors :
    of prison authority, saving of rights of, 12, 167.
    saving of rights of, as regards discontinued prisons, 50, 108.

Crime :
    registration and photographing of persons convicted of, 230—235.
    definition of, in The Prevention of Crimes Act, 1871, 232, note (*r*).

Criminal Prisoners : (See Prisoners—Female Prisoners).

Curacy :
    not to be held by prison chaplain in certain cases, 26, 69.

Custody :
    of prisoners when in prison, 14, 31, 98, 151, 172.
    when prisoners to be deemed to be in legal, 32, 172.
    safe, of debtors, how far gaoler bound to give security for, 32, 99.
    safe, of prisoners, to vest in Secretary of State, 14, 151.
    of prisoners in a substituted prison, 34, 102.
    of journals and other documents, gaoler to be responsible for, 134.

Death:
   jurisdiction, &c., of sheriff as regards prisoners under sentence of. not to be affected, 31, 33, 98, 174.
   provisions as to prisoners under sentence of, 130.
   of prisoners in prison, provisions as to, inquests in case of, 44, 93, 187.
                duty of gaoler on. 133. 291.
                duty of surgeon on, 137.
   visits to prisoners under sentence of, 130, 162, 287.
   prisoners convicted of offences rendering them liable to punishment of. &c., may be committed to house of correction. 205.
   execution of judgment of, to be carried out within prisons, 227.
                to be certified by surgeon, 227.
                declaration of, to be signed by sheriff, &c., 227.
                Secretary of State may make rules, &c., as to, 228.
   rules, &c., so made to be laid before Parliament, 228.
   rules so made, 228.
   duties of sheriff, &c., as to, may be performed by deputies, 229.
   saving clauses as to legality and manner of, 229.
   duty of coroner and jury at inquest on the body of an executed criminal, 227.

Debtors:
   in what prisons to be confined, 31, 171, 259.
   escape of from prison, how far sheriff liable for, 32. 100, 174.
   to be separated altogether from criminal prisoners, 35, 72.
   how far gaoler bound to give security for safe custody of, 32, 99.
   may maintain themselves in prison, 118. 277.
   not to sell food, &c., to other prisoners, 118, 277.
   to receive prison allowance, if unable to maintain themselves, 118.
   what quantity of malt liquor, &c., they may procure or buy, 277.
   may be permitted to work and follow their trades, &c., 121.
   earnings of, provisions as to, 121.
   daily exercise of, in open air. 123.
   how far they may be employed in prison offices, 131.
   certain borough, &c., may be removed to county gaol, 209.
   may be confined in common gaol of county, when, 216.
   special rules for, 276—279.
   to what other persons the special rules for, are to apply, 279.
   when not to be required to take a bath on reception, 277.
   to occupy rooms or cells assigned to them, 277.
   personal cleanliness of, special rules as to, 277.
   attendance of, at Divine Service, 278.
   power and duties of Visiting Committee and gaoler as to granting permission to, in certain cases, 278.
   when visits to, and to criminal prisoners, not to be in same place, 278.
   by whom and how often to be visited, 278.

INDEX. 307

Debtors (continued)—
    what letters may be written and received by, 278.
    power of Visiting Committee to prolong period of visits, or to increase number of visitors to, 278.
    how far to be subject to general prison rules, 279.

Debts:
    existing, to be defrayed by prison authority, 13. 169.
    mortgage, to be paid by prison authority, 13, 169.
    definition of "mortgage debt," 13, 169.
    rules may be made as to treatment, &c., of prisoners confined for non-payment of sums in nature of. 38. 183.
    rules as to debtors to apply to prisoners confined for non-payment of sums in the nature of, except, &c., 279.

Declaration:
    of execution of judgment of death, to be signed by sheriff, &c., 227.
    penalty for making a false declaration, 228.
    to be sent to Secretary of State, 228.
    printed copy of, to be exhibited at or near prison entrance, 228.

Defendant:
    in action may plead the general issue, 46, 94.
    costs of, and against, in action, 46, 94.
    when action to be commenced against, 47, 94.

Definition of Terms:
    general provisions as to, 2, 61, 198.
    "borough," 2, 61, 197.
    "municipal borough," 2, 61.
    "prison," 2, 61, 197.
    "gaoler," 3, 61.
    "clerk of the peace," 3, 61.
    "treasurer," 3, 61.
    "quarter sessions," 3, 61.
    "criminal prisoner," 3, 61.
    "prisoner," 3, 195.
    "prison authorities," 3, 62.
    "justices in sessions assembled," 4, 63.
    "separate prison jurisdiction," 4, 66.
    "Gaol Act," 5, 107.
    "furniture and effects belonging to a prison," 5, 195.
    "maintenance of a prisoner," 5, 195.
    "sufficient accommodation for prisoners," 6 196.
    "cell accommodation for a prisoner," 6, 196.
    "county," 6, 196.
    "riding," 6, 196.
    "mortgage debt," 13, 169.
    "existing officers of a prison," 25, 177.
    "prison service," 27, 180.

Definition of Terms (continued)—
"regulation," 141.
"subordinate officers," 141.

Deputy Gaoler: (See also Gaoler).
appointment of, 26, 69.
powers and duties of, 135.
may appoint a substitute, 135.
may perform duties of gaoler on execution of capital sentences, 229.

Deserters:
military, apprehension and imprisonment of, 240, 241.
justice of peace to make report respecting, 241.
payments by and to gaoler in respect of, 241.
reward to be paid for apprehension of, 241.
transfer of, 241.
temporary custody of, in prisons, 241.
from the marines, apprehension and imprisonment of, 248.
justice of peace to make report respecting, 248.
payments by and to gaoler in respect of, 248.
reward to be paid for apprehension of, 248.
transfer of, 249.
temporary custody of, in prisons, 249.

Diet: (See Food).

Discharge of Prisoners: (See Prisoners).

Discharged Prisoners:
allowance to, 43, 89, 173.
how allowance to, may be paid, 280.
assistance of Visiting Committee as to disposal of allowance to, 266.
provision for, of means of returning to place of settlement, 43, 90.
return of clothing to, 120.
provision of clothing for, 120.

Discontinuance of Prisons:
provisions as to, of certain, 48, 103.
by order of Secretary of State, 50, 175.
effect of, 51, 176.
duties and powers of Secretary of State and of prison authority on 51, 176, 177.
rule as to confinement of prisoners, debtors, &c., on, of certain under P. A., 1877, 259.

Disguise:
conveyance of, into prison, with intent to facilitate escape of prisoner, to be felony, 40, 87.

Divine Service:
when to be performed by chaplain, 124.
attendance of criminal prisoners at, 125.
what prisoners exempt from attendance at, 125.
when chaplain may accept assistance for performance of, 126.

Divine Service (continued)—
non-criminal prisoners may be excused from attending, 261.
attendance at, of prisoners awaiting trial, 272.
attendance at, of misdemeanants of first division, 276.
attendance of debtors at, 278.
when prison minister is to perform, 283, 284.

Divisions of Counties:
maintenance of prison by, 7, 65.
termination of local obligation of, to maintain a prison, 8, 163.
in what, court of sessions for the gaol to be held, 199.
powers of justices of the peace of, as respects gaol sessions, 200.
in what proportions rates to be paid by for gaol expenses, 201.
proportions to be settled by arbitration in case of dispute, 202.
order for payment of proportions to be sent to treasurer of, 203.
court or gaol sessions in, may mortgage county rates, 203.
in what manner rates to be charged upon, 203.
county gaol to be deemed to be within each division, 204.

Documentary Evidence Act, 1868:
certain provisions of, to apply to rules made by Secretary of State under P. A., 1877, 45, 56, 192, 193.

Documents:
description of prison in, 33, 100.
punishment for carrying into, or out of prison, contrary to regulations, 41, 88, 298.
rules as to retention of, by prisoners may be made by Secretary of State, 39, 184.
rule as to retention of, by prisoners awaiting trial, 269.
included in term "furniture and effects," 5, 195.
gaoler to be responsible for safe custody of, 134.

Dress: (See also Clothing).
conveyance of, into prison, with intent to facilitate escape of prisoner, to be felony, 40, 87.
of criminal prisoners before trial, 119.
after conviction, 119.
of misdemeanants of first division, 274.

Earnings:
of debtors in prison, provision as to, 121.
allowance out of, to acquitted prisoners, 121.
Prison Commissioners to examine into amount of prisoners', 18, 156.
to report on, of convicted prisoners, 19, 157.
what portion of, to belong to prisoners awaiting trial, 271.
what portion of, to belong to misdemeanants of first division, 275.

Easement:
may be purchased and held by prison authority, 90.
to be included in term "lands," 91.

Effects: (See Furniture and Effects).

Employment: (See also Hard Labour).
  of prisoners in prison, regulations as to, 121, 122, 123.
  of prisoners, when not sentenced to hard labour, 123.
  of prisoners in prison offices prohibited, 131.
  of prisoners, in instruction of prisoners, prohibited, 131.
  of debtors, in their own trades, &c., 121.
  of debtors in prison offices, 131.
  in necessary prison services, when it may be deemed hard labour of second class, 37, 75.
  in their own trades, &c., of prisoners awaiting trial, 271.
  of misdemeanants of first division in their own trades, &c., 275.
  of prisoners in private capacities, prohibited, 288, 289.

Escape:
  of prisoners from prison, how far sheriff liable for, 32, 100, 174.
    offence of assisting, 40, 87.

Established Church:
  chaplain to be a clergyman of, 24, 67.
  assistant-chaplain to be a clergyman of, 26, 69.
  prayers selected from liturgy of, to be used, 124.
  prisoners of persuasion, &c., differing from, not to be compelled to attend Divine Service, 125.
  when debtors of persuasion, &c., differing from, not to be compelled to attend Divine Service, 278.

Estate (Legal):
  in prisons, &c., to vest in Prison Commissioners, 15, 191.
  how to be disposed of by Prison Commissioners, 15, 191.

Exercise: (See Prisoners—Debtors).

Fast Day:
  prisoners not to be put to hard labour on public, 122.

Faversham:
  borough prison of, to be discontinued, 48, 103.

Felony:
  certain offences in relation to prisons to be, 40, 87.

Female Prisoners:
  for a prison where they are imprisoned, a matron and female officers to be appointed, 24, 67.
  to be attended by female officers, 132.
  matron or female officer to accompany gaoler on visits to, 132.
  to be imprisoned in separate buildings from the men, 35, 72.
  to be searched on admission by female officers, 117.
  admission to, and discharge of, &c., from prison, 117, 280.
  hair of, not to be cut without consent, except, &c., 120.
  employment of, at hard labour, 122.
  locks of cells of, to be different from those of males, 135.
  every part of prison occupied by, to be visited daily by matron, 135.
  matron to see, at least once a day, 135.

Female Prisoners (continued)—
    punishments of, to be entered by matron in her journal, 136.
    when infant children of, may be received into prison with, 280.
    retention and clothing of children of, in prison, 281.
    discharge of children of, from prison, 281.
    duty of matron to accompany, &c., male officers, &c., on entering part of prison allotted to, 292.
    to be visited in presence of a female officer, 285.

Fermented Liquor:
    punishment for carrying into prison, contrary to regulations, 41, 88
    allowance of, to convicted criminal prisoners, 119.
    what quantity prisoner awaiting trial may receive or buy, 269, 270.
    what quantity of, misdemeanants of first division may receive or buy, 274.
    what quantity of, debtors may receive or buy, 277.
    not to be sold to other prisoners, 270, 274, 277.

Food:
    special rules to be made as to, of unconvicted prisoners, 39, 185.
    rules &c., to be made as to supply of, to prisoners, 45, 76.
    of prisoners, when under care of surgeon, 119.
    debtor may provide himself with, 118, 277.
    debtor not to sell to other prisoners, 118, 277.
    debtors to receive prison allowance of, if they do not provide it, 118.
    allowance of, to convicted criminal prisoners, 119.
    prisoners may procure for themselves, before trial, 118, 269.
    prisoners not to sell, &c., to other prisoners, 118, 270.
    prisoner before trial to receive prison allowance of, if he does not provide it himself, 119.
    duty of surgeon respecting quality of bad, 137.
    duty of Visiting Committee and gaoler as to inspection of, 264, 293.
    provision and reception of their own by misdemeanants of first division, rules as to, 265, 274.
    complaints, &c., of prisoners as to, when to be made, 281.
    when repeated complaints as to, may be punished, 281.
    suspension of officers for carrying, into or out of prison contrary to orders, 289.
    articles of, not to be received into prisons until examined, 293.
    when gaoler may refuse admission of articles of, 293.

Franchise:
    of what county to be considered a part, 6, 197.
    maintenance of prison of, 7, 65.
    termination of local obligation of, to maintain a prison, 8, 163.

Friends: (See Communication—Prisoners—Visits).

Furniture and Effects belonging to a Prison:
    definition of, 5, 195.
    to vest in Secretary of State, 14, 151.
    legal estate in, to vest in Prison Commissioners, 15, 191.
    Secretary of State to direct mode of disposal of, 15, 191.

Gaming:
prohibition of, in prison, 121.

Gaol: (See also Prisons).
included in term prison, 2, 61.
abolition of distinction between, and house of correction, 29, 98.
of a county divided into ridings, &c., to be deemed to be within each riding, &c., 204.
when to remain part of county, although within limits of municipal borough, 208, 209.
for what municipal boroughs to be provided, 211.

Gaol Act:
meaning of term, 5, 107.

Gaoler: (See also Deputy-Gaoler).
definition of, 3, 61.
to be appointed for every prison, 23, 66.
to keep visitors' book, 134.
to call attention of Visiting Committee to entries made in the visitors' book, 23, 162.
matron to be deemed to be, when, 24, 67.
prisoners in prison to be deemed to be in legal custody of, 31, 98.
provisions as to giving security by, to sheriff, 32, 99.
description of prison in writ addressed to, 33, 100.
to deliver calendar of prisoners to judges of assize and justices in quarter sessions, 33, 100.
to obey commission of gaol delivery, &c., 34, 109.
limitation of power of, to confine in punishment cells, 40, 186.
power of, to bring up prisoners for trial, &c., 42, 100.
when to discharge prisoners on Saturday, 43, 89.
payment by, of gratuity to discharged prisoners, 43, 89, 173.
when visitors not to sleep in prison without permission of, 115.
to report permission to Visiting Justices, 115.
when to make entries as to ingress and egress from prison, 116.
to retain, and to keep an inventory of, certain effects found on prisoners, 116.
to register name, age, &c., of criminal prisoners, 116.
record of health of criminal prisoners to be kept by, 116.
to seize and destroy all dice, cards, or instruments of gaming, 121.
to report to surgeon names of prisoners wishing to see him, or out of health, 123.
to make certain entries in surgeon's journal, 124.
duty as regards reading prayers, &c., daily, 124.
power of, to exempt prisoners from attending Divine Service, 125.
to keep a catalogue of all books, &c., admitted into prison, 126.
abuses in prison to be communicated to, by chaplain, 126.
powers and duties of, as regards visitors to prisons, 127, 285.
no punishment, &c., for prison offences to be awarded except by, &c., 128.
what offences against prison discipline may be punished by, 128.

INDEX. 313

Gaoler (continued)—
- to make entries in punishment book, as to punishment of prison offences, 128, 160.
- to report to Visiting Committee when prisoners guilty of repeated offences against discipline, 129, 160.
- to report to Visiting Committee when prisoner guilty of offence against discipline, which he cannot punish, 129, 160.
- duty of Visiting Committee as to reports by, of misconduct, &c., of prisoners, 263.
- powers and duties of, as to placing prisoners in irons, &c., 129, 264, 291.
- to attend infliction of corporal punishments, 130.
- to make entries as to corporal punishments, 130, 287.
- duties of, as regards prisoners under sentence of death, 130.
- to reside in prison, 132.
- not to be under-sheriff, &c., nor concerned in any employment, 132.
- to conform to and be responsible for observance of law and regulations of prison, 132.
- to enforce performance of duties by prison officers, 132.
- not to allow subordinate officers to be employed in any private capacity, 132.
- power of, to suspend subordinate officers, 132, 289.
- to visit whole of prison and every male prisoner once, at least, a day, 132.
- in default of daily visits, to enter in journal extent and cause of omission, 132.
- once a week, at least, to go through prison at an uncertain hour of the night, 132.
- to make entry of night visits in journal, 132.
- to be attended by matron, &c., when visiting female prisoners, 132.
- to post up in cells abstract of certain regulations, 133.
- duty of, as to reading, abstract of regulations to prisoners, 133, 280.
- to report to surgeon prisoners disordered in mind, &c., 133.
- to carry out surgeon's directions as to such prisoners, 133.
- to notify illness of prisoners to surgeon, and daily to deliver to him a list of prisoners complaining of illness, removed to infirmary, &c., 133.
- to deliver to chaplain and surgeon daily lists of prisoners confined in punishment cells, 133.
- duty of, on death of a prisoner, 133, 291.
- to report cases of insanity to Prison Commissioners, 133, 156, 289.
- what books and accounts to be kept by, 134.
- to be responsible for safe custody of journals, books, &c., 134.
- absence of, from prison, provisions as to, 134.
- when he may appoint a substitute, 135.
- recommendation of, requisite for absence of matron, 136.
- consent of, required for appointment of deputy matron, 136.
- journal of matron to be laid daily before, 136.
- surgeon to report specially to, in writing, where mind of a prisoner

Gaoler (continued)—
    is, or is likely to be, injuriously affected by discipline or treatment, 137.
    officers of prison to obey, 138, 288.
    subordinate officers to perform duties directed by, 138.
    leave of required, for absence of subordinate officers. 138.
        for reception of visitors by subordinate officers.138.
    keys, &c., of subordinate officers to be left with, during their absence, 138.
    all prohibited articles to be delivered to, when seized, 138.
    notice to be given to, of conveyance of prohibited articles into, or of property out of, prison, 139.
    to transmit calendar of prisoners to Secretary of State, 139.
    what books of, to be examined by the Commissioners, 139, 156, 289.
    to present to the Commissioners a certificate as to requisitions with respect to separation of prisoners and enforcement of hard labour having been complied with, 140, 156, 289.
    to be responsible for safe custody of non-resident officers' book, 141.
    duty of, in producing non-resident officers' book, 141, 156.
    allowances to, in certain cases, to be continued, 217, 289.
    to keep a register of the religion, &c., of prisoners, 223.
    to inform prison minister of names, &c., of prisoners belonging to the church or persuasion of such minister, 223, 283.
    to be present at execution of capital sentences, 227.
    to sign a declaration of due execution of capital sentences. 227.
    duties and powers of, as regards execution of capital sentences, may be performed by, and to be vested in the deputy gaoler, &c., 228.
    penalty for refusal of, to receive bankruptcy prisoners, 230.
    duties of, as to making returns of, and sending photographs of, habitual criminals to registrar of criminals, 231, 233, 234.
    penalty for refusal or neglect of, to make such returns, 231.
    penalty for wilfully making return containing false or imperfect statement, 231.
    duties of, as to reception and custody of military offenders under the Mutiny Act. 236.
    duty of, as to reception &c., of soldiers, 236.
    duty of, on removal of military prisoners, and on their discharge in certain cases, 237, 238.
    to provide subsistence, &c., for military offenders in prison, 239.
    what payment to be made to, in respect of such subsistence, 239.
    duties of, on expiration of imprisonment of soldiers, or of persons suspected to be soldiers, 240.
    what payments to be made by, and to, in respect of military deserters in custody, 240, 241.
    duties of, and payments to, respecting temporary custody of military deserters, 241.
    penalty for refusal of, to receive, &c., military offenders, 242.
    duty of, as to reception and custody of offenders under the Marine Mutiny Act, 242.

INDEX. 315

Gaoler (continued)—
  to receive any marine into custody, 243.
  duty of, on removal of a prisoner of marines, and on his discharge in certain cases, 245, note (*y*), 246.
  to provide subsistence, &c., for marines in prison, 246.
  payments to, for such subsistence, &c., 246, 243, note (*x*).
  duties of, on expiration of imprisonment of marines, or of persons suspected to be marines, 246, 247.
  what payments to be made to, in respect of marines discharged from prison, 247.
  what payments to be made by, and to, in respect of deserters from the marines, 248.
  duties of, and payments to, respecting temporary custody of deserters from the marines, 249.
  power of Visiting Committee as to reports by, of misconduct, &c., of prisoners, 263.
  duty of, when prisoners' diet does not fulfil terms of contract, 264.
  when prison routine may be modified by, as regards prisoners awaiting trial, 265, 269.
  duty of, in regard to visits to prisoner under order for execution, 266.
  may dispense with prisoner awaiting trial taking a bath on admission, 268.
  how money of prisoners awaiting trial, in hands of, to be applied, 269.
  what books, &c., prisoner awaiting trial is to be allowed by, to retain, 269.
  not to permit prisoner before trial providing his own food to have prison allowance at same time, 269.
  power of, as to supply of books to prisoners awaiting trial, and to misdemeanants of first division, 270, 275.
  when to inspect written communications of prisoners awaiting trial, 271.
  money in hands of, belonging to misdemeanants of first division, how to be applied, 274.
  not to permit misdemeanants of first division providing their own food, to have prison allowance at same time, 274.
  not to permit debtor who provides his own food to have prison allowance at same meal, 277.
  duties and powers of, as to granting, &c., permission in certain cases, 268, 273, 278, 291.
  entries to be made by, in journals as to granting, &c., permission in certain cases, 292.
  power of, to use spare cells of prisoners of one class for prisoners of another, 280.
  duty and power of, as to discharge of prisoners under sixteen years of age, 280.
  duty of, as to discharge of children of female prisoners, 281.
  prison minister to confer with, and to co-operate with, 284.
  when school to be under superintendence of, 284.
  prison officers to inform, of prisoners wishing to see him, 287.

316 INDEX.

Gaoler (continued)—
  attention of, to be called to prisoners out of health, &c., 287.
  subordinate officers immediately to report to, misconduct, &c., of prisoners, 288.
  restrictions may be made by, as to use, within prison walls, of tobacco, &c., by officers, 289.
  when he may buy provisions under prison contract, 289.
  when not to have dealings with any tradesman supplying the prison, 289.
  duties of, as regards labour and employment of prisoners, 289.
  orders, &c., relating to any department of prison to be addressed to, 289.
  duty of, as to orders, &c., relating to departments of prison, 289.
  to report to Visiting Committee case of child of tender years in prison, 290.
  duty of, in aiding in identification of prisoners, 290.
  when not to allow persons to view the prison, 290.
  to prevent unauthorised communications between visitors and prisoners, 290.
  to notify to chaplain, &c., when prisoner's life appears in danger, 290.
  to carry out written directions of surgeon as to supply of additional articles, 290.
  to pay attention to ventilation, drainage, &c., of the prison, 290.
  to examine frequently the washing places, baths, &c., 290.
  at what hour to hear reports, 290.
  duty of, as to hearing complaints, and redressing prisoners' grievances, 290.
  when to send reports or complaints by prison officers to Commissioners, 291.
  to inform Visiting Committee of prisoner desiring to see them, 291.
  duties of, in enforcing silence, as to communications between prisoners, &c., 291.
  duties of, as to visits to prisoners in solitary confinement or in punishment cells, 291.
  not to allow punishment of prisoners unable to undergo it, 291.
  to report to Commissioners any doubt as to class of rules applicable to prisoners, 292.
  surgeon to inform, of points likely to aid in identifying prisoners, 292.
  when surgeon to report to, case of a prisoner on medical grounds, 292.
  when to report to Commissioners of prisoner's life being endangered, 292.
  duty of surgeon in reporting to, as to prisoners employed at hard labour, 293.
  surgeon to report to, when discipline, &c., likely to injure prisoner's health, 293.
  power of, to refuse admission of articles likely to be used for improper purposes, 293.

INDEX.   317

Gaol Rate:
    may be made in certain municipal boroughs for payment of money borrowed for prison purposes, 210.
    to be made in the same manner as borough rate, 211.

Gaol Sessions:
    to be held in certain counties, 199.
    power of justices of the peace in, 200.
    clerk of, to be elected by court of gaol sessions, 200.
    powers of clerk of, 200.
    duties of clerk of, in giving notice as to holding of, 200, 201.
    at what place to be held, 201.
    court of, to elect a treasurer of county gaol, 201.
        to fix salaries of clerk and treasurer, 201.
        to fix proportions in which county rate shall be paid for gaol expenses, 201, 202.
    may mortgage county rates, 203.
    duty of clerk of, as to payment of proportions of rates, 202.
    in what manner to charge rates upon ridings and divisions, 203.
    justices assembled at, to be prison authorities, for counties divided into ridings or divisions, 5, 62.
    at what, Visiting Committee to be appointed in Yorkshire and Lincolnshire, 250, 262.

Gate Porter:
    duties of, 139.

General Issue:
    may be pleaded to action, under P. A., 1865, 46, 91.

General Sessions:
    included in term "quarter sessions," 3, 61.

Good Friday:
    prisoners not to be put to hard labour on, 122.
    chaplain to perform Divine Service on, 124.

Government of Prisons:
    regulations and rules for, provisions as to, 44—46; 76, 109, 192.
    schedule of regulations as to, made under P.A., 1865, 115—141.
    general rules as to, made under P. A., 1877, 279—293.
    special rules as to prisoners awaiting trial, 268—272.
                   misdemeanants of first division, 272—276.
                   debtors, 276—279.

Governor of Prison: (See Gaoler—Matron).
    included in term "gaoler," 3, 61.

Gratuity:
    to superannuated prison officers, 27, 70, 179, 180.
    prison officer not to receive, from prisoners or visitors, 131.

Gratuity (continued—)
  assistance by Visiting Committee as to disposal of, earned by a prisoner, 266.

Grounds:
  of prison, included in term "prison," 2, 61.

Habitual Criminals:
  who are to be deemed, 234, 235.
  registration and photographing of, 230—235.
  duty of gaoler as to returns and photographs of, 233, 234.

Hair Cutting:
  hair of female prisoners not to be cut, except, &c., 120.
  hair of male criminal prisoners, regulation as to cutting, 121.
  hair of prisoners awaiting trial, provisions as to cutting, 270.
  hair of misdemeanants of first division, cutting of, 275.
  hair of debtors, provisions as to cutting of, 277.
  prisoners to obey regulations as to, 282.

Hard Labour:
  requisitions of P. A., 1865, as to, 36, 74.
  misdemeanants not sentenced to, to be divided into two divisions, 37, 102.
  when employment in necessary prison services may be deemed, of the second class, 37, 75.
  criminal prisoners not to be put to, before trial, 121.
  of the first class, regulations as to, 121, 122.
  of the second class, regulations as to, 122.
  days of exemption from, 122, 282.
  prisoners sentenced to, or employed at, to be examined by surgeon, 122, 292, 293.
  employment of prisoners not sentenced to, 123.
  hours of instruction not to be deducted from hours of, 127.
  record to be kept of employment of prisoners at, 134.
  gaoler to present to Commissioners a certificate as to the requisitions respecting enforcement of, having been complied with, 140, 156, 289.
  Prison Commissioners to examine into state of prisons for carrying out provisions respecting, 18, 155.
  power of Secretary of State to substitute hard labour of the second for hard labour of the first class, 183.
  employment of prisoners at, when above sixteen years of age, 282.
  prisoners who do not do their best to profit by instruction, may be treated as those idle at, &c., 284.
  duties of gaoler as regards advantageous use of, 289.

Health of Prisoners: (See also Gaoler—Surgeon).
  regulations as to, 123, 124, 270.

INDEX.

Helstone:
borough prison of, to be discontinued, 48, 103.

House:
removal of prison officer from, when occupied officially, 28, 71.

House of Correction: (See also Prisons).
included in term prison, 2, 61.
abolition of distinction between gaol and, 29, 98.
to what, prisoners may be committed, 204.
prisoners convicted of offences for which they are liable to death, &c., may be committed to, 205.
in boroughs, mayor, &c., not to be interested in any contract relating to, 208.
may be built beyond limits of borough, 208.
for what municipal boroughs to be provided, 211.

Hundred:
maintenance of prison of, 7, 65.
termination of local obligation of, to maintain a prison, 8, 163.

Implements:
included in term "furniture and effects," 5, 195.
likely to facilitate escape, not to be left unnecessarily exposed in prisons, 115.
of trade, &c., deductions for, out of earnings of debtors, 121.
of trade, &c., deductions for, out of earnings of prisoners awaiting trial, 271.
deduction for use of, from earnings of misdemeanants of first division, 275.

Industrial Schools:
saving of powers and jurisdiction of prison authorities as to, 14, 193.

Infirmary:
to be provided in every prison, 124.
spirituous liquors for use of, to be under control of surgeon, 117.
list of prisoners removed to, to be delivered daily to surgeon, 133.
power of surgeon to direct prisoners to be removed to, 136.
chaplain to visit daily, 283.

Inquests:
on prisoners dying in prison, 44, 93, 187.
certain persons not to be jurors on, 44, 94, 187.
on the bodies of executed criminals, provisions as to, 227.

Insane Prisoners:
gaoler to call attention of surgeon to, 133.
to be reported to Prison Commissioners by gaoler, 133, 156, 289.

Inspectors of Prisons:
appointment of, under P. A., 1877, provisions as to, 16, 154.

Inspectors of Prisoners (continued)—
    transfer of duties of existing, on commencement of P. A., 1877, 16, 187.
    appointed under 5 & 6 Will. IV. c. 38, to become Inspectors under, P. A., 1877, 16, 188.
    salaries of, under P. A., 1877, 17, 155.
    salaries of, appointed under 5 & 6 Will. IV. c. 38, 17, 188.
    to report any irregularity or complaint against officers, &c., 17, 77.
    cells for confinement of prisoners to be certified by, 35, 73.
    repeal of 5 & 6 Will. IV. c. 38, s. 7, as to appointment of, 53, 188.
    certificates of, may be varied or withdrawn, 36, 73, 74.
    cells certified by, before P. A., 1865, to be deemed certified under, 36, 107.
    duties of, under 5 & 6 Will. IV. c. 38, s. 7, 188, note (*o*), 205.
    penalty on obstructing, 189 note (*o*), 206.
    how persons obstructing, to be proceeded against, 188 note (*o*), 206.
    gaol of county to be certified by, before confinement of debtors, 216.

Instruction of Prisoners : (See also Religious and Moral Instruction).
    provisions as to, 127, 270, 275, 284.
    chapel to be used only for religious or moral, &c., 79.
    prisoners not to be employed in, 131.
    supply of books, &c., to prisoners when awaiting trial, 270.
    supply of books, &c., to misdemeanants of first division, 275.
    library to be provided in every prison, 284.
    issue of books to prisoners from library, 284.
    treatment of prisoners who do not do their best to profit by, 284.

Interest :
    of money borrowed, on and out of what rate or property to be charged and paid, 80.
    mortgagee, &c., may appoint receiver to enforce payment of, 80.
    rate of, on certain loans made to prison authorities to be sanctioned by Treasury, 9, 52, 164, 177.

Inventory : (See also Catalogue).
    of effects of prisoners, when to be kept by gaoler, 116.
    of all furniture, &c., belonging to prison to be kept by gaoler, 134.

Ireland :
    Prison Acts not to extend to, (1865), 1, 60 ; (1877) 1, 150.

Irons :
    when prisoners may be put into, 129.
    duty of gaoler in case of use of, 129, 291.
    limitation of time for keeping prisoners in, 129, 291.
    power and duties of Visiting Committee as to placing prisoners in, for an increased period, 264.
    pattern of, to be approved by Secretary of State, 287.
    order of Visiting Committee required for use of, for extended period, 291.

INDEX. 321

Irregularity:
inspector to make report of any, in prisons, 17. 77.

Jew:
prisoner who is a, not to be compelled to labour on his Sabbath, 282.

Journals: (See Chaplain—Gaoler—Matron—Surgeon).

Judges of Assize:
calendar of prisoners to be delivered to, by gaoler, 33, 100.

Judge of High Court of Justice:
when application may be made to, for removal of prisoner from one prison to another, 30, 172.

Jurisdiction, Separate Prison: (See Separate Prison Jurisdiction).

Jurisdiction:
over prisons. 29. 98, 173.

Jurors:
prison officers and prisoners not to be, on inquests held on bodies of prisoners. 44, 93, 187.
who not to be, on inquests on the bodies of executed criminals. 227.

Justices of the Peace: (See also Visiting Justices—Justices in Sessions Assembled).
members of Visiting Committee to be, 21. 158.
in boroughs, when to hold special sessions for appointment of Visiting Committee, 21, 159. 251, 262.
corporal punishment not to be inflicted on prisoners without inquiry by and certificate of two, 22. 161.
visits to prison and prisoners by, 23. 161.
how far jurisdiction of, over prisons, affected by P. A., 1877. 30, 173.
penalties under P. A., 1865, to be recovered before two. 41. 95.
powers of, as to removal of prison officers from apartments, &c., 71.
presentment of, under P. A., 1865, as to building, &c., prisons, 78.
power of, as to infliction of punishments, &c., in prison. 128.
may in certain cases inquire upon oath respecting alleged offences against prison discipline, and order punishment, 129.
non-resident officers' book to be produced for inspection of, when required. 141.
of ridings or divisions of a county, power, &c., of, as regards common gaol of the county. 204.
to what house of correction they may commit prisoners for trial, 204.
may summon, on complaint, any person obstructing an Inspector of Prisons. 188, note (o), 206.
may be present at execution of capital sentences. 227.
to sign, when present, a declaration of the due execution of suc sentences, 227.
may order conveyances, &c., of land, &c., to be made in the name of the clerk of the peace, 219.

21

Justices of the Peace (continued)—
  to report as to military deserters, 241.
  to report as to deserters from the Marines, 248.

Justices in Quarter Sessions assembled :
  when to be prison authorities, 3, 62.
  when term "justices in sessions assembled" to mean, 4, 63.
  what justices included in the term in construction of the Act, 21 & 22 Vict. c. 92, 12, 64.
  calendar of prisoners to be delivered to, by gaoler, 33, 100.
  power of, to grant certificate to, or to suspend certificate of, Prisoners' Aid Societies, 221.
  appointment by, of Visiting Committee of prisons, 21, 159.
  rules as to appointment by, of Visiting Committee, 250—258, 262.
  when to make first appointment of Visiting Committee, 250.
  number of members of Visiting Committee, and at what sessions to be appointed by, 252—258.
  when to make appointments of Visiting Committee after the year 1878, 262.

Justices in Sessions assembled :
  definition of, 4, 63.
  to have same meaning in P. A., 1877, as in P. A., 1865, 7, 198.
  powers and jurisdiction of, in relation to prisons and prisoners, to vest in Secretary of State, 14, 151.
  powers of, as to appointment of prison officers, 24, 66.
  powers of, as to salaries, &c., of prison officers, 24, 70.
  power of, to appoint assistant-chaplain and deputy gaoler, 26, 69.
  their powers, as to superannuation of prison officers, 26, 70.
  how far transfer of jurisdiction of, is to affect that of sheriff or coroner, 30, 174.
  power to award compensation to officers of prisons scheduled in P. A., 1865, 105.
  their powers as regards removal of prisoners from one prison to another, 42, 101.
  power of, to make rules in addition to prison regulations in first schedule of P. A., 1865, 45, 76.
  powers of, as regards enforcement of hard labour, 36, 37, 74, 75.
  to make rules as to admission of friends of convicted prisoners, 127.
  to impose restrictions on communications and correspondence between prisoners and their friends, 127.
  power of, to make rules as to prisoners not debtors nor criminal prisoners, 141.
  rules, &c., made by, to be deemed regulations within the meaning of P. A., 1865, 141.
  allowance of compensation by, to officers on discontinuance, &c., of prisons, 225, 226.

Keeper of Prison : (See Gaoler—Matron).
  included in term "gaoler," 3, 61.

INDEX. 323

King's Lynn:
borough prison of, to be discontinued, 48, 103.

Labour: (See Hard Labour—Employment—Manufacturing Processes).

Land:
power of prison authority to purchase and hold, 90.
power of prison authority to sell, 50, 92, 93.
Prison Commissioners may hold, 16, 153.
confirmation of title to, when bought for purposes of prison, 91.
provision as to proceedings for recovery of possession of, 91.
belonging to a prison, legal estate in, to vest in Prison Commissioners, 15, 191.
disposal of legal estate in, by Prison Commissioners, 15, 191.
when included in term " prison " in P. A., 1877, 2. 197.
power, &c., of Secretary of State to sell, &c., when bought by a prison authority for purposes of a prison, 197.
justices of the peace may order conveyances, &c., of to be made to Clerk of the Peace, 219.
purchased for county purposes to vest in Clerk of the Peace, 219, 220.

Lands Clauses Consolidation Acts, 1845, 1860, & 1869 :
to be deemed to be incorporated with s. 49 of P. A., 1877, 192.
certain clauses of the Acts of 1845 and 1860, incorporated with P. A., 1865, 90.

Legal Adviser:
meaning of the term explained, 271.
of prisoner, how far to see him alone, 127, 271.
special rules to be made as to communications between an unconvicted prisoner and his, 39, 184, 185.
provisions of rules so made, 271.
visits by, to prisoners under sentence of death, 287.
written instructions to, of prisoner awaiting trial, not to be examined by officer of prison, 271.

Legal Custody: (See Custody).

Legal Estate:
in prison, &c., to vest in Prison Commissioners, 15, 191.
how to be disposed of by Prison Commissioners, 15, 191.

Lessons:
chaplain to direct what are to be taught in prison, 124.

Letters:
punishment for carrying into or out of prison, contrary to regulations, 41, 88, 289.
conveyance of, into prison, with intent to facilitate escape of prisoner, to be felony, 40, 87.
what written communications to be considered as, 271.
power of Visiting Committee to accord additional number of, 275.
how many, debtors may write and receive, 278.

Letters (*continued*)—
when, and with whom, convicted prisoner may be allowed to communicate by, 285.
communication by, when person committed for non-payment of a sum of money. 286.

Libel: (See Seditious Libel).

Liberty:
of what county to be considered a part, 6. 197.
maintenance of prison of, 7. 65.
termination of local obligation of, to maintain a prison, 8, 163.

Library:
to be provided in every prison, 284.
of what books to consist, 284.
issue of books from, to prisoners, 284.

Licence:
chaplain and assistant-chaplain to obtain. from bishop, 26, 69.

Lichfield:
borough prison of, to be discontinued, 48, 103.

Loan: (See Money—Interest).

Local Loans Act, 1875:
power of prison authority to borrow in manner provided by, 189.
Public Works Loan Commissioners may lend on securities issuable under. 190.
how far to be substituted for the Public Works Loans Act, 1875, 191.

Local Obligation:
to maintain prisons and prisoners, when to cease. 8, 163.

Lock-up Houses:
prisons scheduled in P. A., 1865, may be used as, 49, 105.

London (City of):
who to be prison authorities in. 3, 62.
meaning of term "justices in sessions assembled." as regards, 4, 63.
to be deemed to be a county. 6, 196.
prisons belonging to, to be deemed to be within, 6. 196.

Maintenance:
of a prisoner, definition of. 5. 195.
of prisons. by separate prison jurisdiction, 7, 65.
of prisons out of public funds. 8, 150.
termination of local obligation as to, of prisons and prisoners. 8. 163.
determination of contracts between prison authorities relating to, of prisons and prisoners. 12, 168.
deductions for, from earnings of debtors, 121.
deductions for, from earnings of prisoners awaiting trial. 271.
deductions for, from earnings of misdemeanants of first division, 275.

INDEX.

Maldon:
borough prison of, to be discontinued, 48, 103.

Malingering:
provisions as to application of test to detect, 40, 186.

Malt Liquor:
debtor may provide himself with, 118.
not to sell to other prisoners, 118, 277.
what quantity of, debtor may receive or buy, 277.
criminal prisoner before trial may provide himself with, 118.
what quantity prisoners awaiting trial may obtain, 269, 270.
not to sell, &c., to other prisoners, 118, 270.
quantity of, for misdemeanants of first division, 274.
not to sell, &c., to other prisoners, 274.

Manufacturing Processes:
report of Prison Commissioners to contain information as to in prisons, 19, 157.

Marines:
duty of gaoler, &c., of a prison, &c., to receive into custody, 243.

Marine Offenders: (See also Deserters).
duty of gaoler, &c., as to reception and imprisonment of, under the Marine Mutiny Act, 242, 243, 245, note (y).
solitary confinement of, 243, 244, 245 note (y).
corporal punishment of, 244.
subsistence of in prisons, &c., provisions as to, 246, 243, note (x).
removal or discharge of, in certain cases, 245, note (y).
duties of gaoler on expiration of imprisonment of, and of persons suspected to be marines, 246, 247.
what payments to be made to gaoler in respect of marines discharged from prison, 247.

Mask:
conveyance of, into prison, with intent to facilitate escape of prisoners, to be felony, 40, 87.

Matron: (See also Gaoler).
to be appointed for prisons where females are imprisoned, 24, 67.
to be deemed gaoler, where females only are imprisoned, 24, 67.
to perform duties of gaoler as regards female prisoners, 117.
when she may search female visitors, 127.
gaoler to be accompanied by, &c., on visiting female prisoners, 132.
to reside in the prison, 135.
her general duties, 135.
to visit daily every part of the prison occupied by females, 135.
to see female prisoners once a day, at least, 135.
weekly, at least, to go through prison at an uncertain hour of night, 135.
absence of, from prison, provisions as to, 136.
may appoint a deputy, during absence, 136.

Matron *(continued)*—
powers and duties of deputy of, 136.
her duties in keeping a journal, 136.
duty of, to accompany &c., male officers, &c., on entering part of prison allotted to females, 292.

Mayor:
not to be interested in contracts relating to borough gaol, 208.
penalty for being so interested, 208.

Meaning of Terms: (See Definition of Terms).

Mechanical Restraint:
when prisoner may be put under, 129.
duty of gaoler in case of prisoner being placed under, 129, 291.
limitation of time for keeping prisoners under, 129, 291.
power and duties of Visiting Committee as to placing prisoners under, for an extended period, 264.
means of applying, to be approved by Secretary of State, 287.
order of Visiting Committee required for use of for extended period, 291.

Medical Aid:
when additional to be called in by surgeon, 137.

Military Offenders: (See also Deserters).
duty of gaoler etc., as to reception and imprisonment of, under the Mutiny Act, 236.
solitary confinement and corporal punishment of, 236, 237.
removal or discharge of in certain cases, 237, 238.
subsistence of in prisons, &c., provisions as to, 239.
duties of gaoler on expiration of imprisonment of, or of persons suspected to be soldiers, 240.
penalty for refusal by gaoler to receive, &c., 242.

Military Prisons:
P. A., 1865, and P. A., 1877, not to apply to, 1, 61, 150.
provisions of The Prevention of Crimes Act, 1871, as to registering and photographing criminals, not to apply to, 232.

Minister: (See Prison Minister).

Misdemeanants:
when to be divided into two divisions, 37, 102.
of first division, not to be deemed criminal prisoners, 28, 103.
prisoners convicted of sedition, or seditious libel, and persons imprisoned for contempt of court to be treated as first class, 39, 40, 186.
of first division, supply of books, &c., to, and occupation for, 265, 275.
when to be allowed to wear their own clothing, 265, 274.
provision and reception of their own food by, 265, 274.
when to be permitted to occupy special rooms or cells, &c., 265, 273, 274.
of the first division, special rules for, 272—276.

Misdemeanants (continued)—
  to what other persons special rules for, are to apply, 276.
  what persons to be placed in first division of, 273.
  when not to be required to take a bath on admission, 273.
  search of, on admission, 273.
  in what cells to be placed on admission, 273.
  what cells or rooms to occupy, 273.
  not to associate or exercise with criminal prisoners, 273.
  power and duties of Visiting Committee and gaoler, as to granting permission to in certain cases, 273.
  how money belonging to, in goaler's hands, may be applied, 274.
  what quantity of malt liquor, &c., they may procure or buy, 274.
  not to sell or transfer articles introduced for their use, 274.
  personal cleanliness of, rules as to, 275.
  when they may work and follow their own trades, &c., 275.
  when period of visits to, may be prolonged. 275.
  when visits to, and to criminal prisoners, not to be in same place, 276.
  of first division, attendance of at Divine Service, 276.
  restriction of allowance of privileges to, 276.
  how far to be subject to general prison rules, 276.

Money: (See also Interest).
  prison authority empowered to borrow, for building, &c., prisons, 77.
  on what rates or property money so borrowed to be charged, 79.
  repayment of money so borrowed, 80.
  loan of, by Public Works Loan Commissioners, to build prisons, 81.
  found on prisoner, duty of gaoler as to, 116.
  belonging to prisoners awaiting trial, application of, 118, 269.
  belonging to misdemeanants of first division, application of, 274.
  prison officers not to receive from prisoners or visitors, 131.
  prison authority may borrow to pay compensation for unprovided cell accommodation, 9, 164.
  and for making payment on discontinuance of prison, 52, 177.
  may be borrowed as one loan or as several loans under provisions of Local Loans Act, 1875, 189.
  period within which such loans must be repaid, 164, 177.
  when period for repayment to begin, 189.
  rates may be given as security for, and levied in same manner, as if P. A., 1877, had not passed, 189.
  power of Public Works Loan Commissioners to lend, for certain purposes under P. A., 1877, 190, 191.
  court of gaol sessions may raise, on mortgage of county rates, 203.
  town council may borrow for certain prison purposes, 210.
  how repayment of, borrowed by town councils, may be secured, 210.
  suspension of officers for carrying into or out of prison contrary to orders, 289.

Mortgage :
  by or with prison authority, how to be executed, 11, 64.
  certain clauses of Commissioners Clauses Act, 1847, to apply to, 80.

Mortgage (continued)—
  mortgage in respect of a prison scheduled in P. A., 1865, not to be affected by discontinuance of prison. 108.
  court of gaol sessions may raise money on, of county rates. 203.
  town councils may borrow on, for certain prison purposes, 210.

Mortgage Debts:
  to be paid by prison authority, 13. 169.
  what the term is to include, 13, 169.

Mortgagee:
  power of, to obtain payment of loan made to a prison authority, under P. A., 1865. 80.

Municipal Borough:
  definition of, 2, 61.
  definition of term "borough," 2, 61, 197.
  who to be prison authority in. 4, 62.
  special sessions in, for appointing Visiting Committee, 21, 159.
  rules for appointing Visiting Committee in. 251—258. 262, 263.
  time of holding special sessions in, for appointing Visiting Committee. 251, 262.
  termination of local obligation of, to maintain a prison, 8, 168.
  approval of salary of prison officers, by council of, 24, 70.
  how far council of, may appoint gaoler, &c., of prison of, 24, 109.
  conditions under P. A., 1865, as to building, &c., prison of. 78.
  payment of certain sums by, in respect of felonies and misdemeanors. 206.
  payment of expenses of prosecution at assizes of offenders from. 207.
  certain county gaols included within limits of, still to be deemed part of the county. 208. 209.
  mayor, &c., not to be interested in contracts relating to gaol of, 208.
  gaol of, may be built beyond the limits of, 208.
  certain debtors, &c., in, may be removed to county gaol, 209.
  council of, may borrow money for certain prison purposes, 210.
  how repayment of money borrowed by council of, to be secured. 210.
  gaol rate in, to be made, &c., in same manner as borough rate, 211.
  when gaol and house of correction to be provided for, 211.
  expenses of prisoners of, in county prisons, how to be defrayed. 212.
  expenses of prosecution of such prisoners, how to be defrayed, 213.
  account of expenses to be rendered, 213, 214.
  when to be free from county rate, 214.

National Monuments:
  protection and maintenance of prisons, in the nature of, 15, 192.

Naval Prisons:
  P. A., 1865, and P. A., 1877, not to apply to, 1, 61. 150.
  provisions of The Prevention of Crimes Act. 1871 as to registering and photographing criminals, not to apply to, 232.

INDEX. 329

Necessaries:
criminal prisoner may provide himself with before trial, 118.
not to sell, &c., to other prisoners, 118, 270.
to receive prison allowance of, if he does not provide them, 119.
debtor may provide himself with in prison, 118.
not to sell to other prisoners, 118, 277.
to receive prison allowance of, if unable to provide himself with, 118.

Newcastle-under-Lyne:
borough prison of, to be discontinued, 48, 103.

Non-Resident Officers:
when to make entries in non-resident officers' book, 140.

Non-Resident Officers' Book:
to be kept in every prison, 140.
chaplain and other non-resident officers to enter therein the date of their visits, 140.
gaoler to be responsible for safe custody of, 141.
to be produced to the Commissioners, or to any justice of the county, &c., when required, 141, 156, 289.

Notice:
of appointment, of chaplains and assistant-chaplains, to be sent to bishop, 26, 69.
of penalties, for offences in relation to, to be placed outside of, prisons, 41, 88.
what, to be served on prison authority on discontinuance of a prison, 51, 176.
public, to be given of appropriation, &c., of particular prisons to particular classes of prisoners, 84.
of purchase or sale of land, &c., by prison authority, 93.
what, to be given by gaoler, on expiration of imprisonment of military offenders, 240.
what, to be given by gaoler, on expiration of imprisonment of offenders from the Marines, 246.

Obligation:
local to maintain prisons, 7, 65.
termination of local, to maintain prisons, &c., 8, 163.
determination of any existing, between prison authorities, 12, 168.
discharge of an existing, by prison authorities, 13, 169, 170.

Offences against Prison Discipline:
what are, 128, 286.
power of gaoler to hear complaints of, and to punish certain, 128.
what punishment may be awarded for, 128, 286.
yearly return of, to be made to Parliament, 20, 158.
by whom punishment to be awarded for, 128, 161.
entries to be made respecting punishment for, 128.
when prisoner guilty of repeated, &c., gaoler to report same to Visiting Committee, 129, 160.

Offences against Prison Discipline (continued)—
  repeated groundless complaints of food to be punished as, 281.
  prisoners refusing to obey regulations as to their being photographed, to be deemed guilty of, 232.
  punishment cells to be provided for confinement of prisoners guilty of, 35, 72.
  book to be kept for entry of all punishments inflicted for, 134.
  Visiting Committee to furnish information respecting, 264.
  what, to render certain male prisoners liable to corporal punishment, 286.

Offences in relation to Prisons :
  provisions as to, 40, 41, 87, 88.
  notice of penalties for, to be placed outside, 41, 88.
  how to be prosecuted, 41, 94.

Operation (Surgical):
  surgeon not to perform any serious, without consultation with another medical practitioner, 137.

Officers of Prisons: (See Prison Officers).

Order :
  for discontinuing a prison, to be laid before Parliament, 51, 175.
  made under Acts repealed, saving clause as to, 52, 106.
  for infliction of corporal punishment to specify number of lashes, &c., and to be duly entered, 287.

Oxford (City of) :
  commutation of payment to, by University of Oxford, in respect of gaol expenses, 194.

Papers :
  special rules to be made as to retention of, by unconvicted prisoners, 39, 184.
  what, prisoners awaiting trial are to be allowed to retain, 269.
  printed, not to be admitted into prisons without permission, 125.
  for religious instruction, to be chosen by chaplain, &c., 125, 126.
  catalogue of, to be kept by gaoler, 126.
  included in term "furniture and effects," 5, 195.
  suspension of officers for carrying into or out of prison, 289.

Parliament :
  maintenance of prisons and of prisoners out of moneys to be provided by, 8, 150.
  rules made by Secretary of State, to be laid before, 46, 193.
  annual report of Prison Commissioners, to be laid before, 19, 157.
  annual return to be made to, of punishments and offences of prisoners, 20, 158.
  order for discontinuance of a prison, to be laid before, 51, 175.
  salaries of Prison Commissioners, Inspectors, &c., to be paid out of moneys provided by, 17, 155.

INDEX. 331

Parliament (continued)—
  when compensation to prison authorities to be paid out of moneys provided by, 9, 164; 10, 165.
  rules as to execution of judgment of death, to be laid before, 228.
  for offences in relation to prisons, 41, 87, 88.

Penalties:
  notice of, to be placed outside prisons, 41, 88.
  how to be recovered, for offences in relation to prisons, 41, 95.
  for obstructing Inspectors of Prisons, 188, note (*o*), 206.
  for obstructing Inspectors, how to be recovered, 188, note (*o*), 206.
  for signing false certificate, &c., on execution of judgment of death, 228.
  for refusal by gaoler to receive bankruptcy prisoners, 230.
  for refusal or neglect of gaoler, &c., to make returns of convicted criminal prisoners, 231.
  for gaoler wilfully making a return containing a false or imperfect statement, 231.
  for refusal of gaoler, &c., to receive, &c., military offenders, 242.
  for default of gaoler in giving certain notices under Marine Mutiny Act, 247.

Penitentiary: (See Prisons).
  included in term "prison," 2, 61.

Pensions:
  of existing officers of prisons, saving clause as to, 28, 194.

Penzance:
  borough prison of, to be discontinued, 48, 103.

Photographs:
  of prisoners, provisions as to the taking and keeping of, 230—233.
  regulations of Secretary of State respecting, 233—235, 279.
  punishment of prisoners refusing to obey regulations as to, 232.
  to whom copies of, may be given, 279, 280.

Plaintiff:
  costs of, and against in action, under P. A., 1865, 46, 94.
  within what time, and where to bring his action, 47, 94.

Plank Bed:
  when, and how long, convicted criminal prisoner to sleep on, 281.

Police:
  power of, to visit prisoners for purpose of identification, 285.
  gaoler to aid, in identification of prisoners, 290.

Police Station House:
  prisons named in schedule II. of P. A., 1865, may be used as, 49, 105.

Porter (Gate):
  duties of, 139.

Prayers:
  to be read daily by chaplain, or gaoler, &c., 124.

Prevention of Crimes Act, 1871:
  certain provisions of, 230—232.
  Amendment Act, 1876, provisions of, 233.
  regulations made by Secretary of State under, 233, 235.

Printed Papers: (See Books—Papers—Documents).

Prison Authority:
  Prison Acts, 1865, 1877, to apply to all prisons belonging to a, 1, 150.
  definition of, 3, 62.
  term, to have same meaning in P. A., 1877, as in P. A., 1865, 7, 198.
  expenses of, how to be defrayed, 7, 65.
  powers, &c., of, as to enlargement, &c., of prisons, 7, 77, 78, 79.
  power of, to contract for reception of prisoners, 8, 82.
  compensation by, in place of prison accommodation, 8, 163.
  when entitled to deduction from amount of compensation, 9, 164.
  may borrow money for payment of compensation, 9, 164.
  compensation to, in respect of accommodation provided for prisoners of another authority, 9, 164.
  compensation to, in respect of accommodation more than adequate for its own prisoners, 10, 165.
  public department of State included in the term, when, 9, 165.
  average maximum number of prisoners of, how computed, 11, 166.
  may be allowed time to complete an uncompleted prison, 11, 166.
  allowance to be made to, in respect of uncompleted prison, 11, 166.
  how contracts, &c., by, are to be made, 11, 64.
  general saving of rights of creditors of, 12, 167.
  determination of contracts made by one, with another, 12, 168.
  existing and mortgage debts to be defrayed by, 13, 169.
  continuing contracts of, how to be discharged, 13, 169.
  powers, &c., of, to be vested in Secretary of State, 14, 151.
  saving of powers of, as to Reformatory and Industrial Schools, 14, 193.
  power of, to use certain prisons as lock-up houses, &c., 49, 105.
  power of, to buy and hold land, 90.
  power of, to sell unnecessary prison or land, 50, 92, 93.
  notice of intention to buy or sell to be given by, 93.
  notice to be served on, when prison discontinued, 51, 176, 177.
  powers and duties of, on discontinuance of prison, 51, 52, 176, 177.
  how far transfer of powers of, to affect sheriff or coroner, 30, 174.
  power of, to borrow money for building, enlarging, &c., prisons, 77.
  on what rates, &c., money so borrowed by, to be charged, 79.
  repayment of money so borrowed by, 80.
  loan to, by Public Works Loan Commissioners, to build prisons, 81.
  payment of expenses of contracts of, with another authority, 83.
  appropriation by, of prisons to particular classes of prisoners, 83.
  public notice to be given by, of appropriation of prisons, 84.
  duties and liabilities of, as regards inadequate prisons, 85, 86.
  may borrow on, and levy rates, as if P. A., 1877, had not passed, 189.

INDEX. 333

Prison Authority (continued)—
  power of Public Works Loan Commissioners to lend to, 190, 191.
  power of, to settle, &c., or refer to arbitation any matter, 47, 194.
  expenses of prisoners committed from jurisdiction of one, to prison of another, how defrayed, 224.

Prison Commissioners:
  appointment of, provisions as to, 15, 153.
  to be a body corporate, &c., 16, 153.
  power of, to hold land, 16, 153.
  style of, 16, 153.
  provision as to acts of, 16, 153.
  legal estate in prisons, &c., to vest in, 15, 191.
  power of, to dispose of legal estate in prisons, &c., 15, 191.
  report of, as to compensation to a prison authority, 10, 165.
  one of the, may perform duties of an existing Inspector, 16, 187.
  may exercise powers &c., of Visiting Justices, 18, 156.
  appointment of certain officers and servants by, 16, 154.
  salaries of, 17, 155.
  duties of, general provisions as to, 17—20 ; 155—158.
  to have general superintendence of prisons, 17, 155.
  to appoint subordinate officers of prisons, 18, 24, 155.
  to make contracts, 18, 155.
  to visit and inspect prisons, 18, 155.
  when Inspector to report to by letter, 17, 77.
  reports, &c., by officers, ordered by P. A., 1865, to be made to, 18, 155, 289.
  to be subject to control of Secretary of State, 19, 155.
  to make reports to Secretary of State, 19, 157.
  to make an annual report to be laid before Parliament, 19, 157.
  report of, to Parliament, to contain information as to manufacturing processes in prisons, 19, 157.
  to make yearly return to Parliament of punishments and offences of prisoners, 20, 158.
  report by, on good conduct of officer, 27, 180.
  power of, to remove prison officers from house or apartments occupied officially, 28, 71.
  duties of, as regards prisoners convicted of sedition or seditious libel, 39, 186.
  order of one of the, or of Visiting Committee, necessary for application of test of malingering, 40, 186.
  power of, to make allowance to discharged prisoners, 43, 173.
  how far they may pay expenses of return of discharged prisoners to place of settlement, 43, 44, 90.
  duty of Visiting Committee in co-operating with, and in making inquiry into matters referred to them by, 263.
  abuses in prisons to be brought to the knowledge of, by Visiting Committee, 263.
  report of prisoners' complaints to, by Visiting Committee, 264.
  Visiting Committee to report to, respecting injurious effect of prison discipline upon mind, &c., of prisoners, 264.

Prison Commissioners (continued)—
  report to, by Visiting Committee, respecting prisoners' diet. 264.
  to fix sums to be paid for use of special rooms or cells and for certain domestic services, by prisoners awaiting trial, misdemeanants of first division, &c., 265, 261, 269, 273, 274.
  to fix deductions from earnings of prisoners awaiting trial, 271.
  to fix deductions from earnings of misdemeanants of first division, 275.
  power of, to order prisoners to be weighed, 279.
  yearly report to be made to, by chaplain on religious condition, &c., of prisoners, 283.
  upon what matters chaplain to report to, periodically, 283.
  power of, as to performance of Divine service by prison minister, 283, 284.
  sanction of, as to books for prison library, 284.
  may give directions in special cases as to place of admission for visitors, 285.
  prison officers to complain to, if desirous of appealing against decision affecting them, &c., 289.
  approval by. of restrictions as to use of tobacco, &c., by prison officers, 289.
  gaoler to report to, offence by officers of bringing into or carrying out of prison certain articles contrary to orders, 289.
  duty of gaoler in sending reports or complaints by officers to, 291.
  doubt as to class of rules applicable to prisoners to be reported to, 292.
  when gaoler to report to, of prisoner's life being in danger, 292.

Prison Dress: (See Dress—Clothing).

Prisoners: (See also Debtors—Female Prisoners—Misdemeanants).
  " prisoner," definition of, 3, 195.
  " criminal prisoner," definition of, 3, 61.
  what expenses to be included in term "maintenance of," 5, 195.
  not to be exempted from payment of certain costs, &c., 6, 196.
  " cell accommodation " for, defined, 6, 196.
  " sufficient accommodation " for, defined, 6, 196.
  accommodation for, provision of, 7, 65.
  power of prison authority to contract for reception, &c., of, 8, 82.
  termination of local obligation to maintain, 8, 163.
  maintenance of, out of public funds, 8, 150.
  average maximum number of, how computed, 11, 166.
  determination of contracts between prison authorities in relation to maintenance of, 12, 168.
  control and safe custody of, to vest in Secretary of State, 14, 151.
  all powers, &c., of prison authorities, &c., in relation to, to be vested in Secretary of State, 14, 151.
  condition of, to be reported on by Prison Commissioners, 19, 157.
  yearly return of punishments and offences of, to be made to Parliament, 20, 158.

INDEX. 335

Prisoners (continued)—
members of Visiting Committee to have free access to, at all times, 21, 159.
Visiting Committee to be deemed Visiting Justices as regards punishment of, when, 22, 161.
personal correction of, order of two justices required for, 22, 161.
visits to, by Justice of the Peace, 23, 97, 161.
under sentence of death, not to be visited by Justice of Peace who is not a member of Visiting Committee, 23, 162.
prison to be certified as fit for reception of, 29, 98.
commitment and classification of, 29—31 ; 170—172.
when, for a matter arising in one county, may be committed to prison in an adjoining county, 170, 260.
appropriation of prisons to classes of, by prison authority, 83.
public notice to be given of such appropriation, 84.
to what prison commitment of may be, 30, 172.
confinement of, before and during trial, 30, 170, 259.
confinement of, after conviction, 31, 171.
confinement of debtor and of non-criminal, 31, 171, 259.
convicted criminal, when to be taken back at public expense to place of conviction, 31, 44. 171.
in prison, to be deemed to be in legal custody of gaoler, 31, 98.
when to be deemed in legal custody, 32, 172.
escape of, how far sheriff liable for, 32, 100, 174.
under sentence of death, sheriff's jurisdiction, &c., as to, not to be affected, 31, 33, 98, 174.
calendar of, to be delivered by gaoler, 33, 100.
custody and trial of, in a substituted prison, 34, 102.
separation of, provisions as to, 34, 72, 117, 268, 273.
criminal, not to communicate with each other, 35, 72.
cells to be certified for confinement of, 35, 73.
hard labour of, 36, 37, 74, 75. 121, 122, 123, 183, 282.
when to be divided into two divisions of misdemeanants, 37, 102.
of first division of misdemeanants, not to be deemed criminal, 38, 103.
special rules to be made for unconvicted, &c., 38, 184, 185.
rules so made, 268—272.
confined for non-payment of sums in the nature of debts, special rules may be made as to treatment, &c., of, 38, 183.
rules so made, 276—279.
convicted of sedition or seditious libel, treatment of, 39, 186, 276.
imprisoned for contempt of court, treatment of, 40, 186, 276.
malingering of, application of test for, 40, 186.
limitation of time of confinement of, in punishment cells, 40, 186.
assisting to escape from prison, offence of, 40, 87.
removal of, for trial, 42, 100.
removal of, by order of Her Majesty, 42, 101.
removal of, for alteration, &c., of prison, 42, 101.
removal of convicted criminal, by Secretary of State 42, 171.
removal of, by judge's order, 30, 172.

Prisoners (continued)—
discharge of, when term of imprisonment expires on Sunday, 43, 89.
discharge of, when under sixteen years of age. 280.
allowance to, on discharge from prison, 43, 89. 173.
how allowance to, on discharge from prison, may be paid, 280.
discharged, may be provided with means of returning to place of settlement, 43, 90.
not to be jurors on inquests held on bodies of prisoners, 44. 93.
death of, in prison, duties of gaoler and surgeon on, 133, 137, 291.
death of, in prison, provisions as to inquests, 44. 93. 187.
rules, &c., to be made as to diet of convicted criminal, 45. 76.
commitment of, to certain prisons, prohibited, 48. 103.
removal of, from prisons scheduled in P. A., 1865, 48, 104.
expenses of, confined in county, instead of scheduled prisons, 49, 104.
chapel to be provided for in prison, 79.
to be searched on admission to prison. 116.
not to be searched in presence of other prisoners. 116.
duty of gaoler as to keeping an inventory of articles found on, 116.
name, age, &c., of criminal, to be entered in nominal record, 116.
to be examined by surgeon on admission to prison, 116. 279. 292.
to be examined, &c., by surgeon, before removal or discharge, 117.
spirituous liquors, for use of, admission of, into prison, 117.
food, clothing, wine, &c., not to be sold to, by debtors, 118, 277.
awaiting trial may procure food, malt liquor. &c.. 118. 269.
not to sell. &c., food, malt liquor, &c., to other prisoners. 118, 270.
to receive prison allowance of food, if they do not provide it, 119.
food of, to be inspected frequently by Visiting Committee, 264.
when additional clothing and bedding may be issued for, 281.
allowance of food to convicted criminal, 119.
dress of criminal, before trial. 119.
dress of convicted criminal, 119.
convicted criminal, restricted to prison allowance of food, &c., 119.
scales and weights and measures to be provided for use of, 119,
return of clothing to, and provision of for, on discharge, 120.
purification and disinfection of clothing, &c., of, 120. 280.
beds and sleeping of, 120, 270, 281.
personal cleanliness of, 120, 270, 275, 277, 282.
cutting hair of, 120, 270, 282.
gaming not to be permitted amongst, 121.
allowance to certain, out of earnings, 121, 271.
assistance of Visiting Committee, regarding gratuities earned by, 266.
employment of, before trial, 121, 270, 271.
exercise of criminal, in the open air, 123.
to be examined by surgeon when at hard labour, 122, 292, 293.
directions of surgeon as to, to be entered in his journal 123.
employment of, when not sentenced to hard labour, 123.
names of, appearing out of health., &c., to be reported, 123, 287.
infirmary to be provided for sick, 124.
attendance of, at Divine service, 125, 264, 272.
admission of ministers to visit, 125, 283.

INDEX.

Prisoners (continued)—
    books and printed papers for religious instruction of, to be approved by chaplain or minister, 125, 126, 284.
    instruction of, provisions as to, 127, 270, 275, 284.
    visits to, and communications with, 127, 266, 271, 275, 278, 285, 286.
    powers of gaoler as regards visitors to, 127, 285, 286.
    punishment of, for offences against discipline, 128, 129, 286.
    putting into irons or under mechanical restraint, 129, 264, 287, 291.
    under sentence of death, general provisions as to, 130, 287.
    officers of prison not to sell or let to, or have pecuniary dealings with, 131, 288.
    officers of prison not to take gratuities from, 131.
    how far they may be employed in prison offices, 131.
    not to be employed in instruction of other prisoners, 131.
    to be visited daily by gaoler, 132.
    on visits to female, gaoler to be attended by matron, &c., 132.
    illness of, to be notified by gaoler to surgeon, 123, 133.
    daily list of, complaining of illness, removed to infirmary, &c., to be delivered to surgeon, 133.
    daily list of, confined in punishment cells, to be delivered to chaplain and surgeon, 133.
    abstract of regulations to be read to, 133, 280.
    insane, or apparently insane, gaoler to report, 133, 156, 289.
    disordered in mind, &c., to be reported to surgeon, 123, 133.
    gaoler to carry out surgeon's directions respecting, 133.
    record of employment of, sentenced to hard labour, 134.
    register of church or religion of, to be kept, 134, 223.
    nominal record of, to be kept, 134.
    punishments for prison offences, entries to be made of, 134.
    record of articles taken from, to be kept, 134.
    when to be visited by surgeon, 136.
    in punishment cells, chaplain and surgeon to visit daily, 136, 283.
    sick, how often to be visited by surgeon, 136.
    surgeon may order removal of, to infirmary, 136.
    duties of surgeon in keeping daily record of, 137.
    injuriously affected in mind, &c., surgeon to report, 137, 293.
    duty of Visiting Committee as to, 264.
    appearing to need special notice of chaplain, surgeon to report, 137.
    calendar of, to be sent by gaoler to Secretary of State, 139.
    not debtors, &c., making of rules as to, by justices, 141.
    to what house of correction they may be committed, 204.
    convicted of offences for which they are liable to death, &c., may be committed to house of correction, 205.
    borough, in county prisons, how expenses of, defrayed, 212.
    how expenses of prosecution of, to be defrayed, 213.
    for debt and contempt of court, commitment of, to county gaol, 217.
    provisions of Prison Ministers Act as to visits of ministers to, 222, 223.
    who are Jews, not to be compelled to labour on their Sabbath, 282.
    sentenced to death, to be executed within walls of prison, 227.
    bodies of executed, to be buried within the prison, 227.

Prisoners (continued)—
>not to be jurors on inquests on bodies of executed criminals, 227.
>registering and photographing of, 230—235; 279.
>military, duty of gaoler as to reception and imprisonment of. 236.
>>solitary confinement and corporal punishment of, 236, 237.
>>>discharge or removal of, in certain cases, 237, 238.
>from Marines, duty of gaoler, as to reception and imprisonment of, under Marine Mutiny Act, 242. 243. 245, note (*y*).
>solitary confinement of, 242, 244, 245, note (*y*).
>corporal punishment of, 244.
>awaiting trial, not to be placed in view of convicted. 268.
>awaiting trial, when routine of prison may be modified in regard to, 265,*269.
>awaiting trial, supply of books, &c., to, and occupation for, 265, 270.
>awaiting trial, may be allowed use of special room or cell, to exercise separately, &c., 265, 268.
>awaiting trial, how money of, in gaoler's hands, may be applied, 269.
>awaiting trial, what books, &c., to be allowed to retain, 269.
>awaiting trial, when their own medical man may attend, 270.
>awaiting trial, supply of paper and writing materials to. 271.
>awaiting trial, how far to be subject to general prison rules, 272.
>awaiting trial, to what persons special rules for, to apply, 272.
>when to take a bath on reception, 268, 279.
>treatment of, when diseased, &c., on admission, 279.
>when to be weighed, 279.
>use of spare cells of one class of, for those of another, 280.
>provision against exposure of, to public view, 280.
>complaints, &c., of, with regard to food, when to be made. 281.
>when repeated complaints by, as to food may be punished, 281.
>convicted criminal, when to sleep on plank bed. 281.
>to obey regulations as to washing, bathing, hair-cutting, &c., 282.
>to be allowed a proper supply of clean linen, &c., 282.
>not to be stripped or bathed in presence of other prisoners, 282.
>duty of, in keeping their cells, &c., clean, 282.
>who can read, to be supplied with Bible, &c., of denomination, 282.
>religious condition, &c., of, chaplain to report on yearly. 283.
>wishing to receive Holy Sacrament, to give notice to chaplain, 283.
>duty of chaplain in seeing and admonishing, 283.
>chaplain to visit daily in infirmary, when sick, &c., 283.
>under orders for execution, &c., duty of chaplain as to, 283.
>names and other particulars of those of his persuasion to be given to prison minister, 283.
>duty of prison minister in seeing, &c., of his persuasion, 284.
>prison minister to pay particular attention to those of his persuasion under orders for execution, &c., 284.
>duty of prison officers as to treatment of, 287.
>wishing to see gaoler, prison officers to report to him, 287.
>prison officers not to strike, except, &c., 288.
>misconduct, &c., of, to be reported immediately to gaoler, 288.

Prisoners (continued)—
subordinate officers not to converse unnecessarily with, &c., 288.
not to be employed for private benefit of any person, 288.
suspension of officers for carrying into or out of prison certain articles to or for, contrary to orders, 289.
duties of gaoler as regards labour and employment of, 289.
identification of, duty of gaoler in aiding in, 290.
unauthorized communications between, and visitors, to be prevented, 220.
gaoler to notify to chaplain, &c., when life of, in danger, 290.
gaoler's duty in hearing complaints made by, &c., 290.
Visiting Committee to be informed of, desiring to see them, 291.
communications between, &c., duties of gaoler as to, 291.
how often to be visited when in solitary confinement or punishment cells, 291.
Secretary of State's decision final as to class of rules applicable to, 292.
power and duties of Visiting Committee and gaoler as to granting permission to, in certain cases, 264, 268, 273, 278, 291.
identification of, points likely to aid, gaoler to be informed of, 292.
when surgeon to report to gaoler of, on medical grounds, 292.
when gaoler to report to Commissioners, life of endangered, 292.
to be examined, &c., by surgeon, before corporal punishment, 293.
records of health of, to be kept by surgeon, 293.
health of, to be reported on periodically by surgeon, 293.

Prisoners' Aid Society:
payments to, for benefit of discharged prisoners, 43, 89, 173.
how to be certified, 221.
how certificate of may be revoked or suspended, 221.

Prison Jurisdiction, Separate: (See Separate Prison Jurisdiction).

Prison Minister:
regulations as to admission of, into prisons, 125.
when to approve books, &c., for religious instruction, 126.
to have free access to prisoner of his persuasion, under sentence of death, 130.
provisions of Prison Ministers Act, as to admission of, 222, 223.
when absent on leave, &c., may appoint a substitute, 126.
on death of, a substitute to be appointed, 126.
names, &c., to be given to, of prisoners of his persuasion, 223, 283.
when to have access to prisoners of his persuasion, 283.
not to communicate with prisoners not of his persuasion, 223, 283.
when to perform Divine service, 283.
duty of, in seeing and admonishing prisoners, 284.
to visit sick prisoners of his persuasion, 284.
to pay particular attention to prisoners of his persuasion under orders for execution, &c., 284.
power of, to object to the issue of certain books to prisoners of his persuasion, 284.

Prison Minister (continued)—
    not to interfere with established rules, &c., of the prison, 284.
    to confer with the gaoler, and to co-operate with him in promoting good order, 284.
    gaoler to notify to, case of life of prisoner in danger, 290.

Prison Ministers Act, 1863:
    provisions of, 222, 223.
    gaoler to keep register required by, 134.

Prison Offences: (See Offences against Prison Discipline).

Prison Officers:
    chief, included in term "gaoler," 3, 61.
    what to be appointed, 23, 66.
    female, to be appointed where females are imprisoned 24, 67.
    general appointment of, to vest in Secretary of State, 14, 24, 151.
    what, to be appointed by Prison Commissioners, 16, 154.
    salaries of, under P. A., 1877, provisions as to, 17. 155.
    complaint of inspector against, how to be made, 17, 77.
    subordinate, to be appointed by Prison Commissioners, 18, 24, 155.
    tenure of office and salaries of, under P. A., 1865, 24, 70.
    meaning of term, "existing officers of a prison," 25. 177.
    tenure of office, duties and salaries of existing. 25, 177.
    existing. may be distributed amongst the prisons to which P. A., 1877, applies, 25, 178.
    superannuation of, 26, 70, 108. 179.
    in receipt of military or naval half-pay, or who have commuted their pension, not to be subject to deduction, 25, 178.
    abolition of office of, or retirement or removal of, 27, 179, 180.
    apportionment of annuity granted to. 28, 180.
    when not to be entitled to superannuation allowance, &c., 28, 194.
    removal of. from houses or apartments occupied officially, 28, 71.
    jurisdiction of sheriff over, as regards carrying out sentence of death on prisoners. 31, 33, 98, 174.
    when prisoners to be deemed to be in legal custody of, 32, 172.
    cells to be furnished with means of communication with, 35, 73.
    punishment of, for allowing sale or use of spirituous liquors or tobacco in prison, 41, 88.
    punishment of. for carrying letters, &c., into or out of prison, contrary to regulations, 41, 88.
    not to be jurors on inquests on bodies of prisoners. 44, 93, 227.
    buildings occupied by, to be included in term "prison." 2. 61.
    compensation to. of prisons scheduled in P. A., 1865, for loss of salary, &c., 49, 105.
    when visitors not to sleep in apartments of subordinate. 115.
    to report to gaoler names of prisoners wishing to see surgeon, or out of health, 123, 287.
    duties of, as regards prisoners under sentence of death, 130.
    prisoners not to be employed in the capacity of certain, 131.
    how far debtors may be employed as, 131.
    to be constables, 131.

INDEX. 311

Prison Officers (continued)—
not to sell or let to, or to have pecuniary dealings with prisoners, 131, 288.
not to have any interest in contracts for supply of the prison, 131.
when they may purchase provisions under prison contract, 289.
not to receive gratuities, 131.
female, to search female prisoners on admission, 117.
female, to attend female prisoners, 132.
female, or matron, to accompany gaoler on visits to female prisoners, 132.
execution of their duties by, to be enforced by gaoler, 132.
subordinate, not to be employed in any private capacity, 132.
subordinate, power of gaoler to suspend, 132.
to obey the gaoler, 138, 288.
not to be absent without leave, 138.
subordinate, not to receive visitors without leave, 138.
to examine cells, locks, &c., and seize prohibited articles, 138.
non-resident, to enter visits in non-resident officers' book, 141.
duties of, acting as gate porter, 139.
what, to be deemed subordinate, 141.
compensation to, in certain cases where prison discontinued, 225.
what, to be present at execution of capital sentences, 227.
present at execution of capital sentences to sign a declaration, 227.
penalty for signing a false declaration, 228.
power of Visiting Committee to suspend, 263.
to inspect articles of food received for prisoners awaiting trial, 269.
not to examine confidential written instructions of prisoner awaiting trial to his solicitor, 271.
when interview between prisoner awaiting trial and his legal adviser may be in view of one of the, 271.
to be specially appointed to search misdemeanants of first division, 273.
to inspect articles of food procured by misdemeanants of first division, 274.
to inspect articles of food provided by debtors for themselves, 277.
their duty in treatment of prisoners, 287.
to inform gaoler of prisoners wishing to see him, &c., 287.
not to strike prisoners, except, &c., 288.
subordinate, to report to gaoler immediately misconduct, &c., of prisoners, 288.
subordinate, not to converse unnecessarily with prisoners, &c., 288.
not to allow prisoners to be employed for private benefit of any person, 288.
to be held responsible for knowledge of prison rules, &c., 288.
to treat members of Visiting Committee with respect, &c., 263, 288.
to complain to Commissioners, if desirous to appeal against any decision affecting them, &c., 289.
tobacco and spirituous liquors not to be used by, within the prison, except, &c., 289.

Prison Officers (continued)—
suspension of, for bringing into or carrying out of prison certain articles, contrary to orders, 289.
reports ordered to be made by, under P. A. 1865, to be made to Commissioners, 289.
defects in washing places, baths, &c., to be reported by, 290.
when gaoler to send reports or complaints by, to the Commissioners, 291.
duty of matron to accompany, &c., on entering part of prison allotted to females, 292.
health and capability of, to be reported on periodically by surgeon, 293.

Prisons:
convict, military, naval, P. A., 1865, 1877, not to apply to, 1, 61, 150.
definition of the term " prison," 2, 61, 197.
governor, keeper, &c., of, included in term "gaoler," 3, 61.
authorities of, definition of, 3, 62.
" furniture and effects belonging to," definition of, 5, 195.
belonging to City of London to be deemed within the city, 6, 196.
maintenance of, by separate prison jurisdiction, 7, 65.
maintenance of, out of public funds, 8, 150.
termination of local obligation to maintain, 8, 163.
powers, &c., of prison authority as to enlarging, &c., 7, 77, 78, 79.
penalty on inadequate, 8, 84.
power of Secretary of State to close inadequate, 8, 85.
average maximum number of prisoners in, how computed, 11, 166.
uncompleted, allowance to be made in respect of, 11, 166.
uncompleted, time may be allowed for completion of, 11, 166.
determination of contracts between prison authorities in relation to maintenance of, &c., 12, 168.
to vest in Secretary of State, 14, 151.
appointment of officers of, to vest in Secretary of State, 14, 24, 151.
various powers relating to, to vest in Secretary of State, 14, 151.
appropriation of court houses, &c., within precincts of, 14, 191, 192.
legal estate in, to vest in Prison Commissioners, 15, 191.
legal estate in, disposal of, by Prison Commissioners, 15, 191.
protection of, when in nature of national monuments, 15, 192.
appointment of Commissioners of, 15, 153.
appointment of Inspectors, officers, and servants of, 16, 154.
irregularity in, to be reported by Inspector, 17, 77.
general superintendence of, Prison Commissioners to have, 18, 155.
to be visited and inspected by Commissioners or Inspectors, 18, 155.
general duties of Commissioners in relation to, 17—20; 155—158.
Commissioners to have powers of Visiting Justices, as to. 18, 155.
Commissioners to make reports on condition of, 19, 20, 157.
manufacturing processes in, to be reported on, 19, 157.
yearly return to be made of punishments, &c., in, 19, 158.
Visiting Committee of, to be appointed, 21, 158.
rules as to appointment of Visiting Committee of, 250—258; 262.

INDEX. 343

Prisons (continued)—
  members of Visiting Committee to have free access to, at all times, 21, 159.
  members of Visiting Committee not to be interested in contracts relating to, 263.
  Visiting Justices, appointment and duties of, 20, 96, 97.
  repeal of provisions as to appointment of Visiting Justices of, 53, 158.
  visits to, by any justice, 23, 97, 161.
  appointment, salaries, &c., of officers of, 23, 24, 25, 66, 70, 177.
  appointment of chaplain to two, 26, 69.
  appointment of assistant-chaplain and deputy gaoler of, 26, 69.
  abolition of distinction between, and houses of correction, 29, 98.
  wheresoever situate, to be deemed within limits of place for which used, 29, 98.
  when any prison locally situate in a county may be appointed as prison of county, riding, &c., 29, 173.
  saving as to commitment of prisoners to, 30, 172.
  appointment of, for confinement of prisoners before and during trial, 30, 170, 259.
  appropriation of, to convicted criminal prisoners, 31, 171.
  appropriation of, to debtors and non-criminal prisoners, 31, 171, 259.
  prisoners in, to be deemed to be in legal custody of gaoler, 31, 98.
  when prisoners in, to be deemed to be in legal custody, 32, 172.
  jurisdiction of sheriff in, as regards prisoners under sentence of death, 31, 33, 98, 174.
  gaoler of, where debtors confined, how far required to give security to sheriff, 32, 99.
  admission of prisoners to, 116, 117, 268, 273, 277, 279—281.
  escape of prisoners from, liability of sheriff for, 32, 100, 174.
  description of, in writ, &c., 33, 100.
  gaoler of, to deliver calendar of prisoners for trial in, 33, 100.
  custody and trial of prisoners in substituted, 34, 102.
  separation of prisoners in, provisions as to, 34, 35, 72, 117, 268, 273.
  cells in, to be certified by an Inspector of Prisons, 35, 73.
  certificate of Inspector as to cells in, may be varied, &c., 36, 74.
  hard labour in, provisions as to, 36, 37, 74, 75, 121, 122, 123, 183, 282.
  misdemeanants in, when to be divided into two divisions, 37, 102.
  assisting prisoners to escape from, &c., 40, 87.
  conveyance of letters, &c., into, with intent, &c., 40, 87.
  punishment for carrying spirituous liquors or tobacco into, 41, 87.
  carrying letters into, or out of, contrary to regulations, 41, 88.
  notice to be given of penalties for offences in relation to, 41, 88.
  removal of prisoners from, for trial, &c., 42, 100.
  removal of prisoners from, by order of Her Majesty, 42, 101.
                for alteration, &c., of prison, 42, 101.
                by judge's order, 30, 172.
  removal from, of convicted criminal prisoners, 42, 171.

Prisons (continued)—
    discharge of prisoners from, 43, 89, 117, 280.
    allowance to prisoners on discharge from, 43, 89, 173, 280.
    prisoners on discharge from, may be provided with means of returning to place of settlement, 43, 44, 90.
    inquests on prisoners dying in, provisions as to, 44, 93, 187.
    saving as to rules in force in, before P. A., 1865, 45, 109.
    regulations as to, in schedule I. of P. A., 1865, to be binding, 44, 76.
    rules in addition to regulations may be made, 45, 76.
    discontinuance of certain, 48, 103.
    removal of prisoners from those scheduled in P. A., 1865, 48, 104.
    expenses of prisoners confined in county, instead of in scheduled prisons, 49, 104.
    scheduled in P. A., 1865, use of, as lock-up-houses, &c., 49, 105.
    compensation for loss of office by closing of scheduled, 49, 105.
    saving of rights of creditors of scheduled, in P. A., 1865, 50, 108.
    unnecessary, power of prison authority to sell, 50, 92, 93.
    discontinuance of, by Secretary of State, 50, 175.
    effect of discontinuance of, by Secretary of State, 51, 176.
    when chapel to be provided for, 79.
    infirmary to be provided for, 124.
    appointment of Surveyor-General of, 82.
    appropriation of, to classes of prisoners, by prison authority, 83.
    public notice to be given of such appropriation of, 84.
    cleanliness in, regulations as to, 115, 270, 275, 277, 282.
    trees, &c., not to be allowed against outer walls of, 115.
    tools and implements not to be left unnecessarily exposed in, 115.
    temperature of, provision as to, 115.
    visitors to, when not to sleep in, 115.
    hours of locking and unlocking, 116.
    no tap to be kept in, 117.
    spirituous liquors not to be admitted into, except, &c., 117.
    smoking in, and introduction of tobacco into, rule as to, 117.
    scales and weights and measures to be provided in, 119.
    purification and disinfection of clothing, &c., of prisoners in, 120, 280.
    beds, bedding, and sleeping of prisoners in, 120, 270, 275, 281.
    personal cleanliness of prisoners in, 120, 270, 275, 277, 282.
    cutting hair of prisoners in, 120, 270, 275, 277, 282.
    employment of prisoners in, 120, 121, 122, 123, 270, 271, 275.
    prohibition of gaming in, 121.
    permitting debtors to work and follow their trades, &c., in, 121.
    allowance to prisoners out of earnings in, 121, 271, 275.
    health of prisoners in, regulations as to, 123, 124, 270.
    religious instruction of prisoners in, 124—126, 278, 282—284.
    instruction of prisoners in, 127, 270, 275, 284.
    abuses in, to be communicated to gaoler by chaplain, 126.
        Prison Commissioners to inquire into, 18, 156.
        Visiting Committee to report on, 22, 160.
            Visiting Committee to bring to notice of the Commissioners, 263.

INDEX. 345

Prisons (continued)—
abuses in, a justice of the peace may make entries respecting, in Visitors' Book, 23, 162.
visits to, and communications with prisoners in, 127, 271.
powers and duties of gaoler as regards visitors to, 127, 285.
offences against discipline of, punishment of, 128, 129, 286.
use of irons or mechanical restraint in, 129, 264, 287, 291.
infliction of corporal punishment within, 130, 161, 286, 287.
regulations as to prisoners under sentence of death in, 130, 287.
employment of prisoners and debtors in offices of, 131.
officers of, not to have any interest in contracts for supply of, 131.
       compensation to, on discontinuance of certain, 225, 226.
register of religion of prisoners to be kept in, 223.
gaoler of, to reside in, 132.
law and regulations of, gaoler to conform to and enforce, 132.
daily inspection of, by gaoler, 132.
weekly inspection of, by gaoler at night, 132.
abstract of certain regulations, to be posted up in cells in, 133.
death of prisoners in, duties of gaoler on, 133, 291.
gaoler to be responsible for safe custody of all journals, &c., in, 134.
absence of gaoler from, provisions as to, 134.
cells, &c., of females in, to be secured by locks different from those of the males, 135.
matron of, to reside in, 135.
every part of, occupied by females, to be visited daily by matron, 135.
weekly inspection of, by matron at night, 135.
absence of matron from, provisions as to, 136.
when surgeon to visit, 136.
every part of, to be inspected occasionally by the surgeon, 137.
duties of the surgeon on making inspection of, 137.
power of Secretary of State to visit and inspect or to authorise any person to visit and inspect, 206.
judgment of death to be executed within walls of, 227.
what officers of, and persons to be present at executions in, 227.
bodies of executed criminals to be buried within the walls of, 227.
printed copies of certificate, &c., of due execution of judgment of death, to be exhibited at or near to the principal entrance of, 208.
to what, bankruptcy prisoners may be committed, 230.
registration and photographing of prisoners in, 230—235; 279, 280.
returns to be made of convicted criminal prisoners in, 231, 233.
military offenders, under Mutiny Act, to be received into, 236.
soldiers to be received into, 236.
removal or discharge of military offenders from, 237.
subsistence of military offenders in, 239.
commitment of military deserters to, 240, 241.
temporary custody of military deserters in, 241.
penalty for refusal to receive military offenders into, 242.
offenders to be received into, under Marine Mutiny Act, 242.
any marine to be received into, 243.

Prisons (continued)—
    subsistence, &c., of marines in, 243, note (*x*), 246.
    commitment to, of deserters from the marines, 248.
    temporary custody in, of deserters from the marines, 249
    when routine of, may be modified in regard to prisoners awaiting trial, 265, 269.
    when spare cells of one class of prisoners in, may be used for those of another, 280.
    provision against exposure of prisoners to public view on removal to or from, 280.
    reception of children of female prisoners into, 280.
    retention and clothing of children of female prisoners in, 280.
    discharge of children of female prisoners from, 280.
    chaplain to attend daily, 283.
    prison minister not to interfere with established rules, &c., of, 284.
    library to be provided in, 284.
    unauthorized communications concerning officers, not to make, 288.
    tobacco and spirituous liquors not to be used within walls of, by officers, except, &c., 289.
    suspension of officers of, for carrying into, or out of, certain articles contrary to orders, 289.
    when officers and gaoler may buy provisions at contract rates 289.
    gaoler not to deal with tradesmen supplying, except, &c., 289.
    orders, &c., relating to departments of, to be addressed to gaoler, 289.
    when persons not to be allowed to view, 290.
    ventilation, drainage, &c., of, to be attended to by gaoler, 290.
    duties of gaoler in enforcing silence in, &c., 291.
    division of, allotted to females, when not to be entered by male officers or visitors, 292.
    general health, &c., of, surgeon to report on periodically, 293.
    articles of food, &c., not to be received into, until examined, 293.
    admission into, of articles likely to be used for improper purposes may be refused, 293.

Prison Service:
    meaning of the term, 27, 180.

Prohibition:
    of commitment to certain prisons, 48, 103.
    of gaming in prisons, 121.

Proof:
    of rules made by Secretary of State, 45, 192.

Prosecution:
    of offences in relation to prisons, 41, 95.
    for anything done in pursuance of P. A., 1865, 47, 94.

Protection:
    of prisons in nature of national monuments, 15, 192.

Provisions:
suspension, &c., of officers for carrying into or out of prisons, contrary to orders, 289.
power of officers to purchase at contract rates, 289.
power of gaoler to purchase at contract rates, 289.

Public Department of State:
when included in term " prison authority," 9, 165.

Public Funds:
maintenance of prisons, &c., out of, 8, 150, 163.

Public Works Loan Commissioners:
power of, to lend money to a prison authority for building, &c., prisons, 81.
within what time money so lent by, must be repaid, 80.
may lend money to prison authority for payment of compensation in respect of unprovided cell accommodation, 9, 164.
may lend money to prison authority for making required payment to the Exchequer on discontinuance of a prison, 52, 177.
on what securities money may be lent by, under P. A. 1877, 190, 191.
The Local Loans Act, 1875, to apply to loans made by, 191.

Punishment Book:
to be kept by gaoler, 134.
entries as to punishment of prison offences to be made in, 128.
particulars of corporal punishment to be entered in, 130, 287.

Punishment Cells: (See Cells).

Punishment of Prisoners:
yearly return of, to be made to Parliament, 20, 158.
for prison offences, not to be awarded except by gaoler, &c., 128.
Visiting Committee to be deemed Visiting Justices as to, 22, 161.
Visiting Committee to furnish information respecting, 264.
corporal, order of two justices required for, 22, 161.
prisoner to hear evidence, &c., against him before infliction of, 286.
dietary and corporal not to be inflicted unless surgeon certifies, 286.

Quarter Sessions: (See Justices in Quarter Sessions).
to include " General Sessions," 3, 61.

Reading:
prisoners to be taught, 127.

Receiver:
may be appointed by mortgagee, &c., to enforce repayment of loan made to prison authority, 80.

Recovery of Penalties: (See Penalties).

Record:
nominal, of prisoners to be kept by gaoler, 134.
of articles taken from prisoners, 134.
of employment of prisoners sentenced to hard labour, 134.

Reformatory Schools:
saving of powers and jurisdiction of prison authority as to, 14, 193.
when a member of a Visiting Committee may name a school to which a youthful offender may be sent, 266.
when a youthful offender is to be sent, &c., to, of his own religious persuasion, 267.

Register:
gaoler to keep, of religious persuasion of prisoners, 134, 223.
of habitual criminals, provisions, &c., as to, 230—235.

Registrar of Habitual Criminals:
duties of gaoler in sending returns and photographs of habitual criminals to, 233, 234, 279.

Regulations: (See also Rules).
contained in first Schedule of P. A., 1865, to be binding, 44, 76.
justices empowered to make rules in addition to, 45, 76.
schedule of, under P. A., 1865, 115—141.
rules, &c., made by justices, under P. A., 1865, to be deemed, 141.
construction of the term "regulation," 141.
made under P. A., 1877, to be laid before Parliament, 46, 193.
abstract of, to be posted up in cells, and read to prisoners, 183, 230.
for execution of judgment of death, Secretary of State to make, 228.
provisions of those so to be observed, 228, note (*q*).
as to registering and photographing criminals, Secretary of State to make, 231, 233.
effect of such, when made, 231, 233.
modification, &c., of such, by Secretary of State. 232.
provisions of, as to registering, &c., criminals, 233—235.
punishment of prisoners refusing to obey such, 232.

Religion:
of prisoners, register of to be kept, 134, 223.

Religious and Moral Instruction:
of prisoners, provisions as to, 124, 125, 126, 278, 282—284.
chapel to be used only for, or for religious worship, 79.

Religious Worship:
chapel of prison to be used only for, or for moral and religious instruction, 79.

Removal:
of prison officer from office, superannuation allowance on, 27, 180.
of prison officers, from houses, &c., occupied officially, 28, 71.
of prisoners, from one prison, &c., to another, for trial, &c., 42, 100.
    by order of Her Majesty, 42, 101.
    for alteration, &c., of prison, 42, 101.
    by judge's order, 30, 172.
    from prisons scheduled in P. A., 1865, 48, 104.
    from prisons closed as inadequate, 86.
of convicted criminal prisoners, by Secretary of State, 42, 171.
prisoners to be examined by surgeon before, 117.

Repeal:
of Acts in schedule III. of P. A., 1865, 52, 106.
saving clauses as to, of Acts in schedule III. of P. A., 1865, and certain other Acts, 52, 45, 106.
of 5 & 6 Will IV., c. 38, s. 7, as to appointment of Inspectors of Prisons, 53, 188.
of ss. 53, 54 of the P. A., 1865, 20, 53, 158.
of s. 55 of the P. A., 1865, 23, 53, 161.
of enactments inconsistent with the P. A., 1877, 54, 192.

Reports:
when to be made to Prison Commissioners, 18, 156, 289.
by Prison Commissioners, when to be made, 19, 157.
to be laid before Parliament, 19, 157.
to contain information as to manufacturing processes, 19, 157.
effect of, of Prison Commissioners as regards compensation to be paid to a prison authority, 10, 166.
by Prison Commissioners as to good conduct, &c., of officer, requisite for superannuation, 27, 180.
when to be made to Secretary of State by Visiting Committee of prisons, 22, 161, 263, 264.
when special, to be made by Visiting Committee to Secretary of State or to the Commissioners, 263.
of chaplain and surgeon, as to condition of prison, &c., 140, 289.
chaplain to make yearly, on religious and moral condition, &c., of prisoners, 283.
on what matters to be made by chaplain periodically, 283.
at what hour to be heard by gaoler, 290.
by prison officers, when gaoler to send to Commissioners, 291.

Restraint: (See Mechanical Restraint).

Retention:
of books, &c., by unconvicted prisoners, special rules to be made as to, 39, 184.
provisions as to, 269.

Retirement:
of prison officers, provisions as to, 27, 180.

Return:
of punishments and offences of prisoners to be made annually to Parliament, 20, 158.
of habitual criminals, to be made by gaoler, 231, 233, 234.

Richmond:
borough prison of, to be discontinued, 48, 103.
meaning of the term "county" as regards, 104.

Ridings:
definition of term "riding," 6, 196.
maintenance of prison by, 7, 65.
termination of local obligation of, to maintain a prison, 8, 163.
in counties divided into, &c., gaol sessions to be held, 199.

Ridings (continued)—
  power of Justices of the Peace of, as respects gaol sessions, 200.
  in what proportions rates to be paid by, for gaol expenses, 201.
  proportions to be settled by arbitration in case of dispute, 202.
  order for payment of proportions to be sent to treasurer of, 203.
  court of gaol sessions in, may mortgage county rates, 203.
  in what manner rates to be charged upon, 203.
  gaol of county divided into, to be deemed within each riding, 204.

Romney Marsh:
  when bailiff and justices of liberty of, to be included in the term "justices in quarter sessions assembled," 12, 64.
  prison of the liberty of, to be discontinued, 48, 103.

Rules: (See also Regulations).
  time for making, under P. A., 1877, 1, 149.
  may be made by Secretary of State as to doing of certain acts by Prison Commissioners, 15, 153.
  made under P. A., 1877, not to restrict visits to prisons and prisoners by members of Visiting Committee, 21, 159.
  may be made by Secretary of State for appointment of Visiting Committee, 21, 158.
  to be made as to duties of Visiting Committee, 22, 160.
  may be made by Secretary of State as to confinement of prisoners before and during trial, 30, 170.
  as to confinement of prisoners after conviction, 31, 171.
  as to confinement of debtors, &c., 31, 171.
  may be made as to treatment, &c., of prisoners confined for non-payment of sums in the nature of debts, 38, 183.
  special to be made as to treatment of unconvicted and certain other prisoners, 38, 184, 185.
  might be made in addition to regulations contained in first schedule of P. A., 1865, 45, 76.
  in force on commencement of P. A., 1865, provisions as to, 45, 109.
  made by Secretary of State, how proved, 45, 192, 193.
  to be laid before both Houses of Parliament, 46, 193.
  not to be in force until laid before Parliament, 46, 193.
  for execution of judgment of death, Secretary of State to make, 228.
  to be laid before Parliament, 228.
  provisions of, 228.
  for first appointment of Visiting Committees, 250, 257.
  as to the number of members of Visiting Committees, and the sessions to appoint them, 252.
  as to appointment of Visiting Committees, in years subsequent to 1878, 262.
  as to duties of Visiting Committees, 263—267.
  as to confinement of prisoners before and during trial, of debtors, and non-criminal prisoners, 259, 260.
  for commitment of prisoners for a matter arising in certain counties to a prison in an adjoining county, 260.

Rules (continued)—
 Visiting Committee to make, for their attendance at prison, 263.
 special, as to prisoners awaiting trial, 268—272.
 special, for prisoners awaiting trial, to what persons to apply, 272.
 special, for misdemeanants of first division, 272—276.
 to what other persons to apply, 276.
 special, for debtors, 276—279.
 to what persons to apply, 279.
 general, made under P. A., 1877, 279—293.
 general, how far prisoners awaiting trial to be subject to, 272.
 how far misdemeanants of first division to be subject to, 276.
 how far debtors to be subject to, 279.
 officers to enforce observance of, 287.
 officers to be held responsible for being fully acquainted with, 288.
 decision of Secretary of State to be final as to class of, applicable to prisoners, 292.

Rye:
 borough prison of, to be discontinued, 48, 103.
 county gaol at Lewes to be deemed county prison for, 104.

Sabbath:
 prisoners who are Jews, not to be compelled to labour on, 282.

Sacrament (Holy):
 when to be administered by chaplain, 124.
 chaplain to give notice, &c., of the administration of, 283.
 prisoners wishing to receive to inform chaplain previously, 283.

Safe Custody of Prisoners: (See Custody).

Salary:
 of Prison Commissioners, Inspectors, and other officers, under P. A., 1877, 17, 155.
 of existing officers of prisons, 25, 70, 177.
 of Inspectors appointed under 5 & 6 Will. IV., c. 38, 17, 188.
 of clerk and treasurer of gaol sessions, 201.

Sale:
 of unnecessary prisons or land by prison authority, 50, 92.
 notice of, and manner of sale, provisions as to, 93.
 of discontinued prison, by prison authority or Secretary of State, 51, 176.

Saturday:
 when prisoner to be discharged on, 43, 89.

Scales and Weights and Measures:
 to be provided for use of prisoners, 119.

School:
 under whose superintendence to be, 284.
 chaplain to report yearly to Commissioners on instruction giv in, 283.

Scotland:
  Prison Acts not to extend to (1865), 1, 60; (1877) 1, 150.

Scriptures:
  portions of, to be read to prisoners at religious instruction, 124.

Search:
  of prisoners, on admission to prison, provisions as to, 116, 273.
  of female prisoners, to be made by female officers, 117.
  power of gaoler as to, of visitors, 127.
  of misdemeanants of first division, 273.

Secretary of State:
  time for making rules by, under P. A., 1877, 1, 149.
  power of, to close, &c., inadequate prisons, 8, 84, 85.
  power of, to decline to recommend payment of compensation to a prison authority, 10, 166.
  powers and duties of, in respect of an uncompleted prison, 11, 166.
  prisons to vest in, 14, 151.
  furniture and effects of prisons to vest in, 14, 24, 151.
  appointment of officers to vest in, 14, 24, 151.
  control and safe custody of prisoners to vest in, 14, 151.
  various powers, &c., to vest in and to be exerciseable by, 14, 151.
  town halls, court-houses, &c., within precincts of prisons not to vest in, 14, 191.
  town halls, court-houses, &c., within precincts of prisons may be bought by, 14, 192.
  legal estate in prisons, &c., not to vest in, 15, 191.
  to direct how legal estate in prisons shall be disposed of, 15, 191.
  prisons used by, when in nature of national monuments, to be protected, 15, 192.
  appointment of Prison Commissioners, on recommendation of, 15, 153.
  may appoint chairman of Prison Commissioners, 16, 153.
  may make rules as to certain acts by Prison Commissioners, 16, 153.
  to determine number of Inspectors and officers, 16, 154.
  to appoint Inspectors, 16, 154.
  to determine salaries of Commissioners, Inspectors, &c., 17, 155.
  Prison Commissioners to be subject to control, and to obey directions of, 19, 155.
  reports to be made to, by Prison Commissioners, 19, 157.
  to make rules as to appointment of Visiting Committee, 21, 158.
  rules of, as to appointment of Visiting Committee, 250, 252, 262.
  to make rules as to duties of Visiting Committee, 22, 160.
  rules of, as to duties of Visiting Committee, 263—267.
  Visiting Committee to report to, 22, 161, 264.
  powers of, as regards existing officers of prisons, 25, 178.
  to certify fitness of prison for confinement of prisoners, 29, 98.
  may appoint any prison locally situate in a county, as prison of county, riding, &c., 29, 173.
  may appoint prisons for confinement of prisoners before and during trial, 30, 170.

Secretary of State (continued)—
appointment of such prisons, 259, 260.
may appoint prison in one county, to which prisoners for trial, &c., may be committed from an adjoining county, 30, 170.
appointment of certain such prisons, 260.
power of, as to confinement and removal of convicted criminal prisoners, 31, 42, 171.
may appoint prisons for confinement of debtors and prisoners who are not criminal prisoners, 31, 171.
appointment of such prisons, 259, 260.
duties of, as regards hard labour in prisons, 36, 74, 75, 183.
may make rules as to classification and treatment of prisoners confined for non-payment of sums in the nature of debts, 38, 183.
rules made by, as to debtors, to apply to such prisoners, 279.
to make special rules as to treatment of unconvicted and certain other prisoners, 38, 184, 185.
special rules of, for prisoners awaiting trial, 268—272.
to what persons special rules of, for prisoners awaiting trial are to apply, 272.
transfer to, of power of justices to make rules, 45, 77.
rules made by, how to be proved, 45, 192, 193.
rules made by, to be laid before Parliament, 46, 193.
rules made by, not in force, until laid before Parliament, 46, 193.
power of, to compromise, settle, or refer to arbitration, any matter, 47, 194.
sanction of, required for use of scheduled prisons as lock-up houses, &c., 49, 105.
discontinuance of prisons by, 50, 175.
duties and powers of, on discontinuance of prison, 51, 176.
sanction of, required under P. A., 1865, for building, &c., prisons, 79.
Surveyor-General of prisons may be appointed by, 82.
calendar of prisoners to be sent to, by gaoler, 139.
power and duty of, as regards land, &c., bought by a prison authority for purposes of a prison, but considered not necessary, 197.
power of, to visit and inspect or to authorize any person to visit and inspect prisons, &c., 206.
authority of, requisite for confinement of debtors in common gaol of county, 217.
power of, as to burial of executed criminals, 227.
to make rules, as to execution of judgment of death, 228.
rules, &c., so made by, to be laid before Parliament, 228.
provisions of rules so made by, 228, note (*q*).
certificate and declaration of due execution of judgment of death to be sent to, 228.
duplicate of coroner's inquisition on the body of an executed criminal to be sent to, 228.
to make regulations as to registering and photographing convicted criminal prisoners, 230, 231, 233.
effect of regulations so made, 231, 233.
power of, to modify, &c., such regulations, 232.

Secretary of State (continued)—
provisions of such regulations, 233—235.
chairman of Visiting Committee to report names, &c., of members to, 263.
duty of Visiting Committee in reporting to, specially, 263.
power of Visiting Committee to report to, generally, 264.
instruments for. infliction of corporal punishment to be approved by, 287.
pattern of irons, &c., to be approved by, 287.
Visiting Committee may report to, when child of tender years imprisoned, 290.
decision of, final as to class of rules applicable to prisoners, 292.

Security:
provisions as to giving of, by gaoler to sheriff, 32, 99.

Sentence of Death: (See Death).

Separate Prison Jurisdiction:
definition of, 4, 66.
maintenance of prisons by, 7, 65.
termination of obligation of, to maintain prison, &c., 8, 150, 163.

Sedition:
treatment of prisoners convicted of, 39, 186, 276.

Seditious Libel:
treatment of prisoners convicted of, 39, 186, 276.

Separation of Prisoners:
provisions as to, 34, 35, 72, 117, 268, 273, 277.
Prison Commissioners to examine into state of prisons for carrying out provisions respecting, 18, 155.

Servants:
of Prison Commissioners, number and appointment of, 16, 154.
salaries of, 17, 155.
prisoners not to be, of prison officers, &c., 131.

Settlement:
discharged prisoners may be provided with means of returning to place of, 43, 44, 90.

Sheriff:
transfer of prisons, not to affect jurisdiction of. 30. 174.
how far liable for escape of prisoners from prison, 32, 100, 174.
as to giving security to, by gaoler, 32, 99.
no longer required to deliver calendar of prisoners, 34, 100.
jurisdiction and responsibility of, as regards prisoners sentenced to death, not to be affected, 31. 33, 98, 174.
power of, in case of prisoners liable to punishment of death being committed to house of correction, 205.
not to receive poundage, on taking any person in execution, 215.
when he may confine prisoners for debt and for contempt of court in the common gaol, 216, 217.

INDEX. 355

Sheriff (continued)—
  to be present at the execution of capital sentences, 227.
  power of, as to admission of relatives of prisoner, or other persons, to be present at execution of capital sentences, 227.
  to sign a declaration of the due execution of such sentences, 227.
  duplicate of coroner's inquisition on body of an executed criminal to be delivered to, 227.
  to send certificate and declaration of due execution of judgment of death to Secretary of State, 228.
  to send duplicate of coroner's inquisition on body of an executed criminal to Secretary of State, 228.
  duties and powers of, as to execution of capital sentences may be performed by, and to be vested in under-sheriff or deputy, 229.

Smoking:
  not allowed in prison, except, &c., 117, 289.

Soldiers:
  duty of gaoler as to reception, &c., of, into prisons, 236.
  duty of gaoler on expiration of imprisonment of, or of persons suspected to be, in prisons, 240.

Solicitor:
  communications between, and unconvicted prisoner, &c., special rules to be made as to, 39, 184, 185.
  provisions of rules so made, 271.
  when prisoner to see him alone, 127, 271.
  visits by, to prisoners under sentence of death, 287.
  written instructions to, of prisoner awaiting trial, not to be examined by officer of prison, 271.

Solitary Confinement:
  of military offenders in, 236, 237.
  of marine offenders in, 243.
  how often prisoners in, to be visited, 291.

South Molton:
  borough prison of, to be discontinued, 48, 103.

Special Case:
  statement of, by arbitrator, 47, 94.

Special Sessions:
  to be held in boroughs for appointing Visiting Committee, 21, 159.
  at what, Visiting Committee to be appointed in boroughs, 251, 262.

Spirituous Liquors:
  punishment for carrying into prison, 41, 87, 88.
  admission of, into prison for use of prisoners, 117.
  for use of the infirmary, 117.
  order of surgeon as to, to be entered by him in his journal, 118.
  when not to be used by officers within prison walls, 289.

State:
  public department of, when included in term "prison authority," 9, 165.

Status of Prison Officers:
provisions as to, 23, 177.

Statutes: (See Acts)

Store Keepers:
appointment of, 16, 154.

Subordinate Officers:
who are to be deemed, 141.
what, and how, to be appointed for prisons, 18, 24, 67, 155.
to obey gaoler and to perform such duties as he may direct, 138.
not to be absent without leave, 138.
to leave their keys, &c., during absence, with the gaoler, 138.
not to receive visitors, without gaoler's leave, 138.
visitors not to sleep in apartments of, without gaoler's leave, 115.
to examine cells, locks, &c., and to seize prohibited articles, 138.
duties of, when acting as gate porter, 141.
not to be allowed to be employed in any private capacity, 132.
may be suspended by gaoler for misconduct, 132.
to report to gaoler immediately misconduct, &c., of prisoners, 288.
not to converse unnecessarily, &c., with prisoners, 288.

Suit: (See Action.)

Sunday:
discharge of prisoner when imprisonment expires on, 43, 89
prisoners not to be employed at hard labour on, 122.
Divine Service to be performed on, 124.
criminal prisoners to attend Divine Service on, 125.
when non-criminal prisoners may be excused from attending Divine Service on, 264.
when prisoners awaiting trial to attend Divine Service on, 272.
attendance of misdemeanants of first division at Divine Service on, 276.
when debtors to attend Divine Service on, 278.
visits to prisoners not to be allowed on except, &c., 285.

Superannuation:
of officers of prisons, 26, 27, 70, 108, 179, 194.

Superannuation Act, 1859:
"existing officers" of prisons to be dealt with under, in respect of abolition of, or retirement from office, &c., 27, 180.

Surgeon:
to be appointed for every prison, 24, 67.
his qualifications, 24, 67.
certificate of, as to superannuation of prison officers, 27, 70, 180.
duty of, as to application of test for malingering, 40, 186.
to examine prisoners on admission to prison, 116, 279, 292.
to enter criminal prisoners' state of health in gaoler's record, 116.
to examine and certify as to health of all prisoners before their removal or discharge, 117.

INDEX. 357

Surgeon (continued)—
    written order of, required for admission of spirituous liquors into prison for use of prisoners, 117.
    to have control of spirituous liquors for use of infirmary, 117.
    when he may allow smoking or introduction of tobacco, 117.
    to enter order as to spirituous liquors or tobacco in his journal, 118.
    diet of prisoners under care of, 119.
    convicted criminal prisoners not to have wine, &c., unless by order of, 119.
    to enter order for allowance of wine, &c., in his journal, 119.
    power of as to sleeping of epileptic or diseased prisoners, 120.
    may give directions as to airing, changing, &c., of bedding, 120.
    may give directions as to cutting hair of female prisoners, 121.
    certificate of, as to unfitness of prisoner for hard labour of first class, 122.
    certificate of, as to unfitness of prisoner for either class of hard labour, 122.
    certificate of, as to unfitness of female prisoner for hard labour, 122.
    duties of, in examining prisoners sentenced to, or employed at, hard labour, 122, 123, 292, 293.
    may regulate exercise of criminal prisoners, 123.
    to enter directions with regard to prisoners in his journal, 123.
    duty of, respecting the infliction of corporal punishments, 130, 293.
    certificate of, required for infliction of corporal and certain other punishments, 286.
    gaoler to report to, prisoners disordered in mind, &c., 133.
    illness of prisoner to be notified to by gaoler, without delay, 133.
    list of certain prisoners to be delivered to, daily, 133.
    when to visit the prison and prisoners, 136.
    to visit daily prisoners in punishment cells, 136.
    when to visit sick prisoners, 136.
    may direct removal of sick prisoners to infirmary, 136.
    duties of, in keeping a daily record of sick prisoners, 137.
    to inspect every part of prison occasionally, 137.
    his duties on making occasional inspection, 137.
    duty of, when the mind or health of a prisoner is likely to be injuriously affected by prison discipline or treatment, 137, 293.
    when to call in additional medical aid, 137.
    duty of, as to performing serious surgical operation, 137.
    to make certain entries in his journal on death of a prisoner, 137.
    when and how he may appoint a substitute, 138.
    leave of Prison Commissioners required for his absence, 138, 156.
    to be present at the execution of capital sentences, 227.
    duty of, as to certifying due execution of capital sentences, 227.
    penalty on, for signing false certificate, 228.
    duties and powers of, as to execution of capital sentences, may be performed by, and to be vested in, chief medical officer, if there is no surgeon, 229.
    power and duty of, as to weighing prisoners, 279.
    duties of, as regards children of female prisoners, in prison, 281.

Surgeon (continued)—
  power of, to order additional clothing and bedding, 281.
  gaoler to carry out written directions of, as to supply of additional articles, 290.
  to examine frequently the washing places, baths, &c., 290.
  to inform gaoler of points likely to aid in identifying prisoners, 292.
  when to report, on medical grounds, case of prisoner to gaoler, 292.
  statistical records to be kept by, of health of prisoners, 293.
  to report periodically on general health of prison, &c., 293.

Surveyor-General of Prisons:
  appointment of, 82.

Tap:
  not to be kept in prison, 117.

Tenterden:
  borough prison of, to be discontinued, 48, 103.

Tenure:
  of office, by existing officers of prisons, 25, 70.

Terms, Definition of: (See Definition of Terms).

Test:
  of malingering, provisions as to application of, 40, 186.

Thanksgiving Day:
  prisoners not to be employed at hard labour on public, 122.

Thermometers:
  to be placed in different parts of a prison, 115.

Title:
  short, of P. A., 1865, 1, 60; P. A., 1877, 1, 149.
  to land, confirmation of, 91.

Tobacco:
  punishment for carrying, into prison, 41, 87, 88.
  not to be introduced into prison without surgeon's order, &c., 117.
  order of surgeon as to, to be entered by him in his journal, 118.
  when not to be used by officers within prison walls, 289.
  suspension of officers for carrying, into or out of prison contrary to orders, 289.

Tools:
  not to be left unnecessarily exposed in prisons, 115.

Town:
  county of a, of what county to be deemed a part, 6, 197.

Town Council: (See also Municipal Borough).
  to be prison authorities in municipal boroughs, 4, 62.
  approval by, of salaries of prison officers, 24, 70.
  as to right of, to appoint certain prison officers, 24, 109.
  members, &c., of, not to be interested in contracts relating to borough prison, 208.
  penalty for being so interested, 208.

Town Council (continued)—
may borrow money for certain prison purposes, 210.
how repayment of money borrowed by, to be secured, 210.

Town Halls:
appropriation of, when situate within precincts of a prison, 14, 191.
may be bought by Secretary of State, 14, 192.

Tradesmen:
dealing with prison, not to be jurors on inquests on bodies of prisoners, 44, 187.
when gaoler not to have dealings with, supplying the prison, 239.

Treasurer:
definition of, 3, 61.
of county gaol, appointment of, 201.
    duties of, 201.
    salary of, 201.
    security to be given by, 201.
of riding, &c., order for payment of contribution to be sent to, 202.
to pay contribution to treasurer of county gaol, 203.
of county, to keep an account of expenses of prosecution at assizes of offenders from certain municipal boroughs, 207.

Treasury:
power of Secretary of State to refuse to recommend payment by, of compensation to a prison authority, 10, 166.
consent of, required for fixing deduction to be made from compensation in respect of an uncompleted prison, 11, 166.
consent of, required for sale of legal estate in prisons, &c., 15, 191.
consent of, required for purchase by Secretary of State of townhall, &c., situate within the curtilage of a prison, 14, 191, 192.
sanction of, required as to number of inspectors, officers, and servants of prisons to be appointed, 16, 154.
consent of, required in fixing salaries of Prison Commissioners and other officers, 17, 155.
power of, to grant annuity or gratuity to "existing officers of prisons," 27, 179.
to determine rate of interest on certain loans to prison authorities by Public Works Loan Commissioners, 9, 52, 164, 177.
when assent of, required for reference to arbitration, 47, 194.

Trees:
not to be allowed to grow against outer walls of a prison, 115.

Under-Sheriff: (See Sheriff).

University of Oxford:
commutation of payment by, in respect of gaol expenses, 194.

Venue:
of action or suit, &c., for anything done under P. A., 1865, 47, 94.

Visiting Committee of Prisons:
general appointment of, 21, 158.

Visiting Committee of Prisons (continued)—
  rules as to first appointment of, in counties and boroughs, 250, 251.
  rule as to the number of members of, and Sessions to appoint, in counties and boroughs, 252.
  rules as to appointments of. after the first appointment, 262.
  when first meeting of to be held in 1878, 251.
  when first meeting of, to be held after the year 1878, 263.
  how long to hold office after election, 263.
  to appoint a chairman and make rules as to their attendance at the prison. 263.
  chairman of, to report names. &c.. of members to Secretary of State, 263.
  appointment of certain members of, for Worcester prison, 21, 159, 251, 257, 263.
  members of, not to be restricted in visiting prisons or prisoners by provisions of P. A., 1877. or rules made under that Act, 21, 159.
  duties of, provision as to. 22, 160, 161.
  duties of, rules as to. 262—267.
  when to be deemed Visiting Justices as regards punishment of prisoners, 22, 160.
  attention of, to be called to entries in visitors' book, 23, 162.
  upon what matters to report to Secretary of State, 22, 161, 264.
  recommendation of, as to aid to discharged prisoners, 43, 173.
  assistance by, as to disposal of gratuities earned by prisoners, 266.
  order of, or of a Prison Commissioner, requisite for application of test for malingering, 40, 186.
  limitation of time of confinement of prisoners by, in punishment cells, 40, 186.
  members of, not to be interested in contracts relating to prison, 263.
  prison officers to treat members of, with respect, &c.. 263, 288.
  duty of, in co-operating with Commissioners and in making inquiries and reports, 263.
  duty of, as regards abuses in prisons, 263.
  power of, to suspend prison officers, 263.
  to keep a book of minutes of their proceedings, 263.
  power of, as to reports of misconduct, &c., of prisoners, 263.
  power and duties of, as regards putting prisoners into irons or under mechanical restraint for an increased period, 264.
  order of, required for use of irons, &c., for extended period, 291.
  to furnish information as to offences and punishments, 264.
  duty of, as to hearing prisoners' complaints, 264.
  duty of, as to reports relating to injurious effect of prison discipline upon mind or body of a prisoner, 264.
  to inspect diets of the prisoners, 264.
  may inspect prison books, 264.
  power of, to excuse non-criminal prisoners from attending Divine Service, 264.
  power and duties of, as to granting permission in certain cases, 264, 268, 273, 278.

INDEX. 361

Visiting Committee of Prisons (continued)—
 their duties in permitting prisoners awaiting trial, and misdemeanants of the first division, to use special rooms or cells, to exercise separately, &c., 265, 266, 268, 273, 274.
 power of to permit modification of prison routine as to prisoners awaiting trial, 265, 269.
 duty of, as to supply of books, &c., to prisoners awaiting trial and misdemeanants of first division, 265, 270, 275.
 when to allow misdemeanants of first division to wear their own clothes, and to provide their own food, 265, 274.
 power of, to prolong period of visits to prisoners, or to extend privilege of communicating with friends, 266, 271, 275, 278, 285.
 when order of, required for visits to prisoners under orders for execution, 266, 287.
 power of members of, to name a reformatory school to which a youthful offender may be sent, 266.
 when a member of, is to cause a youthful offender to be sent, &c., to a reformatory school of the religious persuasion to which he belongs, 267.
 to discharge the duties assigned to them in the special and general rules, 267.
 when they may permit his own medical man to attend prisoner awaiting trial, 270.
 power of, as to discharge of prisoners under sixteen years of age, 280.
 when gaoler to report to, refusal to admit a visitor, 285.
 when gaoler to report to, suspension by him of visits of any person, 286.
 power of members of, to grant permission for conference on important business with prisoners under sentence of death, 287.
 power of members of, to grant orders for visits to prisoners under sentence of death, 287.
 gaoler to report to, case of child of tender years in prison, 290.
 to be informed of prisoners desiring to see them, 291.
 gaoler to inform, when prisoner put in irons or under mechanical restraint, 291.
 death of prisoners in prison to be notified to, by gaoler, 291.

Visiting Justices:
 meaning of the term, 5, 96.
 to mean the same in P. A., 1877, as in P. A., 1865, 7, 198.
 report by letter to, by Inspector, 17, 77.
 powers and jurisdiction of, relating to prisons and prisoners may be exercised by Prison Commissioners, 18, 155.
 reports, &c., required to be made to, or acts to be done by, &c., to be made to, or done by, &c., the Prison Commissioners, 18, 156, 289.
 appointment of, 20, 96.
 rules as to duties of, 20, 97.
 repeal of provisions relating to appointment, &c., of, 20, 53, 158.

Visiting Justices (continued)—
  appointment of Visiting Committee instead of, 21, 158.
  Visiting Committee to be deemed, as regards punishment of prisoners in certain cases, 22, 160.
  powers of, as to removal of prison officers from apartments, 29, 71.
  how far transfer of jurisdiction of, to affect that of sheriff or coroner, 30, 174.
  power of, to order removal of prisoners on emergency, 42, 101.
  power of, as regards employment in necessary services of prison being deemed hard labour of the second class, 37, 75.
  power of, as to allowance to discharged prisoners, 43, 89.
  power of, to provide discharged prisoners with means of returning to place of settlement, 43, 90.
  presentment of, under P. A., 1865, as to building. &c., prisons, 78.
  report of, respecting superannuation of prison officers, 70.
  notice by, of penalties for offences in relation to prisons, 41, 88.
  to enter in minute book copy of Inspector's complaint, 17, 77.
  leave for visitors to sleep in subordinate officer's apartments to be reported to one of the, by gaoler, 115.
  no smoking to be allowed, &c., except under rules of, &c., 117.
  may approve rules as regards debtors maintaining themselves, 118.
  may punish debtors for selling food, &c., to other prisoners, 118.
  to approve rules as to prisoners maintaining themselves before trial, 118.
  may punish such prisoner for breach of regulation, 119.
  to judge of the special circumstances under which a convicted criminal prisoner may receive food, &c., beyond prison allowance, 119.
  may give directions as to airing, &c., prisoners' bedding, 120.
  to direct as to deductions from earnings of certain debtors, 121.
  to determine amount of earnings to be paid to prisoners acquitted, &c., 121.
  to prescribe the hours during which prisoners may be kept to hard labour of the first class, 121.
  when they may substitute hard labour of the first class for hard labour of the second class, 122.
  to make provision for the employment of convicted criminal prisoners not sentenced to hard labour, 123.
  to make rules as to amount and nature of such employment, 123.
  to appoint time for reading of prayers in prison, 124.
  to fix the time with the chaplain for his preaching, 124.
  when they may dispense with prisoner's attendance at chapel, 125.
  when they may permit a minister of a religious persuasion differing from that of the Established Church, to visit a prisoner, 125.
  books and printed papers not to be admitted into prison without their permission, 125.
  consent of, requisite for appointment of substitute by chaplain, 126.
  consent of, requisite for appointment of a substitute for minister appointed under the Prison Ministers Act, 126.
  to provide a substitute on death of chaplain or assistant-chaplain, 126.

Visiting Justices (continued)—
   to give directions as to instruction of prisoners, 127.
   punishments and privations not to be inflicted except by, &c., 128.
   power of, as regards offences against prison discipline, 129.
   power of, to inquire, upon oath, respecting alleged offences against prison discipline, and to order punishment, 129.
   powers and duties of, with regard to putting prisoners into irons, or under mechanical restraint, 129.
   to approve diet and exercise allowed to prisoners under sentence of death, 130.
   during preparation for, or at the time of an execution, no person, not legally entitled, to enter the prison without order from two or more, 130.
   particulars of suspension of subordinate officer to be reported to, by gaoler, 132.
   notice of death of prisoner to be given to one of the, by the gaoler, 133.
   cases of insanity or of apparent insanity to be reported to, by the gaoler, 133.
   leave of one of the, required for absence of gaoler from prison for a night, 134.
   consent of, requisite for appointment of gaoler's or of deputy gaoler's substitute, 135.
   leave of one of the, requisite for matron's absence from prison for a night, 136.
   approval of, requisite for appointment of a deputy by the matron, 136.
   journal of matron to be laid before at their ordinary meetings, 136.
   leave of, required for absence of surgeon, 138.
   approval of, required for appointment of surgeon's substitute, 138.
   sanction of, requisite as to gaoler's directions respecting duties of subordinate officers, 138.
   once, at least, in each quarter, to examine books, &c., of gaoler, 139.
   to report to justices in sessions assembled any special circumstances respecting such books, 140.
   non-resident officers' book to be produced for inspection of, when required, 141.
   rules, &c., made by, under P. A., 1865, to be deemed regulations, 141.
   power of, to make regulations for admission of ministers, 223.
   power of, as to admission of relatives of prisoner or other persons to be present at execution of capital sentences, 227.
   may make representation to Secretary of State as to burial of executed criminals within prison walls, 227.

Visitors:
   power of gaoler as to, 127, 285, 286.
   prison officers not to receive money, &c., from, 131.
   not to be received, without leave, by subordinate officers, 140.
   powers and duties of gate porter as to, 141.
   name, address, &c., to be given by, before admission, 285.

Visitors (continued)—
    when admission may be refused to certain, 285,
    to what place in prisons, to be admitted, 285.
    when visits of certain, may be suspended, 286.
    when to be prevented from communicating with prisoners, 290.
    male, to be accompanied by matron, &c., on entering part of prison allotted to females, 292.

Visitors' Book:
    to be kept by gaoler, 134.
    observations may be made in, by any Justice of the Peace visiting a prison, &c., 23, 97, 162.
    gaoler to call attention of Visiting Committee to entries made in, 23, 97, 162.

Visits:
    to prison, &c., by member of Visiting Committee not to be restricted by P. A., 1877, 21, 159.
    to prisoners, by friends, &c., regulations as to, 127, 271, 275, 278, 285, 286.
    to prisoners under sentence of death, 130, 287.
    to prison by any Justice of the Peace, 23, 97, 161.
    of chaplain and non-resident officers to prison, to be entered in non-resident officers' book, 140.
    prolongation of time of, by Visiting Committee, 266.
    to prisoners under order for execution, when order of Visiting Committee required for, 266.
    power of Visiting Committee to prolong period or to increase number of, to misdemeanants of first division, 275.
    to misdemeanants of first division, when not to be in same place as those to criminal prisoners, 276.
    to debtors when not to be received in same place as those to criminal prisoners, 278.
    by whom and how often they may be made, 278.
    power of Visiting Committee to prolong period of, &c., 278.

Warrant:
    description of prison in, 33, 100.
    saving as to validity of, in certain cases, 34, 109

Wine:
    debtor may provide himself with, 118.
    what quantity of, debtors may procure or buy, 277.
    when to be allowed to convicted criminal prisoners, 119.
    how much prisoner awaiting trial may receive or buy, 269, 270.
    how much, misdemeanant of first division may receive or buy, 274.
    not to be sold, &c., to other prisoners, 118, 270, 274, 277.

Worcester (City of):
    appointment of certain justices of, on Visiting Committee of Worcester prison, 21, 159, 251, 257 263.

Worcester (City of) (continued)—
at what time Town Council of, to appoint certain members of Visiting Committee of Worcester Prison, 251, 263.
number of members and mode of appointment of Visiting Committee of Worcester prison, 257.

Work:
punishment for neglect of, by prisoners not sentenced to hard labour, 123.

Work and Earnings:
of convicted criminal prisoners, report of Prison Commissioners to contain information respecting, 19, 157.
of debtors, provisions as to, 121.
of prisoners awaiting trial, 271.
of misdemeanants of first division, 275.

Worship: (See Religious Worship).

Writ:
description of prison in, 33, 100.
saving as to validity of, in certain cases, 34, 109.

Writing:
prisoners to be taught, 127.

Youthful Offender:
power of member of Visiting Committee to name a reformatory school for, 266.
when to be sent, &c., to a reformatory school of his own religious persuasion, 267.
gaoler to report to Visiting Committee, when child of tender years imprisoned, 290.

www.ingramcontent.com/pod-product-compliance
Lightning Source LLC
Chambersburg PA
CBHW030359230426
43664CB00007BB/664